D0435883

MOLIÈRE

COMEDIES

Molière

COMEDIES

Translated by Donald M. Frame

With Wood-Engraved Illustrations after Tony Johannot

THE FRANKLIN LIBRARY
FRANKLIN CENTER, PENNSYLVANIA

The illustrations selected for this edition of Molière's *Comedies* are the work of the celebrated nineteenth-century painter and etcher Tony Johannot (1803–1852). Johannot and his family moved to Paris, France, shortly after his birth in Offenbach am Main, Germany. Trained to be an artist and engraver by his older brother Charles, Tony was quickly recognized to be "the instrument by which French book illustration could be renewed." A careful craftsman, he approached his finished designs through preliminary sketches and carefully supervised his engravers. Johannot illustrated the works of such writers as Balzac, Cervantes, Goldsmith, and Hugo. The wood-engraved illustrations in this volume are reproduced from the 1835–1836 edition of *Oeuvres de Molière,* Tomes I and II, published by Paulin, Paris. They are reproduced courtesy of the Villanova University Library, which graciously granted The Franklin Library access to these rare books.

The acid-free paper used in this book conforms with the guidelines for permanence and durability set by the Council of Library Resources and the American National Standards Institute.

Printed in the United States of America.

For information about other Franklin Library programs, write to The Franklin Library, Franklin Center, PA 19091. The Franklin Mint is a quality manufacturer of specialty collector's items.

✧ ✧ ✧ ✧ ✧ ✧ ✧ ✧ ✧ ✧ ✧

Contents

The School for Husbands

CHARACTERS

Sganarelle *Ariste*	brothers
Isabelle *Léonor*	sisters
Lisette,	waiting maid to Léonor
Valère,	suitor of Isabelle
Ergaste,	valet to Valère
Constable	
Notary	

The scene is in Paris.

Act One

SCENE ONE
Sganarelle, Ariste

Sganarelle Brother, let's end this talk, at my request,
And each one live his life as he thinks best.
Although I have to yield to you in age,
And though you're old enough to be a sage,
Yet let me tell you I have no intention
Of being guided by your reprehension;
My own advice is what I choose to heed;
My way of life suits me quite well indeed.

Ariste But everyone condemns it.

Sganarelle Oh yes, cranks
Like you, brother.

Ariste A kind remark; much thanks.

Sganarelle Since I must hear you out, I'd like to know
What these fine critics find to censure so.

Ariste That surly humor, whose severity
Shuns all the pleasures of society,
Gives all your actions an eccentric air,
And lends uncouthness even to what you wear.

Sganarelle Of course, I must be fashion's slave! Oh yes!
And not content myself in how I dress!

Wouldn't you like to see, for all your chat,
My *elder* brother, sir (for you are that,
Thank God, by twenty years, to speak straight out;
But that is hardly worth talking about),
Wouldn't you like to see me ape the ways
Of your young fashionable popinjays,
Wear one of their ridiculous *chapeaux*
That bare weak brains to every breeze that blows,
And a blond wig that takes up so much space
As quite to obfuscate the human face?
A tiny doublet, like to disappear,
And a great collar reaching down to here?
Those sleeves, at dinner sampling every food,
Those petticoats, as breeches misconstrued?
Those ribbons on the shoes, which look as sweet
As feathers look upon a pigeon's feet?
And those great canions, reaching from the knees,
Which rob the legs of freedom and of ease,
And give our gallant fops a straddling gait
As though on shuttlecocks they ambulate?
This is the way you'd like to see me dressed:
Wearing this trash, like you and all the rest.

Ariste Always we must accept the general ways,
And never draw on us the public gaze.
In clothes as well as speech, the man of sense
Will shun all these extremes that give offense,
Dress unaffectedly, and, without haste,
Follow the changes in the current taste.
I have no wish to set men on the road
Of those who always overdo the mode
And, loving its extremes, would feel distress
If anyone outdid them in excess.
But I maintain no reason makes it right
To shun accepted ways from stubborn spite;
And we may better join the foolish crowd
Than cling to wisdom, lonely though unbowed.

Sganarelle This speech betrays your age, and that white hair
You hide beneath the black peruke you wear.

Ariste I never fail to note with some surprise

The importance that my age has in your eyes,
And that you always seem to be on fire
To blame my joyfulness and my attire,
As if old age, debarred from all affection,
Must bend on death alone its whole reflection;
As if it had not ugliness enough
Without becoming slovenly and gruff.

Sganarelle Say what you will, I mean nevertheless
To make no changes in the way I dress.
I want a hat, no matter what is said,
That gives comfortable shelter to my head;
A long closed doublet whose appropriate form
Helps me digest and keeps my stomach warm;
A pair of breeches made to fit my thighs,
And shoes in which my feet won't agonize.
Our fathers wore these, wisely, in their day;
And any fop can look the other way.

SCENE TWO

Léonor, Isabelle, Lisette, Ariste, Sganarelle

Léonor [*to Isabelle*] In case he scolds you, leave it all to me.

Lisette [*to Isabelle*] Still in his room avoiding company?

Isabelle He's built that way.

Léonor But, sister, that's not good.

Lisette Be glad his brother does not share his mood,
Madame; thank fate for its benevolence
That it assigned you to the one with sense.

Isabelle Today's a miracle, beyond a doubt:
He neither locked me in nor took me out.

Lisette Him and his ruff, I'd see him in hell-fire . . .

Sganarelle Where are you going, *if* I may inquire?

Léonor We don't know yet. I asked my sister pray
To take the air with me this lovely day;
But . . .

Sganarelle [*to Léonor and Lisette*] You two, go wherever you see fit.
Go on, both of you, make the most of it.

To Isabelle.

But you, ma'am, if you please, I tell you no.

Ariste Oh, come, brother, why not let all three go?

Sganarelle Brother, your servant.

Ariste When has youth been sage?

Sganarelle Youth is a fool, and so sometimes is age.

Ariste You think it's bad for her and Léonor . . . ?

Sganarelle For her to be with me—I like that more.

Ariste But . . .

Sganarelle But on me her actions must depend,
And I shall do my duty toward our friend.

Ariste You think I care about her sister less?

Sganarelle Lord! We each do as we see fit, I guess.
They have no kin; their father, late our friend,
Consigned them to us as he neared his end,
Charging us each to take one for our bride,
Or, should we not, another mate provide;
Gave us a father's and a husband's power
By contract over them from that sad hour.
For one you took responsibility;
That of the other thus devolved on me.
You govern yours according to your will;
So please let me direct the other still.

Ariste To me . . .

Sganarelle To me it seems, to speak straight out,
I talk as one who knows what he's about.
You let yours run around free, well arrayed:
All right; give her a lackey and a maid:
I don't mind; she can chase about and loaf,
Freely sniffed at by every foppish oaf:
Do as you will. But I intend that mine
Live not by hers, sir, but by my design,

Dress in a decent woolen serge or baize,
And wear black only on the proper days;
That closeted, as girls should be, indoors,
She put her mind all on her household chores,
Mending my clothes when other work is done,
Or knitting me some stockings just for fun;
And that, completely deaf to all sweet talk,
She never go unchaperoned to walk.
In short, I know what's what; the flesh is weak;
Horns are an ornament I do not seek;
And since her lot calls her to marry me,
I mean to answer for her personally.

Isabelle You've no cause . . .

Sganarelle Silence. Nothing to discuss.
I'll teach you how to go out without us.

Léonor How's that, sir . . . ?

Sganarelle The fact is, to be concise,
I'm not talking to you; you're much too nice.

Léonor You don't approve our seeing Isabelle?

Sganarelle I don't. Frankly, you spoil her, Mademoiselle.
Your visits here I can at best deplore;
Oblige me by not making any more.

Léonor Then listen while I speak out frankly too.
On all of this I do not know her view;
But I know what distrust would do to me;
And, born of the same parents though we be,
We hardly can be sisters if, in fact,
She comes to love you for the way you act.

Lisette Indeed, I am appalled at all these quirks.
Imprison women? Are we among Turks?
I hear they treat them there like slaves, or worse,
And that is why God marks them with his curse.
You must think us quite ready to discard
Our honor, that you put it under guard.
Come, do you really think all these precautions
Are any obstacle to our intentions,
And that, when we've a mind, we can't prevail,

And make a fool out of the smartest male?
You act like madmen when you spy on us;
The surest thing is to rely on us.
The greatest danger is for you to hector:
Our honor wants to be its own protector.
You almost give us a desire to sin
When you take such great care to hem us in;
And if a husband used constraint on me,
I just might let him see what he should see.

Sganarelle There is your education for you, master;
Hearing this does not make your heart beat faster?

Ariste Brother, her talk should only make us laugh.
There's much in what she says on her behalf:
Their sex enjoys a little liberty;
There's no great point in such austerity;
Suspicions, locks, and bars are all misplaced,
And will not keep our girls and women chaste.
'Tis honor that must hold them to their duty,
Not our severe confinement of their beauty.
It must be a strange woman, I confess,
Who owes her virtue solely to duress.
We hope to rule their every step in vain;
I say the heart is what we have to gain;
My honor I would think in jeopardy,
For all my worry, in the custody
Of one who, if temptation should assail,
Would lack only a ready chance to fail.

Sganarelle Nonsense.

Ariste Perhaps; but I maintain, in truth,
That with a smile we should instruct our youth,
Be very gentle when we have to blame,
And not put them in fear of virtue's name.
Thus I've raised Léonor up to this time:
Her freedom I have never seen as crime.
Her youthful wishes met with my consent;
Nor have I had, thank God, cause to repent.
I've let her mingle in society,
See dances, entertainments, comedy:

Things I have thought to be of such a kind
As serve to fashion a young person's mind.
Better to have her make the world her school
In how to live, than any book or rule.
She likes to spend on linen, bows, and dress:
What then? My wish is for her happiness;
And those are pleasures that can be allowed
To girls in families suitably endowed.
Her father's order makes her marry me,
But I have no desire for tyranny.
I know our ages set us far apart;
I leave the choice to her unhampered heart.
Four thousand crowns a year on which to live
And all the care a tender heart can give:
If these, in her opinion, compensate
For her so early marrying me late,
She's welcome to my hand; if not, she's free.
She would do better elsewhere, I agree.
I'd rather that another had her hand,
Than have her marry me at my command.

Sganarelle How sweet he is! Sugar and honey yet!

Ariste At least thank God I am no martinet.
I'd hate to practice those forbidding ways
That force children to count their fathers' days.

Sganarelle But when their youth is spent in liberty
You cannot curb them very easily;
And you will not avoid your share of strife
When the time comes to change her way of life.

Ariste Well, then, why change it?

Sganarelle Why?

Ariste Yes.

Sganarelle I don't know.

Ariste Is honor wounded when I treat her so?

Sganarelle What? If you marry her, she'll be as free
As now, when just a girl, she seems to be?

Ariste Why not?

Sganarelle You will look kindly, will you not,
On every ribbon, every beauty spot?

Ariste No doubt.

Sganarelle When the whim strikes her, off she'll prance
To every gathering and every dance?

Ariste Yes, really.

Sganarelle And the fops will find their way?

Ariste What then?

Sganarelle With all their presents and their play?

Ariste Indeed.

Sganarelle Your wife may listen to their line?

Ariste All right.

Sganarelle You'll watch all this without a sign
Of how these gallant calls give you a pain?

Ariste Of course I will.

Sganarelle You're old, and you're insane.

To Isabelle.

Go in; such wicked talk should not be heard.

Ariste I mean to trust my wife in deed and word
And always live my life as I have done.

Sganarelle You'll make a fine cuckold; that will be fun.

Ariste Of course I do not know my destiny;
But I do know that if *you* fail to be
Just that, you will not have yourself to blame,
For that is where all your precautions aim.

Sganarelle Go on, laugh all you like—and while you can:
Practically sixty, and a funny man!

Léonor I'll guarantee him not to meet that fate
If I should be selected as his mate:
He's sure of that; but were I matched with you,
I wouldn't answer for what I might do.

Lisette We hate to cheat someone who treats us right.
But someone like you—'twould be sheer delight.

Sganarelle You, hold your tongue, and hang your head for shame.

Ariste For her remarks you have yourself to blame.
Farewell. But, brother, take this thought to heart:
To lock your wife up is not very smart.
Your servant. *Exit.*

Sganarelle I'm not yours. Oh, what a match!
For each, the other is a perfect catch.
A lovely family! An insane antique
Who plays the rake with a forlorn physique;
A bossy girl who's an accomplished flirt;
Pert servants; no, Wisdom could not convert
This household, and might even go insane,
Counseling sense and reason all in vain.
Such company might easily dispel
The seeds of honor lodged in Isabelle;
And so I mean to take the girl away
Into the country for a little stay.

SCENE THREE

Ergaste, Valère, Sganarelle

Valère [*to Ergaste, from backstage*] Ergaste, there goes the Argus I abhor,
Strict tutor of the girl that I adore.

Sganarelle Sometimes I feel something akin to rage
At the corrupted morals of this age!

Valère I must go up to him and say hello.
He is a man whom I intend to know.

Sganarelle You never see the old austerity
That was the essence of civility;
Young people hereabouts, unbridled, now
Just want . . .

Valère He hasn't even seen my bow.

Ergaste That's his bad eye, or so it would appear;
Let's try this side.

Sganarelle I must get out of here.
From staying in the city there can come
Only . . .

Valère I must gain access to his home.

Sganarelle Eh? . . . I thought someone spoke. The countryside
Offers few follies that I can't abide.

Ergaste Go on.

Sganarelle How's that . . . I'm hearing things, I swear.
There are restraints to girls' amusements there . . .
Is that for me?

Ergaste Go nearer.

Sganarelle There, no fop
Comes . . . What the . . . ! Still? He bows, and will not stop!

Valère Sir, by saluting you do I intrude?

Sganarelle That may be.

Valère At the risk of being rude,
I so desire the honor of knowing you,
I could not keep from saying how do you do.

Sganarelle All right.

Valère And adding, in all honesty,
That I am at your service. Count on me.

Sganarelle That's nice.

Valère That we are neighbors, as we are,
Sir, I attribute to my lucky star.

Sganarelle Well, good for you.

Valère But come, sir, have you heard
What circulates at court as the latest word?

Sganarelle What do I care?

Valère But curiosity

Is naturally piqued by novelty.
No doubt you'll see that wonderful affair
Greeting the birthday of a princely heir?

Sganarelle If I wish.

Valère Paris really is unique;
Its pleasures elsewhere you may vainly seek;
Country people and pastimes are so few. . . .
How do you spend your time?

Sganarelle I've things to do.

Valère Our minds need relaxation, and give way
Unless we mix with work a little play.
What do you do before you go to bed?

Sganarelle Just as I please.

Valère No doubt; that is well said;
And your good sense is fully manifest
In that you do only what suits you best.
But that I fear you have too much to do,
I'd spend an evening now and then with you.

Sganarelle Your servant.

SCENE FOUR

Valère, Ergaste

Valère What do you think about this clown?

Ergaste He has a brusque retort, a werewolf frown.

Valère It drives me mad!

Ergaste What?

Valère What? It drives me mad
To see my love ruled by this cloddish cad,
This watchful dragon, whose severity
Will not allow her any liberty.

Ergaste That helps your cause, and you have grounds for hope

In that he gives your love so little rope.
Be steadfast in the course you have begun:
A woman that is watched is halfway won.
A father's or a husband's gloomy wrath
Has always smoothed a hopeful lover's path.
I am no flirt; I fear I lack the talent;
And I do not profess to be a gallant;
But I have served these predatory men,
Who always said their greatest joy was when
They found one of these husbands full of spleen,
Who never come back home without a scene,
These arrant brutes who, without rhyme or reason
Check on their wives in every hour and season,
And harshly, arrogantly criticize
Their actions right before the suitors' eyes.
"We know," these hunters say, "that here's our chance,
And we can ask no better circumstance
Than feminine resentment at these slurs,
In which the witness readily concurs."
In short, few things could augur quite so well
As this severity toward Isabelle.

Valère But in four months in which my love has grown
I haven't got a word with her alone.

Ergaste Love lends inventiveness—but not to you;
And if I had been . . .

Valère But what could you do
When she is never seen without that churl,
And there is not one servant, man or girl,
Who might be tempted by the hope of gain
To give assistance to a luckless swain?

Ergaste She hasn't learned yet that you love her so?

Valère To tell the truth, I simply do not know.
Where'er she goes, escorted by that bear,
Just like her shadow, she has found me there;
Each day my eyes have tried to tell her of
The extraordinary power of my love.
My eyes have spoken loud; but who can tell
Whether their speech is known to Isabelle?

Ergaste Their language may go by as if unheard
Without the written or the spoken word.

Valère How can I put an end to my dejection
And learn whether she knows of my affection?
Tell me some way.

Ergaste That is what we must find.
Let's come into your house and search our mind.

Act Two

SCENE ONE
Isabelle, Sganarelle

Sganarelle All right, I know the house, the person too,
From the account of him I've had from you.

Isabelle [*aside*] Heaven! Be propitious, and do not condemn
An innocently loving stratagem.

Sganarelle Didn't you say you hear his name's Valère?

Isabelle Yes.

Sganarelle Then rest easy, I'll go on from there;
I'll tell this pert young man a thing or two.

Isabelle [*aside*] I know, this seems a brazen thing to do;
But to a proper judge, my harsh abuse
Should be a full and adequate excuse.

SCENE TWO
Sganarelle, Ergaste, Valère

Sganarelle Let's waste no time. Here we are. [*Knocks.*]
What? I say,

Who goes there? . . . Oh, I'm dreaming. . . . Hey there!
Hey!
I'm not surprised, knowing what I know now,
That he should greet me so, and scrape and bow;
But this mad hope of his, with all due speed,
I . . .

Ergaste comes out of the door abruptly.

Damn the clumsy ox, who pays no heed,
And nearly makes me fall, and blocks the door!

Valère Sir, I regret . . .

Sganarelle It's you I'm looking for.

Valère I, sir?

Sganarelle Yes, you. Isn't your name Valère?

Valère Yes.

Sganarelle Pray, one word, if you've the time to spare.

Valère There's nothing I would not be glad to do.

Sganarelle No, no. I've come to do something for you,
And that is what brings me to see you here.

Valère Here, sir?

Sganarelle Yes. How astounded you appear!

Valère I have good reason, and this honor still
Delights . . .

Sganarelle Forget the honor, if you will.

Valère Will you not come inside?

Sganarelle There is no need.

Valère I beg you, sir.

Sganarelle No further; no, indeed.

Valère Out here I cannot hear a word you say.

Sganarelle I will not budge.

Valère All right! I must give way.

To Ergaste.

Quick, since the gentleman prefers the street,
Bring a chair here.

Sganarelle I will talk on my feet.

Valère Should I allow you . . . ?

Sganarelle What I must endure!

Valère I could not bear to treat you like a boor.

Sganarelle It is no better to refuse your ear.
I come to speak to you; you will not hear.

Valère So, I obey you.

Sganarelle That's the way to be;
I have no use for such formality.
Now will you listen?

Valère Yes, I gladly do.

Sganarelle Then tell me, do you know I'm tutor to
A young and rather pretty demoiselle
Living near by, whose name is Isabelle?

Valère Yes.

Sganarelle Then I fear I do not tell you much.
But do you know, you whom her beauties touch,
That I regard her not as just my ward,
But destine her to share my bed and board?

Valère No.

Sganarelle Well, you know it now. Therefore pray cease
Your pointless suit, and leave the girl in peace.

Valère Who, I, sir?

Sganarelle You. Let's put pretense aside.

Valère Who says I yearn for your intended bride?

Sganarelle Some persons whom I trust to be precise.

Valère But who?

Sganarelle Herself.

Valère Herself?

Sganarelle Does that suffice?
She's loved me from a child, and, as is fit,

Has given me a full account of it;
And furthermore has told me to declare
That since you dog her footsteps everywhere,
Her heart, which your persistence mortifies,
Knows all too well the language of your eyes,
That your secret desires are all too plain,
And that it is superfluous and vain
To labor further to express a plea
Offensive to the love she feels for me.

Valère You say it's she herself that sends you here
To . . .

Sganarelle Yes, to give this message, frank and clear,
And say that having seen how much you yearn,
She would have let you know her mind in turn
Much sooner, if her heart, so strongly stirred,
Had had someone by whom to send you word;
But that the pains of an extreme constraint
Led her to wish to use me to acquaint
You with the fact that, as by now you see,
Her heart is not for anyone but me,
That all your ogling will not help a bit,
And that if you possess your share of wit,
You will make other plans. For now, farewell.
I've told you everything I came to tell.

Valère Tell me, Ergaste, what do you make of this?

Sganarelle [*aside*] He surely is surprised!

Ergaste Unless I miss
My guess, you have no reason for dismay;
This hides some subtle mystery, I'd say;
And this is not the message she would send
To put a suitor's passion to an end.

Sganarelle [*aside*] This really hit him hard.

Valère You think it strange . . .

Ergaste Yes . . . But he's watching; let's get out of range.

Sganarelle How his confusion shows upon his face!
He cannot take this message with good grace.
Let's talk to Isabelle. In her we find

The effect of education on the mind:
Virtue she loves; her heart is so much in it
That a man's glance offends her in a minute.

SCENE THREE

Isabelle, Sganarelle

Isabelle [*alone*] I fear this suitor, on his passion bent,
May not have grasped my message's intent;
So from these fetters, from this prison here,
I'll send one more to make my meaning clear.

Sganarelle Here I am back.

Isabelle Well then?

Sganarelle Your words have had
A plentiful effect; your man is sad.
He first attempted to deny his flame;
But when he learned from whom my message came,
The news straightway left him abashed and mute,
And I believe he's through with his pursuit.

Isabelle I fear we will not be so fortunate
And that he still may be importunate.

Sganarelle And on what do you base this fear of yours?

Isabelle Just now, no sooner had you gone outdoors
Than, at the window for a breath of air,
I saw a young man, at the corner there,
Who first, and in a most audacious way,
Bade me, from that young malapert, good day,
And then, right into my own chamber, threw
A box containing a sealed billet-doux.
I would have tossed it right back at his feet,
But he had vanished quickly down the street,
And my heart swells with anger at this trick.

Sganarelle This is a clever rascal, really slick!

Isabelle Duty demands I send right back again
Letter and box to this accursed swain.

But for that service, on whom could I call?
I would not dare to ask you . . .

Sganarelle Not at all.
You'd show your love and faith; it's all I ask;
And joyfully my heart accepts this task.
You obligate me in the strongest way.

Isabelle Then here.

Sganarelle That's fine. Let's see. What does he say?

Isabelle Heavens! Do not open it.

Sganarelle But I don't see . . .

Isabelle He's sure to think that this was done by me.
A decent girl must never even scan
A letter sent to her by any man:
The curiosity she then displays
Reveals a secret pleasure in his praise;
And so this letter must, to be genteel,
Be taken back unopened, under seal,
To make him recognize today at last
That my disdain for him is unsurpassed,
To lead him to admit he loves in vain,
And not give way to silliness again.

Sganarelle How right she is in everything she says!
Your virtue charms me, and your prudent ways.
I see that you have learned my lessons well
And proved worthy to be my Isabelle.

Isabelle Yet I would never tell *you* what to do:
Open it if you wish; it's up to you.

Sganarelle No, not at all; your reasons are too good;
And I shall do your errand as I should,
Go on to get a few things off my chest,
And then return and set your mind at rest.

SCENE FOUR

Sganarelle, Ergaste

Sganarelle My heart floats in a beatific whirl
When I observe the soundness of that girl.
What a fine sense of honor! What a jewel!
To treat as treachery a swain's pursual,
To see his note as proof of impudence,
And have me take it back to show offense!
Seeing all this, I'd really like to know
Whether my brother's ward would answer so.
Faith! Girls are what we bring them up to be.
Hey!

Ergaste What?

Sganarelle Here. Tell your master this from me:
That henceforth he is not to make so bold
As to send letters in a box of gold;
That Isabelle's annoyance is outspoken.
You see, even the seal has not been broken.
He'll gather what she feels about his love
And what success he may be hopeful of.

SCENE FIVE

Valère, Ergaste

Valère What did he just give you, that surly ox?

Ergaste Why, sir, this letter, which, inside this box,
Isabelle, I am told, received from you,
And which, he says, angered her through and through;
So that she sends it promptly back unread.
Hurry up, read it. What can she have said?

LETTER [*Valère reads.*]

"This letter will no doubt surprise you; and I may be considered very bold for both the plan of writing it to you and my way of getting it to you; but I find myself in a plight that makes me overstep the bounds. My justified horror at a

marriage with which I am threatened in six days makes me risk anything; and in my resolve to free myself from that by any means whatever, I thought I should choose you rather than despair. Do not think, however, that you are indebted for everything to my evil destiny: it is not the constraint I am under that has engendered the feelings I have for you; but that is what makes me hurry so to reveal them, and pass over those formalities which feminine decorum demands. It will depend on you alone that I should soon be yours, and I wait only until you signify to me your love's intentions in order to let you know the resolution I have come to; but above all, bear in mind that time is pressing, and that two hearts in love must understand each other's unspoken thoughts."

Ergaste Well, sir! How's that for ingenuity?
Not bad for a young girl, if you ask me!
Would anybody think her capable
Of lovers' ruses?

Valère She's adorable!
This master stroke of hers on my behalf
Augments my love for her again by half,
And, added to her beauty's potent sway . . .

Ergaste Here comes your dupe; think what you have to say.

SCENE SIX

Sganarelle, Valère, Ergaste

Sganarelle Oh! Thrice, four times that edict* do I bless
That interdicts all luxury in dress!
Husbands may have less worry for their nests,
And wives, a limit set to their requests.
How I do thank the King for these decrees!
And how I wish, for the same husbands' ease,
That the same ban applied to coquetry
As does to lace and to embroidery!

* Of November 27, 1660; one of many given by Louis XIV against luxury in dress.

I bought a copy, and if all goes well
I shall read it aloud to Isabelle;
And shortly, when her day's affairs are done,
We'll have this for our after-supper fun.

Seeing Valère.

Ah! Will you still, you with the yellow locks,
Send tender love-notes in a golden box?
You thought you'd find some silly young coquette,
Keen for intrigue and for an amourette?
You see how she received your proposition:
Believe me, you're just wasting ammunition.
She's a good girl; she loves me; you're *de trop:*
Cast your eyes elsewhere, and pack up and go.

Valère Yes, yes, your merit, everyone agrees,
Is far too great, and overcomes my pleas;
And I am mad, although my love is true,
To vie for Isabelle with such as you.

Sganarelle That's right, you're mad.

Valère My folly was extreme
To let her charms foster this silly dream;
I could not know that my insane ambition
Would meet such formidable competition.

Sganarelle You're right.

Valère My hope is vanished now indeed;
Without a murmur, sir, I do concede.

Sganarelle And you do well.

Valère Alas! It's only right;
And I see all your virtues shine so bright,
That, much as I regret, I must defer
To the fond feelings you arouse in her.

Sganarelle Of course.

Valère I leave you master of the field.
But this I beg you (on this only yield
To the request, sir, of a wretched swain;
Since you alone cause his excessive pain):
I conjure you to say to Isabelle

That if for her I've spent three months in hell,
My love is spotless, and without a thought
Toward her of anything but what it ought.

Sganarelle Yes.

Valère That had it been for me to decide,
I would have fondly sought her for my bride,
If destiny, in giving you her heart,
Had not opposed my ardor from the start.

Sganarelle Good, good.

Valère That she must not think, come what may,
My memory of her could fade away;
That I am destined, till the day I die,
To love her only, to my final sigh;
And that if anything can end my suit,
It is my just respect for your repute.

Sganarelle You're speaking wisely; and I'll give the sense
To her of this, which offers no offense.
But take my word, and strive with might and main
To drive this passion clean out of your brain.
Farewell.

Ergaste [*to Valère*] A goodly dupe.

Sganarelle It is a shame,
This poor wight overpowered by his flame;
But he himself brought on his misery,
Trying to seize a fortress held by me.

SCENE SEVEN

Sganarelle, Isabelle

Sganarelle I've never seen a lover's woe revealed
Like his, on getting back his note still sealed:
Losing all hope at last, he now gives way.
But tenderly he conjured me to say
That in his love for you he had no thought
At which your honor might have been distraught,
And that, had it been for him to decide,

He would have fondly sought you for his bride,
If destiny, in giving me your heart,
Had not opposed his ardor from the start;
That you must not imagine, come what may,
His memory of you could fade away;
That he is destined, till the day he die,
To love you only, to his final sigh;
And that if anything can end his suit,
It is his just respect for my repute.
These are his words: a worthy man, whose flame
Deserves our pity rather than our blame.

Isabelle [*aside*] His love does not betray my own intent;
His eyes always declared it innocent.

Sganarelle How's that?

Isabelle I find you too compassionate
To someone whom like death itself I hate;
And if you loved me quite as you pretended,
You'd see why I have grounds to be offended.

Sganarelle But he knew nothing of your inclinations;
And judging by his honest declarations,
His love deserves . . .

Isabelle Tell me, is this a proof,
His aim to snatch me from beneath your roof?
And would a man of honor have recourse
To violence, and marry me by force?
As if I were a girl who would abase
Myself to live on, after such disgrace.

Sganarelle How's that?

Isabelle Oh yes! Beyond all misconstruction,
I've learned this traitor plans on an abduction;
I do not know what underhand technique
So soon informed him that within a week
You purpose to confer on me your hand,
As only yesterday you said you planned;
But he will try to interfere, they say,
And thus anticipate our wedding day.

Sganarelle Indeed that is not good.

Isabelle Pardon me, please.
A worthy man, whose fault is just that he's . . .

Sganarelle He's wrong, and this has gone beyond a jest.

Isabelle Your mildness feeds this folly in his breast.
If you had spoken with asperity,
He'd fear your wrath and my severity;
For it is since he's seen his note rejected
That he declares his plan shall be effected;
And, so I've learned, his faith is resolute
That I look fondly on his brazen suit,
That I oppose our marriage as does he,
And would rejoice if I could be set free.

Sganarelle He's mad.

Isabelle The role he plays for you is shrewd
And artfully intended to delude.
His own fine words reveal the traitor best.
I am, I must admit it, much distressed
That when a decent life is all I crave,
And to rebuff a lady-killing knave,
I'm subject to the deep humiliation
That he could harbor such an expectation!

Sganarelle There, never fear.

Isabelle I tell you, as for me,
Unless you chasten his effrontery
And find some way in which to rid me soon
Of the attentions of this shameless loon,
I give it up, and will no longer stand
For the affronts I suffer at his hand.

Sganarelle Come, don't be so upset. There, little wife,
I'll go give him the lecture of his life.

Isabelle But tell him that denial is in vain,
That I know what I know; his aim is plain;
That now, whatever be his enterprise,
I challenge him to take me by surprise;
That if there's anything he plans to do,

He must know what my feelings are toward you,
And that he, to avert catastrophe,
Must not oblige me to repeat my plea.

Sganarelle I'll say what's needed.

Isabelle But in such a way
As shows my heart means everything I say.

Sganarelle I'll not forget a thing, I do assure you.

Isabelle Impatiently I shall be waiting for you.
So hurry back as quickly as you can;
When you're away, I'm lost without my man.

Sganarelle I'll be right back, my child, just as I should.

Alone.

How can she be so virtuous and good?
Happy am I! How great is my elation
To find a wife who meets my expectation!
Yes indeed, this is how a wife should be,
And not like some who, fond of coquetry,
Listen to all the men, and everywhere
Expose good husbands to the general stare.
Oho! Our enterprising young Don Juan!

SCENE EIGHT

Valère, Sganarelle, Ergaste

Valère What brings you back here, sir?

Sganarelle Your carryings-on.

Valère What?

Sganarelle You know very well what's on my mind.
Really, I did not think you were so blind.
You try to gull me with your badinage,
Yet secretly you cling to your mirage.
I've tried to treat you gently from the start,
But you force me to say what's in my heart.
Aren't you ashamed that, being what you are,

You carry your effrontery so far,
Aim to abduct an honorable miss,
And threaten her main hope of married bliss?

Valère Who gave you, sir, this bizarre information?

Sganarelle Isabelle did; enough dissimulation.
Through me she bids you note, once and for all,
Her signs of where her preferences fall;
She says your project gives her much offense,
That death is better than such insolence,
And that there's going to be a real explosion
Unless you bring this thing to a conclusion.

Valère If what you tell me now is what she said,
I must admit my loving hope is dead:
All's ended, I can see; her words are clear,
And her decision one I must revere.

Sganarelle If? Do you doubt it, and suspect a feint
In my report of her annoyed complaint?
Must she herself then make her meaning plain?
All right, just so you learn your dreams are vain.
Come in, since you still hope to catch me out:
You'll see her heart is not in any doubt.

SCENE NINE

Isabelle, Sganarelle, Valère

Isabelle What? You could bring him here? What is your plan?
Will you take sides against me with this man?
Must I admire his merit, hold him dear,
And patiently endure his visits here?

Sganarelle No, I love you too well, my dear, for that.
But he treats all my words as idle chat,
Thinks I misrepresent your heart to be
Brimming with hate for him, with love for me.
And so I hoped that you would cure him of
An error that encourages his love.

Isabelle What? Has my soul then not yet spoken out
And made my wishes clear beyond all doubt?

Valère Yes, Madame; all this gentleman has said,
For you, has left confusion in my head:
I doubted, I confess; and your decree,
Determining my passion's destiny,
Concerns me so, I hope you will allow
That once again I hear it from you now.

Isabelle No, you should feel no shock at my decision;
It simply states my feelings with precision;
And these are based on equity, I find,
Enough to make me wish to speak my mind.
I want it to be known to both of you
That chance offers two objects to my view
Which, pulling me in different directions,
Excite my heart with opposite affections.
For one, whom I devotedly admire,
Esteem and tenderness alike conspire;
The other one, for all his adoration,
Has my antipathy and execration;
To me the presence of the one brings joy,
Giving me happiness without alloy,
Whereas the other, by his very sight,
Fills me with hatred and with secret spite.
The one of them I would most gladly wed;
The other—I would much rather be dead.
But I have shown my sentiments too long,
The torment that I suffer is too strong;
The one I love must act with speed and care,
Reduce his hated rival to despair,
And by a happy marriage set me free
From torment worse than death can ever be.

Sganarelle Yes, yes, darling, your wish is my intent.

Isabelle Thus only shall I ever be content.

Sganarelle You shall be soon.

Isabelle A girl may be unwise
To speak so candidly, I realize.

Sganarelle No, not at all.

Isabelle But in my present plight
I think a certain freedom is my right;
And surely without shame I can speak straight
To him whom I consider as my mate.

Sganarelle Yes, my poor itty-bitty turtledove.

Isabelle For heaven's sake, then, let him prove his love.

Sganarelle There, kiss my hand.

Isabelle Let him with all dispatch
Arrange an eagerly awaited match,
And here accept in all sincerity
My vow never to hear another's plea.

She pretends to kiss Sganarelle, and instead gives Valère her hand to kiss.

Sganarelle Oh! Little honeybear, poor little pet,
You needn't languish long; now don't you fret:
Hush, now.

To Valère.

You see, her love for me is true;
She's not just saying what I tell her to.

Valère Well, Madame! You are candid, anyhow:
I see from this just what I must do now,
And soon I'll free you from the insolence
Of one whose presence gives you such offense.

Isabelle No greater pleasure could you offer me,
For this is a repellent sight to see,
Odious, hateful; better to be blind . . .

Sganarelle Oh!

Isabelle Do I hurt you when I speak my mind?
Do I . . . ?

Sganarelle Good Lord, no, that's not what I mean;
But when I look at his pathetic mien,
I think you are too lavish with your spite.

Isabelle I cannot show too much in such a plight.

Valère Yes, you shall be content: three days, no more,
Shall rid you of the person you abhor.

Isabelle So be it. Farewell.

Sganarelle I'm sorry for your lot,
But . . .

Valère I have no complaint, sir, indeed not:
Madame is surely fair to both us two,
And I shall strive to make her wish come true.
Farewell.

Sganarelle Poor lad, he's overcome with woe.

To Valère.

Embrace me. You are both alike, you know.

SCENE TEN
Isabelle, Sganarelle

Sganarelle He's to be pitied.

Isabelle Not if you ask me.

Sganarelle Your love touches me to the last degree,
My sweet, and its reward must be unique:
Why make you be impatient for a week?
I'll marry you tomorrow, and invite . . .

Isabelle Tomorrow?

Sganarelle Bashfulness hides your delight;
You're overjoyed; I know how you react,
And that you wish it were an accomplished fact.

Isabelle But . . .

Sganarelle For this marriage let us now prepare.

Isabelle Oh Heaven, give me help in my despair!

Act Three

SCENE ONE
Isabelle

Isabelle A hundred times I'd rather lose my life
Than let myself be made my guardian's wife;
And since I seek just to escape this fate,
I hope my censors will commiserate.
It's dark, time flies; come on, I now must dare
Entrust my fortunes to my dear Valère.

SCENE TWO
Sganarelle, Isabelle

Sganarelle I'm back. Tomorrow they will expedite . . .

Isabelle Heaven!

Sganarelle You, darling? At this time of night?
Where are you going? When I left, you said
That you were tired and going up to bed,
And asked, finding yourself weary and worn,
To sleep on undisturbed until the morn.

Isabelle That's true; but . . .

Sganarelle What?

Isabelle It's awkward to explain,
And I'm afraid you'll think me quite insane.

Sganarelle What is this all about?

Isabelle A mystery.
You see, my sister first moved in with me,
Then by her pleas effected my removal,
Although her reasons met my disapproval.

Sganarelle What?

Isabelle Just imagine, she is smitten badly
With our young banished swain.

Sganarelle Valère?

Isabelle But madly.
Unparalleled is her infatuation,
And you can judge of its immoderation:
Since all alone, and at this hour, she came
To tell me all about her fretful flame,
Saying that she will certainly expire
Unless she can obtain her heart's desire,
That they had lived for upwards of a year
Bound by a passion secret but sincere,
And that they'd even sworn by heaven above
That marriage soon should consecrate their love.

Sganarelle That wicked girl!

Isabelle That learning the despair
To which my coldness has reduced Valère,
She came to ask me if she might console
Him for a blow that must distress his soul;
If from my window, speaking in my name,
She might hold conversation with her flame,
Recall to him, while mimicking my voice,
Sweet sentiments at which he may rejoice,
And in short make herself the addressee
Of the affection that he feels for me.

Sganarelle And what do you think . . . ?

Isabelle I'm fit to be tied.
"What," said I, "sister, have you lost all pride?

Aren't you ashamed to be under the sway
Of such a man, who changes every day?
Can you forget your sex, and be untrue
To one whom Heaven has ordained for you?"

Sganarelle It serves him right, and I am overjoyed.

Isabelle I thought of reasons—I was so annoyed—
To reprehend her baseness, as is right,
And put off her requests at least tonight;
But she expressed such burning hopes and fears,
Uttered such sighs, and shed so many tears,
Harped so on what would be her desperation
If I obstructed her infatuation,
That finally I could not but give in;
And mindful that it might be thought a sin
To sponsor such a tryst as this would be,
I meant to ask Lucrèce to stay with me,
Whose virtues you extol so every day;
But you came back as I was on my way.

Sganarelle No, I'll not have this, in my house, at night.
If just my brother were concerned, all right;
But someone might observe you from below;
And she on whom my person I bestow
Must not just have a modest disposition
But be beyond all possible suspicion.
Let's turn the hussy out; as for her passion . . .

Isabelle No, no, we must not do it in this fashion;
And she would have good reason to complain
Of counting on my secrecy in vain.
Since go she must, and that without delay,
At least wait while *I* send her on her way.

Sganarelle Do that.

Isabelle But you must not be seen or heard.
Just deign to watch her leave without a word.

Sganarelle Yes, I'll restrain my glee for love of you;
But from the time you've bid her fond adieu,
I shall be off; I'm itching to declare
To poor Ariste this whole sordid affair.

Isabelle I conjure you, my name must not be known.
Good night; right now I'm going up alone.

Sganarelle Until tomorrow—I can hardly wait
To tell my brother of this twist of fate!
He's got a bellyful, poor simpleton;
For twenty crowns I wouldn't miss this fun.

Isabelle [*inside the house*] Yes, sister, to your grief I'm not insensible;
But what you ask of me is reprehensible:
My honor's dear to me, and it's at stake.
Farewell: be on your way, for goodness' sake.

Sganarelle My, she is angry! I need hear no more.
For fear she may come back, I'll lock the door.

Isabelle [*on her way out, veiled*] O Heaven, be gracious! Aid my faltering wit!

Sganarelle Where is she bound? I'll follow along a bit.

Isabelle In my distress, darkness is on my side.

Sganarelle Right to her lover's house! Has she no pride?

SCENE THREE

Valère, Sganarelle, Isabelle

Valère [*coming out hastily*] Yes, yes, tonight somehow I mean to try
To speak . . . Who's there?

Isabelle Quiet, Valère, it's I;
I got ahead of you; it's Isabelle.

Sganarelle It is not, and you lie, you Jezebel:
She lives in honor while you live in shame,
And falsely you've assumed her voice and name.

Isabelle But unless you have marriage as your goal . . .

Valère That's the one aspiration of my soul;
And here I swear that if you'll have it so,
Where'er you'll marry me, there will I go.

Sganarelle Poor self-deluded blockhead!

Valère Never fear:
Your guardian's power I defy, my dear;
And long before he could rob me of you,
A thousand times I'd pierce him through and through.

Sganarelle Ah! I assure you that I do not crave
To take from you this wretch, this passion's slave;
Your plighted troth gives me no jealousy,
And you *shall* wed her, if it's up to me.
Yes, let's break up their little tête-à-tête:
I so revere her father's memory yet,
And labor so her sister to protect,
That I must try to save her self-respect.

Knocks on the Constable's door.

Hello!

SCENE FOUR

Sganarelle, Constable, Notary, Attendant

Constable Who's there?

Sganarelle Constable, how do you do.
Here, in your robe, sir, I have need of you:
Please bring along your light and follow me.

Constable We were just . . .

Sganarelle This is an emergency.

Constable What?

Sganarelle See that house? We must surprise inside
Two persons who must soon be man and bride:
A girl of ours, misled, lured to his house
By one Valère, who vowed to be her spouse.
She is both virtuously and nobly born,
But . . .

Constable In that case, sir, you've no cause to mourn,
Since here we have a notary.

Sganarelle You do?

Notary Notary royal.

Constable Honorable too.

Sganarelle Of course. Now, quiet, be on the *qui vive;*
Go in this door; allow no one to leave.
Your trouble shall be lavishly repaid;
But do not let *them* grease your palm instead.

Constable What? Do you think a man of my profession . . . ?

Sganarelle I meant no harm. Don't get the wrong impression.
I'll get my brother here immediately.
Just bring the torch and light the way for me.
That mild and wrathless man, I'll cheer him up.

Knocks at Ariste's door.

Hello!

SCENE FIVE

Ariste, Sganarelle

Ariste Who's knocking? You, brother? What's up?

Sganarelle Come on, wise guardian, supersenile knight,
I want to have you see a pretty sight.

Ariste How's that?

Sganarelle I've news you were not waiting for.

Ariste What?

Sganarelle May I ask, where is your Léonor?

Ariste Why ask me that? Gone dancing, I believe,
At a friend's house.

Sganarelle Yes. Of course. By your leave,
I'll take you to your dancing demoiselle.

Ariste What are you getting at?

Sganarelle You've trained her well:
"We should not be too strict and too severe;
Better rely on gentleness and cheer;
Suspicions, locks, and bars are all misplaced,
And will not keep our girls and women chaste;
We egg them on by such austerity;
Their sex demands a little liberty."
Your minx has taken all she wants, that's plain;
Her virtue's grown exceedingly humane.

Ariste What in the world is all this leading to?

Sganarelle My elder brother, this is made for you;
And fifty crowns would be a modest price
To see you thus repaid for being nice.
It's plain which sister had the better tutor:
One flees, the other chases, this same suitor.

Ariste You love to talk in riddles, I declare.

Sganarelle Oh, she went dancing—with Monsieur Valère;
I saw her go into his house tonight,
And in his arms she now takes her delight.

Ariste Who?

Sganarelle Léonor.

Ariste Come, no more joking, please.

Sganarelle Joking? . . . You think I'm talking pleasantries?
Poor soul, I'm telling you this one time more
That young Valère has got your Léonor,
And that he was engaged to this same belle
Before he started chasing Isabelle.

Ariste This makes so little sense you cannot mean it.

Sganarelle He won't believe it even when he's seen it.
It makes me mad. My word, age does no good
When this [*pointing to his forehead*] is lacking.

Ariste What, brother, you would . . . ?

Sganarelle I would have nothing. Only follow me:
Your mind shall be contented presently;
You'll see whether I'm fooling; soon you'll know
That they became engaged a year ago.

Ariste I can't believe that she would thus consent
To marry, and not tell me her intent,
I, who, since she was but a little child,
Have always been considerate and mild,
And who have always, without reservation,
Let her follow her every inclination.

Sganarelle Well, well, your eyes shall judge of the affair.
The constable and notary are there:
Her honor, which is what we're anxious for,
Is something that this marriage can restore;
For you are not so doting, I believe,
As still to want to wed your tarnished Eve,
Unless you have some more fine theories
To guard against the gossips' pleasantries.

Ariste I never will accept the weakling's part
Of wanting to possess a loveless heart.
But still I can't believe . . .

Sganarelle You talk on so,
We never shall be done; come on, let's go.

SCENE SIX

Constable, Notary, Sganarelle, Ariste

Constable There is no reason for compulsion here,
Gentlemen; calm your passions, have no fear;
If all you seek is marriage for these two,
You'll find them both impatient for it too;
Already young Valère has certified,
In writing, that he'll take her as his bride.

Ariste The girl . . .

Constable Locked in, and won't come out, she swears,
Unless your wishes coincide with theirs.

SCENE SEVEN

Constable, Valère, Notary, Sganarelle, Ariste

Valère [*at the window*] No, gentlemen; indeed, until I hear
That you agree, no one shall enter here.
You know me; I have signed the document
On which you may see proof of my intent.
If you consent that she shall marry me,
Sign it yourself, to show that you agree;
If not, believe me, you must take my life
Before you take away my darling wife.

Sganarelle No, we don't want to part you from your belle.

Aside.

He still believes that she is Isabelle.
Let's keep it so.

Ariste But is it Léonor?

Sganarelle Shut up.

Ariste But . . .

Sganarelle Hush.

Ariste I want to know . . .

Sganarelle What for?
I tell you, please be quiet.

Valère Come what may,
Isabelle is my lawful fiancée;
And I am not, in fact, so bad a choice
That you can only blame, and not rejoice.

Ariste But what he says is not . . .

Sganarelle Be quiet, you.
I will explain. Yes, without more ado,
We both consent that you take as your bride
The girl that we shall find with you inside.

Constable Those are the terms the deed is drawn in, sir;
The name is blank, since we have not seen her.
The girl can sign it later. Now, you sign.

Valère All right with me.

Sganarelle And I insist. That's fine.
Oh, what a laugh! This will make history.
Brother, sign first . . .

Ariste But all this mystery . . .

Sganarelle Damn it, you poor dunce, sign. I'll hear no more.

Ariste He says it's Isabelle; you, Léonor.

Sganarelle Suppose it is, brother, don't you agree
That each should make her choice completely free?

Ariste I do indeed.

Sganarelle Then sign; for so do I.

Ariste Yes; but I don't see . . .

Sganarelle You will by and by.

Constable We shall be back.

Sganarelle Now then, let me explain
What's happening.

SCENE EIGHT

Léonor, Lisette, Sganarelle, Ariste

Léonor Oh, what an utter pain!
How deadly dull I find these young gallants!
It's on account of them I fled the dance.

Lisette Each one tries hard to please your eye, I'm sure.

Léonor And that is just what I cannot endure.
I'd rather hear good plain talk any day
Than all the silly empty things they say.
To them their blond wig is a smashing hit;
And they assume they are the soul of wit
When they come up with some ironic jest
To the effect that older men love best.
And *I* prefer an older man's true zeal

To all the love these youngsters claim they feel.
But do my eyes deceive me . . . ?

Sganarelle [*to Ariste*] Yes, that's true.
Ah! Now I see her, and her servant too.

Ariste Léonor, I have reason for complaint:
You know I've never used you with constraint;
You have heard me a hundred times insist
That you are free to love whome'er you list;
And yet your heart, without concern for me,
Has plighted faith and love in secrecy.
I am not sorry for my gentleness,
But your behavior gives me real distress;
And this was not a kindly thing to do
To one who cares so tenderly for you.

Léonor I do not know what makes you speak this way;
But as I was before, I am today;
Nothing can ever change my high esteem
For you alone; another bond would seem
A crime; and were my wishes satisfied,
Tomorrow I would gladly be your bride.

Ariste Then, brother, what's this talk of strange affairs?

Sganarelle [*to Léonor*] You mean you're not just coming from Valère's?
You've not been pining for him, Mademoiselle,
And just today confessed to Isabelle?

Léonor Such a portrayal is a real surprise.
Who can have fabricated all these lies?

SCENE NINE

Isabelle, Valère, Constable, Notary, Ergaste, Lisette, Léonor, Sganarelle, Ariste

Isabelle Sister, I beg you to be slow to blame
If by my liberties I've smirched your name.
A sudden and appalling situation
Inspired me to this shameful fabrication:

Though your example censures such a passion,
Fate has not treated us in the same fashion.

To Sganarelle.

To you, sir, I make no apology:
My action favors you as well as me.
We were not meant to share a common life:
Let's say I don't deserve to be your wife;
An honor such as that would be too great,
And I preferred to seek another mate.

Valère Sir, beyond words I glory and rejoice
To accept from you the lady of my choice.

Ariste You'll have to swallow this with grace and tact,
Brother: your training brought about this act.
I'm sorry for your lot, for I predict
You won't be pitied, though you have been tricked.

Lisette I'm grateful to him for this whole affair,
Which shows the outcome of his kind of care.

Léonor I guess this action merits no acclaim,
But I cannot view it with any blame.

Ergaste The stars have made of him a cuckold born;
He's lucky to get off without a horn.

Sganarelle I can't get over it; I am astounded;
Such treachery leaves all my wits confounded;
And I do not believe even the devil
Can match this wench's aptitude for evil.
For her I would have put my hand in fire:
Who can trust womankind, since she's a liar?
The best of them excels at machination;
Their sex was born to be the world's damnation.
To that deceitful sex I say farewell,
And heartily consign them all to hell.

Ergaste Good.

Ariste Come with me. Valère, we shall assuage,
Tomorrow, if we can, my brother's rage.

Lisette [*to the audience*] If any husband is a churlish fool,
This is the place to send him—to our school.

The School for Wives

CHARACTERS

Arnolphe, also known as Monsieur de La Forêt
Agnès, an innocent girl, brought up by Arnolphe
Horace, in love with Agnès
Alain, a peasant, servant to Arnolphe
Georgette, a peasant woman, servant to Arnolphe
Chrysalde, a friend of Arnolphe
Enrique, brother-in-law of Chrysalde
Oronte, Horace's father, a great friend of Arnolphe
Notary

Scene: A house and garden in a small square in a town.

Act One

SCENE ONE
Chrysalde, Arnolphe

Chrysalde You've come, you say, to offer her your hand?

Arnolphe Yes, I'll complete tomorrow what I've planned.

Chrysalde We're here alone, unheard: I think we may
Therefore say freely what we have to say.
May I open my heart and not dissemble?
On your behalf your project makes me tremble.
In short, no matter how you view the fact,
To take a wife, for you, is a rash act.

Arnolphe True, my fine friend. Perhaps at home you see
Cause to fear that disaster threatens me;
The horns that on your brow I think you've got
You take for marriage's predestined lot.

Chrysalde Against these blows of chance there's no defense;
To me our vain precautions make no sense.
My fear for you springs from your mocking scorn,
Which countless hapless husbands now have borne;
For as you know, your satire, after all,
Has hit all benedicts, both great and small;
And everywhere you go, your chief delight
Is in the secrets that you bring to light.

Arnolphe Fine. Is there anywhere another town
Where husbands take such mishaps lying down?
Is there a species that we do not see?
And all accommodated to a tee.
One piles up wealth, with which his wife endows
Those who cause horns to grow upon his brows;
Another, happier but just as vile,
Watches his wife take presents, with a smile;
No jealous fancy ever gives him pause,
Because she says her virtue is the cause.
One loudly—and as vainly—makes a scene,
The other lets things go their way serene,
And when she has a caller, never rude,
Gets coat and gloves, not wanting to intrude.
One clever female tells a soothing tale
About her gallant to her doting male,
Who pities his poor rival's labor lost,
While that same rival labors to his cost.
Another, strangely wealthy, stoutly claims
She won the extra money playing games;
What games, the husband lacks the wit to know,
And thanks the Lord, from whom all blessings flow.
In short, when all around lies comedy,
May I not laugh at all these things I see?
When I see fools . . .

Chrysalde Yes, laugh at all the rest.
But don't forget: he who laughs last laughs best.
I hear how people talk; some make a sport
Of passing on each scandalous report;
But though I hear stories I might well quote,
I never do allow myself to gloat.
I hold my peace; and though upon occasion
I may condemn some kinds of toleration,
Although I've no intention to abide
The things that leave some husbands satisfied,
I prefer not to speak my mind straight out;
For all of us must fear a turnabout,
And we should never, since each case is new,
Swear rashly what we will, or will not, do.

Therefore if Fortune, which ignores our vows,
Should plant a cuckold's horns upon my brows,
My past behavior makes me almost sure
I'd have just quiet laughter to endure,
And that a few good people in this city
Might even say they thought it was a pity.
But you, my friend, would find it otherwise;
You run a real risk of a rude surprise.
Since you have been prolific in your sneers
At husbands too indulgent to their dears,
Since you have always been so quick to blast,
Beware of giving them their turn at last;
For if you offer them the slightest ground,
They'll trumpet it to hear for miles around,
And . . .

Arnolphe Lord, my friend, please don't be so upset:
The one who catches *me* is not born yet.
I know each cunning trick that women use
Upon their docile men, each subtle ruse,
And how they exercise their sleight-of-hand.
And so against this mishap I have planned.
My guarantee against such accident
Is marriage to a perfect innocent.

Chrysalde Why such reliance on a simpleton?

Arnolphe A man's no simpleton to marry one.
No doubt your wife's virtue matches her charm,
But a smart woman is cause for alarm;
And I know just what certain men have paid
For marrying an overgifted maid.
I should take on some lady of *esprit,*
Full of her literary coterie,
Dashing off prose and verse in tender bits,
Attended by the marquises and wits,
While I, known as "the husband of Madame,"
Play the unworshiped saint *ad nauseam?*
No, you can have your lofty minds and such;
A woman who's a writer knows too much.
I mean that mine shall not be so sublime,

And shall not even know what's meant by rhyme;
If she plays *corbillon**—that parlor game
Where everything in the basket ends the same—
Let her reply "Cream tart" to "What goes in?"
In short, I'd have her ignorant as sin;
And frankly, it's enough for her to know
How to spin, love me, say her prayers, and sew.

Chrysalde To have a stupid wife, then: that's your whim?

Arnolphe She can be ugly, so her wits are dim,
But not a brain, even if she's a beauty.

Chrysalde Beauty and wit . . .

Arnolphe I'll take a sense of duty.

Chrysalde But how do you expect an idiot
To learn what is her duty and what's not?
For one thing, it must be a dreadful bore
To have a fool around you evermore.
Then, do you think your theory is sound
And will protect your brow from being crowned?
Now, when a clever woman goes astray,
At least she knows, and means it just that way;
A stupid one may fall in the same snare
Not wishing to and wholly unaware.

Arnolphe That profound thought is met by Rabelais,
Who to Panurge has Pantagruel say:
"Urge on me any but a witless bride,
Talk me to death, preach on till Whitsuntide:
When you're all done, you'll be amazed to find
That nothing you have said has changed my mind."

Chrysalde I say no more.

Arnolphe Right. Every man his way.
I have my own to choose a fiancée.
I'm rich enough, I think, to have felt free
To have my wife owe everything to me.

* The popular game of *corbillon* ("basket"), much like the English crambo, involved answering the question *"Dans mon corbillon qu'y met-on?"* ("What do we put in my basket?") by a word ending in *-on*—which *"tarte à la crême"* ("cream tart") of course is not.

From her dependency has come submission;
She cannot flaunt her wealth or her position.
When she was four, one of a numerous brood,
I came to love her modest rectitude;
Seeing her mother too poor to afford
Her care, I asked to take her for my ward;
And that good peasant woman acquiesced
With much relief, finding it for the best.
In a small convent, undisturbed by man,
I had her raised according to my plan,
Which was to have them try as best they could
To keep her ignorant and therefore good.
Thank God, the outcome answered my intent,
And now she has grown up so innocent
That I bless Heaven for having been so kind
As to give me the wife I had in mind.
And so I brought her out; and since my home
Is one to which all kinds of people come,
Since we must never trust the wayward heart,
I've put her in this other house, apart,
And, to preserve her native purity,
Given her servants as naïve as she.
Now you will ask me: why this long narration?
—To let you know of my deliberation.
So, as a faithful friend, I now invite
You to come sup with her and me tonight
To see if, when you've had a chance to tell,
You will not think that I have chosen well.

Chrysalde Agreed.

Arnolphe And there you can, with confidence,
Judge of her person and her innocence.

Chrysalde In that regard, what you have been relating
Cannot . . .

Arnolphe You'll see, I have been understating.
I simply marvel at her naïvetés,
And could die laughing at the things she says.
Just fancy that, a day or two ago,
She came to me distraught, wanting to know—

So innocent, so candid and sincere—
If children are begotten through the ear.

Chrysalde I'm glad, Seigneur Arnolphe . . .

Arnolphe Come now, for shame!
Must you forever call me by that name?

Chrysalde It always will come out, do what I may,
And never your Monsieur de La Forêt.
At forty-two, what led you thus to dump
The name Arnolphe, and take that of some stump—
Rotten and old—upon your property,
To make a title of nobility?

Arnolphe Because that's now my name among my peers,
Also because it better suits my ears.

Chrysalde But why give up your true ancestral name
To take this empty one? It seems a shame.
Yet this is what most people itch to do;
And, though this tale does not apply to you,
I know a peasant whom they call Fat Pete,
Who owned a tiny lot, a few square feet,
Circled it with a ditch to be genteel,
And from it took the name Monsieur de l'Isle.

Arnolphe Such an example I could gladly spare;
But de La Forêt is the name I bear.
It makes good sense to me; I like its flavor;
And those who spurn it do me a disfavor.

Chrysalde Yet most folk still address you as before,
Even on letters coming to your door.

Arnolphe I don't much mind from those who do not know;
But you . . .

Chrysalde All right, agreed; it shall be so.
And I shall try to school my mouth to say
Not Arnolphe, but Monsieur de La Forêt.

Arnolphe Goodbye. I'll stop here for a word or two,
To tell them I am back and learn what's new.

Chrysalde [*aside, leaving*] My word, he is completely daft, I swear!

Arnolphe On certain matters he's just not all there.
How strange it is to see with how much passion
People see things only in their own fashion!
Hey, open up!

SCENE TWO
Alain, Georgette, Arnolphe

Alain [*opens an upper window*] Who's there?

Arnolphe I'm sure that they
Will welcome me after ten days away.

Alain Who's that?

Arnolphe Me.

Alain Georgette!

Georgette [*opens a lower window*] Well?

Alain Open up, see!

Georgette You open up!

Alain No, you!

Georgette Oh no, not me!

Slams window shut.

Alain Neither will I.

Slams window shut.

Arnolphe I could stand here and freeze
Through this routine of theirs. Hey, come on, please.

Georgette [*opening window*]
Who's there?

Arnolphe Your master.

Georgette Alain!

Alain [*opening window*] What?

Georgette The squire.
Open.

Alain No, you.

Georgette I'm blowing on the fire.

Alain I'm trying to save the sparrow from the cat.

Both windows shut.

Arnolphe Whichever doesn't open up like *that*
Shall get no food for four days, to the day.

Alain and Georgette appear at the door.

Georgette Why are you coming when I'm on my way?

Alain Why you, not me? That's a fine strodegy!

Georgette Get out of here.

Alain No, you get out; let me.

Alain and Georgette run to the gate.

Georgette I want to open the gate.

Alain And I do too.

Georgette You will not.

Alain You won't either.

Georgette Nor will you.

Arnolphe So, on they go, and I am waiting yet.

Alain It's me, Alain, sir.

Georgette No, it's me, Georgette.

Alain If I did not respect our master's frown,
I'd . . .

Swings at Georgette, who ducks; hits Arnolphe instead.

Arnolphe Damn it!

Alain Pardon me.

Arnolphe You stupid clown!

Alain She is too, sir . . .

Arnolphe Now, both of you, enough.
Listen and answer. No more silly stuff.
Well, Alain, how is everybody here?

Alain Why, sir . . .

Arnolphe removes Alain's hat; Alain replaces it.

Why, sir, we . . . [*Same business.*]
Thank the Lord, sir, we're . . . [*Same business.*]

Arnolphe Lord! Will you never learn how to behave?
Take off your hat to me, you saucy knave!

Alain You're right, I'm wrong.

Arnolphe [*to Alain*] Ask Agnès down, then, lad.

To Georgette.

After I left, did she seem pretty sad?

Georgette Sad? No.

Arnolphe No?

Georgette Yes, she did.

Arnolphe Then why . . . ?

Georgette Good lack,
She kept thinking she saw you coming back;
Each time a horse or mule or donkey passed
She was quite sure that it was you at last.

SCENE THREE

Agnès, Alain, Georgette, Arnolphe

Arnolphe Her work in hand! That's a good sign. Well then!
Agnès, my trip is done; I'm back again.
Do you like that?

Agnès God be praised, sir, I do.

Arnolphe And I am very pleased to see you too.
I trust you're well, just as you seem to be?

Agnès Yes, but those fleas: all night they bothered me.

Arnolphe You'll soon have someone to drive them away.

Agnès You'll do me pleasure.

Arnolphe Yes, I trust I may.
What are you doing?

Agnès Some caps that I've begun.
Your nightshirts and your nightcaps are all done.

Arnolphe Well! Very good. Now, go on back upstairs.
I'll soon be back; I'm off for some affairs;
Then we'll talk seriously for a bit.

Exeunt Agnès, Alain, Georgette.

You learned ladies, paragons of wit,
Spouters of sentiment and tenderness,
I challenge all your treasured cleverness,
And every letter, love-note, poem, romance,
To match this decent, modest ignorance.

SCENE FOUR

Horace, Arnolphe

Arnolphe We must not set our minds on property;
And if our honor is . . . What? Can it be . . . ?
Yes . . . No, I'm wrong . . . It *is* . . . Yes. My dear boy,
Horace!

Horace Monsieur Arnolphe!

Arnolphe Why, what a joy!
How long have you been here?

Horace Nine days.

Arnolphe Where, pray?

Horace I came to see you, but you were away.

Arnolphe Yes, in the country.

Horace You'd left two days past.

Arnolphe My! When young people grow, they do grow fast!
I can't believe the stage I see him at,
When I remember him as small as *that*.

Horace Well, here I am.

Arnolphe Tell me: Oronte, my dear
Old friend, your father, whom I so revere:
What is he up to? Is he still robust?
He knows I care about these things, I trust.
We haven't seen each other for four years.

Horace Nor written to each other, it appears.
Monsieur Arnolphe, he is as gay as ever.
I have a letter from him to deliver;
But now he writes he's coming here, although
His reason for it I still do not know.
Do you know someone from this neighborhood
Returning from America for good
With wealth it took him fourteen years to seek?

Arnolphe I don't. Didn't he say his name?

Horace Enrique.

Arnolphe No.

Horace Father speaks about him in the tone
He'd use of someone I had always known,
And says they will discuss, along the way,
Something important—what, he does not say.

Hands Oronte's letter to Arnolphe.

Arnolphe When he returns, I hope to make it plain
How glad I'll be to see my friend again.

Reads the letter.

Friends should not be so ceremonious;
These compliments are pointless between us.
He did not need to ask me; please make free,
For any funds you wish, to call on me.

Horace I'll take you at your word, if you'll permit.
A hundred pistoles would help quite a bit.

Arnolphe Believe me, you oblige me, I avow,
And I am glad I have them on me now.
Keep the purse too.

Horace But . . .

Arnolphe Let me have my way.
Now then. How do you like our city, pray?

Horace Fine buildings; an impressive population;
And fun, I think, beyond my expectation.

Arnolphe As regards pleasures, every man his own.
And for gallants (for thus I think they're known)
This town offers delights beyond compare.
The women here are ripe for an affair:
Blonde or brunette, all are exceeding kind,
And all their husbands suitably resigned.
It is sport for a prince; and what I see
Is an unfailing source of comedy.
Already you have smitten one, I'll bet.
Haven't you had some such adventure yet?
Good looks achieve much more than purses do,
And cuckolds owe their horns to such as you.

Horace Well, since you want the whole truth, I declare
I am involved here in a love affair
Which, as a friend, I'll tell you if you wish.

Arnolphe Another spicy tale! They're just my dish,
And I'll add this one to my growing list.

Horace This is in confidence; I must insist.

Arnolphe Oh!

Horace You must be aware that in these matters
If anything leaks out, the whole thing shatters.
Frankly, then, here is what I have to tell:
My heart's been captured by a local belle.
My first attentions had enough success
To lead the girl to grant me some access;
And, not to boast too much or do her wrong,
I really think my chances now are strong.

Arnolphe [*laughing*] But who?

Horace [*pointing to Agnès's house*] A young girl who, it so befalls,
Lives over in that house with the red walls;
Naïve, indeed, thanks to some simpleton
Who hides her from the sight of everyone,

While she, brought up to be an ignorant slave,
Shows charms designed to make an angel rave,
A most engaging manner, something tender,
To which any man's heart can but surrender.
But you are probably not ignorant of
This lovely creature, this young star of love.
Her name's Agnès.

Arnolphe [*aside*] I'll burst!

Horace The man, they say,
Is Monsieur de la Roche . . . de La Forêt . . .
I paid little attention to his name;
Not very bright, it seems, but rich, they claim;
And, so I gather, quite an imbecile.
Surely you know him?

Arnolphe [*aside*] What a bitter pill!

Horace But you don't answer.

Arnolphe Yes, he's known to me.

Horace Surely he's crazy?

Arnolphe Well . . .

Horace Don't you agree?
Does that mean yes? A fool? A jealous clown?
I see: just as they told me here in town.
In short, I've come to love the fair Agnès.
She is a perfect jewel, I confess.
'Twould be a sin for someone so unique
To languish in the power of such a freak.
My every effort, every aim shall go
To win her heart despite my jealous foe;
And what I borrow from you in this wise
Shall serve this honorable enterprise.
In great affairs, as you know better than I,
Gold is the key, whatever else we try;
And that sweet metal aids the conqueror
In every case, in love as well as war.
But you seem gloomy; can this be a sign
That you do not approve this plan of mine?

Arnolphe No, I was thinking . . .

Horace How I do go on!
Goodbye. I've tired you. I will call anon
To thank you.

Arnolphe [*to himself*] Can it be . . . ?

Horace [*returning*] Please be discreet.
Mine is a secret you must not repeat.

Arnolphe [*aside*] My aching soul . . . !

Horace To father above all:
I fear his anger, and what might befall.

Arnolphe [*thinking Horace is returning*] Oh!

Exit Horace.

How I suffered through that conversation!
Never has anyone known such vexation.
What haste and what imprudence, I declare,
He showed in telling *me* the whole affair!
Although my other name leads him astray,
He is a giddy fool to act this way.
Having endured, I had to persevere
Until I learned just what I had to fear,
And had to listen to his heedless chatter
To reach the center of this secret matter.
I'll try to catch him; he will not take wing;
I need to have him tell me everything.
I hate to think of what may be in store;
We often seek more than we bargain for.

Act Two

SCENE ONE
Arnolphe

Arnolphe I couldn't find Horace, but who can tell?
Now that I think of it, it's just as well;
I would have been unable to conceal
From him the deep anxiety I feel:
My gnawing perturbation would have shown;
And what he does not know is best not known.
But I'm not one to take this lying down
And leave the field open to that young clown.
I want to break this up, and I intend
To learn how far their friendship may extend.
My honor is as precious as my life;
I look on her already as my wife;
A lapse of hers would cover me with shame;
Her acts may be imputed to my name.
Why was I absent? Why did I go away?

Knocks at his gate. Alain and Georgette open the door and come out.

SCENE TWO

Alain, Georgette, Arnolphe

Alain Ah, this time, sir . . .

Arnolphe Enough. Come here, I say,
Both of you. This way, this way. Just come here.

Georgette You frighten me; my blood runs cold from fear.

Arnolphe When I am gone, this is how you obey me?
You put your heads together to betray me?

Georgette Don't eat me, sir. You give me quite a scare.

Alain [*aside*] Some mad dog must have bitten him, I swear.

Arnolphe I cannot say a word, I am so bothered:
I'd like to shed my clothes, not to be smothered.
So you permitted, you accursed scum—

To Alain, who starts to run.

Oh, so you want to flee—a man to come?

To Georgette.

Right now, you . . .

To Alain.

If you move . . .

Upon your oath,
I want you both to tell me . . . Yes, you both . . .

Both Alain and Georgette rise and try to run away.

If either of you moves, you're dead, d'you hear?
Now! How did that man ever get in here?
Well, well, speak up now, promptly, quick and smart.
Speak up, will you?

Alain and Georgette [*on their knees*]

Oh! Oh!

Georgette Oh, sir! My heart!

Alain I'm dying.

Arnolphe [*aside*] Lord! I'm soaked with sweat. I swear
I need a cooling walk, a breath of air.
When he was little, how was I to know
He would grow up—to this? I suffer so!
I think my first step is to have recourse
To her, and draw her out, gently, of course.
I'll try to moderate my irritation.
Gently, my heart, gently; hide your vexation.
[*Aloud.*] Get up. Go in and send me down Agnès.
No, stop. [*Aside.*] That way I would surprise her less.
They'd tell her my distress. No, no, much better
That I myself go in right now and get her.
[*Aloud.*] Wait for me here.

SCENE THREE

Alain, Georgette

Georgette Lord, what an awful sight!
The way he looks at you gives me a fright!
I never saw a Christian look so grim.

Alain That gentleman, I tell you, maddened him.

Georgette But why the devil treat his future spouse
So rough, and make us keep her in the house?
How come he hides her in seclusion here
And won't let anyone at all come near?

Alain Because such things arouse his jealousy.

Georgette But where did he get such a fantasy?

Alain Because . . . because he is a jealous cuss.

Georgette Yes, but why is he? And why all the fuss?

Alain Well, jealousy . . . You understand, Georgette . . .
Is something that . . . well . . . makes a man upset,
And makes him chase all other men away.
I'll give you a comparison, which may
Help you to see the point. Now then, when you
Have got a bowl of soup, isn't it true

That if some hungry man came up to eat it,
You would be angry, and you'd make him beat it?

Georgette I can see that.

Alain Good girl, of course you can:
Well, woman is in effect the soup of man.
When one man sees others ready to swoop
And try to dip their fingers in his soup,
He flies into a fury right away.

Georgette Yes; but why don't all men react that way?
And why do some seem perfectly content
To see their wife go out with some fine gent?

Alain Not everyone is of the greedy kind
That wants all for himself.

Georgette Unless I'm blind,
He's coming back.

Alain Your eyes are good; that's him.

Georgette He's angry!

Alain He has reason to look grim.

SCENE FOUR

Arnolphe, Agnès, Alain, Georgette

Arnolphe A Greek once gave the Emperor Augustus
This advice, full of usefulness and justice:
That when some mishap puts us in a fret,
The first thing is to say the alphabet,
So as to give us time to grow less hot
And not do anything that we should not.
So for Agnès, rather than be severe,
I'm having her come down and join me here
Upon the pretext of a little stroll,
That the suspicions of my ailing soul
May deftly lead her on and sound her out,
And I may learn what this is all about.

To Agnès.

Come out.

To Alain and Georgette.

Go in.

SCENE FIVE

Arnolphe, Agnès

Arnolphe It's nice to walk with you.

Agnès Yes, nice.

Arnolphe A lovely day!

Agnès Lovely.

Arnolphe What's new?

Agnès The little kitten died.

Arnolphe Too bad she's gone,
But we're all mortal, and we're on our own.
Didn't it rain while I was gone, my lamb?

Agnès No, no.

Arnolphe And were you bored?

Agnès I never am.

Arnolphe In those nine or ten days, what did you do?

Agnès Six shirts, I think; yes, and six nightcaps too.

Arnolphe [*after musing a bit*] The world is a strange place my dear Agnès.
People talk about anything, I guess.
Just think: some neighbors came to me to say
That a young man came while I was away,
That you received, and listened to, this male.
But I would not believe this wicked tale,
And I proposed to bet them, to their cost . . .

Agnès Good Lord, don't bet! Oh, my! You would have lost.

Arnolphe You mean to say a man . . . ?

Agnès Indeed I do.
He hardly left here once, I swear to you.

Arnolphe [*aside*] Such candor, I confess, is quite disarming.
And her simplicity at least is charming.

Aloud.

But I had said, Agnès, if I recall,
That you must not see anyone at all.

Agnès Oh yes. I saw him, but you don't know why;
I'm sure you would have done the same as I.

Arnolphe Perhaps. Let's hear about it, by your leave.

Agnès It's quite amazing, quite hard to believe.
Out on the balcony to get the air,
I saw, under those trees right over there,
A most attractive young man passing by,
Who bowed most humbly when he caught my eye.
And I, not wishing to be impolite,
Returned a deep bow, as was only right.
Promptly he makes another bow, and then,
I naturally bow to him again;
And since he then goes on to number three,
Without delay he gets a third from me.
He passes by, comes back . . . well, anyhow,
Each time he does he makes another bow.
And I, observing this most carefully,
Returned him every bow he made to me.
The fact is, if the light had not grown dim,
I would have gone on trading bows with him,
Because I did not want to yield, and be
Inferior to him in courtesy.

Arnolphe All right.

Agnès When I was at the door, next day,
An old woman comes up to me to say:
"My child, God keep you in his loving care,
And make you always look so young and fair!
Now, all his bounties constitute a duty:
You must not make a bad use of your beauty.

You have wounded a heart, which now, in pain,
Is forced at last to cry out and complain."

Arnolphe [*aside*] That tool of Satan! Witch! Accursed scum!

Agnès "I? Wounded someone?" I was overcome.
—"Yes," she said, "wounded, wounded terribly:
The man you bowed to from your balcony."
—"Alas!" said I. "I meant no harm, I swear.
Did I drop something on him unaware?"
—"Oh no, your eyes performed the deadly deed,"
She said, "and caused the damage and his need."
—"Good Lord!" I said. "I do not understand:
Have they some fatal power at their command?"
—"Fatal?" she said. "Oh yes, indeed they do.
They have a poison, dear, unknown to you.
In short, he's dying, and he's nearly gone.
And if," that kind old woman then went on,
"You are so cruel as not to give him aid,
They'll bury him in two days, pretty maid."
—"Good Lord!" I said. "*That* I don't want to see.
But just what help then does he ask of me?"
—"My child," she said, "he only wants to gain
The right to see and talk to you again.
Your eyes alone can end what they've begun,
Prevent his death, undo the harm they've done."
—"Alas! Of course," I said. "Now that that's clear,
He can come all he likes to see me here."

Arnolphe [*aside*] Ah, poisoner of souls! Accursed witch!
May hell repay your plots in boiling pitch!

Agnès That's how he came to see me: as a cure.
Don't you think I did right? I did, I'm sure.
And after all, was I to let him die,
And always have to live with that, when I
Have such compassion on all suffering here,
And when they kill a chicken, shed a tear?

Arnolphe [*aside*] There speaks a soul that's innocent and pure;
I was a fool to go away, that's sure,
And leave alone this girl, so free from guile,

Exposed to tempters and their every wile.
Now what I fear is that this noxious pest
Has carried matters . . . well, beyond a jest.

Agnès What ails you? Why, you seem a little mad.
In what I've told you, was there something bad?

Arnolphe No. But . . . after you met, what *did* ensue?
And when the young man came, what did he do?

Agnès Alas! If you had witnessed his delight,
How he was cured when he came in my sight,
The casket for which I am in his debt,
His gifts of cash to Alain and Georgette,
You'd surely love him, and say, as we do . . .

Arnolphe Yes. But what did he do, alone with you?

Agnès He swore his love for me was *sans pareil,*
And oh! he had the nicest things to say,
Incomparable things, that make me weak,
Whose sweetness, every time I hear him speak,
Tickles my heart, and somehow, in a word,
Stirs in me feelings hitherto unstirred.

Arnolphe [*aside*] O painful probing of a fatal riddle
In which the examiner is on the griddle!

To Agnès.

Now. Besides all this talk, these tendernesses,
Didn't he also give you some caresses?

Agnès Indeed he did! My hands and arms he seized,
And kissed and kissed them, seeming very pleased.

Arnolphe Agnès, was there anything else he took?

Seeing her taken aback.

Ouf!

Agnès Well, he . . .

Arnolphe What?

Agnès Took . . .

Arnolphe Ugh!

Agnès The . . .

Arnolphe Well?

Agnès Now look.
I'm sure you will be angry. I don't dare.

Arnolphe No.

Agnès Yes.

Arnolphe Good Lord, no!

Agnès Promise me, then, swear.

Arnolphe I swear.

Agnès He took . . . You'll be mad, I know you.

Arnolphe No.

Agnès Yes.

Arnolphe No, no. Damn it, what an ado!
What did he take?

Agnès He . . .

Arnolphe [*aside*] I'm in agony.

Agnès He took the ribbon that you'd given me.
I couldn't help it, he insisted so.

Arnolphe [*breathing again*] All right, the ribbon. But I want to know
If kiss your arms is all he ever did.

Agnès What? Are there other things?

Arnolphe No, God forbid.
But as a cure for his so-called disease,
Didn't he press for . . . other remedies?

Agnès Oh, no. You can imagine, if he had,
To help him, I'd have done it and been glad.

Arnolphe [*aside*] I got off easy then, thanks be to God!
If I do that again, call me a clod.
Hush.

Aloud.

This, Agnès, comes of your innocence.

What's done is done. I've spoken. No offense.
Your lover only wishes to deceive,
Win your good graces, and then laugh and leave.

Agnès Oh, no! He told me twenty times and more.

Arnolphe You do not know what empty oaths he swore.
But learn this: to accept caskets—or candies—
And listen to the sweet talk of these dandies,
Languidly acquiesce in their demands,
And let them stir your heart and kiss your hands,
This is a mortal sin, one of the worst.

Agnès A sin, you say? And why is it accursed?

Arnolphe Why? Why, there is a sacred declaration
That Heaven regards these acts with indignation.

Agnès With indignation? Why, then? I repeat,
It's all, alas, so pleasant and so sweet!
I marvel at the joy that all this brings,
And I had never known about such things.

Arnolphe Yes, there's great pleasure in this tenderness,
In each nice word and in each sweet caress;
But these have need of honor's discipline,
And only marriage can remove the sin.

Agnès It's not a sin when you are married, pray?

Arnolphe No.

Agnès Please let me be married right away.

Arnolphe Oh, if you want that, so do I, my dear,
And in fact that is why I've come back here.

Agnès Can this be?

Arnolphe Yes.

Agnès You will delight me so!

Arnolphe You will like marriage; that I think I know.

Agnès You want us two . . . ?

Arnolphe I do, assuredly.

Agnès How I'll caress you, if that comes to be!

Arnolphe Believe me, you won't be the only one.

Agnès I never know when someone's making fun.
You really mean it?

Arnolphe Yes, you'll see all right.

Agnès We shall be married?

Arnolphe Yes.

Agnès But when?

Arnolphe Tonight.

Agnès [*laughing*] Tonight?

Arnolphe Tonight. It makes you laugh?

Agnès Oh, yes.

Arnolphe My greatest wish is for your happiness.

Agnès I shall be grateful to you all my life!
And how I shall enjoy being his wife!

Arnolphe Whose?

Agnès His, of course.

Arnolphe. His . . . No. Let's get this straight.
You're pretty quick to pick yourself a mate.
The husband for you is another man.
As for that gentleman, here is my plan
(And if he really dies of it, too bad):
You are to end all dealings with the lad.
Now, if he comes to see you in this place,
You'll shut the door politely in his face,
And if he knocks and tries another tack,
Throw him a stone so that he won't come back.
You understand, Agnès? I'll hide right near.
Do as I say, for I shall see and hear.

Agnès Alas! He is so handsome!

Arnolphe Hush! Enough.

Agnès I shall not have the heart . . .

Arnolphe Now, stop that stuff.
Go on upstairs.

Agnès What? Do you mean to say . . . ?

Arnolphe Enough. I'm master: when I speak, obey.

Act Three

SCENE ONE

Arnolphe, Agnès, Alain, Georgette

Arnolphe Yes, all went well; I can't contain my glee:
You all followed my orders to a tee,
And put to rout that prince of libertines.
Now that is what good generalship means.
He had abused your innocence, Agnès.
See the result of just such thoughtlessness;
For you were, but for my interposition,
Right on the road to hell and to perdition.
The ways of all these boys are known to me:
Their ribbons, feathers, canions at the knee,
Their pretty talk, great wigs, and shining teeth;
But take my word, they all have claws beneath.
Oh yes, insatiable fiends are they,
And women's honor is their favorite prey.
But, once again, under my careful guard,
You have come off with decency unscarred.
Your manner, when I saw you cast that stone
By which his wicked hopes were overthrown,
Convinces me that I should not delay
Our scheduled marriage for one single day.
But first of all, I think it would be nice
To let you have a little sound advice.

To Alain.

A chair here, where it's cool.

To Georgette.

If ever you . . .

Georgette We know our lesson now, indeed we do.
That gentleman, he took us in; but then . . .

Alain If he gets in, may I never drink again!
And he's a fool: those two gold crowns he gave
To us that time were underweight, the knave!

Arnolphe Supper as ordered, then; get what we lack.
And for the contract, stop on your way back,
One of you, get the corner notary,
And ask him to come here with you to me.

SCENE TWO
Arnolphe, Agnès

Arnolphe [*seated*] Agnès, take heed. Now, no more work tonight.
Head up, now; turn your face a bit. That's right.

He puts his finger on his forehead.

Look at me when I talk—there, that's the way—
And take good note of everything I say.
Agnès, I'm marrying you; and you ought
A hundred times a day to bless your lot,
To keep your former low estate in mind
And marvel that a man can be so kind
As I, who found you just a country lass,
And raise you to the honored middle class,
There to enjoy the bed and the embraces
Of one who's always kicked against such traces,
Denying to all parties hitherto
The honor that he now reserves for you.
Always you ought to keep before your eyes
Your little worth without this splendid prize,

So that you may be all the more intent
On meriting this glorious ascent,
Knowing your place, and acting so that I
Never repent of raising you so high.
Marriage is not a joke, Agnès, my dear!
Its laws are stern, its duties are severe;
And you're not going into it, I claim,
As if it were a pastime or a game.
For frailty your sex is made and reared;
Authority is vested in the beard.
Although you form half of society,
Between our halves is no equality;
One is supreme, the other one abject;
One must submit, the other one direct;
And the obedience a soldier must
Show to his leader to deserve his trust,
That which a servant, monk, or little tot
Owes his lord, abbot, father, by his lot,
Comes nowhere near to the docility,
To the obedient humility
And deep respect a wife should harbor toward
Her husband, as her master, chief, and lord.
Now, when he glances at her seriously,
She should cast down her eyes immediately,
And never dare to look him in the face
Unless his glance is kind and full of grace.
Wives will not understand this nowadays;
But do not follow their abandoned ways.
Don't imitate all those flirtatious jades
Who make the town ring with their escapades;
And guard against the Evil One's attacks,
Who uses handsome fops to make girls lax.
Note that in giving you my life to share,
Agnès, I place my honor in your care;
It is a tender thing, easy to hurt,
Which will not tolerate a playful flirt;
And in hell there are caldrons in which wives
Will boil forever, if they lead bad lives.
This is no idle talk that I impart,
And you should take these lessons to your heart.

Heed them, don't flirt, and then your soul is sure
To be forever lily-white and pure;
But if you let dishonor stain your soul,
Then it will promptly turn as black as coal;
People will shrink in horror, and one day
You will go down to hell, the devil's prey,
And there for all eternity you'll stew.
May Heaven not reserve that fate for you!
Now, make a curtsy. As a novice must
Master her convent's laws, and know her trust,
A future bride must know the marriage pact.
Here in my pocket is a useful tract
[*Rising.*] In which to learn what is to be your role.
The author I don't know: some worthy soul.
On this alone I want your mind to dwell.
Here. Let's just see if you can read it well.

Agnès [*reads*]

THE MAXIMS OF MARRIAGE, OR, THE DUTIES OF THE MARRIED WOMAN, WITH HER DAILY PRACTICE

MAXIM I.
When a woman, duly wed,
Comes to share her husband's bed,
She must keep one thing in mind:
Even in these times she'll find
He takes her for himself alone, not for mankind.

Arnolphe I will explain that later, yes indeed;
But for the present, go ahead and read.

Agnès [*reads on*]

MAXIM II.
She should be nicely dressed
Only to interest
Her husband—not some swain.
His satisfaction must be paramount.
It is of no account
That others find her plain.

MAXIM III.
Not for her the ogling glance
Or cosmetics, to enhance
Her loveliness, and set off her complexion:
These are the bane of honor and of duty;
Wives rarely fuss about their beauty
To guarantee their mate's affection.

MAXIM IV.
Decently she must hide her eyes, that gleam so,
Under her coif, soon as she leaves the house,
Since, to seem lovely to her spouse,
To no one must she seem so.

MAXIM V.
All visitors but those who come to see
Her lord and master, she
In honor must deter.
Those who, with gallant whim,
Come only to see her,
Are sure to displease him.

MAXIM VI.
When men, in a pleasant way,
Offer gifts, she must say no;
All men of the present day
Count upon a *quid pro quo.*

MAXIM VII.
In her possessions, though this rouse her spite,
Must be no desk, no paper, pen, or ink;
It is the husband's job to think,
And what needs writing he will write.

MAXIM VIII.
Those giddy blatherings
Called social gatherings
Are places for the wives to plot and plan.
To ban them all would be good policy

As a conspiracy
Against the married man.

MAXIM IX.
Gambling a wife must shun: its specious charm
Should fill her with alarm
For her dear honor's sake:
Luck comes and goes away
And often makes her play
Her one remaining stake.

MAXIM X.
Let a country promenade
Or a picnic in a glade
Not be something she essays:
Men of prudent counsel find
That for pastimes of this kind
The husband is the one who pays.

MAXIM XI. . . .

Arnolphe Now, finish it alone; and in a while
I will explain all this in thorough style.
I've just remembered something I must do:
It won't take long; I'll come right back to you.
Go in; I leave this booklet in your care.
If the notary comes, I'll soon be there.

SCENE THREE
Arnolphe

Arnolphe No, I could never find a better wife.
I'll shape her soul at will, and mold her life.
Between my hands she's like a piece of clay,
And I can fashion her in any way.
They nearly caught me, though, when I was gone,
Using her innocence to lead her on.

But truly it is better that a bride,
If err she must, should err upon that side.
Such failings are no reason for concern:
A simple person is disposed to learn;
And if she's left the straight and narrow lane,
Two words will bring her back to it again.
A clever woman is another dish;
Our fate depends upon her slightest wish.
Nothing can budge her from her chosen course,
And all our teaching does is make us hoarse.
Her wit helps her make sport of our advice,
Portray as virtuous her every vice,
And, to fulfill her bad intentions, find
Devices to deceive the shrewdest mind.
To try to fend the blow is vain fatigue:
A clever wife's a devil for intrigue;
Her husband's honor hangs upon her whim:
Its verdict reached, there's no appeal for him.
Many good men could amplify that theme.
Well, my young fool will have no cause to beam.
He talked too much, and now he pays the price.
That is our Frenchmen's ordinary vice:
When they are lucky in a love affair,
Secrecy is a thing they cannot bear;
And vanity holds them so much in thrall,
They'd rather hang themselves than not tell all.
Oh! How a woman takes the devil's bait
When she picks up with such an addlepate,
And how . . . ! But here he is . . . Let's play our part,
And learn what disappointment fills his heart.

SCENE FOUR

Horace, Arnolphe

Horace I've just come from your house. You know, I swear
Fate simply will not let me find you there.
But still I'll try to pay a proper call . . .

Arnolphe Lord! Please don't think about such things at all.
These ceremonies are a thing I hate,
And I would like to ban them from the state.
Most people waste some two thirds of their days
Quite stupidly, on these accursed ways.
So, let's put on our hats. [*Puts on his.*] No more ado.
Now, in your love life, Sir Horace, what's new?
Just now I had my mind on other things,
I fear; but with the thoughts that leisure brings,
I marvel at your progress from the start,
And I take your successes to my heart.

Horace Well, since I told you all I had to tell,
My love, I must admit, has not fared well.

Arnolphe Oho! How so?

Horace It's Fortune's cruel frown
Which brought my lady's master back to town.

Arnolphe Oh, what bad luck!

Horace What's more, to my chagrin,
He's learned about the state affairs are in.

Arnolphe Why, how the devil did he come to know?

Horace I've no idea; but it is surely so.
I planned, at just about my usual hour,
To pay a visit to my lovely flower,
When, with a wholly altered tone and face,
The maid and valet barred me from the place,
Saying "You can't come back here any more,"
And then—in my face, mind you—slammed the door.

Arnolphe Right in your face!

Horace My face.

Arnolphe That *is* severe.

Horace Still from outside I tried to make them hear;
But every time I spoke, they answered faster:
"You can't come in, by order of the master."

Arnolphe They didn't open?

Horace No. From up above
I then had confirmation from my love,
Who sent me packing in a haughty tone,
And from her window threw me out a stone.

Arnolphe How's that? A stone?

Horace A stone of no small size,
With her own hands, to greet my enterprise.

Arnolphe The devil take it! That was pretty cruel,
And I'm afraid you've lost your little jewel.

Horace It's too bad that man should come back right now.

Arnolphe It makes me sorry for your sake, I vow.

Horace He breaks up everything.

Arnolphe Well, never mind,
There must be a way out that you will find.

Horace By some device, I certainly must try
Some way to dodge this jealous fellow's eye.

Arnolphe That should be easy. And the girl, you say,
Loves you.

Horace Indeed she does.

Arnolphe You'll find a way.

Horace I hope I shall.

Arnolphe That stone put you to rout,
But that should not astonish you.

Horace No doubt,
And I knew right away my man was there,
Unseen, but managing the whole affair.
What I did marvel at—and you will too—
Was something else I must report to you:
That lovely girl hit on a bold device
Startling for one so innocent and nice.
Love is a great teacher, you must agree,
Making us what we never thought to be;
And in a moment, under his direction,
Our character can change its whole complexion.
He breaks down even natural obstacles,

And seems to manage sudden miracles;
In no time he can make a miser kind,
A coward valiant, and a boor refined;
He makes the dullest soul agile and fit,
And gives the most naïve its share of wit.
That miracle has happened to Agnès;
Her terms in breaking with me were express:
"I want no further visits, so goodbye;
I've heard you out, and this is my reply."
And then the stone—and this was really neat—
Fell, with this note attached, right at my feet.
And I'm amazed at how, in sense and tone,
This note goes with her throwing of the stone.
Aren't you surprised at how her action fits?
And isn't love a sharpener of wits?
Can one deny its power to impart
Wondrous resources to the human heart?
Come! How about this letter and her trick?
Don't you admire her wit? Wasn't she quick?
And what about my jealous rival's role
In all this nonsense? Don't you find it droll?
Tell me.

Arnolphe Yes, very droll.

Horace Then how about
A laugh?

Arnolphe forces a laugh.

This man, in arms to keep me out,
Entrenched at home, with stones for ammunition,
As if I were a storming expedition;
Who goads his servants, in his antic fear,
To hinder me from even coming near;
And whom this girl, that he's kept so naïve,
Through his own scheme has managed to deceive!
I must say that although his coming back
Forces my love to take another tack,
I never heard of anything so funny;
I can't help laughing, not for love or money.
But you're not laughing very hard, I'd say.

Arnolphe [*forcing a laugh*] I'm laughing—pardon me—as best I may.

Horace But here's her note. Please read it, as my friend.
All that was in her heart, her hand has penned,
But that in touching terms of kindliness,
Of simple innocence and tenderness.
In short, in just the way I'm speaking of,
Nature expresses the first pangs of love.

Arnolphe [*aside*] So that's why you were taught to write, you tart!
I never wanted you to learn the art.

Horace [*reads*]
"I want to write you, and I am at a loss how to set about it. I have thoughts that I would like you to know; but I don't know how to go about telling them to you, and I mistrust my own words. As I am beginning to realize that I have always been kept in ignorance, I am afraid of putting down something that may not be right and saying more than I ought. Truly, I don't know what you've done to me; but I feel that I am mortally unhappy over what they're making me do to you, that it will be terribly hard for me to get along without you, and that I would be very glad to be yours. Perhaps it's a bad thing to say that; but anyway I can't help saying it, and I wish it could be done without its being wrong. They keep telling me that all young men are deceivers, that I mustn't listen to them, and that everything you say to me is only to take advantage of me; but I assure you that I have not yet been able to imagine that of you, and I am so touched by your words that I cannot possibly believe they are lies. Tell me frankly what the truth is in all this; for after all, since there is no malice in me, you would be doing a terrible wrong if you deceived me, and I think I would die of sorrow."

Arnolphe [*aside*] Hellcat!

Horace What's wrong?

Arnolphe I coughed; just a sore throat.

Horace Could anything be sweeter than that note?

The tyrant's damned precautions are in vain;
This letter makes her lovely nature plain.
Shouldn't it be a punishable crime
To smother such a spirit all this time,
And to have tried to dim her brilliant mind
By keeping her ignorant and confined?
Love has begun to tear away the veil;
And if some lucky star lets me prevail,
I hope to teach him what it's all about,
That traitor, hangman, scoundrel, brutish lout . . .

Arnolphe Goodbye.

Horace So soon?

Arnolphe Something I have to do,
Which I'd forgotten as I talked to you.

Horace But since they keep close watch, could you suggest
How to get to her; who could help me best?
I'm free in asking favors without end;
I hope I'm not imposing on a friend.
I've only foes inside; their eyes are keen;
And maid and servant, whom I just have seen,
No matter what cajoleries I try,
Keep me away with a suspicious eye.
I used to have, for such things, an old woman
Whose gifts, to tell the truth, were superhuman.
It helped at first to have her on my side;
But just four days ago the poor thing died.
Can't you see any way to help me out?

Arnolphe You don't need me; you know what you're about.

Horace Goodbye then. See how I confide in you.

SCENE FIVE
Arnolphe

Arnolphe What torment that young fellow put me through!
How I have struggled to conceal my hurt!
How could a simple girl be so alert?

Either her innocence is just a role,
Or Satan breathed this cunning in her soul.
That cursed note of hers! I could have died.
I see the traitor's got her on his side.
He rules her mind; he's firmly anchored there;
And that's my mortal pain and my despair.
The stealing of her heart afflicts me twice:
My honor and my love both pay the price;
I'm furious that he's usurped my domain,
And furious that my schemes have been in vain.
She will be punished for her lewd romance,
I know, by the sheer force of circumstance:
And she will give herself her just deserts;
But still, to lose the one you love—it hurts.
I made my choice like a philosopher.
Heavens! Why am I so bewitched by her?
She has no relatives, wealth, or protection;
She spurns my cares, my kindness, my affection;
Yet I love her, for all this turnabout:
Her love is something I can't do without.
You fool, you make me mad; you're a disgrace!
A thousand times I'd like to slap my face.
I'll go indoors awhile, only to see
The face she puts upon such treachery.
Heaven, keep my forehead free from any horn;
Or, if it was for that that I was born,
Grant me at least, to help me bear the shame,
The fortitude of some whom I could name!

Act Four

SCENE ONE
Arnolphe

Arnolphe I cannot seem to stay put anywhere,
And my poor mind is torn with many a care,
Trying, indoors and out, to put a stop
To the designs of that obnoxious fop.
With what aplomb the traitress met my gaze!
No care about the error of her ways!
And though she nearly was the death of me,
You never saw such peaceful purity.
The more I saw her sweet and tranquil smile,
The more I felt the boiling of my bile;
And as these angry transports racked me harder,
They seemed to reinforce my loving ardor;
Of bitter, hopeless spite my heart was full:
Yet never has she looked so beautiful.
Her eyes have never seemed so much afire,
Nor ever roused in me such keen desire;
And I shall burst—I feel it deep inside—
If I cannot have Agnès for my bride.
Shall I have trained her under close direction,
With such precautions and with such affection,
Brought her up in my house from infancy,

Cherished the tenderest expectancy,
Admired her budding charms, now almost grown,
Pampered her thirteen years, for me alone,
Only to watch while some young popinjay,
With whom she's smitten, carries her away?
And *that* when she is half married to me?
No, by God! No, by God! It shall not be!
My silly little friend, I'll take such care
That I will wreck your foolish hopes, I swear,
And we shall see which one of us laughs best.

SCENE TWO

Notary, Arnolphe

Notary Ah, here you are! I've come at your behest
To draw that contract that you want. Good day.

Arnolphe [*not seeing him*] How shall I do it?

Notary In the regular way.

Arnolphe [*not seeing him*] Now, what are the precautions I must take?

Notary I'll not forget your interests are at stake.

Arnolphe [*not seeing him*] I must protect myself against surprises.

Notary I'll handle any problem that arises.
Your worries can be easily allayed:
Don't sign the contract till the money's paid.

Arnolphe [*not seeing him*] My fear is that, if anything gets out,
All over town it may be noised about.

Notary It's easy to prevent publicity;
Your contract can be drawn up privately.

Arnolphe [*not seeing him*] But for this, how can I win her assent?

Notary Jointure and dowry should be congruent.

Arnolphe [*not seeing him*] I love her, and by love my hands are tied.

Notary Then one may give some extra to the bride.

Arnolphe [*not seeing him*] How shall I treat her now? What shall I say?

Notary The husband to his fiancée shall pay
One third her dowry; but one may ignore
This rule and, if one wants to, pay her more.

Arnolphe [*not seeing him*] Now if . . .
He sees the notary.

Notary Survivors' shares concern them both.
He may endow his bride, if he's not loath,
Just as he likes.

Arnolphe Eh?

Notary Set her up for life
(If he adores and wants to please his wife)
By stipulated jointure, as they say,
Which would be lost if she should pass away;
It could go to the heirs of the said bride;
Or else by common law, as specified;
Or further, by contractual stipulation,
Through simple or through mutual donation.
Why do you shrug? Don't I make sense? Do you doubt
I know my marriage contracts inside out?
Who is to teach me? Just name anyone.
Don't I know spouses hold in unison
Property, chattels, monies, real estate,
Save what they formally repudiate?
And that one third of the fiancée's share
Enters the joint estate . . . ?

Arnolphe Yes, I'm aware
You know that; but who asked to hear about it?

Notary You seemed as though you could not do without it:
You with your shoulder shrugs and your grimace.

Arnolphe A plague upon him and his ugly face!
Goodbye: I hope that makes you disappear.

Notary Isn't the contract why you called me here?

Arnolphe Yes, I did send for you; but it's deferred,
And when the time is set I'll send you word.
What can possess the man, with all his chatter?

Notary He's had a bellyful, that's what's the matter.

SCENE THREE

Notary, Alain, Georgette, Arnolphe

Notary Wasn't it you your master sent for me?

Alain Yes.

Notary I don't know what you take him to be,
But give this message to that imbecile:
That he's an arrant fool.

Georgette We surely will.

SCENE FOUR

Alain, Georgette, Arnolphe

Alain Monsieur . . .

Arnolphe Come here: you both are tried and true,
My real, good friends; and I've had news of you.

Alain The notary . . .

Arnolphe Wait; time for him anon.
Now hear me. Someone has designs upon
My honor. Children, what would be your shame
If your master were robbed of his good name!
Nowhere in public would you dare appear,
And everyone would point you out and jeer.
So, since you are involved in this affair
As much as I, keep watch with such great care
That this young gallant never may get through.

Georgette A while ago you showed us what to do.

Arnolphe Don't listen to a word he has to say.

Alain Of course we won't.

Georgette We'll send him on his way.

Arnolphe Suppose he's very sweet: "Alain, please deign
To help me out a bit and ease my pain."

Alain You are a fool.

Arnolphe That's good.

To Georgette.

"My sweet Georgette,
You seem as kind a person as I've met."

Georgette You are an ass.

Arnolphe [*to Alain*] "How can you blame
My virtuous and honorable aim?"

Alain You are a rascal.

Arnolphe Fine. [*To Georgette.*] "My death is sure
Without your pity for what I endure."

Georgette You're an impudent booby.

Arnolphe Good enough.

To Alain.

"I do not ask for favors on the cuff.
I've a good memory for service done.
Here's an advance, Alain; go have some fun.
Here's for another petticoat, Georgette.

He holds out money; both reach out and take it.

That's just a sample; I'll do better yet.
And in return I merely ask to see
Your lovely mistress; that's my only plea."

Georgette [*pushing him*]
Try someone else.

Arnolphe That's good.

Alain [*pushing him*] Out!

Arnolphe Good.

Georgette [*pushing him*] But quick!

Arnolphe Good. Hey! Enough.

Georgette Oh, did I miss a trick?

Alain Is that the way? Aren't we pretty adept?

Arnolphe The money, though, you never should have kept.

Georgette Oh yes, that is a point that we forgot.

Alain Shall we begin again?

Arnolphe I should say not.
Enough. Go on back in.

Alain One word from you . . .

Arnolphe I tell you, no; go in, I want you to.
There, keep the money; I'll be right along.
Keep watch, and see that not a thing goes wrong.

SCENE FIVE

Arnolphe

Arnolphe I need to get a careful, keen-eyed spy;
The corner cobbler is the man to try.
I mean to hold her under lock and key
At all times, and to keep the household free
Of hairdressers, wigmakers, ribbon peddlers,
Milliners, glovers, and assorted meddlers,
All those who make a covert business of
Encouraging the mysteries of love.
I've been around, and I know every trick.
In short, this fellow will be very slick
If he can get a message past my guard.

SCENE SIX

Horace, Arnolphe

Horace What luck to find you in your own back yard!
I had a really narrow squeak, I swear.

Just after leaving you, all unaware,
I saw Agnès come to her balcony,
Alone, in the cool shade of the nearby tree.
She, having given me a sign to wait,
And got downstairs, opened the garden gate;
But when we'd barely got inside her room,
Up the stairs came her jealous would-be groom;
And all that she could do in such a plight
Was shut me in a wardrobe good and tight.
He came right in; I could not see, but heard;
He strode around the room without a word,
Uttering frequent sighs that spoke his woes,
Beating the tables with horrendous blows,
Striking a friendly dog, and when he found
Some things of hers, tossing them all around.
He knocked some vases, with a furious hand,
From off the mantel where they used to stand.
This hornèd goat, I'm very much afraid,
Has got some inkling of the trick she played.
When he had vented his discomfiture
At length upon the helpless furniture,
At last, speechless and vexed, he went away,
And I came out into the light of day.
Fearing my rival, we decided not
To stay together longer in that spot:
His jealousy would make the risk too great;
But tonight I shall come to see her late.
I'll cough three times, and she, upstairs, inside,
Will at the signal open the window wide.
A ladder and her help are all I need,
I trust, to reach her side with loving speed.
I tell you all this as to my sole friend.
With joy, it seems, to share is to extend;
And perfect happiness, if it's unknown,
Tastes flat; we cannot savor it alone.
I trust that my success will please you too.
Goodbye. I have some urgent things to do.

SCENE SEVEN

Arnolphe

Arnolphe What? Shall the star that drives me to despair
Not give me time to catch a breath of air?
Blow upon blow! Then must my vigilance
Be overcome by their intelligence?
And at my age, am I to be the dupe
Of a young girl and a young nincompoop?
For twenty years, a philosophic sage,
I've watched the hapless husbands of this age,
Studied all their disasters, tried to know
How even the most prudent are brought low.
Applying all these lessons learned from life,
I sought a way, wanting to take a wife,
To escape the dismal horns of cuckoldry
Which on so many other brows I see.
To serve this noble aim, I put to use
All that human invention can adduce;
And as if fate had chosen to ordain
That men seek such security in vain,
After all my experience, my cares,
My hard-won insight into these affairs,
After twenty-odd years of meditation
Leading to caution and deliberation,
I shall have left the other husbands' route
Just to fall into the same disrepute?
No! Hangman fate, I'll still prove you a liar.
I hold her still, in spite of his desire;
If I have lost her heart to this blond pest,
At least I'll see he shall not have the rest;
And this night, which they count on to elope,
Shall not go by as sweetly as they hope.
I take some pleasure, amid so much pain,
To learn about the snares he sets in vain,
And see my foe, this rattle-brained gallant,
Take his own rival for his confidant.

SCENE EIGHT

Chrysalde, Arnolphe

Chrysalde Well then? Before our walk, suppose we sup?

Arnolphe I shall not eat this evening.

Chrysalde Why, what's up?

Arnolphe I've problems on my mind; excuse me, pray.

Chrysalde Why, have your marriage plans then gone astray?

Arnolphe You're too intent on other men's affairs.

Chrysalde Oho! So angry! Well, what are your cares?
Old chap, your love has not, by any chance,
Encountered some unhappy circumstance?
From your expression, I would almost swear it.

Arnolphe Whatever happens, I shall have the merit
Of not resembling certain folk I know
Who meekly watch the suitors come and go.

Chrysalde I marvel that, with your philosophy,
These matters cause you such anxiety,
That you equate security with bliss,
And think the test of honor is just this.
For you, a man may be a wicked brute,
So long as he avoids this disrepute;
His honor's safe, no matter what his life,
Provided he enjoys a faithful wife.
Come now, how can you make our reputation
Depend on such a chance consideration?
Why should a well-born soul have to repent
Brooking a wrong that no one can prevent?
When we select a wife, why should her ways
Decide whether we merit blame or praise?
Why make a bugbear out of the offense
We suffer from her lack of continence?
Know that a gentleman may possibly
Take a much milder view of cuckoldry,
That since none can ward off this accident,
It should be, by itself, indifferent,
And that the harm, whatever people say,

Comes from our viewing it with such dismay;
For in this plight, as everywhere, it seems
That we should find our way between extremes:
Not imitate the overdebonair
Who pride themselves on every such affair,
Are always mentioning their wives' young gallants,
Singing their praises, dwelling on their talents,
Who take them and their interests to their heart,
And in their treats and parties have their part,
Till, when they turn up in some public place,
Men wonder that they dare to show their face.
But, even as we blame such silliness,
We must condemn the opposite excess.
Friendship with suitors seems a sorry joke;
Yet neither do I praise those stormy folk
Whose reckless anger and tempestuous cries
Bring their anxiety to all men's eyes,
Whose outbursts seem intended to invite
The world's attention to their sorry plight.
Between these courses lies a proper way
In which a prudent man will often stay.
We need not blush, if we are men of sense,
Not even at our partner's worst offense.
In short, say what men will, then, cuckoldom
Is not as frightful as it seems to some;
And our ability, just as I say.
Consists in taking it the proper way.

Arnolphe After that pretty speech, your lordship should
Be thanked by all the cuckolds' brotherhood;
And anyone who hears your rhapsody
Will soon enroll in their society.

Chrysalde I don't say that; I look at that askance.
But since we owe our choice of wives to chance,
As in a game of dice we should behave,
Where, when you do not get the roll you crave,
You must reduce your stakes, control your play,
And change your luck by caution and delay.

Arnolphe In short, sleep and eat well; don't fret a minute;
And make yourself believe there's nothing in it.

Chrysalde You think you're joking; but, pretense aside,
We have more reason to be terrified
At countless sources of much greater woe
Than at this accident that scares you so.
For if I had to choose, do you suppose
I would not rather be—well, one of *those*—
Than have one of those wives without a taint
Whose life is one perpetual complaint,
Dragons of virtue, devils full of piety,
Entrenched in their self-satisfied propriety,
Who, for the one fault they're not guilty of,
Assume the right to look down from above,
And on the grounds that they are chaste and pure,
Indulge their tempers, which we must endure?
Once more, my friend, the state of cuckoldry
Is only what we make it out to be;
It even may be in our interest,
And has its compensations, like the rest.

Arnolphe Then go ahead, if you're contented by it;
But as for me, I have no wish to try it;
And rather than endure the cuckold's horn . . .

Chrysalde Good Lord! Don't swear, lest you should be forsworn.
If fate has willed it, nothing you can do
Can change it; it won't come consulting you.

Arnolphe What, *I* a cuckold?

Chrysalde You're not making sense.
A thousand people are—please, no offense—
Whose wealth, birth, courage, and attractive air
Make them literally beyond compare.

Arnolphe I crave comparison with no such folk.
But come, I'm tired of your elaborate joke:
Let's let it go at that.

Chrysalde My, how you fret!
I don't know why. Goodbye. But don't forget,
Whatever oaths your honor may suggest,
You're halfway toward the fate that you detest
As soon as you have sworn it shall not be.

Arnolphe Again I swear it, and immediately
I'll test my preparations for loose ends.

SCENE NINE

Alain, Georgette, Arnolphe

Arnolphe It's now that I implore your aid, my friends.
Your loyalty gives me great satisfaction.
Now I must see it manifest in action;
And if your service now repays my trust,
Your recompense shall be secure and just.
Now—not a word—the man you know about
Intends, I've learned, to try to catch me out
And enter Agnès' room by escalade;
But you and I will set an ambuscade.
I want each one of you to take a stick,
And when he's at the topmost rung, be quick—
(At the right time I'll open the window wide)
—And set upon the traitor from inside;
Give him a thorough lesson on his back,
So that he won't return to the attack;
But in all this you must not speak my name
Or hint that I'm a party to this game.
Have you the wit to do what I desire?

Alain If beating, sir, is all that you require,
Trust us. Now, when I hit, I hit. You'll see.

Georgette My blows are harder than they look to be,
And in a thrashing they will play their role.

Arnolphe Go in then, and don't tell this to a soul.
Ah, this will teach the neighbors and this clown!
And if each husband living in this town
Gave this response to suitors' provocation,
It would reduce the cuckold population.

Act Five

SCENE ONE
Alain, Georgette, Arnolphe

Arnolphe Traitors, what have you done? He may be dead.

Alain But, sir, we did exactly what you said.

Arnolphe You try such an excuse on me in vain:
I said he should be beaten up, not slain,
And ordered that the brunt of your attack
Should fall not on his head but on his back.
Heavens! What disaster fate reserved for me!
And with him dead, what is my course to be?
Go back into the house, and not a word
Of any harmless order that you heard.
It's almost dawn, and I must make my plans
On how I should behave in this mischance.
What will become of me in my despair?
What will his father say to this affair?

SCENE TWO

Horace, Arnolphe

Horace I must try to find out who that can be.

Arnolphe Could I have known . . . ? Who goes there?
Answer me.

Horace Seigneur Arnolphe?

Arnolphe Yes, but . . .

Horace Horace. It's true.
I was just coming to get help from you.
You are up early!

Arnolphe [*aside*] What is my confusion!
Is it enchantment? Can it be illusion?

Horace Really, I was in great distress of mind,
And I bless Heaven, which was extremely kind
To let me find you now. I came to say
That things turned out in a delightful way,
Both better than I could have hoped, and faster,
Thanks to a plan that seemed to bring disaster.
I can't imagine how the man—can you?
Got his suspicions of our rendezvous;
But, near the window, ready to climb in,
I found some people there, to my chagrin;
And when I saw them swing, and their intent,
I lost my footing—and then down I went.
Though I was bruised, I have no doubt at all
That I was spared a drubbing by my fall.
These folk—my foe among them, I suppose—
Assumed my tumble followed from their blows;
And since for quite a while I did remain
Motionless in considerable pain,
They obviously thought that I was dead—
A notion which filled all of them with dread.
I heard each hold the other ones at fault
For the intensity of their assault;
Cursing their fate, they came, without a light,
To check, and judged that I was dead all right:

And in the darkness, be it understood,
I played a corpse's part as best I could.
Then, terrified, they disappeared from view,
And as I thought about withdrawing too,
Hearing of the disaster, young Agnès
Came down to me in haste and in distress;
For from the outset she had overheard
These people's conversation, every word,
And had, in the confusion, made her way
Out of the house to me without delay;
But finding me uninjured, her relief
Displayed itself in joy beyond belief.
How can I tell you? Well, that charming creature
Followed the counsels of her loving nature,
Flatly refused to go on back in there,
And placed her fate, her honor in my care.
Think how that madman's utter lack of sense
Exposes her in all her innocence,
And of the perils that she might go through
If I did not adore her as I do.
But it is far too purely that I love her;
I'd rather die than take advantage of her.
Her charms are worthy of a better fate,
And death alone can make us separate.
My father, I foresee, will be displeased;
But in due time his wrath can be appeased.
This is the girl I always shall adore;
A man would be a fool to ask for more.
Now I beg leave to give my lady fair,
In utter secrecy, into your care;
Please make her welcome under your protection
A day or two, to favor my affection.
Her flight must be concealed from everyone,
Though soon a search will surely be begun;
And such a beauty, seen with a young male,
Is promptly thought to be beyond the pale.
Now, since, from the beginning to the end,
I've told you everything, my trusted friend,
I come to ask you this one favor more:
To guard for me the woman I adore.

Arnolphe Believe me, I will serve you all I can.

Horace You'll help me carry out this cherished plan?

Arnolphe Most willingly; I feel the greatest joy
To have this chance to help you out, my boy;
Heaven be praised you trust me with Agnès:
Nothing could give me greater happiness.

Horace My debt to you is great in every way.
This is one step I feared you might gainsay;
But you have been around, and from above
You understand the ardor of young love.
She's at the corner, and my man stands guard.

Arnolphe It's getting light; this will be rather hard.
Someone may see me if I take her here;
And at my house, if you were to appear,
Servants are sure to talk. No, just in case,
You'd better bring her to some darker place.
My garden alley's hid from prying eyes.

Horace All these precautions you suggest are wise.
I'll simply turn her over then to you.
And go back home without further ado. *Exit.*

Arnolphe [*alone*] Ah, fortune! This propitious accident
Makes up for all the troubles you have sent!

He muffles his face in his cloak.

SCENE THREE

Agnès, Arnolphe, Horace

Horace Don't worry at my bringing you this way;
I had to find you some safe place to stay.
All would be ruined if you stopped with me.
Go in this door and you'll be safe; you'll see.

Arnolphe, unrecognized by her, takes her hand.

Agnès [*to Horace*] Why are you leaving me?

Horace I must, my dear.

Agnès Then come back soon and end my waiting here.

Horace My love will bring me back soon, dear Agnès.

Agnès When you're away I have no happiness.

Horace Out of your presence, I too am in pain.

Agnès Alas! If that were so, you would remain.

Horace What? Can you doubt then that my love is true?

Agnès You don't love me as much as I love you.

Arnolphe pulls her away.

He pulls too hard.

Horace It's dangerous, my dear,
For us two to be seen together here;
This is a perfect friend, who knows what's best,
And will act wisely in our interest.

Agnès But I don't know him, and . . .

Horace Don't worry, please:
In hands like his you should feel quite at ease.

Agnès Those of Horace would give me more delight.
And I would . . .

To Arnolphe, still pulling her.

Wait.

Horace Goodbye; it's getting light.

Agnès When shall I see you?

Horace Soon. Depend on me.

Agnès Until that time, how wretched I shall be!

Horace My happiness, thank Heaven, now is sure,
And I can go at last and sleep secure.

SCENE FOUR
Arnolphe, Agnès

Arnolphe [*concealed in his cloak and disguising his voice*]
Come on now, you will not be living *there,*
And lodgings are prepared for you elsewhere.
I mean to put you in a safer place.

Throwing back his cloak, in his normal voice.

You recognize me?

Agnès Oh!

Arnolphe You wretch, my face
Frightens your senses more than you'll allow,
And you're dismayed to see me here and now.
I'm interrupting all your amorous schemes.

Agnès looks around for Horace.

You can't bring back the sweetheart of your dreams;
He's too far off to help in such a fix.
Oh! Oh! So young still, and so full of tricks!
Your innocence, that seems without a peer,
Asks whether we make children through the ear;
But you know how to set a midnight tryst
And join your lover without being missed!
Lord! How your tongue can twitter on with him!
Your schooling can't have been so very prim.
Who the devil taught you so much so fast?
And is your fear of ghosts a thing of the past?
Was it he gave you such temerity?
Cruel girl, how could you show such perfidy?
And after all my kindness! I'm distressed.
You serpent, whom I fostered at my breast,
And who, at your first thankless inclination,
Pursue your benefactor's ruination!

Agnès Why do you shout so?

Arnolphe Wouldn't anyone?

Agnès I see no wrong in anything I've done.

Arnolphe Follow a suitor? That's not infamy?

Agnès That suitor says he wants to marry me.
I've heard you preach; your lessons have sunk in:
One must be married to avoid the sin.

Arnolphe Yes, but married to me was what I meant,
And I believe you knew of my intent.

Agnès Yes, but to speak quite frankly, *entre nous,*
He suits my taste for this better than you.
With you, marriage is tiresome and austere;
You always represent it as severe.
But he makes it so pleasureful instead,
He really makes me eager to be wed.

Arnolphe Traitress, you love him then?

Agnès I love him; yes.

Arnolphe You have the gall to tell me that, Agnès?

Agnès Since it is true, shouldn't I be sincere?

Arnolphe And ought you to have loved him, minx?

Agnès Oh, dear!
He made it happen. What am I to do?
And when it did, I wasn't meaning to.

Arnolphe You should have banned that amorous desire.

Agnès How can you ban what sets your heart on fire?

Arnolphe Didn't you know I'd frown on this affair?

Agnès I? Not at all. Why on earth should you care?

Arnolphe Oh, this should fill my cup with happiness!
In short, you do not love me then.

Agnès You?

Arnolphe Yes.

Agnès Alas! No.

Arnolphe What, no?

Agnès Would you have me lie?

Arnolphe And why not love me, hussy? Tell me why.

Agnès He made me love him; I am not to blame.
Why couldn't you have tried to do the same?
I surely didn't stop you, did I now?

Arnolphe Really, I did the best that I knew how;
But all my pains were wasted, I confess.

Agnès He must know how better than you, I guess;
He made me love him without half a try.

Arnolphe Just hear this peasant argue and reply.
Damn it! Would a *précieuse* say any more?
Oh, I've misjudged her; or else, on that score,
A stupid girl knows more than any sage.
Since disputation is your present rage,
My pretty reasoner, does it make sense
To bring you up, for him, at my expense?

Agnès Oh, no. He'll pay each penny back again.

Arnolphe [*aside*] She finds expressions that increase my pain.

Aloud.

Will he discharge, able as he may be,
The obligations, minx, you have to me?

Agnès You find these great; I find them rather small.

Arnolphe I've brought you up; is that nothing at all?

Agnès Indeed, that was a wondrous operation,
And you gave me a pretty education!
Do you think I fool myself, and fail to see
That I'm as ignorant as I can be?
I am ashamed, myself; and at my age,
It's time for me to leave the idiot stage.

Arnolphe You're tired of ignorance, and, come what may,
Want lessons from this dandy?

Agnès I should say.
It is from him I know all that I know:
Much more than you, he is the one I owe.

Arnolphe Lord, what bravado! I don't understand
Why I don't take revenge with this right hand.

Her tantalizing coldness drives me mad,
And a few cuffs would make my spirit glad.

Agnès Alas! You have the power, if you desire.

Arnolphe [*aside*] Her words, her glance, how they disarm my ire!
How they bring back my tenderness to stay,
And drive my evil thoughts of her away!
How strange a thing is love! How soft the male
Is proven by each feminine betrayal!
All are aware of women's frailties,
Their indiscretion, their absurdities,
Their fragile soul and their pernicious spirit;
Nothing could be more weak, devoid of merit,
Nothing more faithless: why, they're hardly human!
Yet man does almost anything for woman.

Aloud.

Well, let's make peace. Traitress, live and let live.
Take back my heart; I'm ready to forgive.
Thus you may judge the love with which I burn,
And, seeing me so good, love me in turn.

Agnès I'd like to grant your wish, I really would:
What would it cost me—if I only could?

Arnolphe Poor little doll, you can if you just try.

He sighs.

Consider well that tender, loving sigh,
That dying glance, the person that I am;
Give up that urchin and his love, my lamb.
He must have charmed you by some sorcery,
And you will be far happier with me.
Clothing and finery are your great passion:
I swear you shall be always in the fashion.
I will caress you always, night and noon,
Fondle you, kiss you, eat you with a spoon;
And you may do whatever you like best.
I've said enough; you can work out the rest.

Aside.

How far passion can lead a man astray!

Aloud.

Nothing can match my love in any way.
Ungrateful girl, what proof would you suggest?
Am I to weep for you, or beat my chest?
Tear out half of my hair for love of you?
Or kill myself? Just tell me what to do.
I'll prove my love to you in any way.

Agnès My soul is deaf to all these things you say,
And two words from Horace would have more weight.

Arnolphe You've flouted me too long. Let's get things straight.
I'll carry out my plan, you stubborn pretty,
And pack you off this instant from this city.
You scorn my suit and put me on the rack;
But now a convent cell shall pay you back.

SCENE FIVE

Alain, Arnolphe, Agnès

Alain I don't know how it is, sir, but I guess
The corpse must have departed with Agnès.

Arnolphe Here she is. Shut her up inside my room.
He won't go looking there, her would-be groom;
And in just half an hour we'll take the road
To carry her to some secret abode.
I'll get a carriage. Lock yourselves up tight,
And never let her get out of your sight.

Exeunt Alain and Agnès.

She may be of the sort that one can wean
From her affection by a change of scene.

SCENE SIX

Arnolphe, Horace

Horace Seigneur Arnolphe! I've had a frightful blow!
Heaven has certainly decreed my woe.
A deadly plot seeks to drive us apart
And tear from me the darling of my heart.
My father traveled hither all last night.
I met him here, just ready to alight.
And listen to the reason why he's here—
Which, as I said, had never been made clear—
All unbeknownst, he's made a match for me,
And comes to honor this solemnity.
Imagine—you will sympathize, I know—
If I could suffer any greater blow!
Enrique, whom I inquired about of late,
Has been the cause of my disastrous fate.
He comes here with my father, on his side;
His only daughter is my destined bride.
I thought I'd faint at what they had to say;
And soon, finding I could not bear to stay,
Since Father planned to visit you, he said,
In consternation I came on ahead.
I beg you, do not say a word about
My new attachment which might put him out.
And, since he has great faith in you, please try
To change his mind about this other tie.

Arnolphe Of course.

Horace Just show him the advantage of
A short delay, and thus assist my love.

Arnolphe I shall.

Horace I put my trust in you alone.

Arnolphe Good.

Horace You're a truer father than my own.
Say that my age . . . He's here! Let's step aside.
Listen: I've many reasons to provide.

They move to a corner of the stage.

SCENE SEVEN

Enrique, Oronte, Chrysalde, Horace, Arnolphe

Enrique [*to Chrysalde*] The moment I first saw you, I could tell
There's something in your face that I know well.
I find in you your lovely sister's features,
My wife, dearest to me of all God's creatures;
And happy I would be if cruel fate
Had let me bring back home that faithful mate,
After our miseries, to join me in
The happiness of seeing all her kin.
But since the fatal power of destiny
Has taken her away from you and me,
Let us accept our loss, and spend our pains
On planning for the one child that remains.
You are concerned; and therefore I would not,
Without your full consent, decide her lot.
The choice of Oronte's son is glorious,
Provided that it pleases both of us.

Chrysalde You pay my judgment no great compliment
If you can doubt my unreserved assent.

Arnolphe [*to Horace*] Yes, I shall serve your interests as I must.

Horace Be sure to keep . . .

Arnolphe I shall repay your trust.

Arnolphe leaves Horace, joins the others, and embraces Oronte.

Oronte How full of tenderness is this embrace!

Arnolphe What a joy once again to see your face!

Oronte I have come here . . .

Arnolphe You need not say a word;
I know what brings you.

Oronte You've already heard?

Arnolphe Yes.

Oronte Very good.

Arnolphe Your son has set his heart
Against this marriage from the very start.
He even begged me to defend his side;
But here's all the advice I can provide:
Do not put off these nuptials, but rather
Exercise the authority of a father.
Young people must be shown that we know best;
Indulgence is against their interest.

Horace [*aside*] Traitor!

Chrysalde I urge you not to have recourse,
Against his wishes, to the use of force.
My brother feels as I do, I believe.

Arnolphe What? Shall he have to beg his youngster's leave?
And should a father be so soft and bland
That he would let his son flout his command?
I cannot think that he'd be such a fool
As to be ruled by one whom he should rule!
No, he's my friend, I share in his repute:
His word is given, let him execute,
Show that he can be firm, not merely fond,
And make his son break off this other bond.

Oronte I quite agree with everything you say
About this match; I warrant he'll obey.

Chrysalde [*to Arnolphe*] I am astonished at your eagerness
To see these young folks married, I confess;
And I can't guess what's brewing in your head . . .

Arnolphe I know what must be done and must be said.

Oronte Seigneur Arnolphe . . .

Chrysalde Not that name, *s'il vous plaît;*
I told you, it's Monsieur de La Forêt.

Oronte No matter.

Horace How is that?

Arnolphe Yes, now you know,
And that is why I had to treat you so.

Horace In what confusion . . .

SCENE EIGHT

Georgette, Enrique, Oronte, Chrysalde, Horace, Arnolphe

Georgette Sir, come quick; I fear
We can't restrain Agnès unless you're here;
She's dying to escape, and possibly
Might jump right out the window to get free.

Arnolphe Bring her to me; my plans are fully made
To take her promptly off.

To Horace.

Don't be dismayed.
Success may well bring pride, do what one may.
The proverb says that turnabout's fair play.

Horace Can any troubles, Heaven, match my woe?
And has a man ever been brought so low?

Arnolphe [*to Oronte*] Schedule the ceremony soon, old friend:
I am concerned, and eager to attend.

Oronte Just what we plan.

SCENE NINE

Agnès, Alain, Georgette, Oronte, Enrique, Arnolphe, Horace, Chrysalde

Arnolphe [*to Agnès*] Come, beautiful, come here,
You whom we couldn't hold, you mutineer.
Here he is: curtsy nicely to your swain
As his reward for all his zeal and pain.

To Horace.

Farewell. Your aspirations are belied;
But lovers are not always satisfied.

Agnès Horace, you'd let me be abducted so?

Horace I don't know where to turn, so great is my woe.

Arnolphe Come, chatterbox.

Agnès I want to stay right here.

Oronte This mystery will have to be made clear.
Try as we may, we cannot comprehend.

Arnolphe I'll tell you when I have some time to spend.
Goodbye for now.

Oronte Where are you going, pray?
You're not explaining in the proper way.

Arnolphe I urge that you, despite his discontent,
Put on the wedding.

Oronte But for that intent,
If you heard everything, did you not hear
That this same girl is staying with you here,
The daughter of the lovely Angélique,
Who married, secretly, Seigneur Enrique?
So all your talk—what was it getting at?

Chrysalde I was vastly astonished too at that.

Arnolphe What's this . . . ?

Chrysalde My sister bore, a secret bride,
One daughter, whose fate she contrived to hide.

Oronte The father sent the child, with a false name,
To be the nursling of a country dame.

Chrysalde And then, while she was there, a hostile fate
Made of the father an expatriate.

Oronte A thousand different risks he underwent
Across the seas in a far continent.

Chrysalde And there he won what in his native land
Deceit and envy formerly had banned.

Oronte And back in France, he promptly went to see
The one who had his daughter's custody.

Chrysalde This peasant woman told him all she knew:
That she had passed the girl, aged four, to you.

Oronte Since you were noted for your charity,
And she was in the throes of poverty.

Chrysalde Enrique, transported with relief and bliss,
Has brought the woman here to witness this.

Oronte And you shall see her soon arriving here
So that this mystery may at last be clear.

Chrysalde I think I can imagine your despair;
But fate is kind to you in this affair.
Since you so fear your marriage may miscarry,
Your surest policy is not to marry.

Arnolphe Ouf!

Exit overcome, unable to speak.

Oronte What! Without a word?

Horace You soon shall know
In full, Father, what mystifies you so.
In all this, chance has managed, as you'll find,
Exactly what your wisdom had in mind:
By the sweet ties of mutual love and duty,
I had become engaged to this same beauty;
She, whom you came to seek and whom you choose,
Is just the one I thought I must refuse.

Enrique I had no doubt about this at first sight;
And ever since she fills me with delight.
My daughter, I have loved you from the start.

Embraces Agnès.

Chrysalde I'd do the same, brother, with all my heart;
But this is not the place. So, if you please,
Let's go in and resolve these mysteries,
Repay Arnolphe for all his interest,
And thank Heaven, which does all for the best!

The Misanthrope

CHARACTERS

Alceste, in love with Célimène
Philinte, friend of Alceste
Oronte, in love with Célimène
Célimène, beloved of Alceste
Éliante, cousin of Célimène
Arsinoé, a friend of Célimène
Acaste
Clitandre } marquis
Basque, servant of Célimène
An *Officer* of the Tribunal of Marshals of France
Du Bois, servant of Alceste

The scene is a salon in Célimène's house in Paris.

Act One

SCENE ONE
Alceste, Philinte

Philinte Well then? What's wrong?

Alceste I pray you, let me be.

Philinte Won't you explain this sudden wrath to me?

Alceste Leave me alone, I say; run off and hide.

Philinte Without such anger you should hear my side.

Alceste Not I. I *will* be angry. I *won't* hear.

Philinte The reasons for your fits escape me clear;
And though we're friends, I feel I must insist . . .

Alceste What? I, your friend? Just scratch me off your list.
Till now I have professed to be one, true;
But after what I have just seen in you,
I tell you flatly now that here we part;
I want no place in a corrupted heart.

Philinte Then in your eyes, Alceste, I'm much to blame?

Alceste You should go off and die for very shame;
There's no excuse for such an act as yours;
It's one that any decent man abhors.
I see you greet a man like a long-lost friend
And smother him in sweetness without end;

With protestations, offers, solemn vows,
You load the frenzy of your scrapes and bows;
When I ask later whom you cherish so,
Even his name, I find, you barely know.
As soon as he departs, your fervor dies,
And you tell *me* he's nothing in your eyes.
Good Lord! You play a base, unworthy role
By stooping to betray your very soul;
And if (which God forbid) I'd done the same,
I'd go right out and hang myself for shame.

Philinte To me the case does not deserve the rope;
Pray you, allow me to retain the hope
That I may exercise some leniency
And need not hang myself from the nearest tree.

Alceste With what bad grace this jesting comes from you!

Philinte But seriously, what would you have me do?

Alceste A man should be sincere, and nobly shrink
From saying anything he does not think.

Philinte But when a man embraces you, I find
You simply have to pay him back in kind,
Respond to his effusions as you may,
And try to meet offers and vows half-way.

Alceste No, I cannot endure this fawning guile
Employed by nearly all your men of style.
There's nothing I so loathe as the gyrations
Of all these great makers of protestations,
These lavishers of frivolous embraces,
These utterers of empty commonplaces,
Who in civilities won't be outdone,
And treat the good man and the fool as one.
What joy is there in hearing pretty phrases
From one who loud and fulsome sings your praises,
Vows friendship, love, esteem for evermore,
Then runs to do the same to any boor?
No, no; a soul that is well constituted
Cares nothing for esteem so prostituted;
Our vanity is satisfied too cheap
With praise that lumps all men in one vast heap;

Esteem, if it be real, means preference,
And when bestowed on all it makes no sense.
Since these new vices seem to you so fine,
Lord! You're not fit to be a friend of mine.
I spurn the vast indulgence of a heart
That will not set merit itself apart;
No, singled out is what I want to be;
The friend of man is not the man for me.

Philinte But one who travels in society
Must show some semblance of civility.

Alceste No, I say; an example should be made
Of hypocrites who ply this shameful trade.
A man should be a man, and let his speech
At every turn reveal his heart to each;
His own true self should speak; our sentiments
Should never hide beneath vain compliments.

Philinte But utter frankness would, in many a case,
Become ridiculous and out of place.
We sometimes—no offense to your high zeal—
Should rather hide what in our heart we feel.
Would it be either fitting or discreet
To air our views of them to all we meet?
Dealing with someone we dislike or hate,
Must we always be sure to set him straight?

Alceste Yes.

Philinte What? Old Émilie you'd promptly tell
That she has passed the age to be a belle,
And that her makeup is a sorry jest?

Alceste No doubt.

Philinte Tell Dorilas that he's a pest,
That all his talk has wearied every ear
About his noble blood and brave career?

Alceste Assuredly.

Philinte You're joking.

Alceste I am not,
I'll spare no one on this point, not one jot.

It hurts my eyes to see the things I've seen,
And court and town alike arouse my spleen.
Dark melancholy seizes me anew
Each time I watch men act the way they do;
Cowardly flattery is all I see,
Injustice, selfishness, fraud, treachery;
I've had my fill; it makes me mad; I plan
To clash head-on with the whole race of man.

Philinte You overdo your philosophic bile;
I see your gloomy fits and have to smile.
We two are like the brothers in *The School*
For Husbands, who, though reared by the same rule,
Yet . . .

Alceste Heavens! spare us these inane charades.

Philinte No, really, you should drop your wild tirades.
Your efforts will not change the world, you know,
And inasmuch as frankness charms you so,
I'll tell you, frankly, that this malady
Is treated everywhere as comedy,
And that your wrath against poor humankind
Makes you ridiculous in many a mind.

Alceste By heaven! so much the better! that's first-rate.
It's a good sign; my joy in it is great.
All men are so abhorrent in my eyes
That I'd be sorry if they thought me wise.

Philinte Toward human nature you are very spiteful.

Alceste I am; the hate I feel for it is frightful.

Philinte Shall all poor mortals, then, without exception,
Be lumped together in this mass aversion?
Even today you still find now and then . . .

Alceste No, it is general; I hate all men:
For some are wholly bad in thought and deed;
The others, seeing this, pay little heed;
For they are too indulgent and too nice
To share the hate that virtue has for vice.
Indulgence at its worst we clearly see
Toward the base scoundrel who's at law with me:

Right through his mask men see the traitor's face,
And everywhere give him his proper place;
His wheedling eyes, his soft and cozening tone,
Fool only those to whom he is not known.
That this knave rose, where he deserved to fall,
By shameful methods, is well known to all,
And that his state, which thanks to these is lush,
Makes merit murmur and makes virtue blush.
Whatever notoriety he's won,
Such honor lacks support from anyone;
Call him a cheat, knave, cursèd rogue to boot,
Everyone will agree, no one refute.
Yet everywhere his false smile seems to pay:
Everywhere welcomed, hailed, he worms his way;
And if by pulling strings he stands to gain
Some honor, decent men compete in vain.
Good Lord! It fairly turns my blood to ice
To see the way men temporize with vice,
And sometimes I've a strong desire to flee
To some deserted spot, from humans free.

Philinte Let's fret less over morals, if we can,
And have some mercy on the state of man;
Let's look at it without too much austerity,
And try to view its faults without severity.
In this world virtue needs more tact than rigor;
Wisdom may be excessive in its vigor;
Perfected reason flees extremity,
And says: Be wise, but with sobriety.
The unbending virtue of the olden days
Clashes with modern times and modern ways;
Its stiff demands on mortals go too far;
We have to live with people as they are;
And the greatest folly of the human mind
Is undertaking to correct mankind.
Like you I note a hundred things a day
That might go better, done another way,
But notwithstanding all that comes in view,
Men do not find me full of wrath like you;
I take men as they are, with self-control;

To suffer what they do I train my soul,
And I think, whether court or town's the scene,
My calm's as philosophic as your spleen.

Alceste But, sir, this calm, that is so quick to reason,
This calm, is it then never out of season?
If by a friend you find yourself betrayed,
If for your property a snare is laid,
If men besmirch your name with slanderous lies,
You'll see that and your temper will not rise?

Philinte Why yes, I see these faults, which make you hot,
As vices portioned to the human lot;
In short, it's no more shock to my mind's eye
To see a man unjust, self-seeking, sly,
Than to see vultures hungry for their prey,
Monkeys malicious, wolves athirst to slay.

Alceste Then I should be robbed, torn to bits, betrayed,
Without . . . ? Good Lord! I leave the rest unsaid;
Such reasoning is patently absurd.

Philinte Less talk would help your cause, upon my word:
Outbursts against your foe are out of place;
You should give more attention to your case.

Alceste I'll give it none. That's all there is to say.

Philinte Then who will speak for you and pave the way?

Alceste The justice of my cause will speak for me.

Philinte Is there no judge that you will stoop to see?*

Alceste No; don't you think my case is just and clear?

Philinte True, but intrigue is what you have to fear,
And . . .

Alceste No, I'll take no steps, I'll not give in;
I'm either right or wrong.

Philinte Don't think you'll win.

Alceste I shall not budge.

* It was normal practice in Molière's France for a litigant to visit his judge while his case was pending.

Philinte Your enemy is strong.
And by collusion he . . .

Alceste What then? He's wrong.

Philinte You're making a mistake.

Alceste All right; we'll see.

Philinte But . . .

Alceste Let me lose my case; that will please me.

Philinte But after all . . .

Alceste In this chicanery
I'll see if men have the effrontery,
And are sufficiently base, vile, perverse,
To wrong me in the sight of the universe.

Philinte Oh, what a man!

Alceste My case—despite the cost,
For the sheer beauty of it—I'd see lost.

Philinte People would really laugh at you, you know,
Alceste, if they could hear you talking so.

Alceste Too bad for those who laugh.

Philinte Even this rigor
Which you require of all with so much vigor,
This rectitude that you make so much of,
Do you observe it in the one you love?
It still amazes me when I see you,
Who censor humankind the way you do,
And see in it so much that you abhor,
Find in it anyone you can adore;
And what astonishes me further yet
Is the strange choice on which your heart is set.
The candid Éliante finds you attractive,
Arsinoé the prude would like you active;
Meanwhile your unconcern with them is plain;
Instead you are bewitched by Célimène,
One whose sharp tongue and whose coquettish ways
Are just the things in fashion nowadays.
How is it that in her you tolerate

Failings which, found in others, rouse your hate?
Are they no longer faults in one so dear?
Are they unseen? Are others too severe?

Alceste No, love for this young widow does not blind
My eyes to all the faults that others find,
And I, despite my ardor for her, am
The first to see them and the first to damn.
But still, for all of that, she has an art;
She finds and fills a soft spot in my heart;
I see her flaws and blame them all I will,
No matter what I do, I love her still;
Her grace remains too strong. My love, no doubt,
Will yet prevail and drive these vices out.

Philinte If you do that, it will be no small coup.
You think she loves you, then?

Alceste Indeed I do!
I'd not love her unless I thought she did.

Philinte But if her fondness for you is not hid,
Why do your rivals cause you such concern?

Alceste A smitten heart wants to possess in turn,
And all I've come here for is to reveal
To her all that my passion makes me feel.

Philinte For my part, if mere wishes had a voice,
Her cousin Éliante would be my choice.
Her heart esteems you and is stanch and true;
She'd be a sounder, better match for you.

Alceste You're right, my reason says so every day;
But over love reason has little sway.

Philinte Your loving hopes I fear that she may flout,
And . . .

SCENE TWO

Oronte, Alceste, Philinte

Oronte Éliante, I hear downstairs, is out,
And likewise Célimène, with things to do,

But since they told me that I might find you,
I came to tell you frankly, anyway,
That I esteem you more than tongue can say,
And that I long have wished and now intend
To ask you to accept me as a friend.
Yes, yes, I would see merit have its due;
In friendship's bond I would be joined with you.
An ardent friend, as nobly born as I,
Can surely not be easily passed by.

To Alceste.

For you if you don't mind, my words are meant.

At this point Alceste is lost in thought and seems not to hear that Oronte is speaking to him.

Alceste Me, sir?

Oronte You. Are they something to resent?

Alceste No, but your praise of me comes unexpected;
Such high regard I never had suspected.

Oronte My great esteem should come as no surprise,
And you can claim the like in all men's eyes.

Alceste Sir . . .

Oronte Our whole State possesses nothing higher
Than all your merit, which men so admire.

Alceste Sir . . .

Oronte Yes, you are far worthier, say I,
Than all I see that others rate so high.

Alceste Sir . . .

Oronte If I lie, may heaven strike me dead!
And, to confirm to you what I've just said,
Allow me, sir, a heart-to-heart embrace,
And in your friendship let me find a place.
Shake on it, if you please. Then it is mine,
Your friendship?

Alceste Sir . . .

Oronte What? Then do you decline?

Alceste Sir, most excessively you honor me;
But friendship asks a bit more mystery,
And surely we profane its name sublime
By using it on all, and all the time.
Upon enlightened choice this bond depends;
We need to know each other to be friends,
And we might prove to be so different
That both of us might presently repent.

Oronte By heaven! That's wisely spoken on that score,
And I esteem you for it all the more.
Let us let time prepare friendship's fruition;
But meanwhile I am at your disposition.
If you need help at court for anything,
You know I have some standing with the King.
He listens to me, and in every way
Treats me more decently than I can say.
In short, consider me as all your own;
And, since your brilliant mind is widely known,
I've come to ask your judgment as a friend
Upon a sonnet that I lately penned,
And learn whether I ought to publish it.

Alceste For such a judgment, sir, I'm hardly fit.
So please excuse me.

Oronte Why?

Alceste For this defect:
I'm always more sincere than men expect.

Oronte Exactly what I ask; I could complain
If, when I urged you to speak clear and plain,
You then disguised your thought in what you said.

Alceste Since you will have it so, sir, go ahead.

Oronte "Sonnet . . ." It is a sonnet. "Hope . . ." You see,
A lady once aroused some hope in me.
"Hope . . ." This is nothing grandiose or sublime,
But just a soft, sweet, tender little rhyme.

At each interruption he looks at Alceste.

Alceste We shall see.

Oronte "Hope . . ." The style may not appear
To you sufficiently easy and clear,
And you may think the choice of words is bad.

Alceste We shall see, sir.

Oronte Moreover, let me add,
A quarter hour was all the time I spent.

Alceste Come, sir; the time is hardly pertinent.

Oronte Hope does, 'tis true, some comfort bring,
And lulls awhile our aching pain;
But, Phyllis, 'tis an empty thing
When nothing follows in its train.

Philinte That is a charming bit, and full of verve.

Alceste [*aside*] You call that charming? What! You have the nerve?

Oronte My flame you once seemed to invite;
'Twas pity that you let it live,
And kept me languishing, poor wight,
When hope was all you had to give.

Philinte Oh, in what gallant terms these things are put!

Alceste [*aside*] You wretched flatterer! Gallant, my foot!

Oronte Should an eternity to wait
Render my ardor desperate,
Then my decease shall end my pains.

Your fond concern you well may spare;
Fair Phyllis, it is still despair
When hope alone is what remains.

Philinte That dying fall casts a seductive spell.

Alceste [*aside, to Philinte*] Poisoner, you and your fall may go to hell.
I wish you'd taken one right on your nose.

Philinte I've never heard verses as fine as those.

Alceste Good Lord!

Oronte You flatter me; perhaps you're trying . . .

Philinte I am not flattering.

Alceste [*aside*] No, only lying.

Oronte [*to Alceste*] But you, sir, you recall what we agreed;
Please be sincere. How do these verses read?

Alceste Questions of talent, sir, are ticklish matters,
And we all yearn to hear the voice that flatters;
But when a man—no matter who—one day
Read me his verses, I made bold to say
A gentleman must have the will to fight
Our universal human itch to write,
That he must overcome his great temptations
To make a fuss about such recreations,
And that our eagerness for self-display
Can give us many a sorry role to play.

Oronte I think I gather what you're getting at:
That I am wrong to want . . .

Alceste I don't say that.
But frigid writing palls, and can bring down—
So I told him—a worthy man's renown;
Though one had every other quality,
Our weakest points are what men choose to see.

Oronte Then with my sonnet, sir, do you find fault?

Alceste I don't say that; but urging him to halt,
I pointed out to him how, time and again,
This thirst has spoiled extremely worthy men.

Oronte Am I like them? Don't I know how to rhyme?

Alceste I don't say that. But, I said, take your time:
Have you some urgent need to versify
And see yourself in print? I ask you, why?
The authors of bad books we may forgive
Only when the poor wretches write to live.
Take my advice and overcome temptations,
Hide from the public all these occupations,
Against all urgings raise a stout defense,
And keep your good name as a man of sense;
Don't change it in some greedy printer's stall

For that of author ridiculed by all.
—That's what I tried to make this man perceive.

Oronte All right. I understand you, I believe.
About my sonnet, though: may I be told . . . ?

Alceste Frankly, your sonnet should be pigeonholed.
The models you have used are poor and trite;
There's nothing natural in what you write.
What is this "lulls awhile our aching pain"?
This "nothing follows in its train"?
Or "kept me languishing, poor wight,
When hope was all you had to give"?
And "Phyllis, it is still despair
When hope alone is what remains"?
This mannered style, so dear to people's hearts,
From human nature and from truth departs;
It's purest affectation, verbal play,
And Nature never speaks in such a way.
Standards today are wretched, I maintain;
Our fathers' taste, though crude, was far more sane.
What men now prize gives me far less delight
Than this old song which I will now recite:
If the king had given me
Great Paris for my own,
And had said the price must be
To leave my love alone,
I would tell the king Henri:
Then take back your great Paris,
I prefer my love, hey ho,
I prefer my love.
The rhyme's not rich, the style is old and rough,
But don't you see this is far better stuff
Then all this trumpery that flouts good sense,
And that here passion speaks without pretence?
If the king had given me
Great Paris for my own,
And had said the price must be
To leave my love alone,
I would tell the king Henri:

Then take back your great Paris,
I prefer my love, hey ho,
I prefer my love.
That's what a really loving heart might say.

To Philinte.

Laugh on. Despite the wits who rule today,
I rate this higher than the flowery show
Of artificial gems, which please men so.

Oronte And *I* maintain my verse is very good.

Alceste I'm sure that you have reasons why you should;
But grant my reasons leave to disagree
And not let yours impose themselves on me.

Oronte Enough for me that others rate it high.

Alceste They have the art of feigning, sir; not I.

Oronte No doubt you think you've quite a share of wit?

Alceste To praise your verse, I should need more of it.

Oronte I'll get along without your praise, I trust.

Alceste I hope you're right, sir, for I fear you must.

Oronte I'd like to see you try, in your own way,
On this same theme, to show what you could say.

Alceste My verses might be just as bad, I own,
But I'd be careful not to make them known.

Oronte Your talk is high and mighty, and your ways . . .

Alceste Look elsewhere for a man to sing your praise.

Oronte My little man, don't take this tone with me.

Alceste Big man, my tone is just what it should be.

Philinte [*stepping between them*] Come, gentlemen, enough! I pray you, no!

Oronte My fault, I do admit. And now I'll go.
With all my heart, I am your servant, sir.

Alceste And I, sir, am your humble servitor.

SCENE THREE

Philinte, Alceste

Philinte Well, there you are! You see? By being candid,
Just note in what a nasty mess you've landed;
Oronte's desire for praise was obvious . . .

Alceste Don't speak to me.

Philinte But . . .

Alceste Finis between us.

Philinte You're too . . .

Alceste Leave me.

Philinte If . . .

Alceste Not another word.

Philinte But what! . . .

Alceste I'm deaf.

Philinte But . . .

Alceste More?

Philinte This is absurd.

Alceste Good Lord! I've had enough. Be off with you.

Philinte You don't mean that. Where you go, I go too.

Act Two

SCENE ONE
Alceste, Célimène

Alceste Madame, shall I speak frankly and be brief?
Your conduct gives me not a little grief;
It rouses too much bile within my heart,
And I can see that we shall have to part.
I have to tell you this for conscience' sake:
Sooner or later we must surely break.
A thousand pledges to the contrary
I might make, but I could not guarantee.

Célimène Indeed, your wish to bring me home was kind,
When scolding me was what you had in mind.

Alceste I do not scold; but what is my dismay,
Madame, that the first comer makes his way
Into your heart? By suitors you're beset;
And I cannot see this without regret.

Célimène You blame me for my suitors, this I see.
Can I prevent people from liking me?
And when they try to visit me, no doubt
I ought to take a stick and drive them out?

Alceste A stick, Madame, is not what I suggest,
Merely a heart less easily impressed.

I know that everywhere you cast a spell;
But those your eyes attract you greet too well;
Your graciousness to all who yield their arms
Completes the conquering action of your charms.
The over-brilliant hopes that you arouse
Surround you with these suitors and their vows;
If only your complaisance were less vast,
This sighing mob would disappear at last.
But by what spell, Madame, if I may know,
Does your Clitandre contrive to please you so?
In worth and virtue is he so supreme
That you should honor him with your esteem?
His little fingernail is very long:
Is that why your regard for him is strong?
Has his blond wig, which has such great effect
Upon society, won your respect?
Do you love him for the ruffles at his knees?
Or do his multitudinous ribbons please?
Is it the charm of his vast German breeches
That, while he plays the slave, your soul bewitches?
Is it his laugh and his falsetto voice
That make of him the suitor of your choice?

Célimène To take offense at him is most unfair!
You know why I must handle him with care,
And that he's pledged his many friends' support
To help me when my lawsuit comes to court.

Alceste Then lose your suit, as bravely as you can,
And do not humor that offensive man.

Célimène Why, everyone excites your jealousy.

Alceste You welcome everyone so charmingly.

Célimène But this should reassure your anxious mind:
That all who seek, this same complaisance find;
And you would have more cause for discontent
If there were only one recipient.

Alceste But I, Madame, whose jealousy you blame,
In what way is my treatment not the same?

Célimène Knowing that you are loved sets you apart.

Alceste How can I prove this to my burning heart?

Célimène To say what I have said exacts a price;
I think such an avowal should suffice.

Alceste But how can I be certain, even then,
You do not say the same to other men?

Célimène My! That's a charming way to pay your court,
And that makes me appear a pretty sort!
Well then, to give you no more cause to sigh,
All I have said I here and now deny.
There's no deceiving to be fearful of
Except your own.

Alceste Lord! And I'm still in love!
If I could just get back my heart, I'd bless
Heaven above for such rare happiness!
I do my best—and this I don't conceal—
To break the cruel attachment that I feel;
But I have toiled in vain, and now I know
That it is for my sins I love you so.

Célimène It's true, your love for me is matched by none.

Alceste Yes, on that score I'll challenge anyone.
My love is past belief, Madame; I say
No one has ever loved in such a way.

Célimène Indeed, your way is novel, and your aim;
The only token of your love is blame;
Your ardor shows itself in angry speech,
And never was a love so quick to preach.

Alceste It rests with you that this should pass away.
Let's call a halt to quarreling, I pray,
Speak out with open hearts, then, and begin . . .

SCENE TWO

Célimène, Alceste, Basque

Célimène What is it?

Basque It's Acaste.

Célimène Well, show him in.

Alceste What? Can one never talk to you alone?
Must you then always welcome everyone?
And can you not for just one moment bear
To have a caller told you are not there?

Célimène You'd have me quarrel with him too, for sure?

Alceste Some of your courtesies I can't endure.

Célimène That man would bear a grudge for evermore,
If he knew I find the sight of him a bore.

Alceste And why should this make you put on an act?

Célimène Heavens! Influence is an important fact.
I don't know why, but people of his sort
Can talk loud and importantly at court.
They push their way into each interview;
They cannot help, but they can damage you;
And even if your other aid is stout,
Don't quarrel with these men who love to shout.

Alceste No matter what the reason or the base,
You find cause to receive the human race;
And the precautions that you take, perforce . . .

SCENE THREE
Basque, Alceste, Célimène

Basque Madame, here is Clitandre as well.

Alceste [*showing that he wants to leave*] Of course.

Célimène Where are you going?

Alceste Leaving.

Célimène Stay.

Alceste What for?

Célimène Stay here.

Alceste I can't.

Célimène I want you to.

Alceste No more.
These conversations weary me past cure;
This is too much to ask me to endure.

Célimène You shall remain, you shall.

Alceste It cannot be.

Célimène All right, then, go; it's quite all right with me.

SCENE FOUR

Éliante, Philinte, Acaste, Clitandre, Alceste, Célimène, Basque

Éliante Here are the two marquis who've come to call.
Were they announced?

Célimène Indeed [*To Basque.*] Bring chairs for all.
[*To Alceste.*] You haven't left?

Alceste No, Madame. I demand
That you declare to all just where you stand.

Célimène Oh, hush.

Alceste You shall explain yourself today.

Célimène You're mad.

Alceste I am not. You shall say your say.

Célimène Ah!

Alceste You'll make up your mind.

Célimène I think you're joking.

Alceste No, you *shall* choose; this doubt is too provoking.

Clitandre My word! I've just come from the King's levee,
Where Cléonte played the fool for all to see.
Has he no friend who could, with kindly tact,
Teach him the rudiments of how to act?

Célimène Indeed, in social life the man's a dunce;
His manner startles every eye at once;
And when you see him, later on, once more,
You find him more fantastic than before.

Acaste Speaking of characters fantastical,
I've just endured the greatest bore of all:
Damon, the talker, kept me, by your leave,
One hour in the hot sun without reprieve.

Célimène Yes, his strange mania for reasoning
Makes him talk on, and never say a thing;
His discourse in obscurity abounds,
And all you listen to is merely sounds.

Éliante [*to Philinte*] Not a bad opening. Soon the entire nation
Will be in danger of annihilation.

Clitandre Timante is quite a character, you know.

Célimène The man of mystery from top to toe,
Who gives you a distracted glance, aside,
Does nothing, yet is always occupied.
Grimaces lend importance to each word;
His high portentousness makes him absurd;
He interrupts your talk, in confidence,
To whisper a secret of no consequence;
At making trifles great he has no peer;
Even "Good day" he whispers in your ear.

Acaste Géralde, Madame?

Célimène He tells a tedious tale.
All but great nobles are beyond the pale;
He mingles with those of the highest note,
And none but duke or princess will he quote.
He is obsessed with rank; his monologues
Are all of horses, carriages, and dogs;
He uses *tu* in speaking to the great,
And seems to think *Monsieur* is out of date.

Clitandre They say Bélise appreciates his merit.

Célimène How dry she is in talk, and poor in spirit!
I find it torture to receive her call:
You labor to say anything at all,
And the sterility of her expression
At every moment kills the conversation.
In vain, her stupid silence to annul,

You try each commonplace, however dull:
Sunny or rainy weather, heat or frost
Are topics that you rapidly exhaust;
Meanwhile her visit, draining all your strength,
Drags on and on at terrifying length;
You ask the time, you yawn and yawn, but no:
She sits there like a log and will not go.

Acaste What of Adraste?

Célimène Oh, what colossal pride!
His love of self has puffed him up inside,
At court he misses due consideration;
So railing at it is his occupation;
No post or benefice goes to anyone,
But that he thinks injustice has been done.

Clitandre On young Cléon what will your verdict be?
He entertains the best society.

Célimène He has a cook who is extremely able;
And what they come to visit is his table.

Éliante He serves you nothing but the finest food.

Célimène He serves himself as well, and that's less good:
His stupid person is a sorry dish
That spoils the taste of fowl and roast and fish.

Philinte Some think Damis, his uncle, rather fine.
What do you say?

Célimène He is a friend of mine.

Philinte He seems a decent sort, I must admit.

Célimène Yes, but he tries too hard to be a wit;
He talks so stiltedly you always know
That he's premeditating some *bon mot*.
Since he has set his mind on being clever,
He takes delight in nothing whatsoever;
In all that's written he finds only flaws,
And thinks that cleverness forbids applause,
That criticism is a sign of learning,
Enjoyment only for the undiscerning,
And that to frown on any book that's new

Places him high among the happy few;
He looks on common talk with condescension
As much too trivial for his attention;
Folding his arms, from high above the rabble,
He glances down with pity on our babble.

Acaste Damme, Madame, that is exactly true.

Clitandre There's no one can portray a man like you.

Alceste That's right, my courtly friends, be strong, spare none,
Strike hard, and have your sport with everyone;
Yet when one of these victims comes in sight,
Your haste in meeting him is most polite,
And with a kiss and offer of your hand,
You demonstrate that you're at his command.

Clitandre But why blame us? If what is said offends you,
'Tis to Madame that your remonstrance sends you.

Alceste By God, no! 'Tis to you; your fawning laughter
Affords her wit just the applause she's after.
Her bent for character assassination
Feeds constantly upon your adulation;
For satire she would have less appetite
Were it not always greeted with delight.
Thus flatterers deserve our main assaults
For leading humans into many faults.

Philinte But why so eager to defend the name
Of those in whom you damn the things we blame?

Célimène Don't you see, he must be opposed to you?
Would you have him accept the common view,
And not display, in every company,
His heaven-sent gift for being contrary?
The ideas of others he will not admit;
Always he must maintain the opposite;
He'd fear he was an ordinary human
If he agreed with any man—or woman.
For him contrariness offers such charms,
Against himself he often turns his arms;
And should another man his views defend,
He will combat them to the bitter end.

Alceste The laughers are with you, Madame; you've won.
Go on and satirize me; have your fun.

Philinte But it is also true you have a way
Of balking at whatever people say;
And that your spite, which you yourself avow,
Neither applause nor censure will allow.

Alceste My God! That's because men are never right;
It always is the season for our spite;
I see them on all matters, in all ways,
Quick with rash censure and untimely praise.

Célimène But . . .

Alceste No, Madame, you *shall* learn, though it kill me,
With what distaste some of your pleasures fill me,
And that I find those persons much to blame
Who foster faults that damage your good name.

Clitandre As for me, I don't know; but I aver
That up to now I've found no fault in her.

Acaste Her charms and grace are evident to me;
But any faults I fear I cannot see.

Alceste I see them all; she knows the way I feel;
My disapproval I do not conceal.
Loving and flattering are worlds apart;
The least forgiving is the truest heart;
And I would send these soft suitors away,
Seeing they dote on everything I say,
And that their praise, complaisant to excess,
Encourages me in my foolishness.

Célimène In short, if we're to leave it up to you,
All tenderness in love we must eschew;
And love can only find its true perfection
In railing at the objects of our affection.

Éliante Love tends to find such laws somewhat austere,
And lovers always brag about their dear;
Their passion never sees a thing to blame,
And everything is lovely in their flame:
They find perfection in her every flaw,
And speak of her with euphemistic awe.

The pallid one's the whitest jasmine yet;
The frightful dark one is a sweet brunette;
The spindly girl is willowy and free;
The fat one bears herself with majesty;
The dowdy one, who's ill-endowed as well,
Becomes a careless and neglectful belle;
The giantess is a divinity;
The dwarf, a heavenly epitome;
With princesses the proud one can compete;
The tricky one has wit; the dull one's sweet;
The tireless talker's charmingly vivacious,
The mute girl modest, womanly, and gracious.
Thus every man who loves beyond compare
Loves even the defects of his lady fair.

Alceste And *I*, for my part, claim . . .

Célimène Let's end this talk
And step outside for just a little walk.
What? You are leaving, sirs?

Clitandre and Acaste No, Madame, no.

Alceste You're certainly afraid that they may go.
Leave when you like, sirs; but I'm warning you,
I shall not leave this place until you do.

Acaste Unless Madame should be a little tired,
There's nowhere that my presence is required.

Clitandre I must go later to the King's *couchée*,
But until then I am quite free today.

Célimène You're joking, surely.

Alceste No. I need to know
Whether you wish for them, or me, to go.

SCENE FIVE

Basque, Alceste, Célimène, Éliante, Acaste, Philinte, Clitandre

Basque Sir, there's a man to see you in the hall
Who says his business will not wait at all.

Alceste Tell him I have no business of such note.

Basque He has a uniform, a great tailcoat
With pleats and lots of gold.

Célimène Please go and see,
Or let him in.

Alceste [*to the Officer*]
What do you want with me?
Come in, sir.

SCENE SIX

Officer, Alceste, Célimène, Éliante, Acaste, Philinte, Clitandre

Officer Sir, with you I crave a word.

Alceste You may speak up, sir; let your news be heard.

Officer The Marshals,* sir, have ordered me to say
You must appear before them right away.

Alceste Who, I, sir?

Officer You yourself.

Alceste What can they want?

Philinte It's that ridiculous business with Oronte.

Célimène How's that?

Philinte They are about to take the sword
Over some verse with which Alceste was bored.
The Marshals want of course to quash the matter.

Alceste They'll never force me to back down and flatter.

Philinte You'll have to follow orders; come, let's go.

Alceste What can they reconcile, I'd like to know?
Shall I now, after everything that's passed,
Be sentenced to admire his verse at last?

* The Tribunal of Marshals regulated quarrels among gentlemen. By this time dueling was on the wane.

I don't take back a single thing I said,
I think they're bad.

Philinte But with a calmer head . . .

Alceste I won't back down; his verse is a disgrace.

Philinte Intransigence like yours is out of place.
Come on.

Alceste I'll go; but I shall not unsay
One thing I've said.

Philinte Come, let's be on our way.

Alceste Unless I have the King's express command
To like these verses, I have made my stand.
That they are bad, on this I'll never falter,
And that their author well deserves the halter.

To Clitandre and Acaste, who laugh.

By God! Messieurs, I never really knew
I was so funny.

Célimène Come, be off with you.
Go where you must.

Alceste I go, Madame, but straight
I shall return to settle our debate.

Act Three

SCENE ONE
Clitandre, Acaste

Clitandre You glow with satisfaction, dear Marquis:
You're free from worriment and full of glee.
But do you think you're seeing things aright
In taking such occasion for delight?

Acaste My word! When I regard myself, I find
No reason for despondency of mind.
I'm rich, I'm young, I'm of a family
With some pretension to nobility;
And through the rank that goes with my condition,
At court I can aspire to high position.
For courage, something we must all admire,
'Tis known I have been tested under fire,
And an affair of honor recently
Displayed my vigor and my bravery.
My wit is adequate, my taste discerning,
To judge and treat all subjects without learning;
When a new play is shown (which I adore),
To sit upon the stage, display my lore,

Determine its success, and stop the show
When any passage merits my "Bravo!"
I make a good appearance, rather chic;
I have fine teeth, an elegant physique.
And as for dress, all vanity aside,
My eminence can scarcely be denied.
I could not ask for more regard; I seem
To have the ladies' love, the King's esteem.
With all this, dear Marquis, I do believe
That no man anywhere has cause to grieve.

Clitandre When elsewhere easy conquests meet your eyes,
Why linger here to utter useless sighs?

Acaste I? 'Pon my word, I'm not the sort to bear
A cool reception from a lady fair.
It is for vulgar men, uncouth in dress,
To burn for belles who will not acquiesce,
Pine at their feet, endure their cold disdain,
Seek some support from sighs and tears—in vain,
And strive to win by assiduity
What is denied their meager quality.
But men of my class are not made to yearn
For anyone, Marquis, without return.
However fair the girls, however nice,
I think, thank God, we too are worth our price;
If they would claim the heart of one like me,
They should in reason pay the proper fee;
And it would be no more than fair that they
Should meet our every overture halfway.

Clitandre Then you are pleased, Marquis, with prospects here?

Acaste They offer me, Marquis, good grounds for cheer.

Clitandre Believe me, leave these fantasies behind;
Dear chap, your self-delusion makes you blind.

Acaste Of course, delusion makes me blind; ah, yes.

Clitandre But what assures you of such happiness?

Acaste Delusion.

Clitandre Have you grounds for confidence?

Acaste I'm blind.

Clitandre What constitutes your evidence?

Acaste I tell you, I'm all wrong.

Clitandre Well, have you, then,
Received some secret vow from Célimène?

Acaste No, I am badly treated.

Clitandre Tell me, please.

Acaste Nothing but snubs.

Clitandre A truce on pleasantries;
Tell me what makes you set your hopes so high.

Acaste Yours is the luck, and I can only sigh.
So great is her aversion for my ways
That I shall hang myself one of these days.

Clitandre Come now, Marquis, to mend our rivalry,
Let us agree on one thing, you and me:
If either one can show beyond a doubt
That in her heart he has been singled out,
The other shall admit defeat and yield,
Leaving the victor master of the field.

Acaste My word! Your notion matches my intent;
With all my heart and soul I do consent.
But hush!

SCENE TWO

Célimène, Acaste, Clitandre

Célimène Still here?

Clitandre Love will not let us go.

Célimène I heard a carriage in the court below:
Who is it?

Clitandre I don't know.

SCENE THREE

Basque, Célimène, Acaste, Clitandre

Basque Arsinoé
Is here, Madame.

Célimène Why, what can bring her, pray?

Basque She's now downstairs talking with Éliante.

Célimène What can be on her mind? What can she want?

Acaste She plays the perfect prude where'er she goes;
Her ardent zeal . . .

Célimène Yes, yes, it's quite a pose:
Her soul is worldly, and her fondest plan
Is, by some miracle, to catch a man.
She can see only with an envious eye
The suitors someone else is courted by.
Left all alone, but not the least resigned,
She rages at the world that is so blind.
She tries to hide, by acting like a prude,
Her obvious and frightful solitude.
Rather than find her feeble charms to blame,
She calls the power they lack a cause for shame.
A suitor, though, is what would please her best,
Especially if that suitor was Alceste.
His visits to me make her feel bereft,
And she pronounces this a kind of theft.
In jealous spite, which she can hardly bear,
She covertly attacks me everywhere.
In short, a sillier soul I never saw;
In her absurdity there's not a flaw,
And . . .

SCENE FOUR

Arsinoé, Célimène

Célimène Ah! Madame! Why, what a nice surprise!
I've missed you so! I can't believe my eyes.

Arsinoé There's something that I think I ought to say.

Célimène Just seeing you makes this a perfect day.

Exit Acaste and Clitandre, laughing.

Arsinoé Their leaving now was apropos indeed.

Célimène Shall we sit down?

Arsinoé I do not see the need,
Madame. True friendship should be manifest
In subjects that concern our interest;
And since none matter more to you or me
Than those of honor and propriety,
I come to tell you something, as a friend,
On which your reputation may depend.
I spent the other day with virtuous folk,
And, as it happened, 'twas of you they spoke.
And there, Madame, the freedom of your ways
Had the misfortune not to meet with praise.
The many men from whom you seek applause,
The rumors your coquettish manners cause,
Found far more censors than they ever ought,
And harsher than I could have wished or thought.
On this, you can imagine where I stood:
I sprang to your defense—as best I could,
Excusing your behavior as well-meant,
And stating I would vouch for your intent.
But there are things, you know as well as I,
We can't excuse, however hard we try;
And so I had to grant the others' claim
That your behavior does not help your name,
That it affords you anything but glory,
And makes of you the butt of many a story,
And that your ways, if you amended them,
Might offer less occasion to condemn.
Not that I think you grant more than you ought:
Heaven preserve my mind from such a thought!
But people hanker so for signs of vice,
To live well for oneself does not suffice.
Madame, I think you have too wise a heart
Not to accept this counsel in good part,

And to suspect a motive in my breast
Other than fervor for your interest.

Célimène Madame, do not misjudge my attitude:
Advice like yours is cause for gratitude;
Now let me show my deep appreciation
By counsel that concerns your reputation,
And since I see you show your amity
By telling me what people say of me,
I'll take your kind example as my cue,
And let you know the things they say of you.
I visited some friends the other day—
People of merit—and it chanced that they
Sought to define the art of living well.
On you, Madame, the conversation fell.
Your prudery, your ready indignation
Were not, alas! held up for admiration.
That affectation of a pious face,
Eternal talk of honor and of grace,
Your screams and airs of outraged innocence,
When a harmless word allows a doubtful sense,
The self-esteem that gratifies your mind,
The pitying eye you cast upon mankind,
Your frequent lessons, and the wrath you vent
On matters that are pure and innocent:
All this, to speak without equivocation,
Madame, gave rise to general condemnation.
"Why does she wear," they said, "this modest guise,
This pious mask which all the rest belies?
Though she would never miss a time to pray,
She beats her servants and withholds their pay.
In church she flaunts her zealous sense of duty,
Yet paints her face and strives to be a beauty.
She covers up the nude when it's in paint,
But of the thing itself makes no complaint."
Against them all I spoke right up for you,
Assuring them that none of this was true;
Still nothing would they do but criticize,
And they concluded that you would be wise
To leave the acts of others more alone,
And think a little more about your own;

That we should take an earnest look within
Before we censure other people's sin;
That only those whose lives approach perfection
Are licensed to administer correction;
And that we leave this better, even then,
To those whom Heaven has chosen among men.
Madame, you too have far too wise a heart
Not to accept this counsel in good part,
And to suspect a motive in my breast
Other than fervor for your interest.

Arsinoé I know we run a risk when we exhort,
But I did not expect quite this retort;
And since, Madame, it is so very tart,
I see my frank advice has stung your heart.

Célimène Why, not at all, Madame; if we were wise,
Such chance for mutual counsel we would prize;
And honesty would banish from our mind
The blindness toward oneself that plagues mankind.
So, if you wish it, we need never end
This helpful interchange from friend to friend,
And we can tell each other, *entre nous,*
All that you hear of me, and I of you.

Arsinoé Why, nothing can be heard against your name,
Madame, and it is I whom people blame.

Célimène Madame, we either praise or blame, in truth,
According to our taste and to our youth.
And thus there is one season for romance,
Another fitter for a prudish stance.
The latter may be suited to the time
When our attractiveness has passed its prime:
It helps to cover our pathetic lacks.
Some day I may well follow in your tracks:
Age brings all things; but who is in the mood,
Madame, at twenty, to become a prude?

Arsinoé You flaunt a scant advantage there, in truth,
And preen yourself a lot about your youth.
If I am just a bit older than you,
This is no reason for such great ado;

And I confess, Madame, I do not know
What passion drives you to attack me so.

Célimène And I, Madame, would like to know the reason
Why hunting me is never out of season.
Why do you blame me for your unsuccess?
And can I help it if men seek you less?
If I inspire so many men with love,
If I am offered daily proofs thereof,
Proofs that you wish might be addressed to you,
It's not my fault; there's nothing I can do:
The field is free, and I do not prevent
Your charming menfolk to your heart's content.

Arsinoé Come, do you think I envy you that crowd
Of suitors whose attentions make you proud,
And that it is so hard for us to tell
At what a price you hold them in your spell?
Would you have us believe, the way things go,
That it is just your merit charms them so?
That it is with a proper love they burn,
And that they hope for nothing in return?
Vain explanations never do ring true,
No one is fooled; and I know women who,
Though made for every mortal to adore,
Yet do not summon suitors to their door.
From this I think we safely may conclude
That such devotion springs from gratitude,
That no one courts us for our lovely eyes,
And that we pay a price for all their sighs.
So be a little less inclined to gloat
On conquests that deserve such little note;
Correct your disposition to be vain,
And show your fellow humans less disdain.
If we were envious of such as you,
I rather think we could, as others do,
Let ourselves go; and then you soon would find
All can have suitors who are so inclined.

Célimène Then help yourself, Madame, and we shall see
If you can lure them with this recipe;
And if . . .

Arsinoé Madame, let's leave things as they are;
More talk would carry both of us too far;
I would have taken leave, as soon I will,
But that my carriage keeps me waiting still.

Célimène Madame, believe me, you are free to stay
As long as you like; please do not rush away;
But, lest more formal talk from me fatigue you,
Here's someone much more likely to intrigue you;
This gentleman, who comes just when he should,
Will entertain you better than I could.
Alceste, I have a letter I must send,
Or else I shall antagonize a friend.
Please stay here with Madame; I have no doubt
She'll graciously excuse my stepping out.

SCENE FIVE

Alceste, Arsinoé

Arsinoé She wants the two of us to talk, you see,
While waiting till my carriage comes for me;
And she could show me no consideration
As nice as such a private conversation.
Truly, people whose merit is supreme
Attract unanimous love and esteem;
And by its charm your high distinction earns
The interest of my heart in your concerns.
I only wish the court would have the grace
To set your merit in its proper place:
You are ill-treated, and I swear it hurts
To see you fail to get your true deserts.

Alceste Who, I, Madame? And what should be my claim?
What service to the state adorns my name?
What splendid thing have I achieved, in short,
To justify my preference at court?

Arsinoé The court regards some with a kindly eye
Which their achievements hardly justify.
Merit requires a chance to meet some test;

And yours, which is so plainly manifest,
Should . . .

Alceste Heavens! forget my merit; be so kind.
How can the court keep such things on its mind?
It would be quite a task for it to scan
The merit that resides in every man.

Arsinoé True merit is most difficult to hide;
Yours commands high esteem on every side;
And yesterday, in two distinguished places,
I heard important persons sing your praises.

Alceste But undiscerning praise today is cheap,
Madame, and lumps us all in one great heap:
With merit all are equally endowed;
Applause no longer makes us justly proud;
We toss bouquets in one another's face;
And in the news my valet has his place.

Arsinoé I wish your quality was more in view,
And that a post at court appealed to you.
If you would show the slightest inclination,
Machinery would be in operation;
And I have influence to bring to bear
To make your progress smooth beyond compare.

Alceste And there, Madame, what role am I to play?
My character demands I stay away.
And Heaven did not make me of the sort
To get along contentedly at court;
I do not have the virtues that you need
To do your business there and to succeed.
Only in honesty can I compete,
I simply have no talent for deceit;
And anyone who can't equivocate
Should leave the place before it is too late.
Away from court we lack support, no doubt,
And all the titles that are handed out;
But there is consolation for our soul:
We do not have to play a silly role,
Brook the rebuffs that all must undergo,
Admire the verse of Mr. So-and-So,

Burn incense at the shrine of Madame Blank,
And suffer every noble mountebank.

Arsinoé All right; about the court I shall be mute;
But I am much distressed about your suit,
And I could wish, if I may speak my mind,
To see your love more suitably assigned.
You certainly deserve a better fate,
And Célimène is not your proper mate.

Alceste One thing, Madame, I do not comprehend:
Do you forget this lady is your friend?

Arsinoé Yes; but my conscience has been grieved too long
At watching you endure so great a wrong;
Seeing you in this state, I am dismayed,
And you should know your passion is betrayed.

Alceste Your tender sentiments I now discover,
Madame: what welcome tidings for a lover!

Arsinoé Yes, though she is my friend, I do declare
That she does not deserve your loving care,
And that her kindness to you is but show.

Alceste Perhaps, Madame; the heart we cannot know;
But could you not in charity decline
To plant such a disloyal thought in mine?

Arsinoé If you would rather look the other way,
There's no use talking, and I've said my say.

Alceste Whatever we are told in this domain,
Doubt is the thing that gives the greatest pain;
And I would rather not have information
Without the chance for clear verification.

Arsinoé Enough said. Very well. To set things right,
On this score you shall have abundant light.
Yes, with your own eyes you shall clearly see:
All you need do is to come home with me;
Convincing proof I will provide you there
Of your betrayal by your lady fair;
And if you're cured of your infatuation,
You might even be offered consolation.

Act Four

SCENE ONE
Éliante, Philinte

Philinte I've never seen such stubborn indignation,
Or such a difficult accommodation:
We could not budge the man, hard as we tried,
With all our arguments from every side,
Nor has a case of such a curious sort
Ever, I think, preoccupied this court.
"No, gentlemen," he said, "to this I cling:
I'll concede all, except for this one thing.
Why must he bridle and strike out so madly?
Is his honor at stake in writing badly?
Why must he twist my judgment for the worse?
Even a gentleman can write bad verse.
These things concern our honor not a whit.
That he's a gentleman I do admit,
A man of quality, merit, and heart,
All that you like—his authorship apart.
I'll praise his lavish get-up for its charms,
His skill at dancing, horsemanship, or arms,
But praise his verse? That takes a diplomat.
And if a man can't write better than that,
He should resist rhyming to his last breath—
At least, unless it's under pain of death."

In short, the best grace and accommodation
He found to cover up his irritation
Was to seek—thus—to put Oronte at ease:
"Sir, I regret that I'm so hard to please,
And for your sake I wish with all my heart
I'd thought your sonnet was a work of art."
After these words, they had the two embrace,
And hastily concluded the whole case.

Éliante His actions are peculiar and extreme,
But, I admit, I hold him in esteem,
And the sincerity that is his pride
Has a heroic and a noble side.
It's an uncommon virtue in this day
Which I wish others had in the same way.

Philinte The more I see the man, the more I wonder
At the impassioned spell his heart is under:
Considering what Heaven made him of,
I cannot think how he can fall in love;
And why he loves your cousin, I confess,
Is something I can fathom even less.

Éliante This clearly shows that love, in human hearts,
Need not imply community of parts;
And theories of mutual admiration
In this case show themselves without foundation.

Philinte But as you see it, is he loved in turn?

Éliante That point is far from easy to discern.
Whether she really loves him, who can tell?
She knows her own emotions none too well:
Sometimes she's been in love, and never knew it,
Or thought she was, when there was nothing to it.

Philinte With this cousin of yours, I think he'll find
More sorrow than has ever crossed his mind;
And if he had this heart of mine, I swear,
He promptly would bestow his love elsewhere,
And, turning in a far better direction,
Would take advantage of your deep affection.

Éliante I am not ceremonious, I fear,

And on these points I like to be sincere:
His love for her causes me no distress;
With all my heart I wish her happiness;
And if the thing were up to me alone,
I'd let him have her for his very own.
But if in such a choice, as just might be,
His love should not be crowned by destiny,
If she should spurn him for some substitute,
I could be willing to receive his suit;
And in this case I would not take offense
To know she had his earlier preference.

Philinte And I do not begrudge him, for my part,
Madame, the feeling for him in your heart;
And he himself can tell you even more
Just how I have advised him on that score.
But if the bonds of marriage joined those two
So that he could not pay his court to you,
My hope would be that I might take his place
And seek to win some measure of your grace,
Happy if his poor judgment left you free,
And if that grace, Madame, might fall on me.

Éliante Philinte, you're jesting.

Philinte No indeed, Madame,
No one could be more earnest than I am,
And eagerly I wait upon the day
When I can tell you all I long to say.

SCENE TWO

Alceste, Éliante, Philinte

Alceste Ah, Madame! You must help me gain redress
For an offense that cracks my steadfastness.

Éliante What is it? What has made you so upset?

Alceste I've had . . . I cannot understand it yet;
And the collapse of the whole firmament
Could never crush me as has this event.
It's done . . . My love . . . There's nothing I can say.

Éliante Try to regain your mind's composure, pray.

Alceste Just Heaven! Must such graces be combined
With vices worthy of the meanest mind?

Éliante But still, what . . . ?

Alceste Everything is devastated;
I'm . . . I'm betrayed; why, I'm assassinated!
Yes, Célimène—can such things be believed?—
Yes, Célimène untrue, and I'm deceived.

Éliante Have you strong reasons for this supposition?

Philinte This might be just an ill-conceived suspicion.
Your jealous mind, an easy prey to snares . . .

Alceste Good Lord, sir! Won't you mind your own affairs?
I've proof of her betrayal, all too clear,
In her own hand, right in my pocket, here.
Madame, a letter bearing Oronte's name
Has shown me my disfavor and her shame:
Oronte, whose suit I thought she viewed askance,
The one I feared the least of her gallants.

Philinte A letter often gives the wrong impression
And bears a false likeness to a confession.

Alceste Once more, sir, if you please, leave me alone
And mind your business; let me mind my own.

Éliante Alceste, control your temper; all this spite . . .

Alceste Madame, this task belongs to you by right;
It is with you my heart now seeks relief
From the torment of overwhelming grief.
Avenge me on that cousin without shame
Who basely has betrayed so true a flame;
Avenge me for what I trust your soul abhors.

Éliante Avenge you? How?

Alceste Madame, my heart is yours.
Take it, replace the faithless Célimène.
Oh, I'll have my revenge upon her then!
I want her punished by the deep emotion,
The heartfelt love, the assiduous devotion,

The eager duties and the service true
Which now my heart will sacrifice to you.

Éliante Of course I sympathize with what you suffer,
And I do not disdain the heart you offer;
But it may be the harm is not so great,
And you may drop your vengeance and your hate.
When it's a charming person does us wrong,
Our plans for vengeance do not linger long:
Whatever the offenses we resent,
A guilty loved one is soon innocent;
The harm we wish her has no aftermath;
And nothing passes like a lover's wrath.

Alceste No, Madame, that is not the way I burn;
I'm breaking off with her; there's no return;
Nothing could ever change what I project;
I'd be ashamed to view her with respect.
—Here she is. My blood boils at her approach;
Her turpitude deserves a sharp reproach;
I shall confound her utterly, and then
Bring you a heart quite free of Célimène.

SCENE THREE

Célimène, Alceste

Alceste Great Heavens! Can I control my indignation?

Célimène Oh dear! What has brought on your agitation?
What do you mean by these portentous sighs
And by the somber passion in your eyes?

Alceste Nothing can match, no, not the ugliest crimes,
The faithlessness you've shown these many times;
The worst that Fate, Hell, wrathful Heaven could do
Never made anything as bad as you.

Célimène I marvel at these sweet amenities.

Alceste No, no, this is no time for pleasantries.
You should be blushing; you have ample reason,
And I have certain tokens of your treason.

The cause of my distress is all too plain;
My apprehensiveness was not in vain;
My doubts, which you thought odious and unsound,
Have led me to the ill my eyes have found;
My star, though you were skillful to pretend,
Warned me of what I had to apprehend.
But don't presume to make a fool of me
And hope to flout me with impunity.
I know that we cannot control desire,
That love's autonomy must be entire,
That force won't strike a heart's responsive chord,
And that each soul is free to choose its lord.
So I would find no subject for complaint
If you had spoken frankly, without feint;
Had you spurned my advances from the first,
I'd have blamed fate and waited for the worst.
But thus to fan my hopes with false acclaim
Is faithless treachery, quite without shame,
Deserving the severest castigation;
And I can freely vent my indignation.
Yes, after such a slight, avoid my path:
I am beside myself with righteous wrath:
Pierced by the mortal blow with which you slay me,
My reason cannot make my sense obey me;
Ruled by the anger that I feel for you,
I cannot answer for what I may do.

Célimène Come, please explain this latest of your fits.
Tell me, have you completely lost your wits?

Alceste Yes, yes, I lost them at that fatal hour
When first I fell into your poisonous power,
And when I sought sincerity as well
In the false charms that caught me in their spell.

Célimène Pooh! Of what treachery can you complain?

Alceste Oh, what duplicity! How well you feign!
But I have ready proof at my command.
Just look at this, and recognize your hand.
This note at least should leave you mortified;
Its evidence is not to be denied.

Célimène Then *this* explains your mood, and all you've said?

Alceste Can you behold this note, and not turn red?

Célimène If I should blush, perhaps you'll state the reason?

Alceste What? Are you adding shamelessness to treason?
Do you disown it, as an unsigned note?

Célimène But why disown a letter that I wrote?

Alceste And you can look at it without dismay
Although its very style gives you away?

Célimène You really are too patently absurd.

Alceste Against this witness, who could take your word?
And how can you offend me so, and flaunt
Your clear infatuation with Oronte?

Célimène Oronte! Who says he is the addressee?

Alceste The person who today gave it to me.
But let's assume it's for some other swain:
Does that give me less reason to complain?
Will that make you less guilty in the end?

Célimène But if it's written to a lady friend,
Where is the guilt, and what's this all about?

Alceste Oh! that's an artful dodge, a neat way out.
I grant I'd not expected such deceit,
And that just makes my certainty complete.
How can you stoop to such a lame excuse?
And do you really think me that obtuse?
Come, come, let's see in just what way you'll try
To lend support to such an obvious lie,
And by what artifice you will pretend
This ardent note was for a lady friend.
Just tell me how you will explain away.
What I shall read . . .

Célimène I do not choose to say.
I don't concede to you or anyone
The right to talk to me as you have done.

Alceste Don't take offense; just tell me, if you please,
How you can justify such terms as these.

Célimène No, I'll do nothing of the kind, I swear.
Think what you like of me; I just don't care.

Alceste Please, show me how this letter could be meant
For any woman, and I'll be content.

Célimène No, no, it's for Oronte; you must be right;
I welcome his attentions with delight;
In all he says and does, he has a way;
And I'll agree to anything you say.
Make up your mind, let nothing interfere;
But I have heard from you all I will hear.

Alceste Heavens! How could such a cruel trick be invented?
And has a heart ever been so tormented?
I come to tax her with her perfidy,
I'm the complainant—and she turns on me!
My pain and my suspicions she provokes.
She won't deny her guilt, but boasts and jokes!
And yet my heart is still too weak and faint
To break the chains that hold it in constraint
And arm itself with generous disdain
Against the object that it loves in vain!
Ah, faithless girl, with what consummate skill
You play upon my utter lack of will
And make capital of the vast excess
Of my ill-omened, fatal tenderness!
At least defend yourself for this offense
And drop this claim of guilt, this vain pretense;
Show me the innocence of what you wrote;
My fond heart will forget about the note.
Just try your best to seem faithful, and know
That I will try my best to think you so.

Célimène Your jealous frenzies make you mad, I swear,
And you do not deserve the love I bear.
What makes you think that I would condescend,
On your account, to brazen and pretend?
And why, if my heart leaned another way,
Shouldn't I quite sincerely have my say?
What? Can the way in which I've spoken out
About my feelings leave you any doubt?

Has that such weight against this guarantee?
Can you regard it and not outrage me?
And since it's hard for women to confess
Their sentiments of love and tenderness,
Since honor bids us never to reveal
The force of any ardor we may feel,
A man for whom this hurdle is surmounted
Should know our word is not to be discounted.
Shouldn't he be ready to stake his life
On what costs us so much internal strife?
Come, such suspicions earn my indignation;
And you are not worth my consideration.
I am a fool; I'm sorry this is true
And that I still have some regard for you;
I should look elsewhere, that is all too plain,
And give you proper reason to complain.

Alceste Treacherous girl! How can I be so weak?
I cannot trust the sugared words you speak;
Yet fate enjoins—and follow it I must—
That my soul be abandoned to your trust;
Although you may betray me, even so
I must learn to what lengths your heart will go.

Célimène No, you don't love me in the proper fashion.

Alceste Ah! Nothing can be likened to my passion.
My eagerness to prove it goes so far
That I could wish you worse off than you are.
Yes, I could wish that no one found you charming,
That your predicament was quite alarming,
That Heaven had given you nothing at your birth,
Not rank, nor family, nor any worth,
So that my heart, a gleaming sacrifice,
Might compensate and might alone suffice;
'Twould be my pride and joy, all else above,
To have you owe everything to my love.

Célimène You surely wish me well in your own way!
I hope to Heaven I never see the day . . .
But here's . . . Monsieur Du Bois. I do declare!

SCENE FOUR

Du Bois, Célimène, Alceste

Alceste What does this outfit mean, this frightened air?
What's wrong?

Du Bois Sir . . .

Alceste Well?

Du Bois I have strange things to tell.

Alceste What are they?

Du Bois Our affairs aren't going well.

Alceste What?

Du Bois Shall I speak?

Alceste Yes, yes, speak up, and quick.

Du Bois Isn't that someone . . . ?

Alceste Oh! You'll make me sick.
Will you speak up?

Du Bois Monsieur, we must give ground.

Alceste How's that?

Du Bois We must decamp without a sound.

Alceste And why?

Du Bois I tell you, sir, we've got to fly.

Alceste What for?

Du Bois We mustn't stop to say good-bye.

Alceste But for what reason? What's this all about?

Du Bois This reason, sir: we promptly must get out.

Alceste Honestly, I will break your head in two,
You knave, if that's the best that you can do.

Du Bois Sir, a black somber man, in face and dress,
Came to our place—the kitchen door, no less—
And left a paper filled with such a scrawl
You'd have to be a demon to read it all.
It's all about your lawsuit, I've no doubt;
But even Satan couldn't make it out.

Alceste Well then? What of it? Just explain to me:
Why should this paper mean we have to flee?

Du Bois A little later, sir, an hour or more,
A man who's been to visit you before
Came in great haste, and finding you not there,
Gave me a message that I was to bear
(Knowing I'm the most dutiful of men),
To tell you . . . Wait, what *is* his name again?

Alceste What did he tell you, wretch? Forget his name.

Du Bois Well, he's a friend of yours; it's all the same.
He told me you have got to get away,
And you could be arrested if you stay.

Alceste But why? Nothing specific? Think, man, think.

Du Bois No; but he did ask me for pen and ink,
And wrote this note, in which I think you'll see
The explanation of this mystery.

Alceste Well, give it to me.

Célimène What's this all about?

Alceste I don't know, but I hope soon to find out.
Come on, you oaf, what are you waiting for?

Du Bois [*after a long search*] My goodness, sir! I left it in your drawer.

Alceste I don't know why I don't . . .

Célimène No, that can wait;
You'd better go and set this matter straight.

Alceste It seems that fate, no matter what I do,
Will never let me have a talk with you;
But let me come again ere day is done,
And I shall think for once my love has won.

Act Five

SCENE ONE
Alceste, Philinte

Alceste No use. My mind is quite made up, I tell you.

Philinte But must this blow, however hard, compel you . . . ?

Alceste No, you may talk and argue all you can,
Nothing that you can say will change my plan:
On every side such wickedness I find
That I mean to withdraw from humankind.
What? Honor, virtue, probity, the laws
Impugn my enemy and plead my cause;
Everyone knows of my integrity;
I put my trust in right and equity;
And yet the outcome leaves me destitute:
Justice is with me, and I lose my suit!
A man whose shame is written on his face
Perjures himself outright, and wins the case!
Good faith gives way before his treachery:
He cuts my throat, and puts the blame on me!
His artificial grimace is so strong
As to taint justice and turn right to wrong!

He gets a court decree to crown his sin,
And not content with having done me in,
There's a revolting book in circulation,
A book subject to solemn condemnation,
Deserving to be banned by law—and he
Foully ascribes the authorship to me!
And thereupon Oronte, that evil cheat,
Nods his assent, and seconds the deceit!
Oronte, whose name at court shines bright and clear,
With whom I've always been frank and sincere,
Who comes to me to wheedle and coerce,
And make me comment on his wretched verse;
And just because I answer in good sooth,
Refusing to betray him or the truth,
He attests a crime that never did exist
And sets me up as his antagonist!
I'll never have his pardon, count upon it,
For failing to appreciate his sonnet!
Lord! What a sordid and familiar story:
Men led to evil by their itch for glory!
Yes, this is the good faith, the virtuous zeal,
The equity and honor they reveal!
Come, I've endured more than enough from men:
Let's flee this ugly wood, this robbers' den.
And since you men behave the way you do—
Like wolves—I bid my last farewell to you.

Philinte I think your plan's a little premature,
And men are not all that depraved, I'm sure;
Your enemy's charges, it is manifest,
Have not availed to bring on your arrest.
His false report has burst like any bubble,
And might well get him into serious trouble.

Alceste He? He need have no fear at any time:
He has some sort of privilege for crime;
And far from hurting him, this added shame
Will only serve to magnify his name.

Philinte At any rate, I think you will concede
His rumors have been given little heed:

You have no cause at all for worry there;
As for your lawsuit, which was most unfair,
A higher court will surely countermand
This verdict . . .

Alceste No! I mean to let it stand.
The wrong it does me is so manifest,
I won't appeal it; no, I'll let it rest.
It shows the right downtrodden and maligned,
And I want it exposed to all mankind
As a clear testimony and display
Of all the evil of the present day.
At twenty thousand francs the cost is high;
But for those twenty thousand francs I'll buy
The right to rail against man's wicked state
And look upon it with undying hate.

Philinte But still . . .

Alceste But still, don't press me any more.
What can you tell me further on this score?
Do you mean to justify, right to my face,
The evil conduct of the human race?

Philinte No, no, all that I'll readily concede:
The world is ruled by pure intrigue and greed;
Nothing but trickery prevails today,
And humans should be made some other way.
But should their disaffection for the right
Lead us to try to flee their very sight?
These human flaws give us the satisfaction
Of testing our philosophy in action:
In such employment virtue can take pride;
And if goodness were found on every side,
If all men's hearts were docile, frank, and just,
Most of our virtues would but gather rust,
Since they can serve to help us calmly bear
The injustices that face us everywhere.
Just as a heart instinct with virtue can . . .

Alceste Sir, you can talk as well as any man.
Your stock of arguments is most profuse,
But now your eloquence is just no use.

Reason bids me retire for my own good:
My tongue will not obey me as it should;
I could not answer for what I might say,
And I'd have a new quarrel every day.
Don't argue, let me wait for Célimène:
I've got to try to talk with her again.
Whether she really loves me, I don't know;
And I must have her answer, yes or no.

Philinte Let's wait for her with Éliante upstairs.

Alceste No, I am too oppressed with anxious cares.
Go on and see her; I'll sit here apart
In this dark corner with my gloomy heart.

Philinte That's not good company for any man;
I'll ask Éliante to join us if she can.

SCENE TWO

Oronte, Célimène, Alceste

Oronte Yes, Madame, it is for you to decide
Whether a bond between us shall be tied.
I must ask you to answer with precision:
A lover will not stand for indecision.
If you're at all responsive to my flame,
You can reveal that to me without shame;
And as you know, the proof that I request
Is that you end the courtship of Alceste,
Sacrifice him, Madame, and promptly break
All your relations with him for my sake.

Célimène But why do you attack him with such spirit,
When I've so often heard you praise his merit?

Oronte Madame, let's let such explanations be;
The question is just how you feel toward me.
So kindly make your choice between us two,
And my decision will depend on you.

Alceste [*coming out of his corner*] Madame, the gentleman's request is just,

And I support it; yes, decide you must.
The same ardor, the same concern are mine;
My love can't do without some clearcut sign;
Matters have gone too far for more delay,
And now's the time for you to have your say.

Oronte Sir, I've no wish to be importunate
And bother you, if you're so fortunate.

Alceste Sir, I've no wish to have you share a part—
Even if this be jealous—of her heart.

Oronte If your love is more precious in her view . . .

Alceste If she can have the slightest taste for you . . .

Oronte I swear I'll leave her to you there and then.

Alceste I swear I'll never see her face again.

Oronte Madame, pray tell us what we've come to hear.

Alceste Madame, you can speak freely, without fear.

Oronte All you need do is say how you're inclined.

Alceste All you need do is to make up your mind.

Oronte What? When we ask your choice, you seem put out?

Alceste What? Your soul hesitates and seems in doubt?

Célimène Good Lord! This urgency is out of place,
And both of you show no more sense than grace.
My mind's made up about this situation,
And in my heart there is no hesitation;
Between you two it is in no suspense,
And I could well declare its preference.
But I think it a painful indiscretion
To utter such a face-to-face confession;
I think these words that are so hard to bear
Should not be spoken when both men are there;
I think our hearts betray our inclinations
Without being forced to such harsh revelations,
And that there are much gentler ways to use
When we must tell a lover such bad news.

Oronte No, no, the truth! I have no cause to fear it.
Come, please speak up.

Alceste And I demand to hear it.
There's nothing in your openness to scare us;
Believe me, I've no wish to have you spare us.
You don't need everyone under your sway;
Enough uncertainty, enough delay:
Now is the time to answer our demand.
If you decline, I shall know where I stand;
Your silence will amount to an admission
That will corroborate my worst suspicion.

Oronte I'm grateful for your indignation, sir;
And what you say is what I say to her.

Célimène Oh, how you weary me with this caprice!
Can't you be fair, and let me have some peace?
Haven't I told you why I will not budge?
But here comes Éliante: I'll let her judge.

SCENE THREE

Éliante, Philinte, Célimène, Oronte, Alceste

Célimène Cousin, I find myself beset indeed
By these two men, who seem to have agreed.
With equal warmth they both insist, my dear,
That I should make my choice between them clear,
And, by a sentence uttered face to face,
That I make one of them give up the chase.
Has anyone ever behaved this way?

Éliante Don't seek my frank opinion on this, pray:
I'm not the one to ask, as you will find,
And I'm for people who will speak their mind.

Oronte Madame, you may defend yourself in vain.

Alceste No use in being devious, that's plain.

Oronte You must speak up, you must, and end this doubt.

Alceste Or if you won't, your silence will speak out.

Oronte One word from you, and there'll be no more scenes.

Alceste And if you're silent, I'll know what that means.

SCENE FOUR

Acaste, Clitandre, Arsinoé, Philinte, Éliante, Oronte, Célimène, Alceste

Acaste Madame, with no offense, we two are here
To try to get a little matter clear.

Clitandre Your presence, sirs, is timely, I declare,
And you are both involved in this affair.

Arsinoé Madame, my coming must be a surprise,
But these men would not have it otherwise:
They both came to me angry and aggrieved
Over an act too mean to be believed.
I think there is a goodness in your soul
That would not let you play so base a role:
My eyes belied their strongest evidence,
My friendship overlooked our difference,
And so I came to keep them company
And see you overthrow this calumny.

Acaste Yes, Madame, let's see, with a peaceful mind,
What sort of explanation you can find.
You wrote Clitandre this note, now didn't you?

Clitandre It was you wrote Acaste this billet-doux?

Acaste To you this handwriting is not obscure,
Messieurs, and her indulgence, I am sure,
Has made it known to every person here;
But this is something for you all to hear.

He reads.

"You're a strange man to condemn my sprightliness and reproach me with never being so happy as when I'm not with you. Nothing could be more unjust; and if you don't come very soon and ask my pardon for this offense, I shall never forgive you for it as long as I live. Our great lout of a Viscount . . ."

He *should* be here.

"Our great lout of a Viscount, whom you complain about first, is a man I never could fancy; and since I watched him for a good three-quarters of an hour spitting into a well to make circles in the water, I have never been able to think well of him. As for the little Marquis . . ."

All vanity aside, gentlemen, that's me.

"As for the little Marquis, who held my hand so long yesterday, I don't know anything as insignificant as his whole person; and the only merit of his kind lies in his cloak and sword. As for the man with the green ribbons . . ."

[*To Alceste.*] Your turn, sir.

"As for the man with the green ribbons, he sometimes amuses me with his bluntness and his surly grouchiness; but there are hundreds of times when I find him as tiresome as can be. And as for the man with the jacket . . ."*

[*To Oronte.*] Here's your bundle.

"And as for the man with the jacket, who has gone in for wit and wants to be an author in spite of everyone, I can't give myself the trouble to listen to what he says; and his prose wearies me as much as his poetry. So get it into your head that I don't always have as good a time as you think; that I miss you more than I could wish in all the parties that I'm dragged into; and that a marvelous seasoning for the pleasures we enjoy is the presence of the persons we love."

Clitandre And now here I am.

He reads.

"Your Clitandre, whom you mention, and who puts on such sweetish airs, is the last man I could be fond of. He is absurd to suppose he is loved; and so are you, to think you are not. To be reasonable, exchange your beliefs for his; and see me as much as you can to help me endure the vexation of being beleaguered by him."

It's a fine character these portraits show,
Madame, and there's a name for it, you know.

* In all editions from 1682 on, this reads "And as for the man with the sonnet . . ."

Enough: we two shall everywhere impart
This glorious self-portrait of your heart.

Acaste I could well speak, I've ample provocation;
But you're not worthy of my indignation;
And there are nobler hearts, as you shall see,
Ready to comfort a *petit marquis.*

Exit Acaste and Clitandre.

Oronte What? You can tear me into shreds this way
After the things I've seen you write and say!
And your false heart, which seems for love designed,
Offers itself in turn to all mankind!
Go to, I've been a dupe too much, too long;
I *should* be grateful that you've proved me wrong.
You give me back my heart, a welcome prize,
And in your loss of it my vengeance lies.

To Alceste.

If I was in your way, I no longer am,
So pray conclude your business with Madame.

Exit Oronte.

Arsinoé Really, that is the blackest action yet.
I can't keep silent, I am too upset.
How can such treachery be justified?
I leave the other gentlemen aside;
But take a man of honor like Alceste,
Whose heart by your good fortune you possessed,
Who worshiped you beyond what tongue can say,
Should he have been . . . ?

Alceste Madame, allow me, pray,
To guard my interest here; that's all I ask;
Don't charge yourself with this superfluous task.
My heart, though grateful for your vindication,
Is in no state to pay its obligation;
And if—I have to tell you, for it's true—
I sought revenge, it would not be with you.

Arsinoé Do you think, sir, that that was in my mind,
And that I look on you as such a find?

To tell the truth, I find you very vain
If that's the kind of thought you entertain.
To hanker for the leavings of Madame,
I'd have to be less choosy than I am.
Come down a peg, open your eyes, give heed:
I'm not the kind of person that you need;
Keep sighing for her; she is quite a catch;
I can hardly wait to see so fine a match.

Exit Arsinoé.

Alceste Well! I have held my tongue, for all I see,
And let everyone speak ahead of me:
Have my feelings been long enough suppressed?
And may I now . . . ?

Célimène Yes, tell me all the rest.
You've every reason to complain your fill
And reproach me for everything you will.
I'm wrong, I do confess; my consternation
Leads me to seek no vain extenuation.
The others' wrath I treated with disdain,
But I agree, my crime toward you is plain;
I've earned your bitterness, lost your esteem;
I know full well how guilty I must seem,
That everything proclaims I have betrayed you,
And if you hate me, it's because I've made you.
Go ahead; I consent.

Alceste Ah! traitress, how?
Can I conquer my passion even now?
And though I burn to hate you, as you say,
Do you think my heart is ready to obey?

To Éliante and Philinte.

See what unworthy tenderness can do;
Bear witness to my frailty, you two.
But this is not yet all, I must confess,
And you shall see me push it to excess,
Proving that those who call us wise are wrong,
And that mere human nature is too strong.

To Célimène.

I'm willing to forget the things you've done;
My soul will find excuse for every one;
And I'll contrive to view your blackest crimes
As youthful foibles caused by evil times,
Provided only that your heart agree
To flee human society with me,
And that you'll follow me without delay
To the seclusion where I've vowed to stay:
Only thus, in the minds of everyone,
Can you repair the harm your note has done,
And after a scene which noble hearts abhor,
Enable me to love you as before.

Célimène What! *I* renounce the world before I'm old,
And molder in some solitary hold?

Alceste If your love matches mine and is as true,
Why should all other men matter to you?
Why can't I be sufficient to your need?

Célimène At twenty, solitude is grim indeed.
I fear I lack the loftiness of soul
To undertake so difficult a role.
If marriage can fulfill your aspiration,
I think I could resolve on that relation,
And thus . . .

Alceste No, never did I hate you so,
And this refusal is the final blow.
Since this is something that you cannot do—
Find all in me, as I find all in you—
Go, I refuse you, and at last I sever
My most unworthy ties to you forever.

Exit Célimène.

To Éliante.

Madame, your beauty is adorned with worth,
You only are sincere in all the earth;
For you my admiration is extreme.
But now please be content with my esteem;
Forgive me if the turmoil in my soul

No longer lets me seek a suitor's role:
I feel unworthy, and that Heaven's plan
Did not create me for a married man;
That you deserve a hand better than mine,
And not the discard of a heart less fine,
And that . . .

Éliante Follow this notion to the end;
I do not find myself without a friend;
And if I asked Philinte, I understand
He might be happy to accept my hand.

Philinte Madame, if I could have you for my wife,
I'd gladly sacrifice my blood, my life.

Alceste May both of you forever feel like this,
And thus experience true wedded bliss!
While I, betrayed, and overwhelmed with wrong,
Leave an abyss where vices are too strong,
And seek some solitary place on earth
Where one is free to be a man of worth.

Exit Alceste.

Philinte [*to Éliante*] Come, Madame, let's do everything we can
To thwart the aims of this unhappy man.

Tartuffe or, The Impostor

CHARACTERS

Madame Pernelle, mother of Orgon
Orgon, husband of Elmire
Elmire, wife of Orgon
Damis, son of Orgon
Mariane, daughter of Orgon, in love with Valère
Valère, in love with Mariane
Cléante, brother-in-law of Orgon
Tartuffe, religious hypocrite
Dorine, lady's maid to Mariane
Monsieur Loyal, a bailiff
A *Gentleman* of the King's Guard
Flipote, maid to Madame Pernelle

The scene is the salon of Orgon's house in Paris.

Act One

SCENE ONE

Madame Pernelle, Flipote, Elmire, Mariane, Dorine, Damis, Cléante

Madame Pernelle Come on, Flipote, come on, out of this place.

Elmire I can't keep up, you set so fast a pace.

Madame Pernelle Daughter-in-law, I'll find my way out. Please,
I have no need for these amenities.

Elmire We merely show you the regard we owe.
But, Mother, why are you so quick to go?

Madame Pernelle I can't abide the goings-on in there,
And no one in the household seems to care.
Yes, child, I'm leaving you, unedified,
My good advice ignored, if not defied.
Everyone speaks right out on everything:
It's like a court in which Misrule is king.

Dorine If . . .

Madame Pernelle You're a maid, like many of your kind,
Too saucy and too quick to speak your mind.
Nobody asks you, but you *will* be heard.

Damis But . . .

Madame Pernelle Here is what you are, boy, in one word:
A fool. I am your grandmother. I know.
A hundred times I've told your father so:
That you were getting wilder every day,
And that you'd bring him nothing but dismay.

Mariane I think . . .

Madame Pernelle His sister now! A startled fawn,
Too sweet to understand what's going on.
Still waters may run deep; they're rarely pure.
You can't fool me by acting so demure.

Elmire But, Mother . . .

Madame Pernelle Daughter-in-law, let me say
You're doing everything in a bad way.
Set an example for them to revere,
As their late mother always did, poor dear.
You spend too much, and I'm distressed to see
You dressed the way a princess ought to be.
If it's your husband that you seek to please,
My dear, you don't need all these fineries.

Cléante But, Madame, may I . . . ?

Madame Pernelle As her brother, sir,
I love you and respect you; but if I were
My son, her husband, I would make it clear
That I preferred you anywhere but here.
You preach a way of life to everyone
That decent people really ought to shun.
I guess that's pretty frank, but that's my way:
When I feel strongly, I must have my say.

Damis Monsieur Tartuffe is virtuous, no doubt . . .

Madame Pernelle He is a good man; you should hear him out;
And I am irritated through and through
To hear him criticized by fools like you.

Damis What? Would you have me sit back overawed
By that despotic, sanctimonious fraud?

And may we have no fun, no merriment,
Unless that gentleman deigns to consent?

Dorine He loves to preach an ethic so sublime
That anything we do becomes a crime.
He frowns on everything and runs it down.

Madame Pernelle And everything he frowns on earns his frown.
He leads the way to Heaven, and my son
Should make you love him, each and every one.

Damis Not even Father ever could compel
Me, Grandmother, to wish that fellow well.
I can't speak otherwise and be sincere:
I can't abide the things I see and hear.
I see a showdown coming with that lout,
And he and I will have to have it out.

Dorine I think it's scandalous, a real disgrace,
To see this stranger seize the master's place.
When he came here, for shoes, he hadn't any,
And all his clothes were hardly worth a penny.
And now this beggar's acting like a king,
Wanting to be obeyed in everything.

Madame Pernelle Things would go better here, if you ask me,
If you were governed by his piety.

Dorine You *will* make him a saint, but I submit
That he is nothing but a hypocrite.

Madame Pernelle My, what a tongue!

Dorine Him and Laurent, his minion!
You can't trust either one, in my opinion.

Madame Pernelle Though for his man I haven't any proof,
I'll guarantee the virtue of Tartuffe.
The reason you dislike him as you do
Is that the things he says to you are true.
Sin is the only thing that makes him burn,
And Heaven's interest is his sole concern.

Dorine So be it; but just recently how is it

That he opposes any sort of visit?
Does this so anger Heaven against us
That he must put up such a dreadful fuss?
I'll tell you what I think, between us here:
I think he's jealous of Madame Elmire.

Madame Pernelle Be still, and take some care of what you say.
Others condemn these calls in the same way.
The consequent commotion and uproar,
The carriages forever at your door,
The racket the assembled lackeys make:
These things keep all the neighborhood awake.
In all of this there may be no real harm;
But people talk; that's reason for alarm.

Cléante What then, Madame? Would you forbid their chatter?
I think that it would be no laughing matter
If in our fear that gossip might ensue
We had to bid our dearest friends adieu.
And even if we did this, and stood by it,
Could we, do you think, keep the whole world quiet?
To gossip seems to be a human need;
Our best protection is to pay no heed.
Let's live in innocence as best we may,
And let the gossipmongers have their say.

Dorine Our neighbor Daphne and her little mate:
Are they the ones who are so quick to prate?
Those whose behavior is most asinine
Are always more than ready to malign;
They always take the greatest satisfaction
In spotting the most innocent attraction,
And joyfully go off to spread the news,
Twisting it in whatever way they choose.
They paint other men's deeds a darker tone,
Thinking thereby to justify their own,
Hoping to blur the contrast, and present
Their own intrigues as wholly innocent,
Or else to cast on someone else's name
Part of the burden of the public blame.

Madame Pernelle All right, criticize Daphne all you want;
But how about the virtuous Orante?
She thinks of Heaven alone; and her devotion,
I hear, makes her condemn all your commotion.

Dorine A fine example, quite without a peer!
It's true that now her life is most austere;
Her years have brought her purity; but still
She's only virtuous against her will.
As long as men were at her beck and call,
She took advantage, and enjoyed it all;
But now, her charms not being what they were,
She wants to leave the world, that's leaving her,
And put on virtue as a proud disguise
To hide her faded beauty from our eyes.
These are the tactics of the modern flirt.
She hates to see her gallant swains desert.
Uneasy in her dreary solitude,
She finds her one vocation as a prude,
And people feel this worthy woman's sting.
Forgiving nothing, blaming everything,
She rants against the morals of the age,
Not out of charity, but jealous rage,
Determined for all others to destroy
The pleasures she no longer can enjoy.

Madame Pernelle [*to Elmire*] These are the fairy tales that please your ear.
No one else has a chance to talk in here,
While Madame Chatterbox goes on all day.
But all the same, I mean to have my say.
In taking in that pious man, my son
Did much the wisest thing he's ever done.
I tell you, he is truly heaven-sent,
In your dire need, to make you all repent.
For your salvation, listen to Tartuffe:
Whatever he reproves deserves reproof.
These visits, dances, chats in which you revel
Are nothing but inventions of the Devil.
Here no one speaks of any pious matter;
There's only idle talk and songs and chatter;

The neighbor usually gets his share,
As universal slander fills the air.
Besides, a sober person's head goes round,
At such assemblies, just from all the sound;
For everyone at once must have his say,
And as a preacher said the other day,
It really is the Tower of Babylon,
For all the people there just babble on;
And then, to illustrate his point, he spoke . . .

Cléante smiles.

Laughing already, sir! Well, what's the joke?
Go find your silly friends and laugh your fill.
Farewell, Elmire; I have said all I will.
I could say more about this house; but then,
You will not catch me in it soon again.

Slapping Flipote.

Come on, you slut, stop gaping at the moon,
Or else I'll slap some sense into you soon.
Come on now.

SCENE TWO
Cléante, Dorine

Cléante I won't see her to the door
For fear she may start in on me once more.
My, that old lady . . . !

Dorine Really, it's a shame
That she can't hear you call her by that name;
She'd surely tell you that you're quite a wit,
And that she's not yet old enough for it.

Cléante What a fuss over nothing! What a blast!
And what a spell her dear Tartuffe has cast!

Dorine You think she's bad? Wait till you see her son,
And you'll admit that he's the crazy one.

During our civil wars he showed good sense,
And served with courage in his king's defense;
But since he's taken Tartuffe as his hero,
His sanity has been reduced to zero;
He calls him brother, holds him far above
Mother, wife, son, or daughter in his love.
There's not a secret he will not confide
To him, as to his spiritual guide.
He pets and spoils him with such tenderness,
A mistress would be satisfied with less;
Gives him the place of honor when they dine,
And beams to see him eat enough for nine.
He saves the choicest bits for that man's part,
And when he belches, he says "Bless your heart!"
In short, he dotes upon his dear Tartuffe,
Worships his goodness, quotes his words for proof,
Sees miracles of virtue in his ways,
And oracles in every word he says.
Tartuffe, who knows his dupe and means to use him,
Has countless saintly poses to bemuse him,
Receives good sums, thanks to his pious mask,
And has the nerve to take us all to task.
Even his servant, a presumptuous fool,
Treats us like little children in a school;
He deafens us with wild-eyed homiletics,
And confiscates our ribbons and cosmetics.
Finding a handkerchief a while ago
Inside a *Fleur des Saints,* he tore it—so—
Saying it was a frightful crime to pair
A holy object with the devil's snare.

SCENE THREE

Elmire, Mariane, Damis, Cléante, Dorine

Elmire You're lucky that you did not stay for more
And hear the speech she gave us at the door.
But here's my husband. I'll go up and wait
And try to greet him in a proper state.

Cléante To save his time, I'll merely say hello
To him down here, and then I'll have to go.

Damis One thing. You know my sister wants to marry.
Tartuffe seems anxious that her plans miscarry,
And forces Father to procrastinate.
You know my interest in all this is great:
Just as love binds my sister and Valère,
As you know, for *his* sister I've my share.
Speak to him . . .

Dorine Here he is.

SCENE FOUR

Orgon, Cléante, Dorine

Orgon Brother, good day.

Cléante I'm glad to see you back; but I can't stay.
I guess you miss the flowers and the trees.

Orgon Dorine . . . Brother-in-law, one moment, please:
Though to be sure I have no cause for fear,
Let me find out what has been happening here.

To Dorine.

These last two days, how has everything gone?
What are you up to? How is everyone?

Dorine Madame had a bad fever, two days ago,
And a headache that really brought her low.

Orgon Yes. And Tartuffe?

Dorine Tartuffe? Fit as a fiddle:
Red mouth, pink cheeks, and bulging at the middle.

Orgon Poor fellow!

Dorine Then she had no appetite,
And therefore couldn't eat a thing that night.
Her headache still was just too much to bear.

Orgon Yes. And Tartuffe?

Dorine Piously, with her there,
He ate a brace of partridge like a flash,
Then half a leg of mutton in a hash.

Orgon Poor fellow!

Dorine Well, then the whole night went by
Without her managing to close an eye;
Fever denied her even a wink of sleep;
It was a nightlong watch we had to keep.

Orgon Yes. And Tartuffe?

Dorine When he had supped, he rose,
Went to his room, already in a doze,
Got into his warm bed without delay,
And slept his carefree fill till the next day.

Orgon Poor fellow!

Dorine When we'd reasoned and we'd pled,
She finally consented to be bled,
And that gave her immediate relief.

Orgon Yes. And Tartuffe?

Dorine He struggled with his grief,
And, girding up his soul at any cost,
To make up for the blood Madame had lost,
He downed at breakfast four great drafts of wine.

Orgon Poor fellow!

Dorine Yes. In short, they both are fine.
I think I'd better go upstairs and tell
Madame how glad you are she's getting well.

SCENE FIVE

Orgon, Cléante

Cléante She's laughing in your face. Did you see her smile?
Brother, I hesitate to rouse your bile,
But I don't blame her, in this situation.
Who ever heard of such infatuation?
And can you really be so hypnotized

That you've forgotten all you ever prized,
Given him food, taken him in with you,
And now you plan . . . ?

Orgon No more, sir; that will do.
You're speaking of a man you do not know.

Cléante All right, I don't, if you must have it so;
But if we ever really are to learn . . .

Orgon Brother, you'd be enchanted in your turn
To know him. I can see it! Oh, I can!
He's a man . . . who . . . a man . . . in short, a man.
Follow him: you will be serene, secure,
And look on everyone as just manure.
He guides me on new paths in new directions,
Trains me to mortify all my affections,
And liberates my soul from every tie.
My brother, children, mother, wife could die,
And I could see it without [*snaps his fingers*] *that* much
pain.

Cléante Brother, your sentiments are most humane!

Orgon Ah, if, that day we met, you'd been on hand,
You'd feel as I do now—you'd understand.
Each day he came to church, meek as you please,
And, right across from me, fell on his knees;
He caught the eye of every person there,
Such warmth and zeal he put into his prayer;
His transports were extreme, his sighs profound;
Each moment he would stoop and kiss the ground;
And when I left, he always went before
To offer me holy water at the door.
His man, who imitates his every deed,
Informed me of his background and his need.
I gave him gifts; but in his modest way,
He'd give me back a part and humbly say:
"That is too much, that's twice too much for me;
I am not worthy of your sympathy";
And then when I refused to compromise,
He'd give half to the poor, before my eyes.
At last Heaven prompted me to take him in;

And ever since, how splendid things have been!
I see him censure everything, and take
Great interest in my wife, all for my sake;
He warns me when men ogle her on the sly,
And acts far jealouser of her than I.
Upon himself he lays his hardest sentence:
A trifle, like a sin, demands repentance;
The merest nothing fills him with dismay.
He came and blamed himself the other day
Because while praying he had caught a flea
And killed the creature much too angrily.

Cléante Good Lord! Brother, you're mad, I do believe.
Are you sure you're not laughing up your sleeve?
Why, this is nonsense! Or do you insist . . . ?

Orgon Brother, you're talking like an atheist;
Your soul's been spattered with freethinking grime.
I've warned you more than once, an ugly time
Awaits you if you will not change your mind.

Cléante These are the arguments of all your kind:
Since they can't see, they think that no one ought;
Whoever does, is tainted with free thought;
Whoever balks at pious affectation
Fails to hold piety in veneration.
Come now, for all your talk, I'm not afraid;
Heaven sees my heart, and I know what I've said;
Your simulators don't disarm my wits.
Like courage, piety has its hypocrites.
Just as we see, where honor beckons most,
The truly brave are not the ones who boast;
The truly pious people, even so,
Are not the ones who make the biggest show.
What? Do you really see no difference
Between devoutness and devout pretense?
Do you want to give them both the selfsame place,
Honor the mask just as you do the face,
Equate artifice with sincerity,
And take similitude for verity?
Isn't there any difference for you
Between phantoms and men, false coins and true?

Most men are strangely made; they always stray
Out of the natural and proper way;
Rejecting reason's bounds as limitations,
They range about amid their aberrations;
Even the noblest things they often mar
By forcing them and pushing them too far.
I mention this because it's apropos.

Orgon Oh yes, you are a learned sage, I know;
The sapience of the world within you lies;
You alone are enlightened, truly wise,
An oracle, a Cato through and through;
All other men are fools compared to you.

Cléante I don't possess the wisdom of the ages,
And I am not a learned sage of sages;
My only knowledge and my only art
Is this: to tell the true and false apart.
And, as there are no heroes I revere
More than those whose devoutness is sincere,
And nothing worthier of veneration
Than genuine religious dedication,
So, nothing seems more odious to me
Than the disguise of specious piety,
Than those breast-beaters in the public square
Whose sacrilegious and deceitful air
Turns to its own advantage, with a sneer,
All that men hold most holy and most dear;
Men whom the lust for gain has so possessed
That they turn piety to interest,
And try to purchase honor and high places
By simulated zeal and false grimaces,
Those men, I say, whose vehement devotion
By way of Heaven seeks temporal promotion,
Who, while they pray, still manage to extort,
And preach of solitude—but stay at court,
Who know how to make zeal and vices mix;
Vengeful, quick-tempered, faithless, full of tricks;
And, when they want to ruin someone, make
It seem they do it all for Heaven's sake;
Most dangerous in that their bitter hate

Makes use of weapons that we venerate,
And that their zeal, which merits our applause,
Seeks to destroy us in a holy cause.
Though far too many fakers meet our eyes,
True piety's not hard to recognize.
Even today, brother, there may be found
Admirable examples all around:
Consider Ariston and Périandre,
Oronte, Alcidas, Polydore, Clitandre:
No one contests their claim to piety,
Yet they do not parade their sanctity;
Their modest zeal is never out of season,
But human and accessible to reason.
They do not lay about in all directions;
They find excessive pride in such corrections,
And leave to others all the lofty speech,
While all they do is practice what they preach.
They do not censure every bagatelle,
But judge with charity and wish men well.
They don't promote intrigue or petty strife,
But mainly seek to lead a virtuous life;
Rather than rage against a reprobate,
They think the sin alone deserves their hate,
And don't espouse, with such intensity,
The cause of Heaven beyond Heaven's own decree.
These are the men that win my admiration,
These are the models for our emulation.
You know your man is not at all like these,
And you may vaunt his fervor all you please;
I think appearances lead you astray.

Orgon Dear brother-in-law, have you had your say?

Cléante I have.

Orgon Your servant.

Starts to leave.

Cléante Brother, please don't go.
One more thing. Valère has, as well you know,
A promise of your daughter's hand from you.

Orgon Yes.

Cléante You had even set a date.

Orgon That's true.

Cléante Why do you put it off, then?

Orgon Don't ask me.

Cléante Have you some other plan in mind?

Orgon Maybe.

Cléante You'd break your promise? Is that what you mean?

Orgon I don't say that.

Cléante But what could intervene
To keep you from accomplishing your pledge?

Orgon Depends.

Cléante Why not speak out? Why always hedge?
Valère wants me to sound you out again.

Orgon Praise be to Heaven!

Cléante What shall I tell him, then?

Orgon Why, what you like.

Cléante But how can you delay?
He has to know your plans.

Orgon I shall obey
The will of Heaven.

Cléante Oh yes, so I've heard.
But to the point now: will you keep your word?

Orgon Farewell.

Cléante This looks ominous for Valère.
And I'll go let him know what's in the air.

Act Two

SCENE ONE
Orgon, Mariane

Orgon Mariane.

Mariane Father.

Orgon Come over here to me.

Mariane What are you looking for?

Orgon [*looking into a small closet*] I want to see
That no one is around to overhear.
It's a bad place for privacy, my dear.
There, we're all right. Mariane, I've always found
In you a spirit mild and duty-bound,
And therefore I have always loved you dearly.

Mariane I'm grateful for that, Father, most sincerely.

Orgon Well said, daughter. Now, to deserve it still,
You must aspire only to do my will.

Mariane In that regard I'm proud to do my best.

Orgon Good. What do you think about Tartuffe, our guest?

Mariane I, sir?

Orgon Answer, but think before you do.

Mariane Alas! I'll say whatever you want me to.

Orgon That's a good girl. Then say, so I can hear it,
That everything about him tells his merit,
That you are fond of him, and would rejoice
To take him as your husband, by my choice.
Well?

Mariane [*starts back in surprise*]
What?

Orgon What's wrong?

Mariane You mean . . . ?

Orgon What?

Mariane Tell me, pray . . .

Orgon What?

Mariane Father, *who* is it I am to say
I am so fond of that I would rejoice
To take him as my husband by your choice?

Orgon Tartuffe.

Mariane But that's not so, I swear it. Why
Do you want to have me tell you such a lie?

Orgon But you forget: I want it to be true.
My mind's made up, and that's enough for you.

Mariane You mean, Father . . . ?

Orgon I mean to bring Tartuffe
Into this family, under this roof.
He is to be your husband; that I swear;
And since you owe . . .

SCENE TWO

Dorine, Orgon, Mariane

Orgon [*to Dorine*] What are you doing there?
I gather that you find a fascination
In trying to overhear our conversation?

Dorine There is a rumor going around here,
Chance or conjecture, I have no idea;

But when I heard these two were to be wed,
I just assumed someone was off his head.

Orgon What? Do you doubt it then?

Dorine Indeed I do;
Yes, even though I've heard it now from you.

Orgon You will believe it soon, before I'm done.

Dorine Yes, yes, I know; you like to have your fun.

Orgon I'm telling you what soon you will attest.

Dorine Nonsense!

Orgon [*to Mariane*] I tell you, daughter, it's no jest.

Dorine [*to Mariane*] Don't mind the games your father plays with you:
Just jokes.

Orgon I say . . .

Dorine No matter what you do,
They won't believe you.

Orgon I am getting mad . . .

Dorine All right, they will, then; and that *is* too bad.
What, sir? Can you, who always have appeared
So wise, with your mustache and solemn beard,
Be fool enough to try . . .

Orgon Listen to me:
You give yourself a lot of liberty,
My girl. I won't put up with it, I swear.

Dorine Now, let's not get excited, sir; there, there.
How could you dream up such a silly plot?
Your daughter for a bigot? I hope not.
He has to have his mind on other things.
Besides, what do you think this union brings?
And when you are so wealthy, why select
A beggar son-in-law . . . ?

Orgon What disrespect!
If he is poor, that is no cause to sneer.
His is a misery we must revere.
He stands above our pomp by his austerity,

Since he has sacrificed his own prosperity
By his disdain for all things transitory
And his concern for true, eternal glory.
But my assistance may facilitate
His restoration to his old estate.
In his district he holds important lands,
And he's a gentleman just as he stands.

Dorine Oh yes, he says so, and that vanity
Does not sit well, sir, with his piety.
If holy living really is his aim,
He should prate less about his birth and name;
And true devoutness seeks a low condition
Which will not suffer outbursts of ambition.
So why this pride? . . . But you are looking grim.
Enough about his rank; how about him?
Is he the sort of man you could prefer
To have possession of a girl like her?
And shouldn't you consider what is seemly,
And fear the consequences most extremely?
The danger to a girl's virtue is great
When she is wed to an unwelcome mate;
Her aim to live in modesty and honor
Rests on the type of man you wish upon her,
And many a man with horns upon his brow
Has made his wife the person she is now.
Fidelity is difficult, in short,
Toward certain husbands of a certain sort.
Marry your daughter where she cannot love,
You'll answer for her sins to Heaven above.
The dangers of your enterprise are grave.

Orgon [*to Mariane*] Now *I* must learn from *her* how to behave!

Dorine Take my advice, and you'd do well enough.

Orgon Daughter, let's not waste time upon this stuff.
I am your father; I know what's best for you.
I *had* promised you to Valère, that's true;
But I am told he gambles more than he ought,

And, worse yet, I suspect him of free thought.
I don't often see him at church, I know.

Dorine Should he go running there just when you go,
Like some who go there only to be seen?

Orgon I did not ask for your advice, Dorine.
At all events, Heaven views Tartuffe with pleasure;
And that is, after all, our greatest treasure.
This marriage will be all you could desire,
Full of sweet joys of which you'll never tire.
You'll live together, in your faithful loves,
Just like two children, like two turtledoves;
No quarrel will take place between you two;
You'll do with him just as you want to do.

Dorine She'll make a fool of him; just wait and see.

Orgon What talk!

Dorine He's built for it, believe you me.
Against the power of his horoscope
Your daughter's virtue, sir, has little hope.

Orgon Stop interrupting me, and just be quiet.
We're minding our affairs; why don't you try it?

Dorine I speak of this, sir, only for your sake.

She interrupts Orgon every time he turns to speak to his daughter.

Orgon Just hush; spare me the interest you take.

Dorine If I didn't love you . . .

Orgon Just don't love me, pray.

Dorine I *will* love you, no matter what you say.

Orgon Oh!

Dorine Your good name fills me with too much pride
To see you ridiculed on every side.

Orgon Quiet!

Dorine My conscience will not let me rest
If I allow this match and don't protest.

Orgon Quiet, you serpent! Wipe that impudent smile . . .

Dorine Oh! So much piety, and so much bile!

Orgon Yes, all this nonsense heats my bile, that's true;
And I don't want another word from you.

Dorine All right, but just the same, my thoughts are there.

Orgon Think, if you like; but better have a care.
Not a word, or . . . enough.

To Mariane.

Now, I have weighed
Everything wisely.

Dorine Silence, I'm afraid,
Will drive me mad.

Orgon turns his head toward her; she is silent.

Orgon True, he's no pretty boy.
And yet Tartuffe . . .

Dorine That snout! Oh, what a joy!

Orgon . . . Without his other gifts, would be a catch
Well worth considering . . .

Turns to Dorine, crosses his arms, and watches her.

Dorine A splendid match!
If I were she, no man would marry me
Against my will and with impunity.
Soon after, I would make him understand
That women have their vengeance close at hand.

Orgon [*to Dorine*] You disregard my orders, is that true?

Dorine What's your complaint? I'm not speaking to you.

Orgon Who *are* you talking to?

Dorine To me; that's all.

Orgon All right. To punish her colossal gall,
I'll have to let her have the back of my hand.

Dorine is behind Orgon, encouraging Mariane to speak up and resist. At this and each of the following pauses, Orgon turns and sets to slap Dorine, who each time either freezes, silent and motionless, or changes her signal to Mariane into an innocent gesture.

Daughter, you should approve of what I've planned . . .
The man I've chosen . . . for your fiancé . . .
[*To Dorine.*] Not talking to yourself?

Dorine Nothing to say.

Orgon Just one more little word.

Dorine The word is mum.

Orgon I'm waiting for you.

Dorine I should be so dumb!

Orgon In short, you must obey the master's voice,
And show yourself compliant to my choice.

Dorine [*fleeing*] I wouldn't marry that man on a bet.

Orgon tries to slap her, but misses.

Orgon That pest will make me lose my temper yet;
I'd best dismiss her, to avoid that sin.
I can't go further in the state I'm in.
Her insolence has vexed me so, I swear,
I'd better go and get a breath of air.

SCENE THREE

Dorine, Mariane

Dorine Well, have you lost your tongue completely, Miss?
And do I have to play your part in this?
Let him propose a project that absurd,
And not combat it with a single word!

Mariane What can I do? My father is the master.

Dorine Do anything to block such a disaster.

Mariane What?

Dorine Tell him you can't love just on his whim;
That you are marrying for yourself, not him.

This is arranged for *you,* supposedly;
Then you must love the husband, and not he.
Tell him that if Tartuffe enchants him so,
Then he should marry him; we shan't say no.

Mariane I know, but Father holds such awful sway,
There's nothing I can bring myself to say.

Dorine Come, let's talk sense. You're courted by Valère.
Well, do you love him, now, or don't you care?

Mariane Oh, come, Dorine, be fairer to my love!
You ask me that? What are you thinking of?
I've held back nothing from you, Heaven knows.
Surely you know how far my ardor goes?

Dorine How do I know you're saying what you feel,
And that your passion for Valère is real?

Mariane Truly, Dorine, you wrong me by your doubt;
My sentiments have clearly spoken out.

Dorine In short, you love him?

Mariane I should say I do.

Dorine Right. And apparently he loves you too?

Mariane So I believe.

Dorine Your hearts are both on fire
To join in marriage?

Mariane That is our desire.

Dorine About this other match: what is your plan?

Mariane To kill myself, if I must have that man.

Dorine That's fine! I hadn't thought of that resource.
Just die, and end your problems! Why, of course.
A fine solution! Oh, it drives me wild
To hear you talking like a silly child!

Mariane Good Lord! Dorine, don't take it out on me!
You've no compassion for my misery.

Dorine I've no compassion left for all this drivel,
When, once the chips are down, you simply shrivel.

Mariane But I'm so timid! What am I to do?

Dorine But love requires a touch of firmness too.

Mariane I'm firm in my devotion to Valère.
Surely Father's consent is his affair.

Dorine But if your father's utterly insane,
Since passion for Tartuffe has rocked his brain,
And breaks his promise that you two should wed,
Why place the blame upon your suitor's head?

Mariane But if I show defiance to a parent,
Won't my love for Valère be too apparent?
Shall I give up, for all his charm and beauty,
The modesty that is a woman's duty?
And is my love a thing you'd have me flaunt . . . ?

Dorine I wouldn't have a thing. I see you want
To be Madame Tartuffe. I'd be unkind,
Were I to try to make you change your mind.
Why should I argue, since you want this match?
Just in himself, he's certainly a catch.
Monsieur Tartuffe! That's quite a thing to be!
In fact Monsieur Tartuffe, it's plain to see,
Is not a man to eat peas with a knife,
And it would be a joy to be his wife.
He basks in honor and in good repute.
He's noble—back at home—a handsome brute:
With that florid complexion, those red ears,
Think what delight you'll have over the years.

Mariane Good Lord! . . .

Dorine Your soul will know eternal bliss,
Wedded to such a handsome man as this!

Mariane Oh! Please don't torture me; I just can't stand it.
How can we break this match, when Father's planned it?
I give up. I'll do anything you say.

Dorine When Father speaks, his daughter must obey,
And even take a monkey for her mate.
You've no complaint; you'll have a lovely fate:
In his small town a coach will take you round.
His uncles and his cousins will abound,
And you will find them a delight to meet.

First you'll be introduced to the elite:
A round of jolly calls will fill your life,
To the bailiff's and the tax collector's wife,
Who'll patronize you with a folding chair.
Then once a year there's dancing at the fair,
With a big orchestra—of two musettes—
Sometimes a monkey act and marionettes,
Though if your husband . . .

Mariane Oh! You're killing me.
I need your help, and not this mockery.

Dorine Madame, your servant.

Mariane Dorine, I beseech you . . .

Dorine No, this will have to happen, just to teach you.

Mariane Dorine, dear!

Dorine No.

Mariane If I declare my will . . .

Dorine Tartuffe's your man, and you shall have your fill.

Mariane You know how much I always have relied . . .

Dorine No, you shall be—my word!—Tartuffified.

Mariane All right! As long as that is all you care,
Henceforth leave me alone with my despair;
In that at least my heart will find a cure;
I know a remedy that's swift and sure.

She starts to go.

Dorine There now, come back. I can't be angry long.
Do what you will, my pity is too strong.

Mariane If this cruel torture is what lies ahead,
I'll kill myself; I'd far rather be dead.

Dorine Come, don't be so upset. This much is plain:
We'll find a way . . . But here's Valère, your swain.

SCENE FOUR

Valère, Mariane, Dorine

Valère Madame, a piece of news is going about,
Unknown to me, but very fine, no doubt.

Mariane What?

Valère That you're marrying Tartuffe.

Mariane Indeed,
That is just what my father has decreed.

Valère Madame, your father . . .

Mariane Has just changed his mind,
And now prefers this other match, I find.

Valère Can he be serious?

Mariane Indeed he can.
He clearly is determined on this plan.

Valère And what have you in mind, this being so,
Madame?

Mariane I do not know.

Valère You do not know?
Delightful!

Mariane No.

Valère No?

Mariane What do you advise?

Valère Marry the man. I'm sure that would be wise.

Mariane That's your advice?

Valère Yes.

Mariane Honestly?

Valère Indeed:
This is a noble choice, which you should heed.

Mariane That's your advice, sir? Well, just as you say.

Valère I think you'll follow it without dismay.

Mariane Just as you offered it, it would appear.

Valère Madame, I offered what you wished to hear.

Mariane And I will do what *you* want *me* to do.

Dorine [*withdrawing to the back of the stage*] Let's see what this affair is coming to.

Valère So that's your love? And it was make-believe
When you . . .

Mariane No more of that, sir, by your leave.
You clearly said I must not hesitate
To take the man presented as my mate.
All right, I'll do precisely that, I vow,
Since that is the advice you give me now.

Valère Just don't make my intentions your excuse.
You'd made your plans already; that's no use.
This pretext that you're seizing is absurd
To justify the breaking of your word.

Mariane Of course. Well said.

Valère No doubt; and in your heart
You've never really loved me from the start.

Mariane Alas! You're free to choose this explanation.

Valère Yes, yes, I'm free; but in my indignation,
I may decide to get ahead of you;
And I know other girls who would be true.

Mariane Indeed they would; I have no doubt of it.
Your merit . . .

Valère Leave my merit out of it:
I haven't much; your act is a reminder.
But I have hopes of finding someone kinder,
And I know one who'll think it no disgrace
To compensate my loss and take your place.

Mariane It's no great loss; you'll easily arrange
To find your consolation for this change.

Valère As you may well believe, I'll do my best.
To be forgotten puts us to the test:

We must forget in turn, even pretend,
If all our efforts don't achieve that end.
To show our love for one who's turned us down
Is to be both a coward and a clown.

Mariane Well, that's a noble, lofty sentiment.

Valère And one to which all men should give assent.
What? Would you have me foster in my breast
The love that, when you wanted, you possessed?
Am I to watch you seek another's arms
And not console my heart with other charms?

Mariane No, that's exactly what I want. Alas!
I wish it had already come to pass.

Valère You do?

Mariane I do.

Valère That's all that I can stand,
Madame; I'll go and do as you command.

Here and later, he starts to leave, then returns.

Mariane All right.

Valère [*returning*] At least remember that it's you
Who's driving me to what I'm going to do.

Mariane Oh, yes.

Valère And that by acting in this way,
I follow your example.

Mariane As you say.

Valère Enough: I'll carry out your wishes, then.

Mariane That's fine.

Valère You see me now, but never again.

Mariane Of course.

Valère [*goes, but turns back at the door*]
Eh?

Mariane What?

Valère Didn't you call?

Mariane Not I.
You're dreaming.

Valère Then, Madame, my last goodbye.
I'm off.

Mariane Goodbye, sir.

Dorine Well, if you ask me,
We've had enough of this tomfoolery.
I've let you bandy insults to and fro
To see how far the two of you would go.
Seigneur Valère! Hey!

She goes and holds his arm to stop him, and he makes a great show of resistance.

Valère What is it, Dorine?

Dorine Come here.

Valère No, no, I've got to vent my spleen.
Don't turn me back from what she has decreed.

Dorine Stand still.

Valère No, don't you see? We've both agreed.

Dorine Oh, my!

Mariane He hates my sight, he wants to leave;
And I'm the one should go, I do believe.

Dorine [*leaves Valère and runs to Mariane*] Now you! Where to?

Mariane Let go.

Dorine You stay right here.

Mariane Dorine, don't try to hold me back, do you hear?

Valère Why, she's in torment at the sight of me.
I'd better disappear, and set her free.

Dorine [*leaves Mariane and runs to Valère*] You again? No, you don't. Confound you two!
Now stop this nonsense. Come here, both of you.

She pulls first at one, then at the other, bringing them together.

Valère What are you trying to do?

Mariane Why all this bother?

Dorine To bring you back to sense and to each other.

To Valère.

Fighting like that! Are you out of your head?

Valère Didn't you hear the heartless things she said?

Dorine [*to Mariane*] Aren't *you* a fool, to work up such a passion?

Mariane Didn't you see him treat me in that fashion?

Dorine Nonsense on both sides.

To Valère.

Why, her only care
Is to preserve herself for you, I swear.

To Mariane.

He loves you, and he wants you for his wife,
Above all else; on this I'll stake my life.

Mariane Why give me such advice? Now, was that right?

Valère Why ask for it at all in such a plight?

Dorine You're both insane. Now, your hands, both of you.
Come on, you.

Valère [*giving Dorine his hand*]
What's that for?

Dorine All right, yours too.

Mariane [*giving Dorine her hand too*] What good will that do?

Dorine Heavens! Come on, let's go!
You love each other better than you know.

Valère [*after a pause, to Mariane*] It doesn't hurt that much, you must confess.
Look at a fellow without bitterness.

Mariane glances at Valère with just a bit of a smile.

Dorine To tell the truth, lovers are all insane!

Valère But look, haven't I reason to complain?
In all sincerity, weren't you unkind
To enjoy driving me out of my mind?

Mariane If I have ever seen ingratitude . . .

Dorine Suppose we just postpone this little feud,
And try to block this marriage if we can.

Mariane Tell us, what shall we do? What is your plan?

Dorine We shall use everything we can invoke.
Your father's mad; this thing is a bad joke;
But you had best indulge his antic bent
By the appearance of a meek consent,
So that you may more easily prolong
The waiting period, should things go wrong.
Time is the very best of remedies.
At first your reason may be some disease,
Which, coming suddenly, demands delay;
A bad omen will do another day:
You dreamed of muddy water, chanced to pass
A funeral, or broke a looking glass.
And don't forget: however hard they press,
You can't be married without saying yes.
But you'd be foolish, in this situation,
To let yourselves be seen in conversation.

To Valère.

Go on, get your friends busy on our side
To make him keep the promise he's denied.
We'll get his son to join us in the strife,
And try to gain assistance from his wife.
Goodbye.

Valère [*to Mariane*] For all the rest of us may do,
The one I'm really counting on is you.

Mariane [*to Valère*] I can't be sure what Father may decide;
But I shall never be another's bride.

Valère How happy you have made me! Come what
may . . .

Dorine Lovers never run out of things to say!
Come on, be off.

Valère [*takes one step and comes back*]
In short . . .

Dorine No time for chat.
You go out this way, and you go out that.

Pushes them by the shoulder toward opposite exits.

Act Three

SCENE ONE
Damis, Dorine

Damis Let lightning right this moment strike me down,
Let me be called a villain and a clown,
If reverence or power holds me back
When everything within me cries: Attack!

Dorine Please moderate your anger if you can:
Your father's only talked about this plan.
Not all that men propose becomes a fact,
Nor does intention always lead to act.

Damis I'll block that coxcomb's plans, just wait and see;
It won't be long before he hears from me.

Dorine Gently! See what your stepmother can do
To get around him and your father too.
She seems to have Tartuffe under her sway;
He treats her in the most obliging way,
And may well feel a certain fascination . . .
Would God he did! That *would* be a sensation.
She has to see him, in your interest,
Sound him out on this marriage you detest,
Learn where he stands, and make him realize
What altercations surely will arise
If he persists in pressing this affair.

His servant says he's busy now in prayer,
But shortly will be on his way down here.
Please go along, and do not interfere.

Damis I have a right to hear this interview.

Dorine No. They must be alone.

Damis I promise you,
I will not speak.

Dorine You can't avoid extremes.
You'll throw a fit, and shatter all our schemes.
Go on.

Damis I want to watch; I won't make trouble.

Dorine Not much! He's coming. In there, on the double.

At Dorine's direction Damis hides in a closet at the back of the stage.

SCENE TWO

Tartuffe, Laurent (offstage), Dorine

Tartuffe [*seeing Dorine; to Laurent offstage*] Put back my scourge and hair shirt in their place,
Laurent, and pray for Heaven's enlightening grace.
If someone asks for me, I may be found
Among the prisoners, giving alms all round.

Dorine What affectation! What pretentious cheek!

Tartuffe What do you want?

Dorine To say . . .

Tartuffe [*taking a handkerchief from his pocket*] Good Lord! Don't speak
Until you take this handkerchief.

Dorine Who, me?

Tartuffe Cover that bosom, which I must not see.
Souls can be harmed by objects of that kind;
And they bring sinful thoughts to a man's mind.

Dorine You must be very weak against temptation
And very prone to fleshly stimulation.
I don't know what can set you so on fire:
For my part, I am slower to desire,
And if I saw you bare from tip to toe,
Your epidermis wouldn't tempt me—so!

Tartuffe Unless you speak more modestly, I vow
That I shall have to leave you here and now.

Dorine No, *I'll* leave *you* in peace; I'm on my way;
And I have only these few words to say:
Madame is coming down, and asks of you
The signal favor of an interview.

Tartuffe Alas, most happily!

Dorine [*aside*] Ah, how polite!
My word! I still believe that I am right.

Tartuffe Will she be coming soon?

Dorine Yes, I believe
I hear her. Here she comes; I'll take my leave.

SCENE THREE

Elmire, Tartuffe

Tartuffe For you may Heaven's grace ever abound,
Preserve your soul and body safe and sound,
And bless your days, according to the love
I humbly offer to the Lord above.

Elmire Your wishes are most pious, I declare.
Thank you. But let's sit down; here is a chair.

Tartuffe I trust your recent illness is all past?

Elmire Oh yes, thank you; that fever didn't last.

Tartuffe My prayers, I know, would never qualify
To have drawn down such mercy from on high;
But every supplication I have made
Has been for your good health, and Heaven's aid.

Elmire Your zeal has been concerned for me too much.

Tartuffe Madame, my care for your dear health is such
That I'd have given my own to make it better.

Elmire Such Christian love goes far beyond the letter;
Your kindness leaves me much obliged to you.

Tartuffe Alas, it is far less than is your due.

Elmire I want to talk to you in secrecy,
And I am grateful for this privacy.

Tartuffe You can't be as delighted as I am
To be alone with you this way, Madame:
I've often prayed to Heaven for this boon,
But it has never judged it opportune.

Elmire What I want is a word with you apart,
Where you'll speak frankly with an open heart.

Tartuffe No other grace would I so highly prize
As to reveal my soul unto your eyes,
And swear to you that if I've caused alarms
Over the visits prompted by your charms,
There is no hatred in the way I feel,
But rather just an overpowering zeal,
A pure desire . . .

Elmire A pious aspiration
In which your sole concern was my salvation.

Tartuffe [*squeezing her fingertips*] Yes, Madame, and my
fervent hopes betray . . .

Elmire You squeeze too hard.

Tartuffe Zeal carries me away.
Surely you don't believe I could have planned
To harm you . . . [*Puts his hand on her knee.*]

Elmire What are you doing with your hand?

Tartuffe Feeling your gown: what soft, velvety stuff!

Elmire Please don't, I'm very ticklish. That's enough.

She moves her chair away, and Tartuffe brings his closer.

Tartuffe [*fondling the lace collar of her gown*] Lord, but this needlepoint is marvelous!
The way they work now is miraculous;
I've never seen the like, upon my word.

Elmire Indeed. But to the point. From what I've heard,
My husband now intends Mariane for you,
Though he had pledged her elsewhere. Is that true?

Tartuffe He's spoken of it; but, since you inquire,
That's not the rapture to which I aspire;
And, Madame, it is elsewhere that I turn
For the felicity for which I yearn.

Elmire That's because you love nothing here below.

Tartuffe My heart is not a heart of stone, you know.

Elmire Come now, Heaven's the one object of your sighs,
And nothing here on earth delights your eyes.

Tartuffe To love eternal beauties far above
Is not to be immune to other love;
Our senses may be easily fascinated
By perfect works that Heaven has created.
It shows itself in others by reflection,
But you alone display its true perfection:
The beauties that upon your face it's lavished
Dazzle men's eyes and leave their feelings ravished.
I could not look at you, O perfect creature,
And not admire the Author of all nature,
Feeling my heart most fervently impassioned
For this lovely self-portrait he has fashioned.
My first reaction was to be afraid
This ardor was a snare the Devil had laid;
And I avoided you as a temptation
That might stand in the way of my salvation.
But finally I knew, O gracious beauty,
That passion need not be at odds with duty,
That I can reconcile it with propriety;
And so I yield to it without anxiety.
I know it is audacious on my part
To make you this poor offering of my heart;

But though my efforts are infirm and vain,
I know that you are gracious and humane;
On you depends my hope and quietude,
My wretchedness or my beatitude;
You must decide what lies ahead of me:
Celestial bliss or utter misery.

Elmire That is indeed a gallant declaration,
But one that quite confounds my expectation.
You should, I think, have striven for self-control
And turned this matter over in your soul.
For one so pious to have such a plan . . .

Tartuffe I may be pious, but I'm still a man.
And at the sight of your celestial charms,
Reason and heart alike lay down their arms.
Coming from me, I know these words distress you;
But after all, I'm not an angel, bless you;
And if you think I've put myself to shame,
It's your bewitching charms that are to blame.
For, once I saw their superhuman splendor,
My heart had no recourse but to surrender;
The indescribable sweetness of your eyes
Forced my resistance to demobilize;
It overcame my fasts, my tears, my prayers,
And made your charms the object of my cares.
My eyes, my sighs, a thousand times, no less,
Have told you what my words would now express.
A bit of sympathy is all I crave
For the distress of your unworthy slave.
If your kindness, Madame, should ever deign
To condescend to me, and end my pain,
Nothing could be as constant and as true
As the devotion I shall have for you.
Your honor will not be in jeopardy,
And will not run a single risk with me.
All those court fops, on whom the ladies dote,
Are far too noisy and too prone to gloat;
They cannot bear to keep their luck concealed;
Each favor granted is at once revealed;

And by their loose and faithless declaration
They smirch the object of their adoration.
But men like us burn with a hidden fire;
The secrecy we offer is entire:
The care we take to keep our own good name
Guarantees our beloved against shame;
Accept our hearts, and you will find, my dear,
Love without scandal, pleasure without fear.

Elmire I've heard you out, and found you eloquent
In giving utterance to your intent.
Aren't you afraid that I may take a notion
To tell my husband of this warm devotion,
And that your passion, if he ever knew,
Might undermine his friendliness for you?

Tartuffe I know that you are gracious and benign,
And will forgive this recklessness of mine,
Blame human weakness for the violence
Of this my love, at which you take offense,
And, looking in your mirror, keep in mind
That man is flesh and blood, and I'm not blind.

Elmire Others might take this in another fashion,
But my discretion recommends compassion.
I will not tell my husband; well and good.
But in return I want it understood
That you will bring your influence to bear
To join Mariane in marriage with Valère,
Give up your own inequitable plan
To take a girl pledged to another man,
And . . .

SCENE FOUR

Damis, Elmire, Tartuffe

Damis [*coming out of the closet where he had been hiding*]
No, Madame, this has to be revealed.
I heard it all from where I was concealed;
Heaven's goodness must have put me there inside

To let me dash this noxious traitor's pride,
Avenge his odious impertinence,
His rank hypocrisy and insolence,
Open my father's eyes, and bare to view
This scoundrel soul that talks of love to you.

Elmire No, Damis: he shall merely learn his place,
And study to deserve my promised grace.
Don't let it out. I've given him my word.
A scene about it would be quite absurd:
A wife laughs off a lot of what she hears,
And doesn't din it in her husband's ears.

Damis You have your reasons for this compromise,
But I have mine for doing otherwise.
To want to spare this bigot is all wrong;
His insolence has lorded it too long
Over my righteous anger, and has tried
To spread dissension here on every side.
Too long he's held my father in his spell,
And crossed my sister's love, and mine as well.
His deceit must be bared to Father's glance,
And Heaven offers me a perfect chance.
It has my deepest gratitude for this,
And the occasion is too good to miss.
I would deserve to have it snatched away
If I did not use it without delay.

Elmire Damis . . .

Damis No, please, I'll do as I think right.
My soul is overflowing with delight;
There's no use telling me to be discreet;
An overdue revenge is doubly sweet.
It's time all this was settled, anyhow;
And, sure enough, here comes my father now.

SCENE FIVE

Orgon, Damis, Tartuffe, Elmire

Damis Father, here's a development that's new
And may well come as a surprise to you.

You're well repaid for your beneficence;
Monsieur has his own kind of recompense.
And it's his zeal on your behalf, I guess,
That leads him to dishonor you, no less.
I've just caught him, in the most shameful fashion,
Asking Madame to share his guilty passion.
Discreet and over mild, she did not choose
To have you inconvenienced by the news;
But I cannot condone such impudence
Or hide it without giving you offense.

Elmire I think we should not vex a husband's mind
With incidents of such a foolish kind;
That honor does not rest on points like these:
Enough to check familiarities.
Those are my feelings; and if you, Damis,
Had heeded them, you would have held your peace.

SCENE SIX

Orgon, Damis, Tartuffe

Orgon What have I heard? Heavens! Can this be true?

Tartuffe Yes, brother, I am evil through and through,
Guilty, full of iniquity and sin,
The greatest scoundrel that has ever been;
Each moment of my life is black with grime;
It is a mass of filthiness and crime;
And I am sure that this mortification
Is just a sign of Heaven's indignation.
Whatever sin they charge against my name,
I won't defend myself, such is my shame.
Believe their stories, everything they say,
And like a criminal send me away:
Whatever ignominy lies in store,
I know that I have merited far more.

Orgon [*to his son*] Oh! Traitor! Would you dare to stigmatize
His perfect virtue with this pack of lies?

Damis What? Because this imposter beats his chest,
You give the lie . . . ?

Orgon Silence, accursed pest.

Tartuffe You're wrong to blame him so. Don't cut him short.
Really, you should believe his whole report.
Why favor me, in this case, as you do?
Do you really think you know me through and through?
Brother, how can you trust my semblance so,
And think me better for my outward show?
Appearances are leading you astray,
And I am anything but what men say.
Alas! Everyone views me with respect,
But in truth I am utterly abject.

To Damis.

Dear son, go on; tell me my crimes are great;
Call me thief, killer, traitor, reprobate;
Load me with epithets still more abhorred:
I won't say no; they are my just reward;
After my life of crime, in expiation,
I'll kneel and suffer that humiliation.

Orgon [*to Tartuffe*] Dear brother, that's too much.

To his son.

Have you no heart,
Traitor?

Damis How's this? You still will take his part?

Orgon Be quiet, scoundrel.

To Tartuffe.

Brother, pray you, rise.

To his son.

Wretch!

Damis He can . . .

Orgon Hush!

Damis I don't believe my eyes.

Orgon If you say one word more, I swear I'll break . . .

Tartuffe Brother, control your wrath, for Heaven's sake.
I'd rather suffer pain, in any amount,
Than have him get a scratch on my account.

Orgon [*to his son*] Ingrate!

Tartuffe Leave him alone. Upon my knees
I ask you to forgive him.

Orgon [*also on his knees, embracing Tartuffe as he addresses him*]
Stop it, please!

To his son.

That good man!

Damis So . . .

Orgon Hush!

Damis What! I . . .

Orgon Hush, do you hear?
I know what lies behind this wicked smear:
You all hate him. Why, just today I've seen
My wife, children, and servants vent their spleen.
I'm shocked to see how brazenly you plan
To separate me from this pious man.
The more you try to drive Tartuffe away,
The harder I shall strive to make him stay;
And soon he'll have my daughter as his bride,
Just to confound my family and its pride.

Damis You'd force your daughter to accept that cad?

Orgon Yes, and this evening, just to make you mad.
Oh! You may try your best to interfere:
You must obey; I am the master here.
Take it back, rascal; and for your conceit,
Get down and ask his pardon at his feet.

Damis Who, me! From that dissembling pietist . . . ?

Orgon So! You insult him, wretch, and still resist?

To Tartuffe, who remains motionless.

Give me a stick! A stick! Don't hold me back.

To his son.

Go on, out of this house; no time to pack,
And never have the nerve to show your face . . .

Damis All right, I'll go; but . . .

Orgon Quick, out of this place.
I disinherit you; and, what is worse,
You scoundrel, all I leave you is my curse.

SCENE SEVEN

Orgon, Tartuffe

Orgon To offend a holy man in such a way!

Tartuffe May Heaven forgive him for my pain, I pray!

To Orgon.

If you knew how it hurts when someone tries
To blacken me before my brother's eyes . . .

Orgon Alas!

Tartuffe The thought of this ingratitude
Inflicts a torment of such magnitude . . .
My heart is torn . . . I'm simply horrified . . .
I cannot speak . . . 'Twere better that I died.

Orgon [*in tears, runs to the door through which he drove out his son*] Villain! I spared your life! Now I repent.
I should have struck you down before you went.

To Tartuffe.

Forgive him, brother; set your mind at peace.

Tartuffe I can't endure these scenes; they've got to cease.
And since I bring dissension, I believe
That it is time, brother, for me to leave.

Orgon What? Are you joking?

Tartuffe No, they hate me here,
And try to make you think I'm not sincere.

Orgon So? Do you really think I hear them out?

Tartuffe They will keep persecuting me, no doubt;
And these same stories, which you now reject—
You'll listen to them some day, I expect.

Orgon No, brother, never.

Tartuffe Oh, brother, a wife
Affects her husband's soul, his very life.

Orgon No, no.

Tartuffe Let me go soon, without a fuss,
And leave them no excuse to hound me thus.

Orgon No, you shall stay; my very life's at stake.

Tartuffe I'll mortify myself, then, for your sake.
But if you wanted . . .

Orgon Ah!

Tartuffe All right. That's that.
But henceforth I must be a diplomat.
Honor is touchy; and to be your friend,
I must bring all these rumors to an end.
I shall avoid your wife, and thus forestall . . .

Orgon No, you shall see her; I defy them all.
To drive them crazy is my main delight,
And you shall be with her in all men's sight.
Nor is that all; to spite them through and through,
I want to have no other heir than you;
And legally—I don't intend to wait—
I'll see that you inherit my estate.
A good true friend, my son-in-law-to-be,
Is dearer than my son, wife, kin to me.
Won't you accept this offer I suggest?

Tartuffe Let Heaven's will be done as it is best.

Orgon Poor fellow! Let's just get this drawn up right,
And then let envy burst its seams for spite!

Act Four

SCENE ONE
Cléante, Tartuffe

Cléante Yes, it is common gossip, and the story,
Believe me, will add little to your glory;
I'm glad I found you, sir; it's overdue;
Briefly, I want to speak my mind to you.
I'm not examining the accusation;
But even if it is without foundation,
Even supposing Damis is to blame
And that he's falsely slandered your good name,
Shouldn't a Christian pardon the offense
And rid his heart of all malevolence?
For all your quarrel, should you stand aloof
And see a son denied his father's roof?
I tell you once again that what you've done,
Frankly, seems scandalous to everyone;
If you'll take my advice, you'll work for peace,
And stop carrying on against Damis.
No, sacrifice your wrath to God above,
And help the son regain the father's love.

Tartuffe Alas! I would, sir, and with all my heart;
I harbor no resentment, for my part;
He has my full forgiveness, not my blame;

To help him out would be my dearest aim.
But Heaven's interest will not have it so;
And if he comes back in here, I must go.
Since he has charged me with a crime so base,
We can't associate without disgrace.
God knows what everyone's first thoughts would be!
They'd chalk it up to sheer expediency,
And say that, to disguise the guilt I feel,
I'm putting on a charitable zeal,
And trying, out of crass self-interest,
To get my accuser to let matters rest.

Cléante This is a specious case, sir, that you plead,
And your arguments are far-fetched indeed.
Why treat the will of Heaven as your own?
Can't Heaven mete out discipline alone?
Our role is not to punish or reward,
But to forgive. Leave vengeance to the Lord.
And whether men speak of you well or ill,
Don't worry; merely follow Heaven's will.
What? Shall your fear to be misunderstood
Make you pass up a chance for doing good?
No, no; let's do what Heaven has assigned,
And not let other things disturb our mind.

Tartuffe My heart forgives him, as you've heard me say;
And thus, when Heaven orders, I obey;
But Heaven has not ordered me, I know,
To live with him, when he has hurt me so.

Cléante And does it order you to listen rather,
Sir, to the sheer caprice of the boy's father,
And to accept his making you his heir,
When equity rejects this as unfair?

Tartuffe All those who know me will believe, I'm sure,
That all my motives in this case are pure.
I do not care for this world's goods, you see;
Their specious luster does not dazzle me;
And if I am prevailed upon to take
This present that Orgon has willed to make,

I do so because honestly I dread
That it may fall in wicked hands instead,
In those of men who, playing fast and loose,
May put these riches to some evil use,
And not employ them, as I surely would,
For Heaven's glory and my neighbor's good.

Cléante Oh! Sir, give up this conscientious care
That may cause lawsuits by the rightful heir;
Leave him, with less concern about his fate,
To all the risks of owning his estate.
He may not use it so one may applaud him,
But better thus than that you should defraud him.
When Orgon spoke to you of his intent,
How could you hear without embarrassment?
Must genuine devotion be so prone
To rob an heir of all that is his own?
And if it's true that Heaven won't allow
You and Damis to live together now,
Why not make your departure in good season,
And not stand by while, contrary to reason,
A father undertakes, in your behoof,
To drive his son from underneath his roof?
This is a strange example, believe me,
Of virtue, sir . . .

Tartuffe Sir, it is half-past three:
I have devotions at this time of day,
And you'll excuse me if I do not stay.

Cléante Oh!

SCENE TWO

Elmire, Mariane, Dorine, Cléante

Dorine Sir, please help us out, for Heaven's sake:
She's suffering so, I fear her heart will break;
Her father's plan to marry her tonight
Has put her in a really desperate plight.

He's coming now. Together, if you will,
Let's try to undermine, by strength or skill,
This wretched match that we deplore and fear.

SCENE THREE

Orgon, Elmire, Mariane, Cléante, Dorine

Orgon I'm glad to see you all together here.

To Mariane.

Here is the contract that assures your bliss,
Mariane, and you know what I mean by this.

Mariane [*on her knees*] Father, by Heaven, which knows the pain I feel,
And by whatever else hears my appeal,
Waive some of your paternal rights, I pray,
And in this, do not force me to obey;
Don't use your power to constrain me so
That I begrudge the duty that I owe;
And do not make this life, which I possess,
Alas, from you, one long unhappiness.
If I must be denied my dearest prayer,
Of marrying the man I love, Valère,
At least be kind, and spare me, I implore,
A marriage to a person I abhor;
And do not drive me into desperation
By using all the powers of your station.

Orgon [*touched*] Be firm, my heart! No human weakness now!

Mariane Pamper him all you like, no matter how:
I am not jealous of the things you do;
Give him your property, and add mine too;
For all this you shall have my full consent.
But as regards my person, please relent,
And let me drag my sad steps toward the tomb
Within a convent's consecrated gloom.

Orgon Oh, that's a daughter for you! Every one,

When once her love is crossed, must be a nun!
Get up! The more you think you cannot bear it,
The more by your acceptance you will merit.
So, by this marriage, mortify your senses,
And spare me all your feminine defenses.

Dorine But what . . . ?

Orgon Shut up, you! Talk to your own kind:
From now on I won't let you speak your mind.

Cléante Might I put in a word of counsel, though?

Orgon Your counsel, brother, I have cause to know,
Is wonderful; I care a lot about it;
But please don't mind if I just do without it.

Elmire [*to her husband*] Words fail me when I see the things I see,
And your persistent blindness baffles me.
You must be quite bewitched by him, I'd say,
To doubt our word on what went on today.

Orgon I trust evidence more than anyone.
I know you dote upon my rascal son,
And that you were afraid to disavow
His little plot against Tartuffe just now.
You were too calm for me to be impressed;
In fact, you didn't seem the least distressed.

Elmire If someone simply tells us of his passion,
Must our honor take arms in martial fashion?
And where it is involved, must we reply
Only with scornful lip and blazing eye?
I take such propositions with a smile,
And do not find explosiveness worthwhile;
I like to see our virtue free of spite,
And do not think those pious prudes are right
Whose honor arms itself with teeth and claws
To scratch men's eyes out for the slightest cause:
Heaven keep me from a virtue such as that!
I just want to be decent, not a cat.
And I believe that it is quite enough
To check a suitor with a cool rebuff.

Orgon I know what's what, and I won't be put off.

Elmire I marvel at your readiness to scoff.
How would your incredulity react
If you should see that what we say is fact?

Orgon See it?

Elmire Yes.

Orgon Nonsense.

Elmire If I found a way
To show it to you in the light of day?

Orgon Fairy tales.

Elmire Answer me; don't be absurd.
I am not asking you to take our word.
But if you hid so you could see and hear
Everything that went on, perfectly clear,
What would you say if you saw your idol fall?

Orgon In that case, I would say . . . nothing at all.
It can't be true.

Elmire You've been too long deceived,
And I am tired of not being believed.
For our contentment, without more ado,
You shall observe all we've been telling you.

Orgon All right. I'll take you up on that, you know.
We'll just see what it is you have to show.

Elmire [*to Dorine*] Have him come here.

Dorine He is a hypocrite,
And may not be so easy to outwit.

Elmire Oh, no! A lover is not hard to cheat,
And self-deception springs from self-conceit.
Have him come down.

To Cléante and Mariane.

Go along, *s'il vous plaît.*

SCENE FOUR

Elmire, Orgon

Elmire Bring up this table. Get under, right away.

Orgon How's that?

Elmire You must be out of sight, you see.

Orgon Why under there?

Elmire Good Lord! Listen to me:
I have my plan; you'll judge this whole affair.
Get underneath, I say; and when you're there,
Make sure that you are neither seen nor heard.

Orgon I'm being very patient, 'pon my word.
But just go right ahead; I'll see it through.

Elmire And you may come to thank me if you do.

To her husband, who is now under the table.

These are strange matters that I shall discuss,
And you must listen and not make a fuss.
Whatever I say, it must be understood:
It's to convince you, as I said I would.
By sweet enticements it will be my task
To lure this hypocrite to drop his mask,
Flatter his passion and his shameless lust,
And countenance his boldness, as I must.
Since it is for your sake, and for his shame
That I shall seem responsive to his flame,
As soon as you're convinced, just let me know,
And that will be as far as things will go.
It's up to you to check his wild desire
When matters are as clear as you require,
To spare your wife, and not expose her to
More than you need to disillusion you.
Your interest is at stake; you are the judge,
And . . . Here he comes, Keep quiet, and don't budge.

SCENE FIVE

Tartuffe, Elmire, Orgon

Tartuffe They told me that you wished to see me here.

Elmire Yes. I have secrets for your private ear.
But shut that door, before I say a word,
And look and see that we're not overheard.

Tartuffe closes the door, looks in the closet, and comes back.

A mishap like that one just now, indeed,
Is certainly the last thing that we need.
I really can't remember such a fright;
Damis had me in terror at your plight,
And you could see I did my very best
To calm his fury, in your interest.
True, I was so confused I never thought
To contradict his story as I ought;
But even that, thank Heaven, worked out well,
And things are that much safer, I can tell.
Your reputation makes it all auspicious;
My husband simply cannot be suspicious.
So as to show the gossips they are wrong,
He wants us two together all day long;
And that's what makes it possible for me
To see you freely in such privacy
And to lay bare to you, in such a fashion,
A heart perhaps too heedful of your passion.

Tartuffe I do not understand. A little while
Ago, Madame, you used a different style.

Elmire Oh! If such a refusal makes you smart,
How little do you know a woman's heart,
And what it is endeavoring to convey
When it resists in such a feeble way!
Our modesty combats the stimulus
Of the sweet feelings you arouse in us.
However strong and justified our flame,
We never can admit it without shame.
Even our first resistance is too tender
Not to give notice of our heart's surrender.

Though honor makes our lips combat temptation,
Such a refusal is an invitation.
I know that this avowal is too free
And too unsparing of my modesty;
But since I have resolved to speak my piece,
Would I have struggled to restrain Damis,
Would I have sat so long, composed and mute,
I ask you, while I listened to your suit?
Would I have taken things in such a fashion
If I'd been unresponsive to your passion?
And when I urged you not to carry through
The marriage that my husband planned for you,
What could such great insistency suggest,
If not my overwhelming interest,
And fear that soon I could not call my own
A heart I want to have as mine alone?

Tartuffe Of course, Madame, it's very sweet to hear
Such words as these spoken by lips so dear:
Their honeyed flavor floods my every sense.
Such bliss I never did experience.
To please you is my one solicitude,
And your love is my heart's beatitude;
But please allow that heart the liberty
To dare to doubt its own felicity.
These words might be a scheme, and nothing more,
To have me break a marriage that's in store;
To be quite candid, as I fear I must,
Sweet words are not enough to win my trust,
Unless some of your favors, which I burn for,
Should give the reassurance that I yearn for,
And fill my soul with lasting confidence
In all the charming bounties you dispense.

Elmire [*coughs to warn her husband*] How fast you move against a woman's heart!
Must you exhaust our kindness from the start?
She immolates herself to offer you
A sweet avowal, but that will not do,
And you will not be satisfied unless
At once she grants her utmost tenderness.

Tartuffe The less we merit, the less we dare expect,
And words alone don't have enough effect.
Such perfect bliss arouses our suspicion,
And our belief awaits its full fruition.
I'm so aware of my indignity,
I cannot credit my felicity,
And I shall not—that is, Madame, until
Your acts attest your genuine good will.

Elmire My, but your love is the despotic kind,
And puts me in a troubled state of mind!
It presses for a dictatorial sway,
And violently wants to have its way!
Must you pursue at such a frantic pace?
And am I not allowed a breathing space?
Is it becoming to employ such rigor,
To urge your points with such relentless vigor,
And, when our weakness puts us in your hands,
Press your advantage with such strong demands?

Tartuffe But if you countenance this suit of mine,
Why do you then refuse me such a sign?

Elmire But thus I would offend, beyond a doubt,
That Heaven that you love to talk about.

Tartuffe If Heaven is all that leads you to resist,
Such obstacles are easily dismissed;
Do as I ask, and set your mind at ease.

Elmire But they frighten us so with Heaven's decrees!

Tartuffe These foolish fears, Madame, I can dispel,
And all your scruples won't be hard to quell.
It's true, there are some pleasures Heaven denies;
But there are ways to reach a compromise.
Yes, now there is a science that succeeds
In stretching consciences to meet our needs,
And can correct, by a sublime invention,
An evil deed just by a pure intention.
To all this there are keys I can provide you;
All you need do, Madame, is let me guide you.
Content my longings, free yourself of dread:

If there is sin, I'll take it on my head.
You've a bad cough, Madame.

Elmire I'm tortured by it.

Tartuffe I have a bit of licorice; won't you try it?

Elmire It's a persistent cold, and I can tell
That all your licorice won't make it well.

Tartuffe That is a shame.

Elmire Yes, more than words can say.

Tartuffe Your scruple, then, is easy to allay:
Our secret will be safe with us alone,
And there's no evil if the thing's not known.
The one offense lies in the public shame,
And secret sin is sin only in name.

Elmire [*coughs again*] I see I'll have to yield to your behest
And grant you everything that you request;
Since nothing else will do, I guess I must,
To make you happy and to win your trust.
I wish you were not so demanding, though;
You press me further than I want to go;
But since you so insist on nothing less,
And doubt my word unless I acquiesce,
Since full conviction is what you require,
I must give in, and do as you desire.
If this is bad, if I am wrong to do it,
So much the worse for you, who drive me to it;
And I am not to blame, assuredly.

Tartuffe I'll take the full responsibility.

Elmire Open the door, will you, and take a glance;
See if my husband's there by any chance.

Tartuffe Why bother with precautions such as those?
He is a man to lead round by the nose;
And he's so glad I have these talks with you,
He'd see the worst and swear it wasn't true.

Elmire No matter; for a moment, please go out
And have a very careful look about.

SCENE SIX
Orgon, Elmire

Orgon [*coming out from under the table*] Yes, he's an evil man, I do admit!
I'm really stunned; I can't get over it.

Elmire What? Coming out so soon? Don't be absurd.
It's not yet time; get back, and not a word;
Don't trust conjecture; don't be premature,
But wait until the end, to be quite sure.

Orgon No, nothing worse ever came out of hell.

Elmire You can't believe the things that people tell.
Don't yield till you're convinced; I'll get along.
And take your time, for fear you might be wrong.

As Tartuffe returns, she has her husband hide behind her.

SCENE SEVEN
Tartuffe, Elmire, Orgon

Tartuffe Madame, my satisfaction is complete:
I've had a look around the entire suite.
No one is there; and now I am delighted . . .

Orgon [*stopping him*] Hold on, lover, you're getting too excited:
You mustn't let your passions run so free.
You holy man, you'd make a fool of me!
Oh, how you let temptations rule your life!
Marry my daughter, and seduce my wife!
I kept on doubting what I might have known,
And kept looking for you to change your tone;
But now my fears are verified indeed:
I am convinced, and that is all I need.

Elmire [*to Tartuffe*] I do not like the part I've had to play,
But I was forced to treat you in this way.

Tartuffe What? You believe . . . ?

Orgon That's enough out of you.
Get out of here without further ado.

Tartuffe My aim . . .

Orgon There's nothing more for me to hear:
Come on, right now, I want you out of here.

Tartuffe You are the one to leave, despite your tone:
This house is mine, and I will make it known,
And show you that you have recourse in vain
To these low tricks, thinking to cause me pain,
That to insult me thus is most unwise,
That I can both expose and punish lies,
Avenge offended Heaven, and bring low
Anyone here who wants to make me go.

SCENE EIGHT

Elmire, Orgon

Elmire What does he mean? And what is all this chatter?

Orgon Faith, I'm dismayed. This is no laughing matter.

Elmire What?

Orgon From his talk I see I've been mistaken;
And that donation has me rather shaken.

Elmire Donation?

Orgon Yes, the thing's already signed.
But that is not what most disturbs my mind.

Elmire What else?

Orgon I'll tell you. First let's go and see
If that strongbox is where it ought to be.

SCENE ONE

Orgon, Cléante

Cléante Where are you off to?

Orgon Alas! I couldn't say.

Cléante I think we should confer about a way
To try to cope with this unhappy turn.

Orgon That strongbox is by far my main concern;
More than all else it drives me to despair.

Cléante Then it conceals some ominous affair?

Orgon It was Argas, a friend whose plight commands
My sympathy, who placed it in my hands:
He picked me out to keep it when he fled;
And these are documents, from what he said,
On which his property and life depend.

Cléante And you gave these to your supposed friend?

Orgon A conscientious scruple made me err.
I went straight to my traitor to confer;
And his persuasion led me to agree
To put the strongbox in his custody,
So that in case of an investigation
I could fall back upon prevarication,

With a clear conscience stifle all I knew,
And take an oath denying what was true.

Cléante I must confess your prospects do look dim;
The deed of gift, your confidence in him
Were both, to speak more frankly than politely,
Dangerous steps, and taken rather lightly.
Holding such weapons, he can lead you far.
Since his advantages are what they are,
To push him to extremes was a mistake,
And you could not afford an open break.

Orgon What? Can it be that such a pious face
Conceals a heart so false, a soul so base?
I took him in without a cent, and then . . .
That does it; I renounce all worthy men:
Henceforth I put them all under my curse,
And I shall be a devil to them, or worse.

Cléante So! There you go, in your exasperation!
You never are content with moderation;
The path of reason's not for you, it seems,
And you fly back and forth between extremes.
You've seen your error now, and fully know
That you were cozened by a pious show;
But to correct yourself, why must you make,
In reason's name, an even worse mistake,
And lump the character of all good men
With that of this repulsive specimen?
Because one rogue has hoodwinked you for fair
By his impressive act and fervent air,
You now think everyone behaves that way,
And that no pious man exists today?
Leave such conclusions to the libertines;
Strip off the mask and learn what virtue means,
And, carefully avoiding each extreme,
Be slower in conferring your esteem.
Refuse to honor falsity as real,
But meanwhile, don't attack authentic zeal;
And if you must fall into one excess,
Err on the side of trusting more, not less.

SCENE TWO

Damis, Orgon, Cléante

Damis What! Father, can it possibly be true
That that ungrateful scoundrel's threatening you,
And that his cowardly and brazen pride
Uses your bounties to support his side?

Orgon It's true, son, and it brings me close to tears.

Damis Leave it to me; I'll cut off both his ears.
His insolence demands to be brought low;
I'll rid you of him with a single blow;
Just let me strike him down, and you'll be freed.

Cléante That's spoken like a young man, yes indeed.
Please simmer down; try not to sound insane:
We're living in a time and in a reign
Where violence is never the way out.

SCENE THREE

Madame Pernelle, Mariane, Elmire, Dorine, Damis, Orgon, Cléante

Madame Pernelle What are these mysteries I've heard about?

Orgon These are strange things, observed with my own eyes;
You've seen my kindnesses, now see the prize.
I raise a man out of his misery,
And like a brother take him in with me,
Load him with favors that should carry weight,
Give him my daughter and my whole estate;
And that vile wretch, that blight upon my life,
Undertakes foully to seduce my wife;
Nor is that all; he's not contented yet,
But dares to hold against me as a threat
The favors I have armed him with too long,
Tries to make use of them to do me wrong,

Take away all I do (or did) possess,
And leave me where I found him, in distress.

Dorine Poor fellow!

Madame Pernelle Son, it cannot be a fact
That he meant to commit so base an act.

Orgon What?

Madame Pernelle Worthy men are prone to be maligned.

Orgon What do you mean, Mother? What's on your mind?

Madame Pernelle People live strangely here, as I have stated,
And anyone can see how much he's hated.

Orgon Is that related to the case at all?

Madame Pernelle I've told you a hundred times, when you were small:
Virtue is always harassed here below;
The envious will die, but envy, no.

Orgon And therefore I suppose he's not to blame?

Madame Pernelle They've made up tales to blacken his good name.

Orgon I've seen the whole thing; that's why I'm indignant.

Madame Pernelle Slanderous people can be quite malignant.

Orgon Mother, you'll have me damned. Listen to me:
With my own eyes I saw this, can't you see?

Madame Pernelle Venom is what their tongues will never lack,
And nothing here below escapes attack.

Orgon This is sheer nonsense. Can't you realize,
I say I saw this, saw with my own eyes,
I mean I *saw!* Now must I spell it out
A hundred times, and stamp my feet and shout?

Madame Pernelle Good Lord, appearances can be deceiving,
And seeing mustn't always be believing.

Orgon I shall go mad.

Madame Pernelle Beware of false suspicions.
Good can seem evil under some conditions.

Orgon And when he tries to make love to my wife,
I am to call this charity?

Madame Pernelle In life,
No accusation should be premature;
You should have waited till you were quite sure.

Orgon The devil! You'd have had me get more proof?
I should have sat and watched, then, while
Tartuffe . . . ?
You make it hard for me to be genteel.

Madame Pernelle His soul is ravished with too pure a zeal;
I simply can't accept it as a fact
That he could be involved in such an act.

Orgon If you were not my mother, I don't know
What I might say, you aggravate me so.

Dorine In all of this, sir, there's a kind of justice:
She won't trust you, but then, you wouldn't trust us.

Cléante We're wasting precious time on idle chatter;
We need a plan of action in this matter.
His is no empty threat, yet here we are.

Damis What? Would he carry insolence so far?

Elmire For my part, I don't think it's possible;
His thanklessness would be too visible.

Cléante Don't be too sure; no doubt he can pull strings
And give the color that he wants to things;
And a cabal has often, for much less,
Entangled people in a nasty mess.
I repeat: with such arms at his command,
You never should have dared to force his hand.

Orgon True, but what could I do? That traitor's pride
Was more than my resentment could abide.

Cléante I wish with all my heart we could renew
Some semblance of a peace between you two.

Elmire If I had known what he held over us,
I wouldn't have occasioned such a fuss,
And my . . .

Monsieur Loyal appears at the door.

Orgon [*to Dorine*] That man, what does he want? What is it?
I'm in a fine state to receive a visit!

SCENE FOUR

Monsieur Loyal, Madame Pernelle, Orgon, Damis, Mariane, Dorine, Elmire, Cléante

Monsieur Loyal Good day, dear sister; kindly let me see
The master of the house.

Dorine He isn't free.
Sorry, but this is a bad time to get him.

Monsieur Loyal My presence isn't likely to upset him.
I'm sure he will be not dissatisfied
At seeing me, but even gratified.

Dorine Your name?

Monsieur Loyal Give him this message, if you would:
Monsieur Tartuffe has sent me, for his good.

Dorine [*to Orgon*] Sir, it's a pleasant-seeming man out there,
Sent by Monsieur Tartuffe on an affair
Which, he declares, will please you.

Cléante You must see
What this man wants, and just who he can be.

Orgon Perhaps he's come to offer me some pact:
If so, how do you think I'd better act?

Cléante Don't let resentment carry you away;
And if he talks peace, let him have his say.

Monsieur Loyal Good day, sir. Heaven smite your enemies,
And, I hope, bring you everything you please!

Orgon [*to Cléante*] This mild opening confirms my
expectation,
And seems to promise some accommodation.

Monsieur Loyal Your family, sir, I cherish and admire;
And once I used to serve your honored sire.

Orgon I beg your pardon, sir, but to my shame,
I cannot place you or recall your name.

Monsieur Loyal My name is Loyal, I'm from Normandy,
A bailiff with a wand, as you can see.
For forty years, thank Heaven, I've enjoyed
Being thus well and honorably employed;
And I am here, sir, if you will permit,
To serve you duly with a certain writ.

Orgon What? You are here . . . ?

Monsieur Loyal Sir, there's no need to shout:
It's nothing but a summons to move out,
Yourself, your furniture, and all your kin,
And clear the place so others may move in,
Without delay and with all proper speed . . .

Orgon I? Leave this house?

Monsieur Loyal Yes, please, sir; yes indeed.
For now the rightful owner, need I mention?
Is good Monsieur Tartuffe, beyond contention.
His ownership of all your goods is clear
By virtue of a contract I have here;
It's in due form, and there is no defense.

Damis My word, I marvel at this impudence.

Monsieur Loyal Sir, you are not involved in this affair,
As is this gentleman; he's mild and fair,
And knows the role a worthy man must play
Too well to flout justice in any way.

Orgon But . . .

Monsieur Loyal Nothing would induce you to rebel,
Sir, not a million francs, I know full well;
And like a gentleman, you will allow
Me to enforce my orders here and now.

Damis Sir Bailiff-with-a-wand, a stick may fall
On that black jacket of yours after all.

Monsieur Loyal Sir, make your son be silent or withdraw.
I'd rather not report you to the law
And have your name on record with the court.

Dorine This Mister Loyal's a disloyal sort!

Monsieur Loyal For all good men my tenderness is large;
And thus I took this matter in my charge
Only to see the thing was nicely done
And keep them from assigning anyone
Who would not share my love and admiration
And would proceed with less consideration.

Orgon Could you do worse than order such a seizure
And drive us from our home?

Monsieur Loyal But you have leisure;
And I shall even grant you one more day
Before you do, sir, what the orders say.
I'll merely bring ten of my men with me
To spend the night, without publicity.
Before you go to bed, though, if you please,
For form's sake, you must let me have your keys.
I shall take care not to disturb your rest,
And allow only what is for the best.
You must remove tomorrow, when you wake,
Any belongings that you want to take;
My men will give you—and I picked them stout—
A helping hand to get everything out.
No one could act more gently than I do;
And since that is the way I'm treating you,
I ask you, sir, for your cooperation
In checking any further aggravation.

Orgon If I still have a hundred louis d'or,
I'd give them happily, and many more,
If I could just land one resounding clout,
My very best, upon that ugly snout.

Cléante Hold on, don't ruin matters.

Damis What a nerve!
I itch to give him what such men deserve.

Dorine You have a handsome back, sir; I can tell
That a few cudgel blows would suit you well.

Monsieur Loyal You could get into trouble, with your jaw,
My girl; women are not above the law.

Cléante Enough; let's have no more, sir; pray you, cease.
Please serve your paper and leave us in peace.

Monsieur Loyal *Au revoir,* one and all. May Heaven content you!

Orgon May it confound you, and the man who sent you!

SCENE FIVE

Orgon, Cléante, Mariane, Elmire, Madame Pernelle, Dorine, Damis

Orgon Well, Mother, now you know about our guest,
And from this summons you can judge the rest.
Is his treachery clear to you at last?

Madame Pernelle Where have I been? I'm utterly aghast!

Dorine You're wrong to blame the poor man, and complain;
And this makes all his pious purpose plain:
He loves his fellow man more than himself;
And, knowing the corrupting power of pelf,
In charity he frees you from temptation
Toward any obstacle to your salvation.

Orgon Shut up! For the last time I'm telling you.

Cléante Let us consider what you'd better do.

Elmire Expose the brazen ingrate's ugly story.
This action makes the contract nugatory;
And his black treachery will be too plain
To yield him the success he hopes to gain.

SCENE SIX

Valère, Orgon, Cléante, Elmire, Mariane, Madame Pernelle, Dorine, Damis

Valère Sir, though I hate to bring unpleasant news,
Such is your danger that I cannot choose.

A dear old friend of mine, who knows how strong
Has been my interest in you all along,
On my behalf has dared to violate
The secrecy owed to affairs of state,
And writes to say that in your present plight
The only course for you is instant flight.
The scoundrel who imposed upon you so
Denounced you to the King an hour ago,
And put into his hands, to bring you down,
The strongbox of an enemy of the crown,
Claiming your failure to reveal it shows
You slight the duty that a subject owes.
I lack details about the charges pressed,
But there's an order out for your arrest.
Tartuffe himself was told to come along
To lend a hand and see nothing goes wrong.

Cléante It's at your property the traitor aims,
And he has weapons to enforce his claims.

Orgon That man is certainly a wicked beast!

Valère Delay is fatal, sir, even the least.
There is my carriage waiting at the door;
And you may need this thousand louis d'or.
Let's waste no time: this is a lightning blow,
Which you can parry only as you go.
Please let me guide you to a safer site
And keep you company throughout your flight.

Orgon Alas! How vastly I am in your debt!
Even the time to thank you is not yet;
Some day, Heaven give me opportunity
To recognize your generosity.
Farewell; be careful, all . . .

Cléante Come on, now, run.
Brother, we'll see that everything is done.

SCENE SEVEN

The Gentleman of the King's Guard, Tartuffe, Valère, Orgon, Elmire, Mariane, Madame Pernelle, Dorine, Cléante, Damis

Tartuffe Hold on, hold on there, sir, stay where you are:
Your new abode is not so very far,
And we arrest you now in the King's name.

Orgon Traitor, you've brought me to this final shame!
This is the stroke, scoundrel, that lays me low,
And all your treachery is in this blow.

Tartuffe Your insults have no power to rouse my gall,
And for the sake of Heaven I'll suffer all.

Cléante That is great moderation, I must say.

Damis To prate of Heaven in such a shameless way!

Tartuffe You cannot anger me, with all your spite;
And all I want to do is what is right.

Mariane I trust this is a source of proud enjoyment.
You've surely picked an honorable employment!

Tartuffe Any employment is a source of pride
When the King's interests are on our side.

Orgon Did you remember that my charity
Rescued you, ingrate, out of poverty?

Tartuffe I know about your help and everything;
But my first duty is to serve my King;
The power of that sacred obligation
Annihilates my own appreciation,
And to it I would sacrifice my wife,
My friend, my relatives, my very life.

Elmire Impostor!

Dorine What a master of pretense!
He cloaks himself in all we reverence!

Cléante But if this pressing zeal that you display
Is quite as perfect as you always say,

Why was it so reluctant to appear
Until he caught you trying to tempt Elmire?
Why did you not denounce him, but hold back,
Until his honor forced him to attack?
I do not mention—it did not dissuade you—
The gift of all his goods that he had made you;
But since you treat him like a culprit now,
What made you take his presents anyhow?

Tartuffe [*to the Gentleman*] Deliver me from every bleeding heart.
You have your orders, sir, pray do your part.

Gentleman Yes, I've been waiting overlong to do it,
And it is fitting that you urge me to it.
Here it is: follow me without delay
Into the prison where you are to stay.

Tartuffe Who? I, sir?

Gentleman You, indeed.

Tartuffe To prison? Why?

Gentleman You're not the one I mean to satisfy.

To Orgon.

Sir, your escape was narrow, but complete.
We live under a king who hates deceit,
A king whose eyes see into every heart
And can't be fooled by an impostor's art.
The keen discernment that his greatness brings
Gives him a piercing insight into things;
Nothing can disconcert his readiness,
And his firm reason always shuns excess.
He honors all the best of humankind;
But zeal for virtue never makes him blind:
The love that for the truly good he fosters
Does not prevent his hatred for impostors.
This fellow could not catch him unawares,
And he has thwarted many craftier snares.
His insight penetrated from the start

The twisted treason of that scoundrel's heart.
Accusing you, Tartuffe revealed his state,
And by an equitable stroke of fate
Led the King to recall his shady fame
For crimes committed under another name.
His record is a long and ugly one
That would fill volumes and still not be done.
Revolted by the black disloyalty
Of that ungrateful wretch, his Majesty
Added this horror to the list at hand
And sent me here, as if at his command,
Only to see how far his gall extends
And bring him here to make you full amends.
Yes, all your papers, which he claims to own,
I shall restore into your hands alone.
The King now chooses to invalidate
The deed of gift that cost you your estate,
And finally he pardons your offense
In shielding even a friend at his expense;
And thus the courage that you once displayed
Against his enemies, shall be repaid,
To show how suddenly, in case of need,
The King can recompense a noble deed,
That merit has no reason for alarm,
Since he remembers help better than harm.

Dorine Heaven be praised!

Madame Pernelle Now I can breathe anew!

Elmire How fortunate!

Mariane Can you believe it's true?

Orgon [*to Tartuffe*] Well, traitor, there you are . . .

Cléante Stop, brother, please,
And do not stoop to such indignities;
Leave the poor wretch to his unhappy course,
And do not add your bit to his remorse;
But rather hope his heart, after today,
May happily return to virtue's way,
That he'll correct his life, detest his crime,
And soften the King's justice in due time,

While you go on your knees before the King
And thank his clemency for everything.

Orgon Well said: let's go and kneel before the throne,
And praise him for the bounties he has shown.
Then, once this first duty is gladly done,
We must start thinking of another one,
And by the marriage of the loving pair,
Reward the deep devotion of Valère.

The Miser

CHARACTERS

Harpagon, father of Cléante and Élise, and suitor to Mariane

Cléante, son of Harpagon, in love with Mariane

Élise, daughter of Harpagon, in love with Valère

Valère, son of Anselme, in love with Élise

Mariane, in love with Cléante, and courted by Harpagon

Anselme, father of Valère and Mariane

Frosine, a woman who lives by her wits

Maître Simon, a broker

Maître Jacques, Harpagon's cook and coachman

La Flèche, Cléante's valet

Dame Claude, servant of Harpagon

Brindavoine, La Merluche, lackeys of Harpagon

The *Officer* and his *Clerk*

The scene is in Paris: Harpagon's living room, with a garden to the rear.

Act One

SCENE ONE
Valère, Élise

Valère What, charming Élise, you are growing melancholy, after the obliging assurances you were good enough to give me of your faith? I see you sigh, alas! in the midst of my joy! Tell me, is it in regret at having made me happy, and do you repent of the signed engagement which my ardor wrung from you?

Élise No, Valère, I cannot repent of anything I do for you. I feel myself drawn to it by too sweet a power, and I haven't even the strength to wish that these things were not so. But to tell you the truth, the outcome gives me some uneasiness; and I am very much afraid that I may love you a little more than I ought.

Valère Oh! What can you fear, Élise, in the kindness you bear me?

Élise Alas! A hundred things at once: a father's anger, a family's reproaches, the censures of society; but more than anything, Valère, a change in your heart, and that criminal coolness with which those of your sex most often repay any too ardent proof of an innocent love.

Valère Ah! Do not do me the wrong of judging me by others. Suspect me of anything, Élise, rather than of failing in what

I owe you; I love you too much for that, and my love for you will last as long as my life.

Élise Ah, Valère, everyone says the same thing. Men are all alike in their words; and it is only their actions that show them to be different.

Valère Since actions alone reveal what we are, then at least wait and judge my heart by these, and don't look for crimes of mine in the unjust fears of dire forebodings. Do not murder me, I beg you, with the painful blows of an outrageous suspicion; and give me time to convince you, by a thousand upon a thousand proofs, of the sincerity of my flame.

Élise Alas! How easily we let ourselves be persuaded by the persons we love! Yes, Valère, I regard your heart as incapable of deceiving me. I believe that you love me with a genuine love, and that you will be faithful to me; I do not in the least want to doubt it, and I confine my concern to my fear of the blame that I may receive.

Valère But why this anxiety?

Élise I would have nothing to fear if everyone saw you with the same eyes as I do, and I find enough in your person to justify the things I do for you. For its defense, my heart has all your merit, supported by the aid of a gratitude by which Heaven binds me to you. At every moment I recall the astounding peril that first brought us to each other's sight; that surprising generosity that made you risk your life to steal mine from the fury of the waves; those most tender cares that you showed me after having drawn me out of the water, and the assiduous homage of that ardent love which neither time nor difficulties have discouraged, and which, making you neglect both kindred and country, detains you here, keeps your fortune disguised for my sake, and has reduced you, in order to see me, to take on the functions of a servant of my father's. All this of course has a marvelous effect on me, and is enough in my eyes to justify to me the engagement I was able to consent to; but perhaps it is not enough to justify it to others, and I am not sure that they will share my feelings.

Valère Of all that you have mentioned, it is only by my love alone that I claim to deserve anything from you; and as for the scruples you have, your father himself takes only too good care to justify you to everyone; and the excess of his avarice and the austere way he lives with his children could authorize even stranger things. Pardon me, charming Élise, if I speak of him thus before you. You know that on that score one can say no good of him. But anyway, if I can find my parents again, as I hope to, we shall not have much trouble in winning him over. I am waiting impatiently for news of them, and if I don't hear any soon I'll go myself and look for it.

Élise Ah! Valère, don't budge from here, I beg you; and just think about getting into my father's good graces.

Valère You see how I am going about it, and the adroit complaisance I have had to employ to make my way into his service; what a mask of sympathy and conformity of feelings I disguise myself under to please him, and what a part I play with him every day so as to win his affection. I am making admirable progress in this; and I find that to win men, there is no better way than to adorn oneself before their eyes with their inclinations, fall in with their maxims, praise their defects, and applaud whatever they do. One need have no fear of overdoing the complaisance; and even though the way you trick them is visible, even the shrewdest are great dupes when it comes to flattery; and there is nothing so absurd or so ridiculous that you can't make them swallow it if you season it with praise. Sincerity suffers a bit in the trade I am plying; but when you need men, you simply have to adjust to them; and since that's the only way to win them over, it's not the fault of those who flatter, but of those who want to be flattered.

Élise But why don't you also try to win my brother's support, in case the maidservant should take it into her head to reveal our secret?

Valère You can't humor them both; and the father's spirit and the son's are things so opposed that it's hard to be in the confidence of both at the same time. But you, for your part, work on your brother, and use the affection there is between you to bring him over to our interests. Here he comes. I'll withdraw. Take this time to speak to him; and don't tell him anything about our affairs except what you see fit.

Élise I don't know whether I'll have the strength to confide this to him.

SCENE TWO

Cléante, Élise

Cléante I'm very glad to find you alone, sister; and I was burning to talk to you, to let you in on a secret.

Élise Here I am ready to listen, brother. What have you to tell me?

Cléante Many things, sister, all wrapped up in a word: I'm in love.

Élise You're in love?

Cléante Yes, I'm in love. But before I go any further, I know that I'm dependent on a father, and that the name of son subjects me to his will; that we should not plight our troth without the consent of those who brought us into the world; that Heaven has made them masters of our affections, and that we are enjoined not to dispose of these without their guidance; that not being prepossessed by any mad ardor, they are in much better shape not to make a mistake than we, and to see much better what is right for us; that we must rather trust the lights of their prudence than the blindness of our passion; and that the impetuosity of youth most often drags us over terrible precipices. I tell you all this, sister, so that you won't take the trouble to tell it to me; for the fact is my love won't listen to anything, and I beg you not to make any remonstrances.

Élise Brother, have you pledged yourself to the one you love?

Cléante No, but I am resolved to; and I conjure you, once again, not to bring up any reasons to dissuade me.

Élise Am I so strange a person, brother?

Cléante No, sister, but you're not in love; you do not know the sweet violence that tender love exerts over our hearts; and I am apprehensive of your wisdom.

Élise Alas, brother! Let's not speak of my wisdom! There is no one who does not lack it, at least once in his life; and if I open my heart to you, I may appear to your eyes much less wise than yourself.

Cléante Ah! Would to Heaven that your heart, like mine . . .

Élise Let's finish with your affair first, and tell me who is the one you love.

Cléante A young person who has lived in this neighborhood only a short time, and who seems to be made to inspire love in all who see her. Sister, nature has formed nothing lovelier; and I felt myself transported from the moment I saw her. Her name is Mariane, and she lives under the guidance of an old mother who is nearly always sick, and for whom this lovable girl has such affection as cannot be imagined. She serves her, sympathizes with her, and consoles her, with a tenderness that would touch your soul. She goes about the things she does in the most charming manner in the world, and a thousand graces shine in all her actions: a most attractive sweetness, an engaging kindness, an adorable modesty, a . . . Ah, sister! I wish you had seen her.

Élise I see much of her, brother, in the things you tell me; and to understand what she is, it is enough for me that you love her.

Cléante I have secretly learned that they are not very well off, and that even with their discreet way of living they are hard put to it to make ends meet with what little they have. Just imagine, sister, what a joy it can be to restore the fortunes of a person we love; to give some little help, adroitly, to the modest needs of a virtuous family; and think how frustrating it is for me to see that because of a father's avarice I am powerless to taste this joy and to display to this beauty any token of my love.

Élise Yes, brother, I can see well enough what your vexation must be.

Cléante Ah! Sister, it's worse than you could believe. For after all, can anything be more cruel than this rigorous economy that is inflicted on us, this extraordinary parsimony in which we are made to languish? And what good will it do us to have money if it comes to us only when we are no longer at a good age to enjoy it, and if, even to maintain myself, I now have to go into debt on all sides, if like you I am reduced to seeking help every day from tradesmen to have enough to wear decent clothes? At all events I wanted to talk to you and ask you to help me to sound out my father about my feelings; and if I find him opposed, I am resolved to go away with this lovely girl and enjoy whatever fortune Heaven may will to offer us. To this end I am hunting everywhere for money to borrow; and if your affairs, sister, are like mine, and if our father must oppose our desires, we shall both leave him and free ourselves from this tyranny in which his insupportable avarice has held us for so long.

Élise It is quite true that every day he gives us more and more reason to regret our mother's death, and that . . .

Cléante I hear his voice. Let's go somewhere nearby to finish our talk in private; and afterward we'll join forces to attack his obduracy.

SCENE THREE

Harpagon, La Flèche

Harpagon Out of here right now, and no back-talk. Come on, get out of my house, you past master of thievery, you gallowsbird!

La Flèche [*aside*] I've never seen anything as mean as this cursed old man, and, subject to correction, I think he has the devil in him.

Harpagon You're muttering between your teeth.

La Flèche Why are you kicking me out?

Harpagon You're a fine one, you scoundrel, to ask me for my reasons. Get out quick, before I beat your brains out.

La Flèche What have I done to you?

Harpagon You've done enough to make me want you to get out.

La Flèche Your son, my master, gave me orders to wait for him.

Harpagon Go wait for him in the street, and don't stay in my house planted bolt upright like a sentry watching what goes on and making your profit from everything. I don't want to have eternally before me a spy on my affairs, a traitor, whose cursed eyes besiege all my actions, devour what I possess, and ferret around everywhere to see if there isn't anything to rob.

La Flèche How the devil do you expect anyone to go about robbing you? Are you a robbable man, when you lock up everything and stand guard day and night?

Harpagon I'll lock up what I see fit and stand guard as I like. Isn't that just like one of those spies, who keep watch on whatever you do? [*Aside.*] I tremble for fear he may have suspected something about my money. [*Aloud.*] Wouldn't you be just the man to start the rumor that I have money hidden in my house?

La Flèche You have money hidden?

Harpagon No, you rogue, I didn't say that. [*Aside.*] He drives me mad. [*Aloud.*] I'm wondering whether maliciously you wouldn't go start a rumor that I have.

La Flèche Heigho! What does it matter to me whether you have or you don't have, if it comes to the same thing for us?

Harpagon A reasoner, are you? I'll give you a piece of that reasoning about your ears. [*He raises his hand to give him a slap.*] Once more, get out of here.

La Flèche All right! I'm going.

Harpagon Wait. Aren't you taking something of mine with you?

La Flèche What would I be taking of yours?

Harpagon Come here, let me see. Show me your hands.

La Flèche Here they are.

Harpagon The others.*

La Flèche The others?

Harpagon Yes.

La Flèche Here they are.

Harpagon [*pointing to La Flèche's breeches*] Haven't you put something in there?

La Flèche See for yourself.

Harpagon [*feeling at the bottom of La Flèche's breeches*] These big breeches are cut out to become receivers for stolen goods; and I wish somebody had been hanged for making them.

La Flèche [*aside*] Ah! How well a man like this would deserve what he fears! And what joy I would have in robbing him!

Harpagon Eh?

La Flèche What?

Harpagon What are you saying about robbing?

La Flèche I say for you to search me everywhere to see if I've been robbing you.

Harpagon That's what I mean to do. [*Searches in La Flèche's pockets.*]

La Flèche A plague on miserliness and misers!

Harpagon How's that? What's that you say?

La Flèche What did I say?

Harpagon Yes, what did you say about miserliness and misers?

La Flèche I said a plague on miserliness and misers.

Harpagon Whom are you referring to?

*This comic bit about the "other" hands is borrowed from Plautus, *Aulularia,* Act IV, scene 4.

La Flèche Misers.

Harpagon And who are these misers?

La Flèche Niggards and skinflints.

Harpagon But whom do you mean by that?

La Flèche What are you worrying about?

Harpagon I'm worrying about what I must.

La Flèche Do you think I mean you?

Harpagon I think what I think; but I want you to tell me whom you're talking to when you say that.

La Flèche I'm talking . . . I'm talking to my hat.

Harpagon And I might just be talking to your thick head.

La Flèche Will you stop me from cursing misers?

Harpagon No, but I'll stop you from chattering and being insolent. Shut up.

La Flèche I'm not mentioning any names.

Harpagon I'll thrash you if you speak.

La Flèche If the cap fits, wear it.

Harpagon Will you shut up?

La Flèche Yes—against my will.

Harpagon Aha!

La Flèche [*turning out one of the pockets in his jerkin*] There, here's another pocket; are you satisfied?

Harpagon Come on, give it back to me without a search.

La Flèche What?

Harpagon What you took from me.

La Flèche I didn't take anything at all from you.

Harpagon Honestly?

La Flèche Honestly.

Harpagon Farewell, and go to all the devils in hell.

La Flèche That's a nice kind of dismissal.

Harpagon Anyway, I charge it against your conscience. [*Alone.*] That's a gallowsbird of a valet, who bothers me a lot, and I don't like to see that limping cur around.*

SCENE FOUR

Élise, Cléante, Harpagon

Harpagon [*alone*] It's certainly no small trouble to keep a large sum of money in the house; and happy is the man who has all his pile well invested, and keeps around only what he needs for his expenses. It's quite a job to think up a safe hiding-place anywhere in the whole house; for to me, strong-boxes are suspect, and I don't ever want to trust them; I regard them as just the right bait for thieves, and they're always the first thing they go for. However, I don't know whether I did well to bury in my garden the ten thousand crowns I was paid back yesterday. Ten thousand crowns in gold in your house is a rather . . . [*Cléante and Élise appear, talking in low voices.*] O Heavens! I must have betrayed myself! My excitement carried me away, and I think I spoke out loud while talking this over with myself. [*To Cléante and Élise.*] What is it?

Cléante Nothing, father.

Harpagon Have you been there long?

Élise We've only just arrived.

Harpagon You heard . . .

Cléante What, father?

Harpagon Just now . . .

Élise What?

Harpagon What I just said.

Cléante No.

Harpagon Oh, yes you did, yes you did.

Élise I *beg* your pardon.

* Louis Béjart, who played La Flèche, had a limp.

Harpagon I see perfectly well that you heard a few words of it. The fact is I was talking to myself about how hard it is to find any money nowadays, and I was saying that any man is fortunate who can have ten thousand crowns in his house.

Cléante We were hesitating to speak to you for fear of interrupting you.

Harpagon I'm very glad to tell you this so you won't get things wrong and imagine I'm saying that I'm the one who has ten thousand crowns.

Cléante We don't enter into your affairs.

Harpagon Would God I had ten thousand crowns!

Cléante I don't think . . .

Harpagon It would be a fine thing for me.

Élise Those are things . . .

Harpagon I could certainly use them.

Cléante I think . . .

Harpagon That would be quite all right with me.

Élise You're . . .

Harpagon And I wouldn't complain as I do that times are hard.

Cléante Good Lord, father! You've no cause to complain, and everyone knows you're well enough off.

Harpagon What? I'm well enough off! Those who say so are liars. Nothing could be more false, and it's a bunch of scoundrels who spread all those rumors.

Élise Don't get angry.

Harpagon It's a strange thing that my own children betray me and become my enemies!

Cléante Is it being your enemy to say that you have money?

Harpagon Yes. That kind of talk, and the expenses you incur, will be the reason why one of these days they'll come and cut my throat in my own house in the belief that I'm made of gold pieces.

Cléante What great expense do I incur?

Harpagon What expense? Is there anything more scandalous than that sumptuous costume that you flaunt around the town? I was scolding your sister yesterday, but this is even worse. That's what cries to Heaven for vengeance; and to take you from head to foot, there'd be enough there to provide a handsome annuity. I've told you twenty times, son, all your ways displease me very much; you're putting on the marquis act like mad; and to go around dressed as you are, you must be robbing me.

Cléante What? How could I rob you?

Harpagon How do I know? Then how do you get the wherewithal to support the way you live?

Cléante I, father? I gamble; and since I'm very lucky, I put all my winnings on my back.

Harpagon That's a very bad way to do. If you're lucky at gambling, you should profit by it, and invest the money you win at decent interest so as to get it back some day. But I'd really like to know, not to speak of the rest, what's the use of all those ribbons you're decked out with from head to foot, and whether half a dozen laces are not enough to fasten a pair of breeches? It's necessary indeed to use money on wigs when you can wear home-grown hair, which costs nothing. I'll bet that in wigs and ribbons you have at least twenty pistoles' worth; and twenty pistoles in a year bring in eighteen francs six sous and eight deniers, even at only one denier interest on twelve.

Cléante You're right.

Harpagon Let's leave that and talk about something else. [*Cléante and Élise exchange glances.*] Huh? [*Aside.*] I think they're making signs to each other to steal my purse. [*Aloud.*] What do those gestures mean?

Élise My brother and I are arguing over who shall speak first; and we both have something to tell you.

Harpagon And I too have something to tell you both.

Cléante It's about marriage, father, that we want to speak to you.

Harpagon And it's marriage too that I want to talk to you about.

Élise Oh, father!

Harpagon Why that exclamation? Is it the word or the thing, daughter, that frightens you?

Cléante Marriage may frighten us both, in the way you may understand it; and we fear that our feelings may not be in accord with your choice.

Harpagon Have a little patience. Don't be alarmed. I know what you both need; and neither of you will have any reason to complain about anything I intend to do. And to begin at one end of the story: [*to Cléante*] tell me, have you seen a young person named Mariane, who lives not far from here?

Cléante Yes, father.

Harpagon [*to Élise*] And you?

Élise I've heard of her.

Harpagon What do you think of the girl, son?

Cléante A very charming person.

Harpagon Her face?

Cléante Extremely modest and full of intelligence.

Harpagon Her air and manner?

Cléante Admirable, beyond a doubt.

Harpagon Don't you think a girl like that is well worth thinking about?

Cléante Yes, father.

Harpagon And would be a desirable match?

Cléante Very desirable.

Harpagon And gives every promise of making a good wife?

Cléante Without a doubt.

Harpagon And a husband would have satisfaction with her?

Cléante Assuredly.

Harpagon There is one little difficulty: I'm afraid she won't bring with her as much money as one might expect.

Cléante Ah, father! The money doesn't matter when it's a question of marrying a good woman.

Harpagon I beg your pardon, I beg your pardon. But there is this to be said, that if she doesn't bring as much money as one would like, one can try to make it up in other ways.

Cléante To be sure.

Harpagon Well, I'm very glad to see that you share my sentiments; for her modest bearing and her gentleness have won my heart, and I'm determined to marry her, provided she has *some* dowry.

Cléante Huh?

Harpagon What's that?

Cléante You are determined, you say . . . ?

Harpagon To marry Mariane.

Cléante Who, you? You?

Harpagon Yes, me, me, me. What does this mean?

Cléante I feel a sudden dizziness, and I'm leaving.

Harpagon It won't amount to anything. Go into the kitchen quick and have a good drink—of fresh water. [*Exit Cléante.*] There's one of your dainty young men for you, with no more vigor than a chicken. Well, daughter, that's what I've decided for myself. As for your brother, I've picked out for him a certain widow that a man came to talk to me about this morning; and as for you, I'm giving you to Seigneur Anselme.

Élise To Seigneur Anselme?

Harpagon Yes, a mature man, prudent and wise, who's not over fifty and who's said to be very wealthy.

Élise [*with a curtsy*] I don't want to get married, father, if you please.

Harpagon [*mimicking the curtsy*] And I, my little daughter, my pet, I want you to get married, if you please.

Élise [*with another curtsy*] I beg your pardon, father.

Harpagon [*mimicking the curtsy*] I beg your pardon, daughter.

Élise [*with another curtsy*] I am Seigneur Anselme's very humble servant; but with your permission, I won't marry him.

Harpagon [*mimicking the curtsy*] I am your very humble valet; but with your permission, you will marry him this evening.

Élise This evening?

Harpagon This evening.

Élise [*with another curtsy*] That shall not be, father.

Harpagon [*mimicking the curtsy*] That shall be, daughter.

Élise No.

Harpagon Yes.

Élise No, I tell you.

Harpagon Yes, I tell you.

Élise That's something you shall not force me to.

Harpagon That's something I shall force you to.

Élise I'll kill myself rather than marry such a husband.

Harpagon You shall not kill yourself, and you shall marry him. But just look at that impertinence! Who ever saw a daughter talk to her father that way?

Élise Who ever saw a father marry off his daughter that way?

Harpagon It's a match to which no one could object; and I bet that everyone will approve of my choice.

Élise And I bet that no reasonable person could approve of it.

Harpagon Here's Valère. Do you want to have him judge between us in this matter?

Élise I consent.

Harpagon Will you be governed by his judgment?

Élise Yes, I'll abide by what he says.

Harpagon That's settled.

SCENE FIVE

Valère, Harpagon, Élise

Harpagon Here, Valère! We've elected you to tell us which of us is right, my daughter or I.

Valère It's you, sir, beyond dispute.

Harpagon Do you know what we're talking about?

Valère No, but you couldn't be wrong, and you are reason itself.

Harpagon I want to give her this evening as her husband a man as rich as he is wise; and the wench tells me to my face that she wouldn't dream of taking him. What do you say to that?

Valère What do I say to that?

Harpagon Yes.

Valère Well, ah . . .

Harpagon What?

Valère I say that fundamentally I agree with you, and you can't fail to be right. But at the same time she's not entirely in the wrong, and . . .

Harpagon What? Seigneur Anselme is an important match, a gentleman who is a nobleman,* mild, sedate, wise, and well off, and who has no children left him from his first marriage. Could she find better?

Valère That's true. But she might say to you that this is hurrying things a bit, and that there ought to be at least some time to see if her inclination can be reconciled with . . .

Harpagon It's an opportunity we must quickly seize by the forelock. I find an advantage here that I wouldn't find elsewhere; he undertakes to take her without dowry.

Valère Without dowry?

Harpagon Yes.

* In Molière's day, gentleman meant a nobleman by birth, while a nobleman might be only recently ennobled.

Valère Ah! I say no more. Do you see? That's a completely convincing reason; you have to give in to that.

Harpagon It's a considerable saving for me.

Valère Assuredly, there's no denying that. It is true that your daughter may point out to you that marriage is a more important affair than some may think; that the happiness or unhappiness of her whole lifetime is at stake; and that a commitment that must last until death should never be made except with great precautions.

Harpagon Without dowry.

Valère You're right. That decides the whole thing, of course. There are people who might tell you that on such occasions a daughter's inclinations are something that should no doubt be considered, and that this great disparity of age, temperament, and feelings makes a marriage subject to very unpleasant accidents.

Harpagon Without dowry.

Valère Ah! There's no answer to that, as anyone knows; who the devil can go against that? It's not that there aren't a lot of fathers who would rather look out for their daughters' satisfaction than for the money they might give away; who would not want to sacrifice them to self-interest, and would seek more than anything else to infuse into a marriage that sweet conformity which maintains in it at all times honor, tranquillity, and joy, and which . . .

Harpagon Without dowry.

Valère That's true; that stops every mouth: *without dowry.* How can anyone resist a reason like that one?

Harpagon [*aside, looking toward the garden*] What's that? It seems to me I hear a dog barking. Could somebody be after my money? [*To Valère.*] Don't move, I'll be right back.

Exit.

Élise Are you joking, Valère, to talk to him the way you do?

Valère It's so as not to exasperate him and to get around him the better. To oppose his feelings head on is the way to spoil everything; and there are some people whom you have to take only from an angle, temperaments hostile to any resistance, restive natures, who shy from the truth, who always balk at the straight road of reason, and whom you can lead only by gradually turning them in the direction you want them to go. Pretend to give your consent to what he wants, you'll get your way better, and . . .

Élise But this marriage, Valère?

Valère We'll find some roundabout way to break it off.

Élise But what can we come up with, if it's to take place this evening?

Valère You must ask for a delay, and pretend to have some illness.

Élise But they'll discover the pretense if they call the doctors.

Valère Are you joking? What do they know about it? Come, come, with them you can have whatever illness you please, they'll find reasons to tell you where it comes from.

Harpagon [*returning; to himself*] It's nothing, thank God.

Valère Finally, our last resort is that flight can make us safe from everything; and if your love, fair Élise, is capable of a strength . . . [*Seeing Harpagon.*] Yes, a daughter must obey her father. She must not consider how a husband looks, and when the great argument of *without dowry* is involved, she must be ready to take whatever is given her.

Harpagon Good. That's the way to talk.

Valère Sir, I ask your pardon if I get carried away a bit and make bold to talk to her as I am doing.

Harpagon What? I'm delighted, and I want you to assume absolute power over her. [*To Élise.*] Yes, it's no use trying to run away. I give him the authority that Heaven gives me over you, and I mean to have you do whatever he tells you.

Valère [*to Élise*] Now will you resist my remonstrances! [*To Harpagon.*] Sir, I'm going to follow her and continue the lessons I was teaching her.

Harpagon Yes, I'll be much obliged. Assuredly . . .

Valère It's good to keep a tight rein on her.

Harpagon That's true. We must . . .

Valère Don't you worry. I think I can bring her around.

Harpagon Do, do. I'm off to take a little turn in town, and I'll be right back.

Valère Yes, money is more precious than anything in the world, and you should thank Heaven for giving you such a fine man for a father. He knows what life is about. When someone offers to take a girl without dowry, one shouldn't look any further. Everything is wrapped up in that, and *without dowry* takes the place of beauty, youth, birth, honor, wisdom, and probity.

Harpagon Ah! Good boy! Spoken like an oracle. Happy the man who can have a servant like him!

Act Two

SCENE ONE

Cléante, La Flèche

Cléante Ah! You scoundrel, where in the world have you been hiding? Didn't I give you orders . . . ?

La Flèche Yes, sir, and I came here to wait for you and not stir; but your honorable father, that most ungracious of men, drove me out against my will, and I ran the risk of a beating.

Cléante How is our affair going? Things are more urgent than ever; and since I last saw you I have found out that my father is my rival.

La Flèche Your father in love?

Cléante Yes, and I had all kinds of trouble not to let him see how much this news upset me.

La Flèche Him, meddling in love! What the devil does he think he's doing? Is he trying to play some kind of a joke on everybody? And was love made for people built like him?

Cléante For my sins, this passion had to come into his head.

La Flèche But why keep your love a mystery to him?

Cléante To give him less reason for suspicion, and to keep the easiest ways open to myself, in case of need, to prevent this marriage. What answer did they give you?

La Flèche My word, sir, people who borrow are very unfortunate; and a person has to put up with some pretty strange things when, like you, he has to pass through the hands of the money-lenders.

Cléante The deal won't come off?

La Flèche Pardon me. Our Maître Simon, the broker they gave us, an active man and full of zeal, says he has done wonders for you; and he insists that your face alone won his heart.

Cléante I'll get the fifteen thousand francs I'm asking for?

La Flèche Yes, but on a few little conditions that you will have to accept if you want these things to be done.

Cléante Did he have you talk to the person who is to lend the money?

La Flèche Oh, really, now, it doesn't work that way. He takes even more care to remain unknown than you, and these are much greater mysteries than you think. They won't tell his name at all, and today they are to bring the two of you together in a house borrowed for the purpose, to learn from your own mouth about your means and your family; and I have no doubt at all that your father's name alone will make things easy.

Cléante And especially since our mother is dead, and they can't keep me from coming into her estate.

La Flèche Here are a few articles that he dictated himself to our go-between, to be shown you before doing anything:

"Provided that the lender see all his securities, and that the borrower be of age and of a family whose estate is ample, solid, secure, clear and free of all encumbrance, a good precise statement of obligation shall be executed before a notary, the most honest man possible, who to this purpose shall be chosen by the lender, to whom it is most important that the act be drawn up in due form."

Cléante There's nothing to object to in that.

La Flèche

"The lender, to have no scruples on his conscience, undertakes to lend the money at only one denier for eighteen."

Cléante One denier for eighteen! Gad! That's honorable. There's no reason to complain.

La Flèche That's true.

"But since the said lender does not have at hand the sum in question, and, to please the borrower, is himself constrained to borrow it from another at the rate of one denier for five, it will be proper that the said first borrower shall pay this interest, without prejudice to the rest, considering that it is only to oblige him that the said lender undertakes to borrow this."

Cléante What the devil! What a bloodsucker! What a robber! That's more than one denier for four.

La Flèche That's true; that's just what I said. That's something for you to see about.

Cléante What do you expect me to see? I need money, and I'll simply have to consent to everything.

La Flèche That's the answer I gave.

Cléante Is there anything else?

La Flèche Just one little article more.

"Of the fifteen thousand francs that are asked, the lender will be able to pay out in cash only twelve thousand, and for the remaining thousand crowns* the borrower will have to take the used clothing, effects, and jewelry listed in the following memorandum, and which the said lender has set, in good faith, at the most moderate price that was possible for him."

Cléante What does this mean?

La Flèche Listen to the memorandum.

"First, one four-poster bed with hangings of Hungarian

* The crown equaled three francs.

lace* very handsomely applied to an olive-colored cloth, with six chairs and a counterpane of the same; the whole lot in very good condition and lined with light shot taffeta in red and blue.

"Plus one tester of good Aumale serge, in old rose, with silk fringes."

Cléante What does he expect me to do with that?

La Flèche Wait.

"Plus one tapestry hanging representing the loves of Gombaut and Macée.

"Plus one big walnut table with twelve columns or turned legs, which can be pulled out at either end, and provided with its six stools to go under it."

Cléante Gad, what have I to do . . . ?

La Flèche Have patience.

"Plus three large muskets all inlaid with mother-of-pearl, with the three forked rests for them.

"Plus one brick furnace with two retorts and three flasks, very useful for those with an interest in distilling."

Cléante I'm going mad.

La Flèche Take it easy.

"Plus one Bologna lute furnished with all its strings, or nearly all.

"Plus one game of 'trou-madame' and one checkerboard, with one game of 'goose' renewed from the Greeks, very suitable for passing the time when one has nothing to do.

"Plus one lizard skin, three and a half feet long, stuffed with hay, a very pleasing curio to hang from the ceiling of a room.

"The whole lot aforementioned, honestly worth more than four thousand five hundred francs, and reduced to a thousand crowns through the discretion of the lender."

Cléante The plague choke him with his discretion, the traitor, the cutthroat! Did you ever hear of such usury? And isn't he

* A very common material.

content with the insane interest he demands without also forcing me to take, for three thousand francs, the old relics he picks up? I won't get two hundred crowns for all that; and yet I've simply got to make up my mind to consent to what he wants, for he's in a position to make me accept anything, and the scoundrel has got me with a dagger at my throat.

La Flèche No offense, sir, but I see you precisely on the highroad to ruin that Panurge took, taking money in advance, buying dear, selling cheap, and eating your wheat in the blade.

Cléante What do you want me to do? That's what young men are reduced to by the cursed avarice of fathers; and after that people wonder why sons wish their fathers would die.

La Flèche I must admit that yours would make the most sedate man in the world angry at his niggardliness. Heaven be praised, I have no great inclination to be hanged; and among my colleagues whom I see dabbling in a lot of little deals, I know how to steer clear, and keep prudently out of all those gallantries that smell the least bit of the gallows; but to tell you the truth, by the way he acts, he would really tempt me to rob him; and in robbing him I would think I was performing a meritorious action.

Cléante Give me that memorandum a second for another look.

SCENE TWO

Maître Simon, Harpagon, Cléante, La Flèche

Maître Simon Yes, sir, it's a young man who needs money. His affairs make it urgent for him to get some, and he'll put up with everything you prescribe.

Harpagon But do you think, Maître Simon, that there's no risk? And do you know the name, the means, and the family of the man you are speaking for?

Maître Simon No, I can't give you full information on all that, and it was only by chance that I was put in touch with him;

but you will be informed about everything by himself, and his man has assured me that you will be satisfied when you know him. All I can tell you is that his family is very rich, he has already lost his mother, and he will guarantee, if you want, that his father will die in the next eight months.

Harpagon Well, that's something. Charity, Maître Simon, obliges us to do favors to people when we can.

Maître Simon Of course.

La Flèche [*softly, to Cléante*] What does this mean? Our Maître Simon talking to your father?

Cléante [*softly, to La Flèche*] Could someone have told him who I am? And would you be the man to betray us?

Maître Simon Aha! You are certainly in a hurry! Who told you it was here? [*To Harpagon.*] At least it wasn't I, sir, who revealed to them your name and address; but in my opinion there's no great harm in that. These are people of discretion, and you can work things out together here.

Harpagon What's this?

Maître Simon This gentleman is the person who wants to borrow from you the fifteen thousand francs I spoke to you about.

Harpagon What, you scoundrel? It's you who abandon yourself to these guilty extremities?

Cléante What, father? It's you who lend yourself to these shameful actions? *Exit Maître Simon and La Flèche.*

Harpagon It's you who are trying to ruin yourself by such disgraceful borrowings?

Cléante It's you who are trying to enrich yourself by such criminal usury?

Harpagon Do you really dare appear before me after this?

Cléante Do you really dare show your face to the world after this?

Harpagon Tell me, aren't you ashamed to descend to such debauch? to plunge headlong into frightful expenses? and to squander shamefully the money that your parents amassed for you by the sweat of their brow?

Cléante Don't you blush to dishonor your position by the deals you make? to sacrifice glory and reputation to the insatiable desire to pile up one crown-piece on another, and to outdo, in the matter of interest, the most infamous dodges that the most notorious usurers ever invented?

Harpagon Get out of my sight, you rogue! Get out of my sight!

Cléante Which one is more criminal, in your opinion, the man who buys a sum of money he needs, or the man who steals a sum of money that he has no use for?

Harpagon Out of here, I tell you, and don't torment my ears.

Exit Cléante.

I'm not sorry about this adventure; and it's a warning to me to keep an eye more than ever on all his actions.

SCENE THREE
Frosine, Harpagon

Frosine Sir . . .

Harpagon Wait a moment; I'll come back and talk to you. [*Aside.*] It's about time I went and took a little look at my money.

SCENE FOUR
La Flèche, Frosine

La Flèche [*not seeing Frosine*] It's an utterly comic adventure. Somewhere he must have a whole big warehouse of used furniture, for we didn't recognize anything in the memorandum we have.

Frosine Oh, it's you, my poor La Flèche? Fancy meeting you!

La Flèche Aha! It's you, Frosine. What are you doing here?

Frosine What I do everywhere else: serving as a go-between, making myself useful to people, and profiting as best I can from the little talents I may have. You know that in this world you have to live by your wits, and that Heaven has given people like me no other revenue than intrigue and ingenuity.

La Flèche Do you have some business with the master of the house?

Frosine Yes, I'm handling a little matter for him for which I hope to be compensated.

La Flèche By him? Oh, my word! You'll be very clever if you get anything out of him; and I warn you that in here money is very expensive.

Frosine There are certain services that are wondrously effective.

La Flèche I am your humble servant, and you don't yet know *Seigneur* Harpagon. Seigneur Harpagon is of all humans the least human human; the mortal of all mortals who is hardest and most close-fisted. There is no service that drives his gratitude to the point of making him open his hands. Praise, esteem, and good will in words, friendliness—all you like; but money—nothing doing. There is nothing more dry and arid than his good graces and his compliments; and *give* is a word for which he has such an aversion that he never says *I give you,* but *I lend you good day.*

Frosine Good Lord! I know the art of milking men, I have the secret of winning their tenderness, tickling their hearts, and finding their soft spots.

La Flèche Useless trifles here. I defy you to soften up the man in question in the matter of money. On that score he's cruel, so cruel as to drive anyone to despair; a person could die and he wouldn't budge. In a word, he loves money, more than reputation, honor, and virtue; and the sight of anyone asking for it throws him into convulsions. That's striking him in his vulnerable spot, that's piercing his heart, that's tearing out his entrails; and if . . . But he's coming back; I'm off.

SCENE FIVE

Harpagon, Frosine

Harpagon [*aside*] Everything is as it should be. [*To Frosine.*] Well, what is it, Frosine?

Frosine Oh my Heavens, how well you look! And what a picture of health you are!

Harpagon Who, me?

Frosine I've never seen you looking so fresh and sprightly.

Harpagon Really?

Frosine What? You've never in your life been as young as you are now; and I see people of twenty-five who are older than you.

Harpagon And yet, Frosine, I'm a good sixty years old.

Frosine Well, sixty, what's that? A lot indeed! That's the flower of life, and you're just coming into your prime.

Harpagon That's true; but nevertheless, as I see it, twenty years less would do me no harm.

Frosine Are you joking? You don't need that, and you're built to live to a hundred.

Harpagon You think so?

Frosine Indeed I do. You show all the indications of it. Hold still a moment. Oh, look, right there between your eyes, there's a sign of long life!

Harpagon You're an expert in those things?

Frosine Certainly. Show me your hand. Oh, my goodness, what a life line!

Harpagon How's that?

Frosine Don't you see where that line goes to?

Harpagon Well, what does that mean?

Frosine My word! I said a hundred; but you'll pass six score.

Harpagon Is it possible?

Frosine They'll have to kill you, I tell you; and you'll bury your children and your children's children.

Harpagon Splendid. How is our business going?

Frosine Need you ask? And do I ever take a hand in anything without making it come out? Above all I have a marvelous talent for matchmaking; there aren't two people in the world that I couldn't find a way to pair off in a short time; and I think that if I took it into my head I could marry the Grand Turk to the Republic of Venice. Of course there were no such great difficulties in this affair. Since I have dealings with the ladies, I've talked to them both about you at length, and I've told the mother about the designs you had formed on Mariane, from seeing her pass in the street and take the air at her window.

Harpagon She answered . . .

Frosine She received the proposal with joy; and when I gave her to understand that you were very anxious to have her daughter present this evening at the signing of your own daughter's marriage contract, she consented without difficulty and entrusted her to me for that purpose.

Harpagon You see, Frosine, I am obliged to give a supper for Seigneur Anselme, and I'd like very much for her to share in the treat.

Frosine You're right. After dinner she's to pay a visit to your daughter, and from there she plans to go and make a trip to the fair, and then come to the supper.

Harpagon Well! They'll go together in my carriage, which I'll lend them.

Frosine That's just the thing for her.

Harpagon But Frosine, have you talked with the mother about the dowry she can give her daughter? Did you tell her that she had to bestir herself, make some effort, and bleed herself, for an occasion like this one? For after all, one does not marry a girl unless she brings something.

Frosine What? She's a girl that will bring you twelve thousand francs a year.

Harpagon Twelve thousand francs a year!

Frosine Yes. In the first place, she's trained and brought up to eat very sparingly; she's a girl accustomed to live on salad, milk, cheese, and apples, and consequently she will have no need of a well-served table, nor exquisite consommés, nor eternal broths of peeled barley, nor the other delicacies that another woman would require; and that is no such small matter but that it will amount every year to three thousand francs at the least. Besides that she has no taste for anything but very simple dress, and does not like fancy clothes or rich jewelry or sumptuous furnishings, which others of her sex go in for so heartily; and this item is worth more than four thousand francs a year. Moreover, she has a horrible aversion to gambling, which is not a common trait in today's women; and I know one in our neighborhood who lost twenty thousand francs at "trente-et-quarante" this year. But let's take only a quarter of that. Five thousand francs a year for gambling, and four thousand francs on clothes and jewelry, that makes nine thousand francs; and a thousand crowns that we put down for food: doesn't that give you your twelve thousand francs of hard money per year?

Harpagon Yes, that's not bad; but there's nothing real in that accounting.

Frosine Pardon me! Isn't it something real to bring you in marriage a great sobriety, the inheritance of a great love of simplicity in adornment, and the acquisition of a great fund of hatred for gambling?

Harpagon It's just a joke to try to make up a dowry for me out of all the expenses that she won't incur. I won't give any quittance for what I don't receive; and I've got to get some money out of this.

Frosine Good Lord! You'll get plenty; and they spoke to me of certain money they have abroad that you will become master of.

Harpagon We'll have to look into that. But Frosine, there's another thing that worries me. The girl is young, as you see; and young folk ordinarily like only those like themselves and seek only their company. I'm afraid that a man of my age may not be to her taste; and that that may come to produce in my house certain little disorders that would not suit me.

Frosine Ah, how little you know her! That's another peculiarity I was going to mention to you. She has a frightful aversion for young men, and loves only old ones.

Harpagon She?

Frosine Yes, she. I wish you had heard her talk on the subject. She can't abide the sight of a young man at all; but she is never more delighted, she says, than when she can see a handsome old man with a majestic beard. The eldest are the most charming for her, and I warn you not to go making yourself look younger than you are. She wants a man at the very least to be in his sixties; and not four months ago, all ready to be married, she flatly broke off the marriage on the grounds that her sweetheart revealed that he was only fifty-six and didn't put on spectacles to sign the contract.

Harpagon Just on those grounds?

Frosine Yes. She says that fifty-six is no satisfaction to her; and most of all, she favors noses that wear spectacles.

Harpagon What you're telling me is a very novel thing.

Frosine It goes further than I could tell you. In her bedroom you see a few pictures and prints; but what do you think they are? Adonises, Cephaluses, Parises, and Apollos? No; fine portraits of Saturn, of King Priam, of old Nestor, and of good father Anchises on the shoulders of his son.

Harpagon That's admirable! I never would have thought it; and I am delighted to learn that her taste runs that way. Indeed, if I'd been a woman, I wouldn't have liked young men.

Frosine I should think not. Young men are a fine lot, for anyone to love! They're pretty boys with running noses, fine show-offs, to make anyone crave their skin; and I'd certainly like to know what relish there is to them.

Harpagon As for me, I don't find any; and I don't know how it is that there are women who love them so.

Frosine You'd have to be raving mad. To find youth attractive! Does that make sense? Those blond youngsters, are they men? And can anybody take to those creatures?

Harpagon That's what I keep saying every day: with their voices like milk-fed hens, and their three little wisps of beard turned up like a cat's whiskers, their wigs of tow, their flowing breeches, and all unbuttoned over the stomach!

Frosine Oh, they're mighty well got up indeed compared with a man like you! Now you, you're a man. There's something here to satisfy the sight; and this is the way you have to be built and dressed to inspire love.

Harpagon You like my looks?

Frosine Do I? You're irresistible, and your face is fit for a painting. Turn around a little, please. Couldn't be better. Let me see you walk. There's a fine figure of a man—trim, free and easy as it should be, and with no sign of imperfection.

Harpagon I've nothing serious, thank God. There's just my catarrh that gets me from time to time.

Frosine That's nothing. Your catarrh is not unbecoming to you, and you cough with grace.

Harpagon Just tell me now: hasn't Mariane seen me yet? Hasn't she noticed me passing by?

Frosine No, but we've talked a lot about you. I've described your person to her, and I did not fail to praise your merit, and the advantage it would be for her to have a husband like you.

Harpagon You've done well, and I thank you for it.

Frosine I *would* like to make one small request of you, sir. [*Harpagon looks severe.*] I have a lawsuit that I'm on the point of losing for lack of a little money; and you could easily enable me to win the case, if you were to show me a little kindness.—You could never believe how delighted she will be to see you. [*Harpagon looks cheerful again.*] Ah, how pleased with you she will be! And what a wonderful effect that old-fashioned ruff of yours will have on her fancy! But above all she'll be charmed with your breeches, attached as they are to your doublet with laces; it's enough to make her crazy about you; and a lover with laced-up breeches will be a wonderful treat for her.

Harpagon Really, I'm enchanted to have you tell me this.

Frosine Truly, sir, this lawsuit is a matter of very great consequence to me. [*Harpagon looks severe again.*] I'm ruined if I lose it; and some small assistance would put my affairs back in order.—I wish you'd seen how delighted she was to hear me talk about you. [*Harpagon looks cheerful again.*] Joy shone in her eyes at the account of your qualities; and in short, I made her extremely impatient to see this marriage all settled.

Harpagon You've given me great pleasure, Frosine; and I confess I'm extremely obliged to you.

Frosine I beseech you, sir, to give me the little assistance I'm asking of you. [*Harpagon looks severe again.*] It will put me on my feet again, and I'll be eternally grateful to you.

Harpagon Good-by. I'm going to finish my letters.

Frosine I assure you, sir, that you could never give me relief in greater need.

Harpagon I'll give orders to have my carriage all ready to take you two to the fair.

Frosine I wouldn't trouble you if I weren't forced to by necessity.

Harpagon And I'll see to it that we have supper early, so as not to make you ill waiting.

Act Three

SCENE ONE

Harpagon, Cléante, Élise, Valère, Dame Claude, Maître Jacques, Brindavoine, La Merluche

Harpagon All right, come here all of you while I give you my orders for this evening and assign everyone his job. Come here, Dame Claude. Let's start with you. [*She is holding a broom.*] Good, I see you're armed. I entrust you with the task of cleaning up everywhere; and above all, take care not to rub the furniture too hard, for fear of wearing it out. Besides that, I assign to you the government of the bottles during the supper; and if there's one missing or anything broken, I'll hold you responsible and deduct it from your wages.

Maître Jacques [*aside*] A politic punishment.

Harpagon Off you go. [*Exit Dame Claude.*] You, Brindavoine, and you, La Merluche, I establish you in charge of rinsing the glasses and serving the drink; but only when people are thirsty, and not in the manner of some impertinent lackeys who egg people on and put them in mind of drinking when they're not thinking about it. Wait until they ask you more than once, and remember always to take around plenty of water.

Maître Jacques Yes, pure wine goes to your head.

La Merluche Shall we be taking off our aprons, sir?

Harpagon Yes, when you see the people coming; and take care not to spoil your clothes.

Brindavoine You know very well, sir, that one of the foreflaps of my doublet is covered with a big spot of oil from the lamp.

La Merluche And me, sir, I got a big hole in the seat of my breeches, and with all respect, people can see . . .

Harpagon Peace. Arrange that adroitly against the wall, and always face the company. [*Harpagon puts his hat in front of his doublet to show Brindavoine what he must do to hide the oil spot.*] And you, always hold your hat thus when you serve. [*To Élise.*] As for you, daughter, you'll keep an eye on what is cleared away, and take care that nothing is wasted. That's quite fitting for a daughter. But meanwhile prepare to receive my fiancée well. She's coming to visit you and take you to the fair with her. Do you hear what I'm telling you?

Élise Yes, father.

Harpagon And you, my fine fop of a son, whom I am kind enough to forgive for that matter just now, don't go and take it into your head to show her a sour face either.

Cléante I, father, a sour face? And for what reason?

Harpagon Oh Lord! We know the way children carry on whose fathers remarry, and how they usually look at what we call a stepmother. But if you want me to lose all remembrance of your latest escapade, I recommend to you above all to greet this person with a friendly face, and in short to give her the best welcome you possibly can.

Cléante To tell you the truth, father, I can't promise you to be very glad that she is to become my stepmother; I'd be lying if I told you so; but as for receiving her well and showing her a friendly face, I promise to obey you to the letter on that score.

Harpagon All right, be sure you do.

Cléante You'll see that you have no reason to complain.

Harpagon You will do wisely. Valère, help me in this. Here now, Maître Jacques, come here, I've kept you for the last.

Maître Jacques Is it your coachman, sir, or your cook that you want to speak to? For I'm both.

Harpagon Both.

Maître Jacques But which one first?

Harpagon The cook.

Maître Jacques Then wait, please. [*He takes off his coachman's overcoat and hat and appears dressed as a cook.*]

Harpagon What the devil kind of a ceremony is that?

Maître Jacques I await your orders.

Harpagon I have committed myself, Maître Jacques, to giving a supper this evening.

Maître Jacques [*aside*] Will wonders never cease?

Harpagon Now tell me, will you give us a good meal?

Maître Jacques Yes, if you give me plenty of money.

Harpagon What the devil, always money! They seem to have nothing else to say but "Money, money, money." Oh, that's the only word in their mouths: "Money." Always talking about money! That's the sword by their bedside, money.

Valère I've never heard a more pointless answer than that. That's a great wonder, to make a good meal with lots of money! It's one of the easiest things in the world, and any poor fool can do as much; but to show some ability you've got to talk about making a good meal with little money.

Maître Jacques A good meal with little money!

Valère Yes.

Maître Jacques Upon my word, Mr. Steward, you'll do us a favor by showing us that secret, and taking over my job as cook, since you're meddling with being a factotum here.

Harpagon Be quiet. What will we need?

Maître Jacques There's Mr. Steward of yours, who'll give you a good meal for little money.

Harpagon Hey! I want you to answer me.

Maître Jacques How many of you will there be at table?

Harpagon There'll be eight or ten of us; but figure on only eight; when there's enough to eat for eight, there's certainly enough for ten.

Valère Obviously.

Maître Jacques Well! You'll need four big soups, and five courses. Soups . . . entrées . . .

Harpagon What the devil! That's enough to treat a whole town.

Maître Jacques. A roast . . .

Harpagon [*putting his hand over Maître Jacques' mouth*] Ah, traitor! You're eating up everything I own.

Maître Jacques Side dishes . . .

Harpagon Still at it?

Valère Do you want to make everybody burst? And did the master invite people in order to kill them with too much food? Go read up a bit on the precepts for health, and ask the doctors if there's anything more prejudicial to man than eating to excess.

Harpagon He's right.

Valère Learn, Maître Jacques, you and the likes of you, that a table overloaded with food is a deathtrap; that to be a true friend to those you invite, frugality must reign in the meals you give; and that, as one of the ancients put it, *we must eat to live, and not live to eat.*

Harpagon Ah! That's well put! Come here, let me embrace you for that saying. That's the finest precept I've ever heard in my life. *We must live to eat, and not eat to li* . . . No, that's not it. How does it go?

Valère *That we must eat to live, and not live to eat.*

Harpagon Yes. [*To Maître Jacques.*] Do you hear? [*To Valère.*] Who was the great man who said that?

Valère I don't remember his name now.

Harpagon Remember to write down those words for me; I want to have them engraved in letters of gold on the mantelpiece in my dining room.

Valère I won't fail to. And for your supper, you need only leave it to me: I'll arrange it all as it should be.

Harpagon Then do.

Maître Jacques All the better; I'll have that much less trouble.

Harpagon We'll have to have some of those things that people don't eat much of and that fill you up right away: a good fat lamb stew, and a potted pie well stuffed with chestnuts.

Valère Rely on me.

Harpagon Now, Maître Jacques, my carriage needs to be cleaned.

Maître Jacques Wait. This is for the coachman. [*He puts his coat on again.*] You were saying . . . ?

Harpagon That my carriage needs to be cleaned and my horses got ready to drive to the fair . . .

Maître Jacques Your horses, sir? My word, they're in no condition at all to walk. I won't tell you that they're down on their litter, the poor beasts don't have any, and it would be no way to talk; but you make them observe such austere fasts that they are nothing any more but ideas or phantoms or shadows of horses.

Harpagon They're sick indeed! They don't do anything.

Maître Jacques And because they don't do anything, sir, don't they need to eat anything? It would be much better for them, poor creatures, to work a lot and eat likewise. It breaks my heart to see them so emaciated; for the fact is I have such a tender feeling for my horses that when I see them suffer, it seems to be happening to me. Every day I take things out of my own mouth for them; and, sir, it's a sign of too harsh a nature if a man has no pity on his neighbor.

Harpagon It won't be any great effort to go as far as the fair.

Maître Jacques No, sir, I haven't the heart to drive them, and it would go against my conscience to give them the whip in the state they're in. How do you expect them to drag a carriage when they can't even drag themselves along?

Valère Sir, I'll get our neighbor Le Picard to take on the job of driving them; and we'll need him here too to get the supper ready.

Maître Jacques So be it. I'd still rather they died under someone else's hand than mine.

Valère Maître Jacques is acting very reasonable.

Maître Jacques Mr. Steward is acting very indispensable.

Harpagon Peace!

Maître Jacques Sir, I can't stand flatterers; and I see that whatever he does, his perpetual checks on the bread and the wine, the wood, the salt, and the candles, are nothing but scratching your back and getting on your good side. That makes me mad, and I'm angered every day to hear what people say about you; for after all I have a soft spot in my heart for you in spite of myself; and after my horses, you are the person I like best.

Harpagon Might I learn from you, Maître Jacques, what people say about me?

Maître Jacques Yes, sir, if I could be sure it wouldn't make you angry.

Harpagon No, not in the least.

Maître Jacques Pardon me. I know very well that I'd put you in a rage.

Harpagon Not at all. On the contrary, it will give me pleasure, and I'm very glad to learn how people talk about me.

Maître Jacques Since you want it, sir, I'll tell you frankly that people everywhere make fun of you; that from every side they toss a hundred jokes at us on your account; and that they couldn't be more delighted than in catching you with your pants down and telling stories constantly about your stinginess. One man says that you have special almanacs printed in which you double the number of fast days and vigils, so as to profit by the fasts that you force upon your household. Another says that you always have a quarrel ready to pick with your valets when it's time for presents or for them to leave you, so you can find a reason for not giving them anything. This man tells how you took the cat of one of your neighbors to court for having eaten up the remains of a leg of lamb of yours. That man tells how you were caught one night going, yourself, to steal your horses' oats; and that your coachman, who was the one before me, in the dark, gave you I don't know how many blows with a stick, which you never wanted to say anything about. In short, do you want me to tell you how it is? A man can't go anywhere where he won't hear you hauled over the coals; you are a byword and a laughingstock to everybody; and nobody ever speaks about you except as a miser, a skinflint, a pennypincher and a usurer.

Harpagon [*beating him*] You are a numbskull, a rogue, and an impudent scoundrel.

Maître Jacques Well! Didn't I guess right? You wouldn't believe me. I told you I'd make you angry if I told you the truth.

Harpagon That'll teach you how to talk.

SCENE TWO

Maître Jacques, Valère

Valère [*laughing*] From what I can see, Maître Jacques, your frankness is ill repaid.

Maître Jacques By gad, Mr. Upstart, you who like to play important, it's none of your business. Laugh at your own beatings when you get them, and don't come laughing at mine.

Valère Ah! Sir Maître Jacques, don't be angry, I beg you.

Maître Jacques [*aside*] Oh! sweet talk! I'll play tough, and if he's fool enough to be afraid of me, I'll give him a bit of a drubbing. [*Aloud.*] Do you realize, Mr. Laugher, that me, I'm not laughing, and that if you make me mad I'll make you laugh out of the other side of your mouth? [*Maître Jacques pushes Valère to the end of the stage, threatening him.*]

Valère Eh! gently.

Maître Jacques What do you mean, gently? That doesn't suit me.

Valère I pray you.

Maître Jacques You're an impertinent fellow.

Valère Sir Maître Jacques.

Maître Jacques I won't give you two cents for your "Sir Maître Jacques." If I take a stick to you, I'll give you a sound thrashing.

Valère [*makes him retreat as much as he had done*] What, a stick?

Maître Jacques Oh, I don't mean that.

Valère Do you realize, Mr. Big Shot, that I'm just the man to thrash *you?*

Maître Jacques I don't doubt it.

Valère That take you all in all you're nothing but a scum of a cook?

Maître Jacques I know that very well.

Valère And that you don't know me yet?

Maître Jacques I beg your pardon.

Valère You'll thrash me, you say?

Maître Jacques I said it as a joke.

Valère And I have no taste for your jokes. [*Beats him.*] Better learn that you're a bad joker. *Exit.*

Maître Jacques A plague on sincerity! It's a bad trade. Henceforth I give it up, and I'll never speak the truth again. All right for my master; he has a certain right to beat me; but as for this Mr. Steward, I'll be revenged on him if I can.

SCENE THREE

Frosine, Mariane, Maître Jacques

Frosine Maître Jacques, do you know if your master is at home?

Maître Jacques Yes indeed he is, I know it only too well.

Frosine Please tell him that we're here.

SCENE FOUR

Mariane, Frosine

Mariane Ah, Frosine, what a strange state I'm in! And if I must say what I feel, how I dread the sight of him!

Frosine But why? And what are you worried about?

Mariane Alas! How can you ask? And can't you imagine the alarm of a person just about to see the torture that's in store for her?

Frosine I see well enough that to die pleasantly, Harpagon isn't the torture that you'd like to embrace; and I can tell by your face that that blond youngster you spoke to me about is a bit on your mind.

Mariane Yes, Frosine, it's something against which I don't even want to defend myself; and the respectful visits he has paid us have, I admit, had some effect on my soul.

Frosine But have you found out who he is?

Mariane No, I don't know who he is; but I know that he's made in such a way as to be loved; that if things could be left to my choice, I'd take him rather than another man; and that he contributes no little to make me find a frightful torment in the husband they want to give me.

Frosine My Lord! All these young fops are attractive, and have a good line; but most of them are poor as church mice; and it's better for you to take an old husband who'll give you plenty of money. I admit that the senses are not so well taken care of on the side I'm talking about, and that there are some distasteful things to put up with with such a husband; but that's not made to last, and his death, believe me, will soon put you in a position to take a more attractive one, who will make up for everything.

Mariane Good Lord, Frosine! It's a strange business when, to be happy, we must wish for someone else's decease; and death does not always fall in with all the plans we make.

Frosine Don't be silly. You're marrying him only on condition that he leave you a widow soon; and that must be one of the articles in the contract. He would be very impertinent not to die inside of three months.—Here he is in person.

Mariane Ah! Frosine, what a face!

SCENE FIVE

Harpagon, Frosine, Mariane

Harpagon Don't be offended, my beauty, if I come to you with spectacles on. I know that your charms strike the eye enough, are visible enough, by themselves, and that there's no need of glasses to perceive them; but after all, it is through glasses that we observe the stars; and I maintain and guarantee that you are a star, but a star that is the loveliest star in the land of stars. Frosine, she doesn't answer a word, and, it seems to me, shows no joy in seeing me.

Frosine That's because she's still all overcome; and then, girls are always ashamed to show at first what they feel in their souls.

Harpagon You're right. There now, my pretty, here's my daughter coming to greet you.

SCENE SIX

Élise, Harpagon, Mariane, Frosine

Mariane I've owed you a visit, Madame, and I'm late in paying it.

Élise You've done what I should have done, Madame, and *I* should have come to see *you* first.

Harpagon You see she's a big girl; but bad weeds always grow.

Mariane [*aside, to Frosine*] Oh, what an unpleasant man!

Harpagon What is the pretty thing saying?

Frosine That she thinks you're admirable.

Harpagon You do me too much honor, adorable pet.

Mariane [*aside*] What a beast!

Harpagon I'm only too obliged to you for these sentiments.

Mariane [*aside*] I can't stand it any longer.

Harpagon Here's my son too, coming to pay his respects to you.

Mariane [*aside, to Frosine*] Ah! Frosine, what an encounter! This is just the one I was telling you about.

Frosine [*to Mariane*] It's an amazing coincidence.

Harpagon I see that you're astonished to see that I have such grown-up children; but I'll soon be rid of them both.

SCENE SEVEN

Cléante, Harpagon, Élise, Mariane, Frosine

Cléante [*to Mariane*] Madame, to tell you the truth, this is a coincidence I certainly wasn't expecting; and my father surprised me no little when he told me just now of the plan he had made.

Mariane [*to Cléante*] I may say the same thing. This is an unforeseen encounter that surprised me as much as it did you; and I was not prepared for such an adventure.

Cléante It is true that my father, Madame, can make no finer choice, and that the honor of seeing you is a real joy to me; but for all that, I will not assure you that I am delighted with the plan you might have to become my stepmother. I confess to you, that compliment is too difficult for me; and by your leave, that is a title I do not wish you. This speech will appear brutal in the eyes of some people; but I am sure that you will be the person to take it aright; that this is a marriage, Madame, for which you may well imagine I must have some repugnance; that you are not unaware, knowing what I am, how it clashes with my interests; and that, in short, you are willing to have me tell you, with my father's permission, that if things depended on me, this marriage would not take place.

Harpagon That's a very impertinent compliment. What a fine confession to make to her!

Mariane And I, to answer you, must tell you that things are very much the same with me; and that if you would feel repugnance to see me as your stepmother, I would doubtless feel no less to see you as my stepson. Please don't believe that it is I who am trying to give you this distress. I would be very sorry to cause you any displeasure; and if I do not find myself forced to it by some absolute power, I give you my word that I shall not consent to this marriage that makes you unhappy.

Harpagon She's right: a stupid compliment demands a like answer. I beg your pardon, my beauty, for my son's impertinence. He's a young fool, who doesn't yet know the consequence of the words he says.

Mariane I promise you that what he said to me did not offend me at all; on the contrary, he gave me pleasure by thus explaining his true feelings to me. I like an avowal of that kind from him; and if he had spoken in any other way, I would esteem him the less for it.

Harpagon It's very kind of you to want to excuse his faults thus. Time will make him wiser, and you'll see that he'll change his feelings.

Cléante No, father, I am not capable of changing them, and I earnestly implore Madame to believe this.

Harpagon Just see how wild he is! He goes on stronger than ever.

Cléante Do you want me to betray my heart?

Harpagon Still at it? How would you like to change your tune?

Cléante Well, since you want me to speak in another vein, allow me, Madame, to put myself in my father's place and admit to you that I have seen nothing in the world as charming as you; that I can conceive nothing equal to the happiness of pleasing you; and that to be called your husband is a glory, a felicity that I would prefer to the destinies of the greatest princes on earth. Yes, Madame, the happiness of possessing you is in my eyes the fairest of all fortunes; I set my whole ambition on that; there is nothing I am incapable of doing to make so precious a conquest; and the most powerful obstacles . . .

Harpagon Gently, son, if you please.

Cléante It's a compliment I'm paying for you to Madame.

Harpagon My Lord! I've a tongue to explain myself with, and I don't need an advocate like you. [*To the Servants.*] Come on, bring some chairs.

Frosine No, it's better that we go to the fair right now, so as to get back sooner and then have plenty of time to talk to you.

Harpagon Then have them put the horses to the carriage. I pray you to excuse me, my beauty, if I didn't think to give you a little refreshment before leaving.

Cléante I've arranged for that, father, and I've had brought here a few basinsful of China oranges, sweet lemons, and preserves,* which I have sent for on your behalf.

Harpagon [*aside, to Valère*] Valère!

Valère [*to Harpagon*] He's out of his mind.

Cléante Do you think it's not enough, father? Madame will please be kind enough to excuse it.

Mariane That was not necessary.

Cléante Madame, have you ever seen a brighter diamond than the one you see my father has on his finger?

* These were all great luxuries in Molière's day.

Mariane It's true that it's very sparkling.

Cléante [*takes it from his father's finger and gives it to Mariane*] You must see it from close up.

Mariane Certainly it's very beautiful and casts great luster.

Cléante [*stands in front of Mariane who tries to return it*] No, Madame, the hands it is in are too beautiful. It's a present that my father has given you.

Harpagon I?

Cléante Isn't it true, father, that you want Madame to keep it for your sake?

Harpagon [*aside, to his son*] What?

Cléante [*to Harpagon*] A fine question! [*To Mariane.*] He's signaling me to make you accept it.

Mariane I don't want . . .

Cléante Are you joking? He wouldn't think of taking it back.

Harpagon [*aside*] I'm getting mad!

Mariane It would be . . .

Cléante [*still keeping Mariane from returning the ring*] No, I tell you, you would offend him.

Mariane Please . . .

Cléante Not at all.

Harpagon [*aside*] Plague take . . .

Cléante Now he's shocked at your refusal.

Harpagon [*aside, to his son*] Ah, traitor!

Cléante You see he's getting desperate.

Harpagon [*aside, to his son, threatening him*] You cutthroat!

Cléante Father, it's not my fault. I'm doing what I can to make her keep it; but she's obstinate.

Harpagon [*aside, to his son, in a fury*] You scoundrel!

Cléante You are the reason, Madame, why my father is scolding me.

Harpagon [*aside, to his son, with the same grimaces*] The villain!

Cléante You will make him ill. Please, Madame, don't resist any longer.

Frosine My Lord! What a to-do! Keep the ring, since the gentleman wants you to.

Mariane So as not to make you angry, I'll keep it for now; and I'll find another time to return it to you.

SCENE EIGHT

Harpagon, Mariane, Frosine, Cléante, Brindavoine, Élise

Brindavoine Sir, there's a man here that wants to speak to you.

Harpagon Tell him I'm busy, and to come back another time.

Brindavoine He says he's bringing you some money.

Harpagon I beg your pardon. I'll be right back.

SCENE NINE

Harpagon, Mariane, Cléante, Élise, Frosine, La Merluche

La Merluche [*comes running in, and knocks Harpagon down*] Sir . . .

Harpagon Oh! I'm dead.

Cléante What is it, father? Did you hurt yourself?

Harpagon The traitor certainly got money from my debtors to make me break my neck.

Valère It won't be anything.

La Merluche Sir, I beg your pardon, I thought I was doing the right thing to come running.

Harpagon What did you come for, you murderer?

La Merluche To tell you that both your horses have lost their shoes.

Harpagon Have them taken promptly to the smith's.

Cléante While we're waiting for them to be shod, father, I'll do the honors of the house for you, and take Madame into the garden, where I'll have the refreshments served.

Harpagon Valère, keep an eye on all this, and please take care to save me as much of it all as you can, to send back to the storekeeper.

Valère Enough said.

Harpagon O you rascal of a son, do you want to ruin me?

Act Four

SCENE ONE

Cléante, Mariane, Élise, Frosine

Cléante Let's come back in here, this place is much better. There are no suspicious people around any more, and we can talk freely.

Élise Yes, Madame, my brother has confided to me the passion he feels for you. I know the chagrins and vexations that such crossings can cause; and, I assure you, it is with extreme tenderness that I take an interest in your adventure.

Mariane It's a sweet consolation to see a person like you espousing one's interests; and I conjure you, Madame, always to keep this generous friendship for me, so capable of softening the cruelties of fortune.

Frosine My word! You are both unfortunate that you didn't inform me about your affair before all this. I would certainly have averted this trouble, and I wouldn't have brought things to the point where they are.

Cléante What's the use? It's my evil destiny that willed it so. But, lovely Mariane, what have you decided?

Mariane Alas! Am I in a position to decide anything? And in my dependent situation, can I do anything but wish?

Cléante No other support for me in your heart than mere wishes? No well-intentioned pity? No helpful kindness? No active affection?

Mariane What can I say to you? Put yourself in my place, and see what there is I can do. Advise me yourself, order me; I put myself in your hands, and I think you are too reasonable to try to require of me anything but what honor and propriety permit.

Cléante Alas! To what straits you reduce me, by confining me to what is allowed by the frustrating feelings of rigorous honor and scrupulous propriety!

Mariane But what would you have me do? Even if I could override a quantity of considerations to which our sex is obliged, I have some consideration for my mother. She has always brought me up with extreme tenderness, and I could not bring myself to cause her any displeasure. Do your best to work on her; use every means to win her over. You can do and say anything you want, I give you my permission; and if all that's needed is for me to declare myself in your favor, I am willing to consent to make her an avowal myself of all that I feel for you.

Cléante Frosine, my poor dear Frosine, would you help us out?

Frosine My word! Need you ask? I would like to with all my heart. You know I'm naturally quite humane; Heaven did not make my heart of bronze, and I'm only too tender in doing little favors when I see people wholeheartedly and honorably in love. What can we do in this matter?

Cléante Please give it a little thought.

Mariane Give us some ideas.

Élise Find some scheme to break up what you've done.

Frosine That's pretty hard. [*To Mariane.*] As for your mother, she's not altogether unreasonable, and it might be possible to win her over and persuade her to transfer to the son the gift she wants to make to the father. [*To Cléante.*] But the problem I find is that your father is your father.

Cléante That's just it.

Frosine I mean that he'll hold a grievance if he finds himself turned down, and he'll be in no mood then to give his consent to your marriage. To do this right, we'd have to have the refusal come from him, and try to find some means to give him a distaste for your person.

Cléante You're right.

Frosine Yes, I know I'm right. That's what we need; but the devil of it is finding the means. Wait! Suppose we had some woman fairly well along, who had my kind of talent, and could act well enough to counterfeit a lady of quality, with the help of a retinue gotten up in haste, and with some strange title of marquise or viscountess, let's suppose from lower Brittany; I would be skillful enough to make your father believe she was a wealthy woman with a hundred thousand crowns in ready cash besides her houses; that she was madly in love with him and so eager to be his wife that she would give him everything she had in the marriage contract; and I have no doubt that he would lend an ear to the proposition. For after all he loves you very much, I know, but he loves money a little bit more. And if, dazzled by this bait, he had once consented to what concerns you, it would make little difference later that he was disillusioned when he came to try to see more clearly into the possessions of our marquise.

Cléante All that is very well thought out.

Frosine Leave it to me. I've just remembered a friend of mine who will be just the person we want.

Cléante Be assured of my gratitude, Frosine, if you can bring this off. But, charming Mariane, let us begin, I pray you, by winning over your mother; it would be a lot accomplished, at any rate, to break off this marriage. For your part, I conjure you, make every possible effort to this end; use all the power you have over her through the fondness she has for you; employ, and don't hold back, the eloquent graces, the all-powerful charms that Heaven has placed in your eyes and mouth; and please don't forget any of those tender words, those sweet prayers, and those touching caresses to which, I am persuaded, nothing can be refused.

Mariane I'll do everything I can, and I won't forget a single thing.

SCENE TWO

Harpagon, Cléante, Mariane, Élise, Frosine

Harpagon [*aside and still unseen*] Well now! My son is kissing the hand of his prospective stepmother, and his prospective stepmother is not defending herself very hard. Can there be some mystery beneath all this?

Élise Here is my father.

Harpagon The carriage is all ready. You can leave when you please.

Cléante Since you're not going, father, I'll take them.

Harpagon No, stay. They'll go all alone perfectly well; and I need you. *The ladies exit.*

SCENE THREE

Harpagon, Cléante

Harpagon Now tell me, apart from her being your stepmother, what do you think of this person?

Cléante What do I think of her?

Harpagon Yes, her manner, her figure, her beauty, her mind?

Cléante Ho, hum.

Harpagon But then what?

Cléante To speak frankly, I didn't find her up to what I'd thought. Her manner is that of an out-and-out coquette; her figure is rather clumsy, her beauty very mediocre, and her mind quite ordinary. Don't think, father, that this is to make you lose your taste for her; for as stepmothers go, I like this one as well as another.

Harpagon And yet you were saying to her just now . . .

Cléante I said a few sweet nothings to her in your name, but that was to please you.

Harpagon So that you would not have any inclination for her?

Cléante I? Not at all.

Harpagon I'm sorry; for that ruins an idea that had come into my mind. Seeing her here, I got to thinking about my age; and it struck me that people may find fault with me to see me marrying so young a girl. That consideration was about to make me give up the plan; and since I've asked for her hand, and have pledged my word to her, I would have given her to you, but for the aversion you show.

Cléante To me?

Harpagon To you.

Cléante In marriage?

Harpagon In marriage.

Cléante Listen: it's true she's not much to my taste; but to please you, father, I'll make up my mind to marry her, if you want.

Harpagon I? I'm more reasonable than you think; I don't want to force your inclination.

Cléante Pardon me; I'll force myself for your sake.

Harpagon No, no; a marriage can't be happy without inclination.

Cléante That's something, father, that may come later; and they say that love is often a fruit of marriage.

Harpagon No; on the man's side this is not a risk to take; and there are unhappy consequences to which I have no wish to commit myself. If you had felt some inclination for her, well and good: I would have had you marry her instead of me; but that not being the case, I'll stick to my original plan and marry her myself.

Cléante Well, father, since that's the way things are, I must open my heart to you, I must reveal our secret to you. The truth is that I have loved her ever since the day when I first saw her, out for a walk; that my plan just now was to ask you to let me have her for my wife; and that all that held me back was your declaration of your feelings, and my fear of displeasing you.

Harpagon Have you paid her any visits?

Cléante Yes, father.

Harpagon Many times?

Cléante A good many, considering the time there has been.

Harpagon Were you well received?

Cléante Very well, but without their knowing who I was; and that's what caused Mariane's surprise just now.

Harpagon Have you declared your passion to her, and the intention you had to marry her?

Cléante Of course; and I've even made some overtures to her mother about it.

Harpagon Did she listen to your proposal on her daughter's behalf?

Cléante Yes, very civilly.

Harpagon And does the daughter fully return your love?

Cléante Judging by appearances, father, I am persuaded that she has some affection for me.

Harpagon [*aside*] I'm very glad to have learned such a secret, and that's just what I wanted to know. [*To Cléante.*] Now then, son, do you know what's ahead? You will have to make up your mind, if you please, to get rid of your love; to stop all your pursuit of a person whom I intend for myself; and shortly to marry the woman who is destined for you.

Cléante So, father, that was the game you were playing with me! Well! Since this is what things have come to, *I* declare to *you* that I will never give up my passion for Mariane, that I will go to any extreme to dispute your conquest of her, and that if you have a mother's consent on your side, I may perhaps have other resources fighting for me.

Harpagon What, you gallowsbird? You have the audacity to poach on my preserves?

Cléante You're the one who's poaching on mine; and I was the first one there.

Harpagon Am I not your father? And don't you owe me respect?

Cléante These are not matters in which children are obliged to defer to fathers; and love is no respecter of persons.

Harpagon I'll make you respect me all right—with a good stick!

Cléante All your threats will have no effect.

Harpagon You shall give up Mariane.

Cléante Absolutely not.

Harpagon Give me a stick immediately.

SCENE FOUR

Maître Jacques, Harpagon, Cléante

Maître Jacques Now, now, now, gentlemen, what is all this? What are you thinking of?

Cléante I don't care a bit.

Maître Jacques Oh, sir, gently!

Harpagon To talk to me with such impudence!

Maître Jacques Oh, sir, please!

Cléante I won't give an inch.

Maître Jacques What? To your father?

Harpagon Let me at him.

Maître Jacques What? Your son? For me it would be another matter.

Harpagon Maître Jacques, I'll make you yourself the judge of this matter, to show how right I am.

Maître Jacques I agree. [*To Cléante.*] Move off a bit.

Harpagon I'm in love with a girl whom I mean to marry; and this gallowsbird has the insolence to love her too, and to aspire to her hand in spite of my orders.

Maître Jacques Oh! He's wrong.

Harpagon Isn't it a frightful thing for a son to want to go into rivalry with his father? And shouldn't he, out of respect, abstain from meddling with my inclinations?

Maître Jacques You're right. Let me speak to him, and you stay there. [*Crosses the stage to Cléante.*]

Cléante Well, yes, since he wants to choose you as judge, I won't back down; I don't care who it is; and I too am willing to leave it to you, Maître Jacques, to judge our difference.

Maître Jacques You do me too much honor.

Cléante I'm in love with a young lady who returns my affection and tenderly accepts the offer of my love; and my father takes it into his head to come and disturb our love by asking for her hand.

Maître Jacques He is certainly wrong.

Cléante Isn't he ashamed, at his age, to think of marrying? Is it becoming to him to be still in love? And shouldn't he leave that occupation to young men?

Maître Jacques You're right, he can't be serious. Let me have a word with him. [*Goes back to Harpagon.*] Well! Your son isn't as strange as you say, and he's listening to reason. He says that he knows the respect he owes you, that he was carried away only in the first heat of anger, and that he will not refuse to submit to whatever you like, provided you are willing to treat him better than you do, and give him some person in marriage that he'll have reason to be pleased with.

Harpagon Ah! Tell him, Maître Jacques, that on those conditions he can hope for anything from me; and that except for

Mariane, I give him the freedom to choose anyone he wants.

Maître Jacques Let me handle it. [*Crosses to Cléante.*] Well, your father isn't as unreasonable as you make him out to be; and he told me that it was your outbursts that made him angry; that all he objects to is your way of acting; and that he will be quite disposed to grant you what you wish, provided you are willing to go about matters nicely, and show him the deference, respect, and submission that a son owes to his father.

Cléante Ah! Maître Jacques, you can assure him that if he grants me Mariane, he will always find me the most submissive of men, and that I will never do anything except by his wishes.

Maître Jacques [*to Harpagon*] That's done. He agrees to everything you say.

Harpagon That's just wonderful.

Maître Jacques [*to Cléante*] Everything is settled. He's satisfied with your promises.

Cléante Heaven be praised!

Maître Jacques Gentlemen, all you have to do is talk it over. Now you are agreed; and you were going to have a quarrel because you didn't understand each other.

Cléante Dear Maître Jacques, I shall be obliged to you all my life.

Maître Jacques Don't mention it, sir.

Harpagon You've given me great pleasure, Maître Jacques, and that deserves a reward. [*Feels in his pocket, while Maître Jacques holds out his hand; then pulls out his handkerchief.*] Go along with you; I'll remember this, I assure you.

Maître Jacques I kiss your hands.

SCENE FIVE
Cléante, Harpagon

Cléante I beg your pardon, father, for having lost my temper.

Harpagon That's nothing.

Cléante I assure you, I'm as sorry as I can be.

Harpagon And I'm as happy as I can be to find you reasonable.

Cléante How good of you to forget my fault so quickly!

Harpagon It's easy to forget children's faults when they remember their duty.

Cléante What? Do you bear me no resentment for all my outrageous conduct?

Harpagon You oblige me not to, by the submission and respect you show me.

Cléante I promise you, father, that to the grave I shall carry in my heart the memory of your goodness.

Harpagon And *I* promise *you* that there is nothing you may not obtain from me.

Cléante Ah! father, I ask nothing more of you; and you've given me enough by giving me Mariane.

Harpagon How's that?

Cléante I say, father, that I'm only too delighted with you, and that I find all I want in your kindness in granting me Mariane.

Harpagon Who says anything about granting you Mariane?

Cléante You, father.

Harpagon I?

Cléante Of course.

Harpagon What? You're the one who promised to give her up.

Cléante I, give her up?

Harpagon Yes.

Cléante Not at all.

Harpagon You haven't given up your hopes for her?

Cléante On the contrary, I'm more determined than ever.

Harpagon What, you blackguard? At it again?

Cléante Nothing can change me.

Harpagon Let me at you, you traitor.

Cléante Do what you like.

Harpagon I forbid you to come into my sight again.

Cléante That's fine with me.

Harpagon I abandon you.

Cléante Abandon all you like.

Harpagon I disown you as my son.

Cléante So be it.

Harpagon I disinherit you.

Cléante Whatever you like.

Harpagon And I give you my curse.

Cléante I have no use for your gifts.

SCENE SIX

La Flèche, Cléante

La Flèche [*coming from the garden with a money-box*] Ah, sir! I was just looking for you! Quick, follow me.

Cléante What's going on?

La Flèche Follow me, I tell you; we're in luck.

Cléante How's that?

La Flèche Here is what we need.

Cléante What?

La Flèche I've had my eye on this all day.

Cléante What is it?

La Flèche Your father's treasure, which I've nabbed.

Cléante How did you manage?

La Flèche I'll tell you everything. Let's run, I hear him shouting.

SCENE SEVEN

Harpagon

Harpagon [*shouting* "Stop, thief!" *from the garden, and coming in without his hat*] Stop, thief! Stop, thief! Assassin! Murderer! Justice, just Heaven! I'm ruined, I'm assassinated, they've cut my throat, they've stolen my money. Who can it be? What has become of him? Where is he? Where is he hiding? What shall I do to find him? Which way shall I run? Which way shall I not run? Isn't he there? Isn't he here? Who is it? Stop! [*Catches his own arm.*] Give me back my money, you scoundrel . . . Oh, it's me. My mind is troubled, and I don't know where I am, who I am, or what I'm doing. Alas! My poor money, my poor money, my dear friend! They've deprived me of you; and since you are taken from me, I've lost my support, my consolation, my joy; all is finished for me, and there's nothing more for me to do in the world; without you, it's impossible for me to live. It's all over, I can't go on; I'm dying, I'm dead, I'm buried. Isn't there anyone who will bring me back to life by giving me back my dear money, or by telling me who took it? Eh? What do you say? . . . It's no one. Whoever it was that did it, he must have watched his opportunity with great care; and he chose just the time when I was talking to my traitor of a son. Let's go out; I'm going to fetch the law, and have everyone in my house put to the torture: maidservants, valets, son, daughter, and myself too. [*Looking at the audience.*] What a lot of people assembled! There's no one my eyes light on but gives me suspicions, and everyone looks like my thief. Eh? What are they talking about over there? About the man who robbed me? What's that noise they're making up there? Is my thief there? For Heaven's

sake, if anyone has any news of my thief, I implore him to tell me. Isn't he hiding there among you? . . . They're all looking at me and laughing. You'll see, beyond a doubt they're all involved in my robbery. Let's go, quick, officers, policemen, provosts, judges, racks, gallows, and executioners. I'll have everybody hanged; and if I don't find my money, I'll hang myself afterward.

Act Five

SCENE ONE

Harpagon, the Officer, his Clerk

Officer Leave it to me: I know my job, thank God. Today's not the first time I've been involved in solving a theft; and I wish I had as many thousand-franc bags as I've had people hanged.

Harpagon It's in the interest of every magistrate to take this affair in hand; and if they don't get me my money back, I'll demand justice of justice itself.

Officer We must take all the necessary steps. You say there was in this money-box . . . ?

Harpagon Ten thousand crowns in cash.

Officer Ten thousand crowns!

Harpagon Ten thousand crowns.

Officer That's a considerable theft.

Harpagon There is no punishment great enough for the enormity of this crime; and if it remains unpunished, the most sacred things are no longer safe.

Officer In what denominations was this sum?

Harpagon In good louis d'or and pistoles of full weight.

Officer Whom do you suspect of this theft?

Harpagon Everyone; and I want you to arrest the whole town and the suburbs.

Officer If you'll take my advice, we must try not to frighten anyone, and seek quietly to collect some evidence, so as then to proceed with full rigor to recover the money that has been taken from you.

SCENE TWO

Maître Jacques, Harpagon, Officer, Clerk

Maître Jacques [*speaking to someone offstage as he enters*] I'll be back. I want his throat cut right away; I want his feet grilled, I want him put in boiling water, and then hung from the rafters.

Harpagon Who? The man who robbed me?

Maître Jacques I'm talking about a sucking pig that your steward has just sent me, and I want to fix him for you according to my fancy.

Harpagon We're not talking about that; and here is this gentleman, to whom there are other things to talk about.

Officer Don't be frightened. I'm not the man to cause a scandal, and things will be done quietly.

Maître Jacques Is the gentleman one of your supper party?

Officer In this matter, my good friend, you must hide nothing from your master.

Maître Jacques My word, sir! I'll show you all I know how to do, and I'll treat you as best I can.

Harpagon That's not the point.

Maître Jacques If I don't give you as good a meal as I'd like, that's the fault of that Mr. Steward of ours, who has clipped my wings with the scissors of his economy.

Harpagon Traitor, we're talking about something besides supper; and I want you to tell me some news about the money that was stolen from me.

Maître Jacques Somebody stole some money from you?

Harpagon Yes, you scoundrel; and I'm going to hang you if you don't give it back to me.

Officer [*to Harpagon*] Good Lord! Don't mistreat him. I can see from his face that he's an honest man, and that without having to be thrown into prison, he'll tell you what you want to know. [*To Maître Jacques.*] Yes, my friend, if you confess it all to us, you won't come to any harm, and you'll be suitably rewarded by your master. Somebody took his money today, and you can't help knowing something about this business.

Maître Jacques [*aside*] Here is just what I need to get revenge on our steward. Ever since he came here he's been the favorite; they listen only to his advice; and I also have that beating of a while ago on my mind.

Harpagon What are you ruminating about?

Officer Let him be. He's preparing to give you satisfaction; and I told you he was an honest man.

Maître Jacques Sir, if you want me to tell you how things are, I think it was your dear Mr. Steward who did the job.

Harpagon Valère?

Maître Jacques Yes.

Harpagon He, who seems so faithful to me?

Maître Jacques Himself. I think he's the one who robbed you.

Harpagon And on what grounds do you think so?

Maître Jacques On what grounds?

Harpagon Yes.

Maître Jacques I think so . . . on the grounds that I think so.

Officer But you have to say what evidence you have.

Harpagon Did you see him hanging around the place where I'd put my money?

Maître Jacques Yes indeed. Where was your money?

Harpagon In the garden.

Maître Jacques Exactly! I saw him hanging around the garden. And what was the money in?

Harpagon In a money-box.

Maître Jacques The very thing. I saw him with a money-box.

Harpagon And that money-box, what is it like? I can easily tell if it's mine.

Maître Jacques What is it like?

Harpagon Yes.

Maître Jacques It's like . . . it's like a money-box.

Officer That's understood. But describe it a bit so we can tell.

Maître Jacques It's a big money-box.

Harpagon The one stolen from me is small.

Maître Jacques Oh, yes, it's small, if you look at it that way; but I call it big for what it contains.

Officer And what color is it?

Maître Jacques What color?

Officer Yes.

Maître Jacques Its color is . . . well, a certain color . . . Can't you help me find the word?

Harpagon Huh?

Maître Jacques Isn't it red?

Harpagon No, gray.

Maître Jacques Why yes, grayish red: that's what I meant.

Harpagon There's no doubt whatever: that's certainly the one. Write it down, sir, write down his deposition. Heavens! Whom can I trust from now on? I mustn't swear to anything any more; and I think after this I'd be capable of robbing myself.

Maître Jacques Sir, here he comes back. For goodness' sake, don't go and tell him that I'm the one who told you this.

SCENE THREE

Valère, Harpagon, Officer, Clerk, Maître Jacques

Harpagon Come here! Come and confess the foulest action, the most horrible crime ever committed.

Valère What do you want, sir?

Harpagon What, traitor, don't you blush for your crime?

Valère Why, what crime are you talking about?

Harpagon What crime am I talking about, you wretch? As if you didn't know what I mean! There's no use your trying to disguise it; the business is uncovered, and I've just learned everything. How could you take advantage of my kindness so, and make your way into my house on purpose to betray me and play a trick like this on me?

Valère Sir, since the whole thing is revealed to you, I won't attempt to get around it and deny it.

Maître Jacques [*aside*] Oho! Could I have guessed right without realizing it?

Valère It was my intention to speak to you about it, and for that I wanted to wait for a favorable occasion; but since things are as they are, I conjure you not to be angry, and to be willing to hear my reasons.

Harpagon And what fine reasons can you give me, you infamous robber?

Valère Ah, sir! I have not deserved those names. It is true that I have committed an offense against you; but after all, my fault is pardonable.

Harpagon What, pardonable? An ambush, a murder like that one?

Valère Please don't get angry. When you've heard me, you'll see that the harm is not as great as you make it out.

Harpagon The harm is not as great as I make it out! What, you gallowsbird? My blood, my entrails?

Valère Your blood, sir, hasn't fallen into bad hands. I am of a rank that will do it no harm, and there is nothing in all this that I cannot well repair.

Harpagon That's my intention all right, and to have you restore what you've stolen from me.

Valère Your honor, sir, shall be fully satisfied.

Harpagon There's no question of honor in this. But tell me, what led you to this act?

Valère Alas! Can you ask?

Harpagon Yes indeed I do ask.

Valère A god who bears his own excuses for everything he makes people do: the god of Love.

Harpagon Love?

Valère Yes.

Harpagon A fine kind of love, a fine kind of love! My word! Love for my louis d'or!

Valère No, sir, it was not your riches that tempted me; that's not what dazzled me; and I protest that I have no aspirations to all your wealth, provided you leave me the one treasure I have.

Harpagon That I won't, by all the devils in hell! I won't leave it to you. Will you look at that insolence, to want to keep what he's stolen from me!

Valère Do you call that stealing?

Harpagon Do I call it stealing? A treasure like that?

Valère It's a treasure, that's true, and beyond a doubt the most precious that you have; but you won't be losing it by leaving it to me. On my knees I ask you for it, this most charming treasure; and to do right, you must grant it to me.

Harpagon I'll do nothing of the sort. What is all this?

Valère We have promised a mutual faith to each other, and have taken a vow never to abandon one another.

Harpagon That's a wonderful vow and a delightful promise!

Valère Yes, we've pledged ourselves to belong to one another forever.

Harpagon I'll put a stop to that, I assure you.

Valère Nothing but death can separate us.

Harpagon That's being devilishly enamored of my money.

Valère I've already told you, sir, that it was not self-interest that drove me to do what I did. My heart did not act for the reasons you think, and a nobler motive inspired that resolution in me.

Harpagon Next we'll find that it's out of Christian charity that he wants my money. But I'll take care of that; and the law, you barefaced rogue, will give me satisfaction for all this.

Valère You will do as you wish about that, and here I am ready to suffer all the violence you please; but I beg you to believe at least that if wrong has been done, I am the only one to accuse, and in all this your daughter is not at all to blame.

Harpagon Indeed, I can believe that; it would be mighty strange if my daughter had had a hand in this crime. But I want to have my own back, and for you to confess what spot you've used for a hiding-place.

Valère I? There is no hiding-place, and your treasure is still in your house.

Harpagon [*aside*] O my dear money-box! [*To Valère.*] Hasn't left my house?

Valère No, sir.

Harpagon Now, just tell me: you haven't touched . . . ?

Valère I, touched? Oh! You wrong us both; and the ardor with which I burn is wholly pure and respectful.

Harpagon [*aside*] Burn for my money-box!

Valère I'd rather die than show any offensive notion to one who is too decent and honorable for that!

Harpagon [*aside*] My money-box too honorable!

Valère I have limited my desires to feasting my eyes; and nothing criminal has profaned the passion that her lovely eyes have inspired in me.

Harpagon [*aside*] The lovely eyes of my money-box! He talks about it like a lover about a mistress!

Valère Dame Claude, sir, knows the truth of the matter, and she can testify to you that . . .

Harpagon What? My serving-woman is an accomplice in the affair?

Valère Yes, sir, she was a witness to our engagement; and it was after recognizing that my love was honorable that she helped me persuade your daughter to plight me her troth and receive mine.

Harpagon [*aside*] Eh! Is fear of the law making his mind wander? [*To Valère.*] What's all this gibberish about my daughter?

Valère I say, sir, that I had all the difficulty in the world in prevailing on her modesty to consent to what my love desired.

Harpagon Whose modesty?

Valère Your daughter's; and it was not until yesterday that she could make up her mind that we should sign a mutual promise of marriage.

Harpagon My daughter has signed you a promise of marriage?

Valère Yes, sir, even as I too have signed one for her.

Harpagon O Heavens! Another disgrace!

Maître Jacques [*to the Officer*] Write it down, sir, write it down.

Harpagon Trouble piled on trouble! Despair on despair! Come, sir, do the duty of your office, and draw me up the indictment against him as a thief and a suborner.

Valère Those names are not due me; and when it is known who I am . . .

SCENE FOUR

Élise, Mariane, Frosine, Harpagon, Valère, Maître Jacques, Officer, Clerk

Harpagon Ah, you wicked daughter! daughter unworthy of a father like me! So this is how you practice the lessons I've given you? You let yourself fall in love with an infamous thief, and you pledge him your troth without my consent? But you'll be surprised, both of you. [*To Élise.*] Four solid walls shall answer for your conduct; [*to Valère*] and a good gallows will give me satisfaction for your audacity.

Valère It will not be your passion that will judge the affair; and I shall at least be heard before being condemned.

Harpagon I was wrong to say the gallows, and you shall be broken alive on the wheel.

Élise [*on her knees before her father*] Ah! father, be a little more humane in your feelings, I implore you, and don't push matters to the utmost violence of paternal power. Don't surrender to the first impulses of your passion; give yourself time to consider what you mean to do. Take the trouble to have a better look at the man you are offended with: he is very different than he appears to your eyes; and you will find it less strange that I have given myself to him when you know that but for him you would long since have had me no longer. Yes, father, he's the one who saved me from that great peril I was in in the water, and to whom you owe the life of that very daughter whom . . .

Harpagon All that is nothing; and it would have been much better for me if he had let you drown than do what he's done.

Élise Father, I conjure you, by your paternal love, to . . .

Harpagon No, no, I won't hear a thing, and justice must take its course.

Maître Jacques [*aside*] You'll pay me for my beating.

Frosine [*aside*] Here's a fine kettle of fish.

SCENE FIVE

Anselme, Harpagon, Élise, Mariane, Frosine, Valère, Maître Jacques, Officer, Clerk

Anselme What is it, Seigneur Harpagon? I find you all upset.

Harpagon Ah! Seigneur Anselme, you see in me the most unfortunate of men; and here's a lot of confusion and disorder over the contract that you have come to sign. I'm being assassinated in my property, I'm being assassinated in my honor; and here is a traitor, a scoundrel, who has violated all the most sacred rights, who has wormed his way into my house under the title of a domestic to steal my money and suborn my daughter.

Valère Who's thinking of your money, that you're making such a strange fuss about?

Harpagon Yes, they've given each other a promise of marriage. This affront concerns you, Seigneur Anselme, and it is you who should become his prosecutor and bring a lawsuit against him to take revenge on his insolence.

Anselme It's not my plan to get myself married by force, and to lay any claim to a heart that has already given itself; but as regards your interests, I am ready to espouse them just like my own.

Harpagon This gentleman here is an honest officer who, from what he has told me, won't forget any part of the duty of his office. [*To the Officer.*] Charge him properly, sir, and make things good and criminal.

Valère I don't see what crime they can make of my passion for your daughter; and as for the punishment you think I may be condemned to for our engagement, when they know who I am . . .

Harpagon I don't care a rap for all these stories; and today the world is full of these people who steal their nobility, these impostors who take advantage of their obscurity to dress themselves insolently in the first illustrious name that comes into their head.

Valère Then know that I have too sound a heart to adorn myself with anything that isn't mine, and that all Naples can bear witness to my birth.

Anselme Easy now! Be careful of what you're going to say. You're taking a bigger risk than you think; and you're speaking in the presence of a man to whom all Naples is known, and who can easily see through any story you tell.

Valère [*proudly putting on his hat*] I am not the man to fear anything, and if Naples is known to you, you know who was Don Thomas d'Alburcy.

Anselme Indeed I do know; and few men have known him better than I.

Harpagon I don't care a rap about Don Thomas or Don Martin. [*He sees two candles burning, and blows one out.*]

Anselme Pray let him speak; we'll see what he wants to say about him.

Valère I want to say that he is the man who gave me life.

Anselme He?

Valère Yes.

Anselme Come, you're jesting. Try some other story that may succeed better, and don't hope to save yourself with this imposture.

Valère Be careful what you say. This is no imposture, and I'm asserting nothing that is not easy for me to justify.

Anselme What? You dare to call yourself the son of Don Thomas d'Alburcy?

Valère Yes, I dare; and I'm ready to maintain this truth against anyone at all.

Anselme This is amazing audacity. Then learn, to your confusion, that at least sixteen years ago the man you're telling us about perished at sea with his wife and children while trying to save their lives from the cruel persecutions that accompanied the disorders in Naples, and that caused many noble families to be exiled.

Valère Yes; but learn, to *your* confusion, that his son, seven years old, was saved from that shipwreck with one servant by a Spanish vessel, and that this son who was saved is the man speaking to you now; learn that the captain of that vessel, touched by my lot, took me into his friendship. He had me brought up as his own son, and arms were my profession as soon as I was old enough; I learned not long ago that my father was not dead, as I had always thought; passing through this town on my way to look for him, an accident arranged by Heaven made me see the charming Élise; the sight of her made me a slave to her beauty; and the violence of my love and the severities of her father made me resolve to enter his household and send someone else in quest of my parents.

Anselme But what other proofs, besides your words, can assure us that this is not some fable that you've built upon a truth?

Valère The Spanish captain; a ruby signet-ring that belonged to my father; an agate bracelet that my mother had put on my arm; old Pedro, the servant who escaped from the shipwreck with me.

Mariane Alas! from your words I myself can attest here and now that this is no imposition; and everything you say makes me know clearly that you are my brother.

Valère You, my sister?

Mariane Yes. My heart was stirred from the moment you opened your mouth; and our mother, who will be delighted to see you, has told me a thousand times about our family's misfortunes. Heaven did not make us perish either in that sad shipwreck; but it saved our lives only at the cost of our freedom; and it was pirates who picked us up, my mother and me, from a bit of the wreckage of our ship. After ten years of slavery, a happy chance restored our liberty to us, and we returned to Naples, where we found all our property sold, without being able to find any news of my father. We took passage to Genoa, where my mother went to collect some wretched remains of an inheritance that had been torn to bits; and from there, fleeing the barbaric injustice of her relatives, she came to these parts, where she has lived little better than a languishing life.

Anselme O Heaven! How great are the works of your power! And how well you show that it is for you alone to work miracles! Embrace me, my children, and both mingle your transports with those of your father.

Valère You are our father?

Mariane It's you my mother mourned so?

Anselme Yes, my daughter, yes, my son, I am Don Thomas d'Alburcy, whom Heaven saved from the waves with all the money he had on him, and who, having thought you all dead for more than sixteen years, was preparing, after much voyaging, to seek, in marriage with a sweet and decent woman, the consolation of a new family. The little safety I could see for my life if I returned to Naples made me renounce that place forever; and having managed to sell what I owned, I have settled down here, where, under the name of Anselme, I have tried to put aside the sorrows of that other name that has caused me so many misfortunes.

Harpagon That's your son?

Anselme Yes.

Harpagon I hold you responsible for paying me ten thousand crowns that he stole from me.

Anselme *He* stole from you?

Harpagon Himself.

Valère Who told you that?

Harpagon Maître Jacques.

Valère [*to Maître Jacques*] You're the one who says that?

Maître Jacques You see I'm not saying a thing.

Harpagon Oh, yes you did; here's the officer who took the deposition.

Valère Can you think me capable of such a cowardly act?

Harpagon Capable or not capable, I want my money back.

SCENE SIX

Cléante, Valère, Mariane, Élise, Frosine, Harpagon, Anselme, Maître Jacques, La Flèche, Officer, Clerk

Cléante Don't worry, father, and don't accuse anyone. I have learned news of your affair, and I come here to tell you that if you will make up your mind to let me marry Mariane, your money will be returned to you.

Harpagon Where is it?

Cléante Don't be concerned about it; it's in a place where I can answer for it, and everything depends on me alone. It's up to you to tell me what you decide; and you can choose either to give me Mariane or to lose your money-box.

Harpagon Hasn't anything been taken out of it?

Cléante Nothing at all. See whether it's your intention to agree to this marriage and join your consent to that of her mother, who gives her her freedom to make a choice between the two of us.

Mariane But you don't know that that consent is not enough, and that Heaven has just restored to me, together with a brother, whom you see, a father, from whom you must obtain me.

Anselme Heaven does not give me back to you, my children, to oppose your wishes. Seigneur Harpagon, you know very well that a young person's choice will fall on the son rather than on the father. Come, don't make anyone tell you what it is not necessary to hear, and consent, as I do, to this double marriage.

Harpagon To take counsel, I must see my money-box.

Cléante You shall see it safe and sound.

Harpagon I have no money to give my children in marriage.

Anselme Well, I have enough for them; don't let that worry you.

Harpagon Will you undertake to meet all the expenses of these two marriages?

Anselme Yes, I undertake that. Are you satisfied?

Harpagon Yes, provided you have a suit made for me for the weddings.

Anselme Agreed. Come, let's enjoy the bliss that this happy day offers us.

Officer Hold on, gentlemen! Hold on! Easy, if you please. Who is going to pay me for my depositions?

Harpagon We want no part of your depositions.

Officer Yes, but *I* don't intend to have taken them for nothing.

Harpagon [*pointing to Maître Jacques*] For your payment, here is a man I give you to hang.

Maître Jacques Alas! What is a man to do? They give me a beating for telling the truth, and they want to hang me for lying.

Anselme Seigneur Harpagon, you must forgive him for this imposture.

Harpagon Then you'll pay the officer?

Anselme So be it. Let's go quickly and share our joy with your mother.

Harpagon And I, to see my dear money-box.

The Would-Be Gentleman

CHARACTERS

Monsieur Jourdain, a bourgeois
Madame Jourdain, his wife
Lucile, their daughter
Nicole, a maidservant
Cléonte, in love with Lucile
Covielle, Cléonte's valet
Dorante, a count, in love with Dorimène
Dorimène, a marquise
Music Master
Music Master's Pupil
Dancing Master
Fencing Master
Philosophy Master
Master Tailor
Journeyman Tailor
Two Lackeys
Several *Singers, Instrumentalists, Dancers, Cooks, Tailor's Apprentices,* and other characters in the ballets

The scene is Paris, in Monsieur Jourdain's home.

Act One

The overture is played by a large group of instruments. The Music Master's Pupil is seen at center stage, at a table, composing a tune that Monsieur Jourdain has commissioned for a serenade.

SCENE ONE

Music Master, Dancing Master, three Singers, two Violinists, four Dancers

Music Master [*to his musicians*] Come on, come into this room and rest here until he comes.

Dancing Master [*to his dancers*] And you, too, on this side.

Music Master [*to the Pupil*] Is it done?

Pupil Yes.

Music Master Let's see . . . That's fine.

Dancing Master Is it something new?

Music Master Yes, it's an air for a serenade that I had him compose here while we're waiting for our man to wake up.

Dancing Master May I see what it is?

Music Master You'll hear it, with the words, when he comes. He won't be long.

Dancing Master Ours are no small jobs now.

Music Master That's true. We've found here just the man we both need. This Monsieur Jourdain is a nice income for us, with the visions of nobility and gallantry that he's taken into his head; and your dance and my music might well wish that everyone was like him.

Dancing Master Not entirely; and I wish he had more understanding than he does of the things we offer him.

Music Master It's true that he understands them badly, but he pays for them well; and that's what our arts need nowadays more than anything else.

Dancing Master As for me, I confess, I get some enjoyment out of appreciation; I care about applause; and I maintain that in all the fine arts it's a pretty painful torture to display ourselves to fools, to endure the barbarous reaction of a stupid man to our compositions. There is pleasure—don't tell me there isn't—in working for people who are capable of sensing the fine points of an art, who can offer a sweet reception to the beauties of a work, and, by gratifying approval, repay you for your labor. Yes, the most delightful reward you can receive for the things you do is to see them understood, to see them fêted by an applause that honors you. There is nothing, in my opinion, that pays us better than that for all our fatigues; and enlightened praises are exquisite delights.

Music Master I agree, and I relish them as you do. There is certainly nothing as gratifying as the applause you speak of. But that adulation does not keep you alive; praise by itself does not make a man well off; you have to mix in something solid; and the best way to praise is to praise with the open hand. Indeed, this is a man of scant understanding, who talks nonsense about everything and applauds only the wrong things; but his money corrects the judgments of his mind; there is discernment in his purse; he praises in cash; and this ignorant bourgeois is worth more to us, as you see, than the enlightened noble lord who brought us in here.

Dancing Master There is something in what you say; but I think you put too much emphasis on money; and self-interest is such a base thing that an honorable man should never show any attachment for it.

Music Master All the same, you are perfectly willing to receive the money our man gives you.

Dancing Master Certainly; but I don't set all my happiness in it, and I wish that with all his money he also had a little taste.

Music Master I wish he did too, and that's what we're both working for as best we can. But in any case, he's giving us a chance to make ourselves known in society; and on behalf of the others he will pay for what the others will praise for him.

Dancing Master Here he comes.

SCENE TWO

Monsieur Jourdain, two Lackeys, Music Master, Dancing Master, Violinists, Singers, and Dancers

Monsieur Jourdain Well, gentlemen, what is it to be? Will you show me your little funny business?

Dancing Master What? What little funny business?

Monsieur Jourdain Why, the . . . what you may call it, your prologue or dialogue of song and dance.

Dancing Master Aha!

Music Master You find us all ready.

Monsieur Jourdain I've kept you waiting a little, but that's because today I'm having myself dressed like people of quality; and my tailor has sent me some silk stockings that I thought I'd never get on.

Music Master We are here only to await your leisure.

Monsieur Jourdain I ask you both not to go away until they've brought me my coat, so you can see me in it.

Dancing Master Whatever you please.

Monsieur Jourdain You'll see me decked out right from head to foot.

Music Master We've no doubt of it.

Monsieur Jourdain [*showing his dressing-gown*] I've had this India print made up for me.

Dancing Master It's very handsome.

Monsieur Jourdain My tailor told me that people of quality went around like this in the morning.

Music Master It's most becoming to you.

Monsieur Jourdain Lackeys! Hey, my two lackeys!

First Lackey What do you wish, sir?

Monsieur Jourdain Nothing. It was just to see if you hear me all right. [*To the two Masters.*] What do you think of my liveries?

Dancing Master They're magnificent.

Monsieur Jourdain [*opening his dressing-gown and displaying his tight red velvet breeches and green velvet jacket*] And here's a little casual outfit to do my exercises in in the morning.

Music Master Very gallant.

Monsieur Jourdain Lackeys!

First Lackey Sir?

Monsieur Jourdain The other lackey!

Second Lackey Sir?

Monsieur Jourdain Hold my gown. [*To the Masters.*] How do I look this way?

Dancing Master Very good; couldn't be better.

Monsieur Jourdain Let's have a look at this thing of yours.

Music Master First I'd like you to hear an air he has just composed for the serenade you asked me for. He's one of my pupils who has a remarkable talent for this kind of thing.

Monsieur Jourdain Yes; but you shouldn't have had it done by a pupil, and you're not too good to have done the job yourself.

Music Master You mustn't let the word *pupil* mislead you, sir. Pupils of this kind know as much about it as the greatest masters, and this air is as beautiful as can be. Just listen.

Monsieur Jourdain Give me my gown so I'll hear better

. . . Wait, I think I'll be better without a gown . . . No, give it back to me, that'll be better.

Singer

I languish night and day; great is my woe
Since my enslavement to your cruelties;
If thus you treat someone who loves you so,
How, Iris, must you treat your enemies?

Monsieur Jourdain That song seems a bit lugubrious to me; it puts a man to sleep, and I wish you could liven it up a bit here and there.

Music Master Sir, the music must be suited to the words.

Monsieur Jourdain I learned a really pretty one some time ago. Wait . . . la, la . . . how does it go?

Dancing Master My word, I don't know!

Monsieur Jourdain There's lamb in it.

Dancing Master Lamb?

Monsieur Jourdain Yes. Ah! [*Sings.*]

I thought my little Pam
Was sweet as she was fair,
I thought my little Pam
Was sweet as any lamb.
Alas! There's nothing like her,
None crueler anywhere;
She's worse than any tiger!

Isn't that pretty?

Music Master Couldn't be prettier.

Dancing Master And you sing it well.

Monsieur Jourdain That's without having learned music.

Music Master You should learn it, sir, just as you are learning the dance. These are two closely related arts.

Dancing Master And they open a man's mind to beautiful things.

Monsieur Jourdain Do people of quality learn music too?

Music Master Yes, sir.

Monsieur Jourdain Then I'll learn it. But I don't know where I'll find the time; for besides the fencing master who's teaching me, I've also taken on a philosophy master, who's due to begin this morning.

Music Master Philosophy is something; but music, sir, music . . .

Dancing Master Music and the dance . . . Music and the dance, that's all you need.

Music Master There's nothing so useful in a state as music.

Dancing Master There's nothing so necessary to men as the dance.

Music Master Without music a state cannot subsist.

Dancing Master Without the dance a man couldn't do anything.

Music Master All the disorders, all the wars we see in the world come only from not learning music.

Dancing Master All the misfortunes of men, all the deadly disasters that history is full of, the blunders of politicians, the mistakes of great captains—all these have come just from not knowing how to dance.

Monsieur Jourdain How's that?

Music Master Doesn't war come from a lack of union among men?

Monsieur Jourdain That's true.

Music Master And if all men learned music, wouldn't that be the way to achieve concord, and to see universal peace in the world?

Monsieur Jourdain You're right.

Dancing Master When a man has committed a lapse in conduct, whether in his family affairs, or in the government of a state, or in the command of an army, don't people always say: "So-and-so has made a misstep in such-and-such a matter?"

Monsieur Jourdain Yes, people say that.

Dancing Master And making a misstep, can that come from anything but not knowing how to dance?

Monsieur Jourdain That's true, you're both right.

Dancing Master That's to show you the excellence and utility of dancing and music.

Monsieur Jourdain I understand that now.

Music Master Do you want to see our two things?

Monsieur Jourdain Yes.

Music Master I've told you already, this is a little essay I once composed on the various passions that music can express.

Monsieur Jourdain Very good.

Music Master [*to the Singers*] Come on, step forward. [*To Monsieur Jourdain.*] You must imagine that they're dressed as shepherds.

Monsieur Jourdain Why always shepherds? That's all you see everywhere.

Dancing Master When you have people speak to music, for verisimilitude you have to go in for the pastoral. Singing has always been assigned to shepherds; and it's hardly natural in dialogue for princes or bourgeois to sing their passions.

Monsieur Jourdain All right, all right. Let's see.

DIALOGUE IN MUSIC
between a *Woman Singer* and two *Men Singers*

Woman

A heart that love holds in its sway
To countless cares must always be a prey;
They talk as though we sigh and languish pleasantly,
And yet, for all they say,
Nothing is quite so sweet as to be free.

First Man

Nothing is quite so sweet as the tender passion
That lovingly can fashion
One single heart of two.
Without loving desires there is no happiness:

Take love from life and you'll confess
You take away its pleasures too.

Second Man

It would be sweet to enter love's domain
If, seeking faith in love, we did not seek in vain;
But alas! Cruel heartlessness!
One cannot find a faithful shepherdess,
And that inconstant sex, unworthy to be born,
Should make men give up love in utter scorn.

First Man

Longing so sweet,

Woman

Freedom and bliss,

Second Man

Sex full of deceit,

First Man

What's dearer than this?

Woman

How you exalt me!

Second Man

How you revolt me!

First Man

Ah! for the sake of love give up this hatefulness.

Woman

You can be made to see
A faithful shepherdess.

Second Man

Alas! Where can she be?

Woman

Since our sex is so maligned,
Here: I give my heart to you.

Second Man

Shepherdess, but shall I find
That it will be always true?

Woman

Well, let's try it out and see
Which of us is the truer lover.

Second Man

Whichever fails in constancy,
Over that one may the gods' wrath hover!

All Three Singers

So fair is love's dart,
Let's yield to its heat;
Ah! loving is sweet
For the faithful in heart!

Monsieur Jourdain Is that all?

Music Master Yes.

Monsieur Jourdain I think it's well worked out, and there are some rather pretty little remarks in it.

Dancing Master Here, for my piece, is a little attempt to show the most beautiful movements and attitudes with which a dance can be varied.

Monsieur Jourdain Is it still shepherds?

Dancing Master They're whatever you like. [*To the Dancers.*] Let's go.

Four Dancers execute all the different movements and all the kinds of steps that the Dancing Master directs them to. This dance makes up the First Interlude.

SCENE ONE

Monsieur Jourdain, Music Master, Dancing Master, Lackeys

Monsieur Jourdain Now that's not bad at all, and those fellows really jig around well.

Music Master When the dance is combined with music, that will be even more effective, and you'll see something gallant in the little ballet we've arranged for you.

Monsieur Jourdain That's for later, anyway; and the person for whom I've had all this done is to do me the honor of coming to dinner here.

Dancing Master Everything's ready.

Music Master Furthermore, sir, this is not enough. A person like you, who does things in a big way and who has an inclination for beautiful things, should give a concert at home every Wednesday or Thursday.

Monsieur Jourdain Do people of quality have them?

Music Master Yes, sir.

Monsieur Jourdain Then I'll have some. Will it be good?

Music Master Beyond a doubt. You'll need three voices: á soprano, an alto, and a bass, which will be accompanied by a bass viol, a theorbo, and a harpsichord for the sustained bass, with two violins to play the refrains.

Monsieur Jourdain We'll have to put in a trumpet marine too. The trumpet marine is an instrument I like, and it's harmonious.

Music Master Let us decide things.

Monsieur Jourdain Anyway, don't forget to send me some musicians soon to sing at table.

Music Master You'll have everything you need.

Monsieur Jourdain But above all, see that the ballet is nice.

Music Master You'll be pleased with it, and, among other things, with certain minuets you'll see in it.

Monsieur Jourdain Ah! The minuet is my dance, and I want you to see me dance it. [*To the Dancing Master.*] Come on, Master.

Dancing Master A hat, sir, if you please. [*Monsieur Jourdain takes a Lackey's hat and puts it on over his nightcap, removing it for the deep bows involved in the dance. The Dancing Master takes his hand, sings the music, and gives directions.*] La, la, la; La, la, la, la, la, la; La, la, la, once again; La, la, la; La, la. Keep time, if you please. La, la, la, la. Your leg straight. La, la, la. Don't move your shoulders so much. La, la, la, la, la; La, la, la, la, la. Your arms look crippled. La, la, la, la, la. Lift your head. Turn your toes out. La, la, la. Body straight.

Monsieur Jourdain Euh?

Music Master That couldn't be better.

Monsieur Jourdain By the way. Teach me how I should make a bow to greet a marquise; I'll soon need it.

Dancing Master A bow to greet a marquise?

Monsieur Jourdain Yes, a marquise named Dorimène.

Dancing Master Give me your hand.

Monsieur Jourdain No. All you have to do is do it; I'll remember.

Dancing Master If you want to greet her with great respect, you must first make a bow stepping backward, then walk toward her with three forward bows, and on the last one bow to the level of her knees.

Monsieur Jourdain Just do it for me. Good.

First Lackey Sir, here's your fencing master.

Monsieur Jourdain Tell him to come in here and give me my lesson. [*To the Dancing Master and the Music Master.*] I want you to watch me perform.

SCENE TWO

Fencing Master, Music Master, Dancing Master, Monsieur Jourdain, two Lackeys

Fencing Master [*after putting a foil in Monsieur Jourdain's hand*] Come, sir, the salute. Body straight. Weight a bit more on the left thigh. Legs not so far apart. Your feet on the same line. Your wrist in line with your hip. The point of your sword level with your shoulder. Arm not extended quite so far. Left hand at eye level. Left shoulder more in quart. Head up. Confident look. Forward. Body firm. Engage my foil in quart, and follow through. One, two. Recover. Thrust again, feet firm. A jump back. When you make your thrust, sir, the sword must start first, and the body must be out of the way. One, two. Come on, engage my foil in tierce, and follow through. Forward. Body firm. Forward. Lunge from there. One, two. Recover. Thrust again. A jump back. On guard, sir, on guard. [*As he calls* "On guard," *the Fencing Master scores two or three touches on Monsieur Jourdain.*]

Monsieur Jourdain Euh?

Music Master You're doing wonders.

Fencing Master I've told you already, the whole secret of swordplay consists in just two things: in giving, and in not receiving; and as I showed you the other day by demonstrative reasoning, it is impossible for you to receive if you know how to turn your opponent's sword away from the line of your body; which depends simply on a tiny movement of your wrist either to the inside or to the outside.

Monsieur Jourdain Then in that way a man, without being brave, is sure of killing his man and not being killed?

Fencing Master Absolutely. Didn't you see the demonstration?

Monsieur Jourdain Yes.

Fencing Master And it's in that way that you see how much consideration we should enjoy in a state, and how far superior the science of arms is to all the useless sciences like dancing, music, and . . .

Dancing Master Gently, Mr. Sword-Waver; don't speak of the dance except with respect.

Music Master I pray you, learn to speak better of the excellence of music.

Fencing Master You are funny people, to try to compare your sciences with mine.

Music Master Just look at this very important person!

Dancing Master That's a funny-looking beast, with his chest-protector!

Fencing Master My little dancing master, I could teach you how to dance! And you, my little musician, I could really make you sing!

Dancing Master Mr. Swashbuckler, I'll teach you your trade!

Monsieur Jourdain [*to the Dancing Master*] Are you mad, to pick a fight with him, when he understands tierce and quart, and knows how to kill a man by demonstrative reasoning?

Dancing Master I don't care a rap for his demonstrative reasoning or his tierce and his quart.

Monsieur Jourdain Gently, I tell you.

Fencing Master What? You impertinent little . . . !

Monsieur Jourdain There now, Fencing Master!

Dancing Master What? You big cart horse!

Monsieur Jourdain There now, Dancing Master!

Fencing Master If I jump on you . . .

Monsieur Jourdain Gently!

Dancing Master If I lay a hand on you . . .

Monsieur Jourdain Easy!

Fencing Master I'll tan your hide so . . .

Monsieur Jourdain Please!

Dancing Master I'll give you such a drubbing . . .

Monsieur Jourdain I beg you!

Music Master Just let us be and we'll teach him how to talk!

Monsieur Jourdain Good Lord! Stop it!

SCENE THREE

Philosophy Master, Music Master, Dancing Master, Fencing Master, Monsieur Jourdain, Lackeys

Monsieur Jourdain Hello, Mr. Philosopher, you've come in the nick of time with your philosophy. Come here a minute and make peace between these people.

Philosophy Master Why, what is it? What's wrong, gentlemen?

Monsieur Jourdain They've gotten angry over the preference of their professions, to the point of exchanging insults and wanting to come to blows.

Philosophy Master How now, gentlemen! Should a man become so angry? And haven't you read the learned treatise that Seneca composed on anger? Is there anything more base and shameful than this passion, which turns a man into a wild beast? And shouldn't reason be the mistress of all our impulses?

Dancing Master Why, sir, he comes and insults us both, sneering at the dance, which I practice, and at music, which is *his* profession!

Philosophy Master A wise man is above all the insults that may be paid him; and the great response we should make to affronts is moderation and patience.

Fencing Master They both have the audacity to want to compare their professions with mine.

Philosophy Master Should that move you? It is not over vainglory and rank that men should dispute among themselves; what distinguishes us perfectly from one another is wisdom and virtue.

Dancing Master I maintain against him that the dance is a science to which one cannot pay too much honor.

Music Master And I, that music is one that all ages have revered.

Fencing Master And I maintain against them that the science of arms is the most beautiful and necessary of all sciences.

Philosophy Master And what is philosophy to be then? I find all three of you mighty impertinent to speak with such arrogance in my presence and impudently to give the name of science to things that should not even be honored with the name of art, and that can only be comprised under the name of miserable trades of gladiator, singer, and mountebank!

Fencing Master Go on, you dog of a philosopher!

Music Master Go on, you good-for-nothing pedant!

Dancing Master Go on, you egregious pedagogue!

Philosophy Master What? Why, you rascals . . . [*He throws himself upon them, and all three beat him, continuing until their exit.*]

Monsieur Jourdain Mr. Philosopher!

Philosophy Master Wretches! Insolent scoundrels!

Monsieur Jourdain Mr. Philosopher!

Fencing Master Confound the brute!

Monsieur Jourdain Gentlemen!

Philosophy Master Impudent clowns!

Monsieur Jourdain Mr. Philosopher!

Dancing Master Devil take the stupid ass!

Monsieur Jourdain Gentlemen!

Philosophy Master Blackguards!

Monsieur Jourdain Mr. Philosopher!

Music Master The devil with him and his impertinence!

Monsieur Jourdain Gentlemen!

Philosophy Master Rogues! Beggars! Traitors! Impostors!

Monsieur Jourdain Mr. Philosopher, Gentlemen, Mr. Philosopher, Gentlemen, Mr. Philosopher!

Exit the four Masters, still fighting.

Oh, fight all you please! There's nothing I can do about it, and I'm not going to ruin my gown trying to separate you. I'd be mighty crazy to butt in there among them and get a smack that would hurt me.

SCENE FOUR

Philosophy Master, Monsieur Jourdain

Philosophy Master [*straightening his neckband as he returns*] Let's get to our lesson.

Monsieur Jourdain Ah, sir, I'm sorry about the blows they gave you.

Philosophy Master That's nothing. A philosopher knows how to take things as they come, and I'm going to compose a satire against them in the style of Juvenal, which will really tear them to shreds. Enough of that. What do you want to learn?

Monsieur Jourdain Everything I can, for I'm just dying to be learned; and I'm furious that my father and mother didn't make me study every kind of learning when I was young.

Philosophy Master That's a reasonable sentiment: *Nam sine doctrina vita est quasi mortis imago.* You understand that, and you know Latin, no doubt.

Monsieur Jourdain Yes, but act as though I didn't know it: explain to me what that means.

Philosophy Master That means that without knowledge, life is little but an image of death.

Monsieur Jourdain That Latin is right.

Philosophy Master Haven't you some first principles, some rudiments of the sciences?

Monsieur Jourdain Oh, yes! I know how to read and write.

Philosophy Master Where do you want to begin? Do you want me to teach you logic?

Monsieur Jourdain What is this logic?

Philosophy Master That's what teaches us the three operations of the mind.

Monsieur Jourdain What are these three operations of the mind?

Philosophy Master The first, the second, and the third. The first is sound conception by means of universals. The second, sound judgment by means of categories; and the third, sound drawing of consequences by means of the figures *Barbara, Celarent, Darii, Ferio, Baralipton,* and so forth.

Monsieur Jourdain Those words are too crabbed. I don't like that logic. Let's learn something else that's prettier.

Philosophy Master Do you want to learn moral philosophy?

Monsieur Jourdain Moral philosophy?

Philosophy Master Yes.

Monsieur Jourdain What does this moral philosophy say?

Philosophy Master It treats of happiness, teaches men to moderate their passions, and . . .

Monsieur Jourdain No, let's leave that alone. I'm as bilious as all the devils in hell; and I don't care what moral philosophy says, I want to get as angry as I like when I feel like it.

Philosophy Master Is it physics that you want to learn?

Monsieur Jourdain What kind of business is this physics about?

Philosophy Master Physics is the science which explains the principles of natural things and the properties of bodies; which discourses on the nature of the elements, of metals, minerals, stones, plants, and animals, and teaches us the causes of all the meteors, rainbows, will-o'-the-wisps, comets, lightning, thunder, thunderbolts, rain, snow, hail, winds, and whirlwinds.

Monsieur Jourdain There's too much racket in that, too much hullabaloo.

Philosophy Master Then what do you want me to teach you?

Monsieur Jourdain Teach me spelling.

Philosophy Master Most gladly.

Monsieur Jourdain After that, you'll teach me the almanac, so I'll know when there's a moon and when there isn't.

Philosophy Master Very well. To follow your idea properly and treat this matter as a philosopher should, we must begin according to the order of these things, by an exact knowledge of the nature of the letters and the different ways in which they are all pronounced. And on that point I have this to tell you, that the letters are divided into vowels, so called because they express the voiced sounds, and into consonants, so called because they sound with the vowels and merely mark the various articulations of the voiced sounds. There are five vowels or voiced sounds: A, E, I, O, U.

Monsieur Jourdain I understand all that.

Philosophy Master The vowel A, pronounced *Ah,* is formed by opening the mouth wide: A.

Monsieur Jourdain A, A. Yes.

Philosophy Master The vowel E, pronounced *Euh,* is formed by bringing the lower jaw close to the upper one: A, E.

Monsieur Jourdain A, E, A, E. My word, yes! Ah, how beautiful that is!

Philosophy Master And the vowel I, pronounced *Ee,* by bringing the jaws even closer together and stretching the corners of the mouth toward the ears: A, E, I.

Monsieur Jourdain A, E, I, I, I, I. That's true! Long live learning!

Philosophy Master The vowel O is formed by opening the

jaws again and bringing the lips closer together both at the corners and above and below: O.

Monsieur Jourdain O, O. Nothing could be more true. A, E, I, O, I, O. That's admirable! I, O, I, O.*

Philosophy Master The opening of the mouth makes precisely a sort of little circle that represents an O.

Monsieur Jourdain O, O, O. You're right. O. Ah, what a beautiful thing it is to know something!

Philosophy Master The vowel U, pronounced Ü,† is formed by bringing the teeth close together but not quite touching, and sticking out both lips, bringing them also close to each other but not quite touching: U.

Monsieur Jourdain U, U. There's nothing truer than that. U.

Philosophy Master Your two lips stick out as if you were making a pout; whence it comes about that if you want to make that kind of a face at someone and deride him, all you can say to him is: U.

Monsieur Jourdain U, U. That's true. Ah! Why didn't I study earlier, to know all that?

Philosophy Master Tomorrow we'll have a look at the other letters, which are the consonants.

Monsieur Jourdain Are there as curious things about them as about these?

Philosophy Master Beyond a doubt. The consonant D, for example, is pronounced by applying the tip of the tongue above the upper teeth: DA.

Monsieur Jourdain DA, DA. Yes. Ah! Beautiful! Simply beautiful!

Philosophy Master The F, by pressing the upper teeth on the lower lip: FA.

Monsieur Jourdain FA, FA. It's the truth! Ah, Father and Mother, how I blame you!

Philosophy Master And the R, by raising the tip of the tongue

* Here the actor imitates a donkey's bray.

† The French *u*, which is like the German *ue* or *ü*.

up against the upper palate, so that, being brushed by the air as it comes out with force, it yields to it, and always returns to the same place, making a kind of vibration: RRA.

Monsieur Jourdain R, R, RA; R, R, R, R, RA. That's true! Oh, what an able man you are! And how much time I've wasted! R, R, R, RA.

Philosophy Master I'll explain all these curious facts to you thoroughly.

Monsieur Jourdain Please do. By the way, I must confide in you. I'm in love with a person of high quality, and I'd like you to help me write her something in a little note I want to drop at her feet.

Philosophy Master Very well.

Monsieur Jourdain It will be gallant, yes?

Philosophy Master Beyond a doubt. Is it verse that you want to write her?

Monsieur Jourdain No, no, no verse.

Philosophy Master You want only prose?

Monsieur Jourdain No, I don't want either prose or verse.

Philosophy Master It has to be one or the other.

Monsieur Jourdain Why?

Philosophy Master For the reason, sir, that there is nothing to express ourselves in but prose or verse.

Monsieur Jourdain There's nothing but prose or verse?

Philosophy Master That's right, sir: whatever isn't prose is verse, and whatever isn't verse is prose.

Monsieur Jourdain And the way we talk, what's that then?

Philosophy Master Prose.

Monsieur Jourdain What? When I say: "Nicole, bring me my slippers and give me my nightcap," that's prose?

Philosophy Master Yes, sir.

Monsieur Jourdain Bless my soul! I've been talking prose for over forty years without knowing it, and I'm ever so grateful to you for teaching me that. So: I'd like to put in a note to her: "Lovely marquise, your beautiful eyes make me die of love"; but I'd like to have that put in a gallant style, and nicely turned.

Philosophy Master Say that the flames from her eyes reduce your heart to ashes; that you suffer for her night and day the torment of a . . .

Monsieur Jourdain No, no, no, I don't want all that; I just want what I told you: "Lovely marquise, your beautiful eyes make me die of love."

Philosophy Master You really should extend the thing a bit.

Monsieur Jourdain No, I tell you, all I want in the note is just those words; but fashionably turned, nicely arranged in the proper style. Please just tell me, to give me an idea, the various ways that can be put.

Philosophy Master First of all, you can put them just as you've said: "Lovely marquise, your beautiful eyes make me die of love." Or else: "Of love make me die, lovely marquise, your beautiful eyes." Or else: "Your eyes beautiful of love make me, lovely marquise, die." Or else: "Die your beautiful eyes, lovely marquise, of love make me." Or else: "Make me your beautiful eyes die, lovely marquise, of love."

Monsieur Jourdain But of all those ways, which is the best?

Philosophy Master The one you said: "Lovely marquise, your beautiful eyes make me die of love."

Monsieur Jourdain And yet I've never studied, and I did that at the very first try. I thank you with all my heart, and please come early tomorrow.

Philosophy Master I shall not fail to. *Exit.*

Monsieur Jourdain [*to his Lackeys*] What? Hasn't my coat arrived yet?

Second Lackey No, sir.

Monsieur Jourdain That confounded tailor is certainly keeping me waiting, for a day when I have so much to do. That makes me mad. A quartan fever seize that blackguard of a tailor! Devil take the tailor! A plague on the tailor! If I had him here now, that detestable tailor, that dog of a tailor, that traitor of a tailor, I'd . . .

SCENE FIVE

Master Tailor, Journeyman Tailor (carrying Monsieur Jourdain's coat), Monsieur Jourdain, Lackeys

Monsieur Jourdain Ah, there you are! I was just about to get angry with you.

Master Tailor I couldn't come any sooner, and I've had twenty of my men at work on your coat.

Monsieur Jourdain The silk stockings you sent me were so tight that I had all the trouble in the world getting them on, and there are already two stitches broken.

Master Tailor They'll stretch all you need, and more.

Monsieur Jourdain Yes, if I keep breaking stitches. Also, the shoes you made me hurt terribly.

Master Tailor Not at all, sir.

Monsieur Jourdain What do you mean, not at all?

Master Tailor No, they don't hurt you.

Monsieur Jourdain And *I* tell *you* they hurt me.

Master Tailor You're imagining it.

Monsieur Jourdain I imagine it because I feel it. That's a fine kind of talk!

Master Tailor Look, here is the handsomest coat in all the court, and the best harmonized. It's a masterpiece to have invented a dignified coat that isn't black, and I defy the most creative tailors to match it in half a dozen tries.

Monsieur Jourdain What in the world is this? You've put the flowers upside down.

Master Tailor You didn't tell me you wanted them right side up.

Monsieur Jourdain Is that something you have to specify?

Master Tailor Yes, really. All persons of quality wear them this way.

Monsieur Jourdain Persons of quality wear the flowers upside down?

Master Tailor Yes, sir.

Monsieur Jourdain Oh, then that's fine.

Master Tailor If you wish, I'll put them right side up.

Monsieur Jourdain No, no.

Master Tailor You have only to say so.

Monsieur Jourdain No, I tell you; you did right. Do you think the coat will look well on me?

Master Tailor A fine question! I defy a painter with his brush to make you anything more becoming. I have one man who for putting together petticoat-breeches is the greatest genius in the world, and another who for assembling a doublet is the hero of our age.

Monsieur Jourdain Are the wig and the plumes as they should be?

Master Tailor Everything is fine.

Monsieur Jourdain [*looking at the Master Tailor's coat*] Aha, Mr. Tailor! There's some of my material from the last coat you made me. I recognize it all right.

Master Tailor The fact is that the material seemed to me so beautiful that I decided to cut a coat from it for me.

Monsieur Jourdain Yes, but you shouldn't have cut it from my material.

Master Tailor Do you want to try on your coat?

Monsieur Jourdain Yes, give it to me.

Master Tailor Wait. It doesn't go on that way. I've brought some men to dress you to music, and this kind of coat is to be put on with ceremony. Hello there! Come in, all of you. Put this coat on the gentleman in the way you do for persons of quality.

Four Tailor's Apprentices enter, of whom two take off the breeches worn for Monsieur Jourdain's exercises, and two others the jacket; then they put his new coat on him; and he promenades among them and shows off his coat to them to see if it looks good—all this to the music of the whole orchestra.

Journeyman Tailor Will the gentleman* please give the apprentices something to drink his health with?

Monsieur Jourdain What did you call me?

Journeyman Tailor The gentleman.

Monsieur Jourdain "The gentleman!" That's what it means to be gotten up as a person of quality! Just go on always dressing as a bourgeois, and nobody will call you "the gentleman." Here, that's for "the gentleman."

Journeyman Tailor My Lord, we're much obliged to you.

Monsieur Jourdain "My Lord," oh, oh, "My Lord!" Wait, my friend: "My Lord" deserves something, and that's no small term, "My Lord." Here, this is what My Lord gives you.

Journeyman Tailor My Lord, we're all going to drink to the health of Your Eminence.

Monsieur Jourdain "Your Eminence!" Oh, oh, oh! Wait, don't go away. "Your Eminence" to me! My word, if he goes on as far as "Your Highness," he'll get the whole purse. Here, this is for My Eminence.

Journeyman Tailor My Lord, we thank you very humbly for your liberality.

Monsieur Jourdain A good thing he stopped; I was going to give him the whole thing.

The four Tailor's Apprentices express their joy in a dance that constitutes the Second Interlude.

* See note in *The Miser,* Act I, scene 5.

Act Three

SCENE ONE
Monsieur Jourdain, Lackeys

Monsieur Jourdain Follow me while I go and show off my coat a bit around town; and above all be careful both of you to walk immediately in my footsteps so that people can clearly see that you belong to me.

Lackeys Yes, sir.

Monsieur Jourdain Call Nicole for me, so I can give her a few orders. . . . Don't move, here she is.

SCENE TWO
Nicole, Monsieur Jourdain, Lackeys

Monsieur Jourdain Nicole!

Nicole What is it?

Monsieur Jourdain Listen.

Nicole Hee, hee, hee, hee, hee!

Monsieur Jourdain What are you laughing at?

Nicole Hee, hee, hee, hee, hee, hee!

Monsieur Jourdain What does that hussy mean?

Nicole Hee, hee, hee! The way you're dressed! Hee, hee, hee!

Monsieur Jourdain How's that?

Nicole Oh, oh, Lord have mercy! Hee, hee, hee, hee, hee!

Monsieur Jourdain What kind of a rascal is this? Are you making fun of me?

Nicole No, sir, I'd hate to do that. Hee, hee, hee, hee, hee, hee!

Monsieur Jourdain I'll give you one on the nose if you laugh any more.

Nicole Sir, I can't help it. Hee, hee, hee, hee, hee, hee!

Monsieur Jourdain Aren't you going to stop?

Nicole Sir, I ask your pardon; but you look so funny that I can't keep from laughing. Hee, hee, hee!

Monsieur Jourdain Will you look at that insolence!

Nicole You're really a sketch like that. Hee, hee!

Monsieur Jourdain I'll . . .

Nicole I beg you to excuse me. Hee, hee, hee, hee!

Monsieur Jourdain Look here, if you laugh the least bit more, I swear I'll give you the biggest slap that ever was given.

Nicole Well, sir, it's all over, I won't laugh any more.

Monsieur Jourdain Take good care that you don't. Now, to get ready, you must clean . . .

Nicole Hee, hee!

Monsieur Jourdain Clean up properly . . .

Nicole Hee, hee!

Monsieur Jourdain You must, I say, clean up the parlor, and . . .

Nicole Hee, hee!

Monsieur Jourdain Again!

Nicole Look here, sir, just beat me and let me laugh to my heart's content. That'll do me more good. Hee, hee, hee, hee, hee!

Monsieur Jourdain I'm getting mad.

Nicole Please, sir, I beg you to let me laugh. Hee, hee, hee!

Monsieur Jourdain If I catch you . . .

Nicole Sir-ir, I'll blow-ow up if I don't laugh. Hee, hee, hee!

Monsieur Jourdain Why, did anyone ever see such a hussy as that? She comes and laughs insolently in my face, instead of taking orders from me!

Nicole What do you want me to do, sir?

Monsieur Jourdain To think, you wench, about getting my house ready for the company that's due to come soon.

Nicole Ah, faith! I've no more wish to laugh; and all your company makes such a mess in here that that word is enough to put me in a bad humor.

Monsieur Jourdain I suppose that for your sake I should close my door to everybody?

Nicole You should at least close it to certain people.

SCENE THREE

Madame Jourdain, Monsieur Jourdain, Nicole, Lackeys

Madame Jourdain Aha! Here's a new one! What in the world, my dear husband, is that get-up? Is this some kind of joke, to have got yourself decked out like that, and do you want to have people everywhere make fun of you?

Monsieur Jourdain My dear wife, there's none but the fools, male and female, who'll make fun of me.

Madame Jourdain Well, really, they haven't waited until now to do it, and it's been a long time now that your carryings-on have been making everybody laugh.

Monsieur Jourdain And just who is this *everybody,* if you please?

Madame Jourdain This everybody is people who are right, and who have more sense than you. For my part, I'm scandalized at the life you're leading. I don't know what our house is any more; you'd think it was Mardi Gras every day; and from morning on, for fear we might miss it, we hear a great uproar of fiddlers and singers that disturbs the whole neighborhood.

Nicole Madame is quite right. I can't keep my house clean any more, with that train of people that you invite home. They have feet that go hunting for mud in every quarter of town to bring it here; and poor Françoise is almost worn out scrubbing the floors that your fine masters come and muddy up regularly every day.

Monsieur Jourdain Well now, Nicole, our servant, you've got a mighty sharp line of chatter for a peasant girl.

Madame Jourdain Nicole is right, and she has better sense than you. I'd like to know what you think you can do with a dancing master at your age.

Nicole And with a great big master sword player, who comes stamping around and shakes the whole house and loosens all the tiles in the parlor floor?

Monsieur Jourdain Be quiet, my maidservant and my wife.

Madame Jourdain Do you want to learn dancing for the time when your legs are gone?

Nicole Or do you have a hankering to kill somebody?

Monsieur Jourdain Be quiet, I tell you: you are both ignoramuses, and you don't know the prerogatives of all that.

Madame Jourdain You should much rather be thinking of marrying off your daughter, who's of an age to be provided with a husband.

Monsieur Jourdain I'll think about marrying off my daughter when a good match for her comes along; but I also want to think about learning the finer things of life.

Nicole I've also heard, Madame, that to top it off, today he took on a philosophy master.

Monsieur Jourdain Indeed I did. I want to have wit and be able to reason about things among people of culture.

Madame Jourdain Won't you be going to school one of these days and having yourself whipped, at your age?

Monsieur Jourdain Why not? Would God I could get whipped right now in front of everybody, and know the things they learn in school!

Nicole Faith, yes! That would do you a lot of good!

Monsieur Jourdain Undoubtedly.

Madame Jourdain All that is mighty necessary for running your house!

Monsieur Jourdain Of course it is. You're both talking like fools, and I'm ashamed of your ignorance. [*To Madame Jourdain.*] For example, you, do you know what it is you're saying right now?

Madame Jourdain Yes, I know that what I'm saying is very well said, and that you should do some thinking about living in a different way.

Monsieur Jourdain I'm not talking about that. I'm asking you, what are the words that you're saying now?

Madame Jourdain They're very sensible words, and your conduct is scarcely that.

Monsieur Jourdain I'm not talking about that, I tell you. I ask you: what I speak with you, what I'm saying to you right now, what is it?

Madame Jourdain Stuff and nonsense.

Monsieur Jourdain Oh, no, it's not that! What we're both saying, the language we're speaking right now?

Madame Jourdain Well?

Monsieur Jourdain What is that called?

Madame Jourdain That's called whatever you want to call it.

Monsieur Jourdain It's prose, ignoramus.

Madame Jourdain Prose?

Monsieur Jourdain Yes, prose. Everything that's prose is not verse; and everything that's not verse is not prose. Well, that's what it means to study. [*To Nicole.*] And you, do you know what you have to do to say U?

Nicole How's that?

Monsieur Jourdain Yes. What do you do when you say U?

Nicole What?

Monsieur Jourdain Just say U, to see.

Nicole Well then, U.

Monsieur Jourdain Well, what is it you do?

Nicole I say U.

Monsieur Jourdain Yes; but when you say U, what do you do?

Nicole I do what you tell me.

Monsieur Jourdain Oh, what a strange business it is to have to deal with idiots! You thrust your lips out and bring the upper jaw close to the lower one: U. Do you see? U. I make a pout: U.

Nicole Yep, that's real purty.

Madame Jourdain That *is* admirable.

Monsieur Jourdain It's something else again if you'd seen O, and DA, DA, and FA, FA.

Madame Jourdain What *is* all this rigmarole?

Nicole What does all this cure you of?

Monsieur Jourdain It makes me mad to see ignorant women.

Madame Jourdain Go on, you ought to send all those people on their way, with their tomfoolery.

Nicole And especially that great lout of a fencing master, who fills my whole house with dust.

Monsieur Jourdain Well, you've certainly got that fencing master on the brain. I want to show you how impertinent you are right now. [*He has the foils brought and gives one to Nicole.*] Here you are. Demonstrative reasoning, the line of the body. When you thrust in quart, all you have to do is this; and when you thrust in tierce, all you have to do is this.

That's the way never to get killed; and isn't that fine, to be certain of how you'll come out when you fight with somebody? There, try a thrust at me, to see.

Nicole [*making several thrusts at Monsieur Jourdain, and as many touches*] Well, what about it?

Monsieur Jourdain Easy now! Hold on! Oh, gently! Devil take the hussy!

Nicole You told me to thrust.

Monsieur Jourdain Yes, but you're thrusting in tierce before thrusting in quart, and you won't wait for me to parry.

Madame Jourdain You're crazy, my dear husband, with all your fancies; and this has all happened to you since you've been taking it into your head to hang around the nobility.

Monsieur Jourdain When I hang around the nobility, I show my judgment, and that's better than hanging around your bourgeoisie.

Madame Jourdain Oh yes indeedy! There's a lot to be gained by going around with your noblemen, and you've done good business with that fine Monsieur le Comte that you're so stuck on.

Monsieur Jourdain Peace. Think what you're saying. Do you know, my dear wife, that you don't know whom you're talking about when you talk about him? He's a person of more importance than you think, a lord who's well considered at court, and who talks to the King just as I'm talking to you. Isn't that a very honorable thing for me, for people to see a person of such quality coming to my house so often, calling me his dear friend, and treating me as if I were his equal? You'd never guess how good he is to me; and in front of everybody he shows me regards that leave me embarrassed myself.

Madame Jourdain Yes, he's good to you and shows you regards; but he borrows your money.

Monsieur Jourdain Well! Isn't it an honor for me to lend money to a man of that rank? And can I do less for a lord who calls me his dear friend?

Madame Jourdain And this lord, what does he do for you?

Monsieur Jourdain Things that would astonish people, if they knew them.

Madame Jourdain And what are they?

Monsieur Jourdain Enough. I can't explain it all. Sufficient that if I've lent him money, he'll give it back to me all right, and before long.

Madame Jourdain Yes, just count on that.

Monsieur Jourdain Of course; hasn't he told me so?

Madame Jourdain Yes, yes; he won't fail—not to do so.

Monsieur Jourdain He's given me his word as a gentleman.

Madame Jourdain Fiddlesticks!

Monsieur Jourdain Well now, you are mighty obstinate, my good wife. I tell you he'll keep his word, I'm sure.

Madame Jourdain And *I'm* sure he won't, and that all the attentions he shows you are only to cajole you.

Monsieur Jourdain Be quiet; here he is.

Madame Jourdain That's all we need. Perhaps he's coming to get another loan from you; and I lose my appetite when I see him.

Monsieur Jourdain Be quiet, I tell you.

SCENE FOUR

Dorante, Monsieur Jourdain, Madame Jourdain, Nicole

Dorante My dear friend Monsieur Jourdain,* how are you?

Monsieur Jourdain Very well, sir, at your service.

Dorante And Madame Jourdain here, how is she?

* As a form of address, *Monsieur* (or *Madame*) alone was polite in Molière's day; the form *Monsieur* (or *Madame*) *Jourdain* was pointedly impolite. Of course Monsieur Jourdain, in addressing Dorante, uses the polite form *Monsieur* (Sir) alone.

Madame Jourdain Madame Jourdain is doing as well as she can.

Dorante Well, Monsieur Jourdain, how elegant you are!

Monsieur Jourdain As you see.

Dorante You look very smart in that coat, and we have no young men at court who are better turned out than you are.

Monsieur Jourdain Heh, heh!

Madame Jourdain [*aside*] He scratches him where he itches.

Dorante Turn around. That's utterly gallant.

Madame Jourdain [*aside*] Yes, just as stupid from the rear as from the front.

Dorante Upon my word, Monsieur Jourdain, I was extraordinarily impatient to see you. You are the man I esteem the most in all the world, and I was talking about you just this morning in the King's bedchamber.

Monsieur Jourdain You do me great honor, sir. [*To Madame Jourdain.*] In the King's bedchamber!

Dorante Come now, put on your hat.

Monsieur Jourdain Sir, I know the respect that I owe you.

Dorante Good Lord, put it on! No ceremony between us, pray.

Monsieur Jourdain Sir . . .

Dorante Put it on, I tell you, Monsieur Jourdain; you are my friend.

Monsieur Jourdain Sir, I am your humble servant.

Dorante I won't put mine on unless you do.

Monsieur Jourdain [*putting his hat on*] I'd rather be uncivil than a nuisance.

Dorante I'm your debtor, as you know.

Madame Jourdain [*aside*] Yes, we know it only too well.

Dorante You have generously lent me money on several occasions, and you have certainly obliged me with the best grace in the world.

Monsieur Jourdain Sir, you're joking.

Dorante But I know how to repay what is lent me, and to recognize favors done me.

Monsieur Jourdain I don't doubt it, sir.

Dorante I want to settle things up with you, and I've come here to clear up our accounts together.

Monsieur Jourdain [*to Madame Jourdain*] Well! You see how silly you were, my good wife.

Dorante I'm a man who likes to pay up his debts as soon as he can.

Monsieur Jourdain [*to Madame Jourdain*] I told you so!

Dorante Let's see now, what do I owe you?

Monsieur Jourdain [*to Madame Jourdain*] There you are with your ridiculous suspicions!

Dorante Do you have a good recollection of all the money you've lent me?

Monsieur Jourdain I think so. I've kept a little memorandum. Here it is. Given to you once, two hundred louis.

Dorante That's true.

Monsieur Jourdain Another time, six score.

Dorante Yes.

Monsieur Jourdain And another time, a hundred and forty.

Dorante You're right.

Monsieur Jourdain These three items make four hundred and sixty louis, which come to five thousand and sixty francs.

Dorante The accounting is very good indeed. Five thousand and sixty francs.

Monsieur Jourdain One thousand eight hundred and thirty-two francs to your plume-seller.

Dorante Precisely.

Monsieur Jourdain Two thousand seven hundred and eighty francs to your tailor.

Dorante That's true.

Monsieur Jourdain Four thousand three hundred and seventy-nine francs twelve sous eight deniers to your clothier.

Dorante Very good. Twelve sous eight deniers: the account is exact.

Monsieur Jourdain And one thousand seven hundred and forty-eight francs seven sous four deniers to your saddler.

Dorante That's all exactly right. What does it come to?

Monsieur Jourdain Sum total, fifteen thousand eight hundred francs.

Dorante Sum total is correct: fifteen thousand eight hundred francs. Now, add another two hundred pistoles that you're going to give me, that will make precisely eighteen thousand francs, which I'll pay you the first chance I get.

Madame Jourdain [*to Monsieur Jourdain*] Well! Didn't I guess it all right?

Monsieur Jourdain [*to Madame Jourdain*] Peace!

Dorante Will that inconvenience you, to give me what I've mentioned?

Monsieur Jourdain Oh, no!

Madame Jourdain [*to Monsieur Jourdain*] This man milks you like a cow.

Monsieur Jourdain Be quiet.

Dorante If it's inconvenient for you, I'll look elsewhere.

Monsieur Jourdain No, sir.

Madame Jourdain [*to Monsieur Jourdain*] He won't be content until he's ruined you.

Monsieur Jourdain [*to Madame Jourdain*] Shut up, I tell you.

Dorante You have only to tell me if it embarrasses you.

Monsieur Jourdain Not at all, sir.

Madame Jourdain [*to Monsieur Jourdain*] He's a real wheedler.

Monsieur Jourdain [*to Madame Jourdain*] Shut up, you.

Madame Jourdain [*to Monsieur Jourdain*] He'll suck you dry to your last sou.

Monsieur Jourdain [*to Madame Jourdain*] Will you shut up?

Dorante I have plenty of people who would be overjoyed to lend me money; but since you are my best friend, I thought I would wrong you if I asked anyone else.

Monsieur Jourdain You do me too much honor, sir. I'll go get what you want.

Madame Jourdain [*to Monsieur Jourdain*] What? Are you going to give him that too?

Monsieur Jourdain [*to Madame Jourdain, as he makes his exit*] What am I to do? Do you want me to refuse a man of that rank, who talked about me this morning in the King's bedchamber?

Madame Jourdain Go on, you're a real dupe.

SCENE FIVE

Dorante, Madame Jourdain, Nicole

Dorante You seem quite melancholy. What's the matter, Madame Jourdain?

Madame Jourdain My head's bigger than my fist, and it's not swollen at that.

Dorante And your charming daughter, where is she? I don't see her.

Madame Jourdain My charming daughter is fine where she is.

Dorante How is she getting along?

Madame Jourdain She's getting along on her own two legs.

Dorante Don't you want to come with her one of these days to see the ballet and comedy that are being performed before the King?

Madame Jourdain Yes indeed, we really want to laugh, really want to laugh we do.

Dorante I think, Madame Jourdain, you had plenty of suitors in your younger days, pretty and good-humored as you were.

Madame Jourdain Land's sakes, sir! Is Madame Jourdain decrepit and doddering already?

Dorante Ah! Faith, Madame Jourdain, I beg your pardon. I wasn't thinking that you're still young, and I'm very absentminded. I beg you to excuse my impertinence.

SCENE SIX

Monsieur Jourdain, Madame Jourdain, Dorante, Nicole

Monsieur Jourdain Here are two hundred louis exactly.

Dorante I assure you, Monsieur Jourdain, that I'm at your service, and I'm burning to do you a favor at court.

Monsieur Jourdain I'm only too obliged to you.

Dorante If Madame Jourdain wants to see the entertainment before the King, I'll see that she gets the best seats in the house.

Madame Jourdain Madame Jourdain kisses your hands.

Dorante [*aside to Monsieur Jourdain*] Our fair marquise, as I told you in my note, will come here soon for the ballet and the meal, and I finally got her to consent to the party you want to give her.

Monsieur Jourdain [*aside to Dorante*] Let's go a little farther away, for good reason.

Dorante It's a week since I've seen you, and I haven't told you the latest about the diamond you placed in my hands to present to her on your behalf; but the fact is I've had all the trouble in the world in overcoming her scruples, and it's only today that she's made up her mind to accept it.

Monsieur Jourdain How did she like it?

Dorante She thought it was wonderful; and unless I'm much mistaken, the beauty of that diamond will set you high in her regard.

Monsieur Jourdain Would God!

Madame Jourdain [*to Nicole*] Once he's with him, he can't leave him.

Dorante I made the most to her of the richness of this present and the greatness of your love.

Monsieur Jourdain These are kindnesses, sir, that overwhelm me; and I am most greatly embarrassed to see a person of your rank lower himself for my sake to do what you're doing.

Dorante Are you joking? Between friends, does one stop at this sort of scruple? And wouldn't you do the same thing for me if the occasion should arise?

Monsieur Jourdain Oh, certainly, and with all my heart!

Madame Jourdain [*to Nicole*] How his presence weighs on me!

Dorante For my part, I don't worry about anything when a friend needs a service; and when you confided to me the passion you had formed for this charming marquise whom I knew, you saw that right away I freely offered myself to serve your love.

Monsieur Jourdain That's true, these are kindnesses that embarrass me.

Madame Jourdain [*to Nicole*] Won't he ever go away?

Nicole [*to Madame Jourdain*] They like to be together.

Dorante You took the right approach to touch her heart. Above all else women like the expenditures people make for them; and your frequent serenades and continual bouquets, that superb display of fireworks on the water, the diamond she has received on your behalf, and the party you are preparing for her—all this speaks to her far better in favor of your love than any words you might have said to her yourself.

Monsieur Jourdain There are no expenditures I would not make if thereby I could find the way to her heart. A woman of quality has ravishing charms for me, and it's an honor I would buy at any price.

Madame Jourdain [*to Nicole*] What can they be talking about for so long? Go up quietly and lend an ear a bit.

Dorante You will soon enjoy at your ease the pleasure of seeing her, and your eyes will have all the time you want to be satisfied.

Monsieur Jourdain To be completely free, I've arranged for my wife to go and dine at her sister's and stay on the whole time after dinner.

Dorante You have acted prudently, and your wife might have embarrassed us. I've given the necessary orders for you to the cook, and for all the things that are needed for the ballet. It's a composition of my own; and provided the execution comes up to my idea, I'm sure it will be found . . .

Monsieur Jourdain [*noticing that Nicole is listening, and giving her a slap*] Well, you're mighty impertinent! [*To Dorante.*] Let's get out of here, if you please.

SCENE SEVEN

Madame Jourdain, Nicole

Nicole Faith, Madame! Curiosity cost me something; but I think I smell a rat, and they're talking about some affair where they don't want you to be.

Madame Jourdain Today's not the first time, Nicole, that I've had suspicions about my husband. Unless I'm utterly mistaken, he's trying to promote some amour, and I'm trying to find out what it may be. But let's think about my daughter. You know about Cléonte's love for her. He's a man I like, and I want to help his suit and give him Lucile if I can.

Nicole To tell the truth, Madame, I'm most delighted to see that this is your feeling; for if you like the master, I like the valet no less, and I could wish that our marriage might take place in the shadow of theirs.

Madame Jourdain Go and speak to him for me, and tell him to come and see me as soon as he can, so that together we can ask my husband for my daughter's hand.

Nicole I'll run and do it with joy, Madame, and I couldn't be given a pleasanter errand.

Exit Madame Jourdain.

I think I'm going to make the men very happy.

SCENE EIGHT

Cléonte, Covielle, Nicole

Nicole Ah, there you are, just at the right time. I am a bearer of joyful news, and I come . . .

Cléonte Go away, perfidious girl, and don't come and beguile me with your traitorous words.

Nicole Is that the way you receive . . . ?

Cléonte Go away, I tell you. Go to your faithless mistress right away and tell her that she will never again in her life delude the too simple Cléonte.

Nicole What sort of caprice is that? My poor dear Covielle, give me some idea of what this means.

Covielle My poor dear Covielle! You little minx! Come on, quick, get out of my sight, wretched girl, and leave me in peace!

Nicole What? You too . . . !

Covielle Get out of my sight, I tell you, and never speak to me again in your life!

Nicole Well! What's bitten the two of them? Let's go and inform my mistress of this fine how-do-you-do.

SCENE NINE

Cléonte, Covielle

Cléonte What? Treat a sweetheart in that way, and a sweetheart who is the most faithful and passionate of all sweethearts!

Covielle It's a frightful thing, what they're doing to the two of us.

Cléonte I reveal for a certain person all the ardor and all the tenderness imaginable; I love nothing in the world but her, and have her alone in my mind; she constitutes all my cares, all my desires, all my joy; I speak of her alone, think of her alone, dream of her alone, breathe through her alone, my heart lives in her alone: and this is the fitting reward for so much affection! I go two days without seeing her, which for me are two frightful centuries; I meet her by chance; my heart, at the sight of her, is all transported, my joy bursts out on my face, I fly toward her in ecstasy; and the faithless creature turns her eyes away from me and passes brusquely by, as if she had never seen me in her life!

Covielle I say the same things as you do.

Cléonte Is it possible, Covielle, for anything to match this perfidy of the ingrate Lucile?

Covielle Or that, sir, of that hussy Nicole?

Cléonte After so many ardent sacrifices, sighs, and vows that I've offered to her charms!

Covielle After so many assiduous homages, so many attentions and services I've done for her in the kitchen!

Cléonte So many tears that I've shed at her knees!

Covielle So many buckets of water that I've drawn from the well for her!

Cléonte So much ardor I've shown in cherishing her more than myself!

Covielle So much heat I've endured turning the spit in place of her!

Cléonte She flees me with disdain!

Covielle She turns her back on me with effrontery!

Cléonte It's perfidy worthy of the greatest punishments.

Covielle It's a betrayal that deserves a thousand slaps in the face.

Cléonte Don't ever take it into your head, I pray you, to speak to me on her behalf.

Covielle I, sir! God forbid!

Cléonte Don't come to me with excuses for this faithless girl's action.

Covielle Have no fear.

Cléonte No, you see, all you may say to defend her will be no use.

Covielle Who has that in mind?

Cléonte I want to preserve my resentment against her, and break off all relations with her.

Covielle I consent to that.

Cléonte Perhaps that Monsieur le Comte who goes to her house has caught her eye; and her mind, I can see, is letting itself be dazzled by rank. But, for my own honor, I must forestall the revelation of her inconstancy. I mean to keep step with her in this change toward which I see her hurrying, and not let her have all the glory of leaving me.

Covielle That's very well said, and I, on my own account, share all your feelings.

Cléonte Lend a hand to my spite, and support my resolve against any remains of love that might speak to me on her behalf. Tell me, I beseech you, all the bad things you can about her; paint me a portrait of her person that will make her contemptible to me; and point out to me clearly, to destroy my taste for her, all the defects you can see in her.

Covielle She, sir! She's a girl who puts on a lot of airs, an affected bit of goods, a fine one for you to be so much in love with! I see nothing in her that isn't very ordinary, and you can find a hundred girls that will be more worthy of you. In the first place, her eyes are small.*

Cléonte That's true, her eyes are small; but they're full of fire;

* There is a tradition that what follows is a portrait of Molière's wife Armande, who played Lucile.

they're the most brilliant, the most piercing in the world, the most touching to be seen anywhere.

Covielle Her mouth is large.

Cléonte Yes; but there are graces to be seen in it that you don't see in other mouths; and that mouth, when you see it, inspires desires, is the most attractive, the most loving in the world.

Covielle As for her figure, it's not tall.

Cléonte No, but it's graceful and well built.

Covielle She affects nonchalance in her speech and in her actions.

Cléonte That's true; but she does so with grace, and her manners are engaging; they have an indefinable charm that insinuates itself into the heart.

Covielle As for wit . . .

Cléonte Ah, that she has, Covielle, of the most subtle and delicate kind.

Covielle Her conversation . . .

Cléonte Her conversation is charming.

Covielle She's always serious.

Cléonte Do you want broad playfulness, everlasting expansive gaiety? And do you find anything sillier than women who laugh at everything?

Covielle But finally, she's as capricious as anybody in the world.

Cléonte Yes, she is capricious, I agree; but in beautiful women everything looks good, we put up with anything from beautiful women.

Covielle Since that's the way it goes, I see perfectly well that you want to love her forever.

Cléonte I? I'd rather die; and I'm going to hate her as much as I've loved her.

Covielle And how, if you find her so perfect?

Cléonte That's how my revenge will be the more brilliant, and how I mean to show my strength of heart all the better, by hating her, by leaving her, beautiful, attractive, and lovable as I find her to be . . . Here she is.

SCENE TEN

Cléonte, Lucile, Covielle, Nicole

Nicole For my part, I was utterly scandalized.

Lucile It can only be what I'm telling you, Nicole. But here he is.

Cléonte [*to Covielle*] I won't even speak to her.

Covielle I'll follow your example.

Lucile Why, what is it, Cléonte? What's the matter?

Nicole What's wrong with you, Covielle?

Lucile What makes you so distressed?

Nicole What's put you in such a bad humor?

Lucile Are you struck dumb, Cléonte?

Nicole Have you lost your tongue, Covielle?

Cléonte What a crime!

Covielle What a couple of Judases!

Lucile I see perfectly well that our recent encounter has troubled your mind.

Cléonte Aha! They see what they've done.

Nicole Our greeting this morning got your goat.

Covielle They've guessed where the shoe pinches.

Lucile Isn't it true, Cléonte, that that's the cause of your vexation?

Cléonte Yes, perfidious woman, it is, since speak I must. And let me tell you that you shall not triumph in your faithlessness as you expect, that I mean to be the first to break with you, and that you shall not have the advantage of sending me away. No doubt I'll have trouble in conquering the love

I have for you, it will cause me distress, I shall suffer for a time; but I'll get over it, and I'll sooner pierce my own heart than be so weak as to return to you.

Covielle Same here.

Lucile That's a lot of fuss over nothing. I want to tell you, Cléonte, what it was made me avoid your greeting this morning.

Cléonte No, I won't listen to a thing.

Nicole I want to let you know the reason we went by so quickly.

Covielle I won't hear a thing.

Lucile Know that this morning . . .

Cléonte No, I tell you.

Nicole Learn that . . .

Covielle No, traitress.

Lucile Listen!

Cléonte No such thing.

Nicole Let me speak.

Covielle I'm deaf.

Lucile Cléonte!

Cléonte No.

Nicole Covielle!

Covielle Not a bit.

Lucile Stop!

Cléonte Nonsense!

Nicole Hear me!

Covielle Fiddlesticks!

Lucile One moment.

Cléonte Not at all.

Nicole A little patience.

Covielle Bunk.

Lucile Two words!

Cléonte No, it's all over.

Nicole One word!

Covielle We're all through.

Lucile Well! Since you won't listen to me, keep on thinking what you're thinking, and do as you please.

Nicole Since that's how you're acting, take it any way you like.

Up to this point the girls have been following the young men around the stage; from now on the young men follow the girls.

Cléonte All right, let's know the reason for such a fine greeting.

Lucile I don't feel like telling it any more.

Covielle All right, just tell us this story.

Nicole Me, I don't want to tell it to you any more.

Cléonte Say what . . .

Lucile No, I won't say a thing.

Covielle Tell me . . .

Nicole No, I'm not telling a thing.

Cléonte Please.

Lucile No, I tell you.

Covielle Out of charity . . .

Nicole Nothing doing.

Cléonte I beg you.

Lucile Let me be.

Covielle I conjure you.

Nicole Get out of here.

Cléonte Lucile!

Lucile No.

Covielle Nicole!

Nicole Not a bit.

Cléonte In the name of the gods!

Lucile I won't.

Covielle Speak to me.

Nicole Not at all.

Cléonte Clear up my doubts.

Lucile No, I'll do nothing of the sort.

Covielle Cure my mind.

Nicole No, I don't feel like it.

Cléonte Well! Since you care so little about ending my pain and justifying yourself for your unworthy treatment of my flame, you see me, ingrate, for the last time, and I'm going far away from you to die of grief and love.

Covielle And I'm going to follow in his footsteps.

Lucile Cléonte!

Nicole Covielle!

Cléonte Eh?

Covielle What is it?

Lucile Where are you going?

Cléonte Where I told you.

Covielle We're going to die.

Lucile You're going to die, Cléonte?

Cléonte Yes, cruel girl, since you want it.

Lucile *I* want you to die?

Cléonte Yes, you want it.

Lucile Who says so?

Cléonte Isn't it wanting it not to want to clear up my suspicions?

Lucile Is that my fault? If you'd been willing to listen to me, wouldn't I have told you that the incident this morning that you're complaining about was caused by the presence of an old aunt of mine who absolutely insists that the mere approach of a man dishonors a girl, who preaches us sermons perpetually on this subject, and who pictures all men to us as devils whom we must flee.

Nicole That's the secret of the matter.

Cléonte You're not deceiving me, Lucile?

Covielle You're not handing me a line?

Lucile Nothing could be more true.

Nicole That's the thing as it is.

Covielle [*to Cléonte*] Do we give in to this?

Cléonte Ah, Lucile! With one word from your lips, how many things you can appease in my heart! And how easily we let ourselves be persuaded by the persons we love!

Covielle How easily we get softened up by these confounded creatures!

SCENE ELEVEN

Madame Jourdain, Cléonte, Lucile, Covielle, Nicole

Madame Jourdain I'm very glad to see you, Cléonte, and you're here at the right time. My husband's coming; take your chance quickly to ask him for Lucile's hand in marriage.

Cléonte Ah, Madame, how sweet these words are to me, and how they flatter my desires! Could I receive a more charming order, a more precious favor?

SCENE TWELVE

Monsieur Jourdain, Madame Jourdain, Cléonte, Lucile, Covielle, Nicole

Cléonte Sir, I didn't want to get anyone else to make a request of you that I have long been meditating. It concerns me closely enough for me to take it on myself; and so, without beating around the bush further, I will tell you that the honor of being your son-in-law is a glorious favor that I beg you to grant me.

Monsieur Jourdain Before giving you an answer, sir, I ask you to tell me if you are a gentleman.

Cléonte Sir, most people don't hesitate much on this question. The word is easy to throw around. People have no scruples about assuming this title, and usage today seems to authorize the theft of it. For my part, I admit, I have slightly more delicate feelings about this matter. I think that any imposture is unworthy of an honorable man, and that there is cowardice in disguising what Heaven had us born to be, in adorning ourselves in the eyes of the world with a stolen title, in trying to pass ourselves off for what we are not. To be sure, I was born of ancestors who have held honorable positions. I have acquired the honor of six years of service under arms, and I have enough means to hold a pretty passable position in society. But with all that, I don't want to give myself a title that others in my place would feel entitled to assume, and I will tell you frankly that I am not a gentleman.

Monsieur Jourdain Shake on it, sir; my daughter is not for you.

Cléonte How's that?

Monsieur Jourdain You're not a gentleman, you shall not have my daughter.

Madame Jourdain What are you talking about with your gentleman business? Are *we* sprung from Saint Louis's rib?

Monsieur Jourdain Be quiet, wife; I can see you coming.

Madame Jourdain Are we both descended from anything but good bourgeois?

Monsieur Jourdain There goes your tongue!

Madame Jourdain And wasn't your father a tradesman just like mine?

Monsieur Jourdain Plague take the woman! She's never failed. If your father was a tradesman, too bad for him; but as for mine, it's only the ill-informed who say so. As for me, all I have to say to you is that I want to have a gentleman for my son-in-law.

Madame Jourdain Your daughter needs a husband who is suited to her, and she'd be much better off with an honorable man who is rich and attractive than with a beggarly and unattractive gentleman.

Nicole That's true. In our village we have the gentleman's son who's the biggest oaf and the stupidest lout I've ever seen.

Monsieur Jourdain Shut up, you, with your impertinence. You're always butting into the conversation. I have enough money for my daughter, all I need is honor, and I want to make her a marquise.

Madame Jourdain A marquise?

Monsieur Jourdain Yes, a marquise.

Madame Jourdain Alas! God forbid!

Monsieur Jourdain It's something I've decided on.

Madame Jourdain It's something *I'll* never consent to. Marriages above your station are always subject to unpleasant drawbacks. I don't want a son-in-law to be able to reproach my daughter for her parents, and for her to have children who are ashamed to call me their grandma. If she had to come and visit me decked out like a grand lady, and by mistake failed to greet someone in the neighborhood, right away people wouldn't fail to say a hundred stupid things. "Do you see that Madame la Marquise," they'd say, "with her high and mighty airs? That's Monsieur Jourdain's daughter, who was only too happy, when she was little, to play at being a fine lady with us. She wasn't always as lofty as she is now, and both her grandfathers used to sell cloth by the Porte Saint-Innocent. They piled up some wealth for their children, which they may be paying mighty dear for now in the other world, and you just don't get that rich by being honest folk." I don't want all that gossip; and in a word, I want a man who will feel obliged to me for my daughter, and to whom I can say: "Sit down there, my son-in-law, and have dinner with me."

Monsieur Jourdain Those are certainly the sentiments of a petty mind, to want to remain always in lowliness. Don't answer me further; my daughter shall be a marquise in spite of everybody; and if you get me angry, I'll make her a duchess. *Exit.*

Madame Jourdain Cléonte, don't lose heart yet. Follow me, my daughter, and come and tell your father resolutely that if you don't get him, you won't marry anyone.

SCENE THIRTEEN

Cléonte, Covielle

Covielle You made a fine success of it with your fine sentiments.

Cléonte Well, what would you have me do? On that score I have scruples that example cannot overcome.

Covielle Are you joking, to take the matter seriously with a man like that? Don't you see he's crazy? And was it costing you anything to accommodate yourself to his fancies?

Cléonte You're right; but I didn't think you had to give your proofs of nobility to be the son-in-law of Monsieur Jourdain.

Covielle Ha, ha, ha!

Cléonte What are you laughing about?

Covielle An idea that comes to my mind to play a trick on our man and have you get what you want.

Cléonte How's that?

Covielle It's a really funny notion.

Cléonte What is it then?

Covielle There has been a certain masquerade performed for a little while that would do perfectly here, and that I'd like to work into a hoax I want to perpetrate on this ridiculous man of ours. The whole thing smacks a bit of low comedy;

but with him you can risk anything, you don't have to be too careful; and he's the man to play his own part in it to perfection, to lend himself easily to all the nonsense we take it into our heads to tell him. I have the actors, I have the costumes all ready; just leave it to me.

Cléonte But tell me . . .

Covielle I'll tell you all about it. Let's leave, he's coming back.

SCENE FOURTEEN

Monsieur Jourdain, Lackey

Monsieur Jourdain What the devil is all this? They have nothing to reproach me for but the noble lords; and I don't think anything is as fine as to associate with noble lords. With them there is nothing but honor and civility; and I wish it had cost me two fingers off my hand, and I'd been born a count or a marquis.

Lackey Sir, here is Monsieur le Comte, and a lady on his arm.

Monsieur Jourdain Oh my Lord! I have some orders to give. Tell them I'll be here right away.

SCENE FIFTEEN

Dorimène, Dorante, Lackey

Lackey The master says like he'll be here right away.

Dorante Very good.

Dorimène I don't know, Dorante; this is another strange thing I'm doing here, letting you take me into a house where I don't know anybody.

Dorante Then what place, Madame, would you have my love choose to entertain you, since, to avoid publicity, you want neither your house nor mine?

Dorimène But you don't mention that I'm becoming involved imperceptibly every day by accepting excessive tokens of your passion. I try to defend myself against these things, but you wear down my resistance; and you have a polite obstinacy which makes me come around gradually to whatever you like. It began with the frequent visits; the declarations came next, which brought after them the serenades and entertainments, which were followed by the presents. I opposed all that; but you don't give up, and step by step you overcome my resolutions. For me, I can no longer answer for anything, and I think that in the end you'll persuade me to marriage, which I have put so far from my mind.

Dorante Faith, Madame! You should be married already. You're a widow, and dependent only on yourself. I am my own master, and I love you more than my life. What is to keep you from making my happiness complete this very day?

Dorimène Good Lord, Dorante! Many qualities on both sides are needed to live happily together; and the two most reasonable people in the world often have trouble in forming a union to their satisfaction.

Dorante You can't be serious, Madame, in picturing so many difficulties in this; and the experience you have had proves nothing about all the others.

Dorimène Anyway, I still come back to this: the expenditures I see you make for me worry me for two reasons: one, they commit me more than I would like; and two, I am sure—no offense—that you do not make them without financial embarrassment; and I don't want that.

Dorante Ah, Madame, those are trifles; and it's not by those . . .

Dorimène I know what I'm saying; and among other things, the diamond you forced me to accept is so valuable . . .

Dorante Oh, Madame! Please don't make so much of something that my love finds unworthy of you; and permit . . . Here's the master of the house.

SCENE SIXTEEN

Monsieur Jourdain, Dorimène, Dorante, Lackey

Monsieur Jourdain [*after making two bows as he steps forward, and finding himself too close to Dorimène*] A little farther back, Madame.

Dorimène How's that?

Monsieur Jourdain One step back, if you please.

Dorimène What?

Monsieur Jourdain Step back a bit, for the third.

Dorante Madame, Monsieur Jourdain knows his etiquette.

Monsieur Jourdain Madame, it's a very great glory for me to find myself so fortunate as to be so happy as to have the happiness that you have had the goodness to grant me the grace of doing me the honor of honoring me with the favor of your presence; and if I also had the merit of meriting a merit like yours, and if Heaven . . . envious of my good fortune . . . had granted me . . . the advantage of finding myself worthy . . . of the . . .

Dorante Monsieur Jourdain, that's enough of that. Madame does not like great compliments, and she knows that you are a man of wit. [*Aside to Dorimène.*] He's a good bourgeois, rather ridiculous, as you see, in all his manners.

Dorimène [*aside, to Dorante*] It's not hard to see that.

Dorante Madame, this is the best of my friends.

Monsieur Jourdain You do me too much honor.

Dorante A complete man of the world.

Dorimène I have much esteem for him.

Monsieur Jourdain I've done nothing yet, Madame, to deserve that favor.

Dorante [*aside, to Monsieur Jourdain*] Be very careful, at any rate, that you don't speak to her about the diamond you gave her.

Monsieur Jourdain [*aside, to Dorante*] Couldn't I just ask her how she likes it?

Dorante [*aside, to Monsieur Jourdain*] What? See that you don't. That would be vulgar of you; and to act as a man of the world, you have to behave as though it wasn't you who gave her that present. [*Aloud.*] Madame, Monsieur Jourdain says he is delighted to see you in his house.

Dorimène He honors me greatly.

Monsieur Jourdain [*aside, to Dorante*] How obliged I am to you, sir, for speaking to her thus for me!

Dorante [*aside, to Monsieur Jourdain*] I had frightful difficulty in getting her to come.

Monsieur Jourdain [*aside, to Dorante*] I don't know how to thank you for it.

Dorante He says, Madame, that he thinks you're the most beautiful person in the world.

Dorimène That's very gracious of him.

Monsieur Jourdain Madame, the graciousness is all on your side; and . . .

Dorante Let's think about eating.

Lackey Everything is ready, sir.

Dorante Then let's sit down, and send in the musicians.

Six Cooks, who have prepared the feast, perform a dance together, which makes up the Third Interlude. After that, they bring in a table covered with various dishes.

Act Four

SCENE ONE

Dorante, Dorimène, Monsieur Jourdain, two Men Singers, a Woman Singer, Lackeys

Dorimène Why, Dorante! This is a really magnificent meal!

Monsieur Jourdain You're joking, Madame, and I wish it was more worthy of being offered to you.

They all take their seats at the table.

Dorante Monsieur Jourdain is right, Madame, to speak in this way, and he obliges me by doing you the honors of his house so well. I agree with him that the meal is not worthy of you. Since it was I who ordered it, and since I do not have the sophistication of our friends in this matter, you don't have a very learned meal here, and you will find in it some gastronomic incongruities and some barbarisms in the matter of good taste. If Damis had had a hand in it, everything would be according to the rules; there would be elegance and erudition everywhere; and he would not fail, himself, to overpraise to you all the parts of the meal that he would serve, and to make you agree to his high capacity in the science of tidbits: to talk to you of his rolls cooked on the edge of the oven, golden brown, crusted all over, crunching delicately under the teeth; of a wine with a velvety savor, armed with a youthful vigor that is not too dominating; a breast of lamb garnished with parsley; a loin of Normandy veal, just so long, white, delicate, and like real almond paste under your teeth; partridges seasoned with a surprising bouquet; and for his masterpiece, a plump young turkey flanked by squabs, in a pearly bouillon, crowned with white onions wedded to chicory. But as for me, I confess my ignorance; and as Monsieur Jourdain has very well said, I wish the meal were more worthy of being offered you.

Dorimène My only reply to this compliment is to eat as I am doing.

Monsieur Jourdain Ah, what beautiful hands!

Dorimène The hands are very ordinary, Monsieur Jourdain; but no doubt you mean to speak of the diamond, which is very beautiful.

Monsieur Jourdain I, Madame! God forbid that I should mean to speak of it; that would not be acting like a man of the world, and the diamond is a very small thing.

Dorimène You're very hard to please.

Monsieur Jourdain You are too kind . . .

Dorante Come, serve some wine to Monsieur Jourdain and to these gentlemen, who will do us the kindness of singing us a drinking air.

Dorimène It's a marvelous seasoning for good cheer, to combine it with music, and I find myself being admirably entertained here.

Monsieur Jourdain Madame, it's not . . .

Dorante Monsieur Jourdain, let's be quiet for these gentlemen; what they will tell us will be better than anything we could say.

The Musicians take glasses and sing two drinking songs, accompanied by the whole orchestra.

FIRST DRINKING SONG

Just a wee drop of wine, Phyllis, to start the round.
Ah! Ah! How in your hands a glass is full of charms!

You and the wine, you lend each other arms,
And for you both my love is doubled at a bound.
So you and I let's swear, between us three,
Love that shall always be.

Wetting your mouth, it is embellished with love's shafts,
And as you see, by it your mouth is set on fire;
Each of the other fills me with desire;
Of you and it I drink intoxicating drafts.
So you and I let's swear, between us three,
Love that shall always be.

SECOND DRINKING SONG

Friends, let's drink, let's pass the glass.
Time invites us, and it's fleeting.
Let's enjoy life and this meeting
All we can, alas!
When we've passed the gloomy brink,
Our links with wine and love we sever,
So let's hurry up and drink;
We can't drink forever.

Leave discussion to the asses
On man's true felicity.
For our own philosophy
Finds it in the glasses.
Riches, learning, and renown
Don't remove care and distress;
Only when we drink it down
Can we taste happiness.

CHORUS

Come on, then, wine all round, come on, then, pour, boys, pour,
Keep pouring, keep pouring, till no one asks for more.

Dorimène I don't think it's possible to sing better, and that's quite lovely.

Monsieur Jourdain I still see something lovelier here, Madame.

Dorimène Well! Monsieur Jourdain is more gallant than I thought.

Dorante Why, Madame, what do you take Monsieur Jourdain for?

Monsieur Jourdain I certainly wish she'd take me for what I could mention.

Dorimène Still at it?

Dorante You don't know him.

Monsieur Jourdain She'll know me whenever she likes.

Dorimène Oh! I give it up.

Dorante He's a man who always has an answer ready. But Madame, you aren't noticing that Monsieur Jourdain eats all the morsels you touch.

Dorimène Monsieur Jourdain is a man who delights me.

Monsieur Jourdain If I could delight your heart, I would be . . .

SCENE TWO

Madame Jourdain, Monsieur Jourdain, Dorimène, Dorante, Musicians, Lackeys

Madame Jourdain Aha! I find nice company here, and I can easily see that I wasn't expected. So it's on account of this fine affair, my worthy husband, that you were so eager to send me to dinner at my sister's? I've just seen a sort of theater downstairs, and here I see a banquet fit for a wedding. This is how you spend your money, and this is the way you entertain ladies in my absence, and offer them music and a play, while you send me packing?

Dorante What do you mean, Madame Jourdain? And what kind of fancies do you have, to take it into your head that your husband is spending his money, and that he's the one who's giving this party for Madame? Pray learn that I'm the one; that all he's doing is just lending me his house, and that you should be a little more careful about the things you say.

Monsieur Jourdain Yes, you impertinent woman, it's Monsieur le Comte who is offering all this to Madame, who is a lady of quality. He is doing me the honor of taking my house and wanting me to be with him.

Madame Jourdain That's a lot of nonsense; I know what I know.

Dorante Madame Jourdain, put on a better pair of spectacles.

Madame Jourdain I have no use for spectacles, sir, and I see clear enough. I've sensed things for a long time, and I'm not a fool. For a great lord, it's very mean of you to lend a hand as you do to my husband's follies. And you, Madame, for a great lady, it's neither nice nor decent of you to sow dissension in a family and allow my husband to be in love with you.

Dorimène Why, what is the meaning of all this? Come, Dorante, this is a poor joke to expose me to the silly delusions of this madwoman. *Exit.*

Dorante Madame, stay! Madame, where are you running off to?

Monsieur Jourdain Madame! Monsieur le Comte, make my excuses to her, and try to bring her back . . .

Exit Dorante.

[*To Madame Jourdain.*] Ah! You impertinent woman, that was a fine performance! You come and affront me in front of everyone, and you drive people of quality out of my house!

Madame Jourdain I don't care a rap about their quality.

Monsieur Jourdain Confound you, I don't know what keeps me from cracking your skull with the leftovers of the meal you came and broke up.

The Lackeys remove the table.

Madame Jourdain I don't care a rap about that. It's my rights I'm defending, and all the women will be on my side.

Exit.

Monsieur Jourdain You do well to avoid my anger. [*Alone.*]

She certainly arrived at a bad time. I was in the mood to say some pretty things, and I never had felt so full of wit. . . . What's all this?

SCENE THREE

Covielle (in Oriental costume, with a long beard), Monsieur Jourdain, Lackeys

Covielle Sir, I don't know whether I have the honor of being known to you.

Monsieur Jourdain No, sir.

Covielle I knew you when you were no bigger than that [*holding his hand not far above the floor*].

Monsieur Jourdain Me?

Covielle Yes, you were the handsomest child in the world, and all the ladies would take you in their arms to kiss you.

Monsieur Jourdain To kiss me!

Covielle Yes. I was a great friend of your honorable late father.

Monsieur Jourdain Of my honorable late father!

Covielle Yes. He was a very fine gentleman.

Monsieur Jourdain What's that you say?

Covielle I say he was a very fine gentleman.

Monsieur Jourdain My father!

Covielle Yes.

Monsieur Jourdain You knew him well?

Covielle Certainly.

Monsieur Jourdain And you knew him to be a gentleman?

Covielle Beyond a doubt.

Monsieur Jourdain Then I don't know what the world is coming to.

Covielle How's that?

Monsieur Jourdain There are some stupid people who try to tell me that he was a merchant.

Covielle He, a merchant? That's sheer calumny; he never was. All he did was that he was very obliging, very helpful; and since he was a real connoisseur of cloth, he went around and picked it out everywhere, had it brought to his house, and gave it to his friends for money.

Monsieur Jourdain I'm delighted to know you, so that you can give that testimony, that my father was a gentleman.

Covielle I'll maintain it in front of everybody.

Monsieur Jourdain I'll be much obliged to you. What brings you here?

Covielle Since the time when I knew your honorable late father—a fine gentleman, as I've told you—I've traveled all over the world.

Monsieur Jourdain All over the world!

Covielle Yes.

Monsieur Jourdain It must be a long way to those parts.

Covielle Yes indeed. I've been back only four days from all my long journeys; and because of the interest I take in all that concerns you, I come to announce to you the best news in the world.

Monsieur Jourdain What's that?

Covielle You know that the son of the Grand Turk is here?

Monsieur Jourdain I? No.

Covielle What? He has an utterly magnificent retinue; everybody's going to see him; and he has been received in this country as a lord of great importance.

Monsieur Jourdain Upon my word! I didn't know that.

Covielle What's advantageous about it for you is that he is in love with your daughter.

Monsieur Jourdain The son of the Grand Turk?

Covielle Yes; and he wants to be your son-in-law.

Monsieur Jourdain My son-in-law, the son of the Grand Turk?

Covielle The son of the Grand Turk, your son-in-law. Since I went to see him and understand his language perfectly, he had a talk with me; and after some other conversation he said to me: *"Acciam croc soler ouch alla moustaph gidelum amanahem varahini oussere carbulath,"** that is to say: "Have you by any chance seen a beautiful young person who is the daughter of Monsieur Jourdain, a Parisian gentleman?"

Monsieur Jourdain The son of the Grand Turk said that about me?

Covielle Yes. When I answered that I knew you personally and had seen your daughter, he said to me: "Ah! *Marababa sahem,*" that is to say: "Ah! How I love her!"

Monsieur Jourdain *Marababa sahem* means "Ah! How I love her!"

Covielle Yes.

Monsieur Jourdain Faith! You do well to tell me so, for personally I would never have thought that *marababa sahem* meant "Ah! How I love her!" What a wonderful language this Turkish is!

Covielle More wonderful than you'd believe. Do you know what *cacaracamouchen* means?

Monsieur Jourdain *Cacaracamouchen?* No.

Covielle It means "My dear heart."

Monsieur Jourdain *Cacaracamouchen* means "My dear heart"?

Covielle Yes.

Monsieur Jourdain That is marvelous! *Cacaracamouchen,* "My dear heart." Who'd have thought it? That amazes me.

Covielle Finally, to complete my embassy, he is coming to ask for your daughter in marriage; and to have a father-in-law who is worthy of him, he wants to make you a *Mamamouchi,* which is a certain great dignity of his country.

* The "Turkish" throughout is mostly gibberish.

Monsieur Jourdain A *Mamamouchi?*

Covielle Yes, a *Mamamouchi;* that is to say, in our language, a paladin. Paladins are some of those ancient . . . In short, a paladin. There's nothing nobler than that in the world, and you'll move on a par with the greatest lords on earth.

Monsieur Jourdain The son of the Grand Turk does me great honor, and I beg you to take me to meet him and give him my thanks.

Covielle What? He's right on his way here.

Monsieur Jourdain He's on his way here?

Covielle Yes; and he's bringing everything for the ceremony of your ennoblement.

Monsieur Jourdain That's very prompt.

Covielle His love can bear no delay.

Monsieur Jourdain All that embarrasses me in all this is that my daughter is a stubborn girl who's gone and set her mind on a certain Cléonte, and she swears she won't marry anyone but him.

Covielle She'll change her feelings when she sees the son of the Grand Turk; and then there's a wonderful coincidence here, that the son of the Grand Turk bears a very close resemblance to this Cléonte. I've just seen Cléonte, he was pointed out to me; and her love for the one may easily pass to the other, and . . . I hear him coming; here he is.

SCENE FOUR

Cléonte (in Turkish costume, with three pages carrying his train), Monsieur Jourdain, Covielle (disguised)

Cléonte *Ambousahim oqui boraf, Iordina, salamalequi.*

Covielle That is to say, "Monsieur Jourdain, may your heart all year round be like a rosebush in bloom!" These are obliging modes of expression in those countries.

Monsieur Jourdain I am the very humble servant of his Turkish Highness.

Covielle *Carigar camboto oustin moraf.*

Cléonte *Oustin yoc catamalequi basum base alla moran.*

Covielle He says: "May Heaven give you the strength of lions and the prudence of serpents!"

Monsieur Jourdain His Turkish Highness does me too much honor, and I wish him all sorts of prosperity.

Covielle *Ossa binamen sadoc babally oracaf ouram.*

Cléonte *Bel-men.*

Covielle He says that you should go with him quickly and prepare for the ceremony, so he may then see your daughter and conclude the marriage.

Monsieur Jourdain All those things in two words?

Covielle Yes, the Turkish language is like that, it says a lot in a few words. Go quickly where he wants you to.

SCENE FIVE

Dorante, Covielle

Covielle Ha, ha, ha! Faith! That's really funny! What a dupe! If he'd learned his part by heart he couldn't play it better. Ha, ha! I beg you, sir, to help us here in something that's going on.

Dorante Ha, ha! Covielle, who would have recognized you? What a get-up that is!

Covielle You see. Ha, ha!

Dorante What are you laughing at?

Covielle At something, sir, that well deserves it.

Dorante What's that?

Covielle I'd give you lots of tries, sir, to guess the stratagem we're using with Monsieur Jourdain to bring him around to give his daughter to my master.

Dorante I can't guess the stratagem, but I can guess that it won't fail to work, since you're undertaking it.

Covielle I know, sir, that the beast is known to you.

Dorante Tell me what it's all about.

Covielle Be good enough to move a little farther away, to make room for what I see coming. You'll be able to see part of the story, and I'll tell you the rest.

The Turkish ceremony ennobling Monsieur Jourdain is performed as a dance to music, and composes the Fourth Interlude.

Six dancing Turks enter gravely, two by two, to a Turkish march. As they dance, they wave three long carpets, and finally raise them high; the Turkish Singers and Instrumentalists pass under them. Four Dervishes accompany the Mufti to close the procession.

The Turks put their carpets on the ground and kneel on them. The Mufti remains standing in the middle, raises his eyes to Heaven in a burlesque invocation, grimaces, and moves his hands beside his head like wings. The Turks bow and touch their foreheads to the floor, singing "Alli," return to a kneeling position, singing "Alla," and continue this alternation until the invocation is over; then all rise to their feet and join in the words "Alla ekber."

Then the Dervishes bring on Monsieur Jourdain dressed as a Turk, clean-shaven, without turban or saber. The Mufti sings.

Mufti

Se ti sabir,
Ti respondir;
Se non sabir,
Tazir, tazir.
Mi star Mufti.
Ti, qui star ti?
Non intendir:
Tazir, tazir.*

Two Dervishes take Monsieur Jourdain out. The Mufti questions the Turks about Monsieur Jourdain's religion.

* If you know,/ You answer;/ If you no know,/ Be quiet, be quiet./ Me be Mufti./ You, who be you?/ You don't understand:/ Be quiet, be quiet.

Mufti Dice, Turque, qui star quista.
Anabaptista, anabaptista?

Turks Ioc.*

Mufti Zwinglista?

Turks Ioc.

Mufti Coffita?

Turks Ioc.

Mufti Hussita? Morista? Fronista?†

Turks Ioc. Ioc. Ioc.

Mufti Ioc. Ioc. Ioc.
Star pagana?

Turks Ioc.

Mufti Luterana?

Turks Ioc.

Mufti Puritana?

Turks Ioc.

Mufti Bramina? Moffina? Zurina?‡

Turks Ioc. Ioc. Ioc.

Mufti Ioc. Ioc. Ioc.
Mahometana? Mahometana?

Turks Hey valla! Hey valla!

Mufti Como chamara? Como chamara?

Turks Giourdina, Giourdina.

Mufti Giourdina.

Leaping and looking in one direction and another.

Giourdina? Giourdina? Giourdina?

* Tell me, Turk, who be this?/ An Anabaptist, Anabaptist?/ No.—*Ioc* (no) is a real Turkish word.

† A Zwinglian?/ No./ A Copt?/ No./ A Hussite?—The meaning of "Morista" (a Moor?) and "Fronista" is not clear.

‡ No. No. No./ No. No. No./ Be he a pagan?/ No./ A Lutheran?/ No./ A Puritan?/ No./ A Brahmin? ("Moffina" and "Zurina" are not clear.)

Turks Giourdina! Giourdina! Giourdina!*

Mufti

Mahameta per Giourdina
Mi pregar ser e matina:
Voler far un Paladina
De Giourdina, de Giourdina.
Dar turbanta, e dar scarcina
Con galera e brigantina
Per deffender Palestina.
Mahameta per Giourdina
Mi pregar ser e matina.†

Star bon Turca Giourdina?
Star bon Turca Giourdina?

Turks

Hey valla. Hey valla.
Hey valla. Hey valla.‡

Mufti [*dancing and singing*] Hu la ba ba la chou ba la ba ba la da.

Exit Mufti.

Turks [*dancing and singing*] Hu la ba ba la chou ba la ba ba la da.

Reenter the Mufti wearing an enormous ceremonial turban set with four or five rows of lighted candles. With him are two Dervishes, wearing pointed hats also adorned with lighted candles, and bearing the Koran. The other two Dervishes bring in Monsieur Jourdain, who is terrified by the ceremony, make him kneel down with his back to the Mufti and rest his hands on the floor, and set the Koran on his back for the Mufti to read. The Mufti gives a burlesque invocation, frowning and opening his mouth without saying a word, then speaking vehemently, now softly, now as if pos-

* No. No. No./ No. No. No./ A Mohammedan? A Mohammedan?/ Yes, by Allah! Yes, by Allah!/ What is his name? What is his name?/ Jourdain, etc.

† To Mahomet for Jourdain/ Me pray evening and morning./ Want to make a paladin/ Of Jourdain, of Jourdain./ Give a turban and a scimitar/ With a galley and brigantine/ To defend Palestine./ To Mahomet for Jourdain/ Me pray evening and morning.

‡ Jourdain be good Turk?/ Jourdain be good Turk?/ Yes, by Allah! etc.

sessed, slapping his sides as if to drive the words out, striking the Koran, turning its leaves very fast. Finally he raises his hands and cries out loudly: "Hou!"

During the invocation the Turks sing "Hou, hou, hou!" alternately bowing and straightening up.

After the invocation the Dervishes take the Koran off Monsieur Jourdain's back; he exclaims "Ouf!" in relief from this tiring posture; and they lift him to his feet.

Mufti [*to Monsieur Jourdain*] Ti non star furba?

Turks No, no, no.

Mufti Non star forfanta?

Turks No, no, no.

Mufti Donar turbanta. Donar turbanta.*

Exit the Mufti.

The Turks repeat his words, singing and dancing, and present the turban to Monsieur Jourdain. Reenter the Mufti with a scimitar.

Mufti [*presenting the scimitar to Monsieur Jourdain*]
Ti star nobile, e non star fabola.
Pigliar schiabola.†

Exit the Mufti.

The Turks draw their scimitars and repeat his words. Six of them dance around Monsieur Jourdain and pretend to strike him with their scimitars. Reenter the Mufti, who orders the Turks to beat Monsieur Jourdain.

Mufti Dara, dara, bastonara, bastonara, bastonara.‡

Exit the Mufti.

The Turks repeat his words, dancing and beating Monsieur Jourdain with sticks in cadence. Reenter the Mufti.

* You no be knave?/ No, no, no./ No be rascal?/ No, no, no./ Give turban, give turban.

† You be noble, that be no fable./ Take scimitar.

‡ Give, give, beat, beat, beat.

Mufti

Non tener honta:
Questa star l'ultima affronta.*

The Turks repeat his words. To the music of the whole orchestra the Mufti, leaning on the Dervishes, who support him with respect, makes a final invocation. The Turks, dancing, lead off the Mufti and Monsieur Jourdain in triumph, thus ending the Fourth Interlude.

* No feel shame:/ This be the final affront.

Act Five

SCENE ONE
Madame Jourdain, Monsieur Jourdain

Madame Jourdain Oh! Lord have mercy! What in the world is all this? What a sight! Are you getting ready for a mummer's play, and is it a time for a masquerade? Speak up; what is all this? Who rigged you out like this?

Monsieur Jourdain Look at your impertinence, to talk that way to a *Mamamouchi!*

Madame Jourdain How's that?

Monsieur Jourdain Yes, you've got to show me some respect now; and I've just been made a *Mamamouchi.*

Madame Jourdain What do you mean with your *Mamamouchi?*

Monsieur Jourdain *Mamamouchi,* I tell you. I'm a *Mamamouchi.*

Madame Jourdain What kind of animal is that?

Monsieur Jourdain *Mamamouchi,* that is to say, in our language, Paladin.

Madame Jourdain A balladin'! Are you at an age for going around a-ballading?

Monsieur Jourdain What an ignoramus! I said a Paladin. That's a dignity that's just been conferred on me with proper ceremony.

Madame Jourdain What kind of a ceremony?

Monsieur Jourdain *Mahameta per Giourdina.*

Madame Jourdain What does that mean?

Monsieur Jourdain *Giourdina,* that is to say Jourdain.

Madame Jourdain Well then, Jourdain? What about it?

Monsieur Jourdain *Voler far un Paladina de Giourdina.*

Madame Jourdain What?

Monsieur Jourdain *Dar turbanta con galera.*

Madame Jourdain What does that mean?

Monsieur Jourdain *Per deffender Palestina.*

Madame Jourdain What is it you mean by that?

Monsieur Jourdain *Dara dara bastonara.*

Madame Jourdain Just what is this jargon?

Monsieur Jourdain *Non tener honta: questa star l'ultima affronta.*

Madame Jourdain Just what is all this?

Monsieur Jourdain [*dancing and singing*] *Hou la ba ba la chou ba la ba ba la da.*

Madame Jourdain Alas! Good Lord! My husband's gone crazy.

Monsieur Jourdain [*on his way out*] Peace, insolent woman! Show respect to Monsieur le *Mamamouchi.*

Madame Jourdain Why, where can he have lost his wits? Let's run and keep him from leaving. [*Sees Dorante and Dorimène entering.*] Aha! Sure enough, this is all we needed. I see nothing but trouble on every side. *Exit.*

SCENE TWO

Dorante, Dorimène

Dorante Yes, Madame, you'll see the most amusing thing you ever could see; and I don't think it's possible still to find in all the world a man as crazy as that one. And then, Madame, we must try to serve Cléonte's love, and support his

whole masquerade; he's a very decent chap who deserves our taking an interest on his behalf.

Dorimène I think a lot of him, and he deserves to have good fortune.

Dorante Besides that, Madame, we have a ballet coming to us here, which we shouldn't allow to be wasted; and I really must see whether my idea can work out.

Dorimène I saw some magnificent preparations there; and these are things, Dorante, that I can no longer put up with. Yes, I want to put a stop to your extravagance at last; and to cut short all the expenditures I see you making for me, I have resolved to marry you promptly. That's the real solution; all these things end with marriage.

Dorante Ah, Madame! Is it possible that you could have made such a sweet resolve on my behalf?

Dorimène It's only to keep you from ruining yourself; and without this I can easily see that in a short time you wouldn't have a penny.

Dorante How obliged I am, Madame, to your concern for preserving my property. It is entirely yours, as well as my heart, and you will use it in any way you please.

Dorimène I shall have good use for them both. But here's your man; he's a wonderful sight.

SCENE THREE

Monsieur Jourdain, Dorante, Dorimène

Dorante Sir, Madame and I come to pay homage to your new dignity, and to rejoice with you at your daughter's coming marriage to the son of the Grand Turk.

Monsieur Jourdain [*after making his bows in Turkish fashion*] Sir, I wish you the strength of serpents and the prudence of lions.

Dorimène I was very glad to be one of the first, sir, to come and congratulate you on the high degree of glory you have risen to.

Monsieur Jourdain Madame, I hope your rosebush may be in flower all year long. I am infinitely obliged to you for taking part in the honors that are coming to me, and I take great joy in seeing you here again so I can offer you my very humble apologies for my wife's outlandish behavior.

Dorimène That's nothing; I can excuse such an impulse in her. Your heart must be precious to her, and it's not strange that the possession of a man like you can give her some alarms.

Monsieur Jourdain The possession of my heart is a thing that is entirely yours.

Dorante You see, Madame, that Monsieur Jourdain is not one of those people who are blinded by prosperity, and that in all his glory he still knows how to recognize his friends.

Dorimène That's the mark of a wholly noble soul.

Dorante Now where is his Turkish Highness? As friends of yours, we would like to pay him our respects.

Monsieur Jourdain Here he comes, and I've sent for my daughter to give him her hand.

SCENE FOUR

Cléonte, Covielle, Monsieur Jourdain, Dorante, Dorimène

Dorante [*to Cléonte*] Sir, as friends of your honorable father-in-law, we come to make obeisance to Your Highness and respectfully assure Your Highness of our very humble services.

Monsieur Jourdain Where is the interpreter, to tell him who you are and make him understand what you're saying? You'll see that he'll answer you, and he speaks Turkish wonderfully. Hello! Where the deuce has he gone? [*To Cléonte.*] *Strouf, strif, strof, straf.* This gentleman is a *grande Segnore, grande Segnore, grande Segnore;* and Madame is a *granda Dama, granda Dama, granda Dama.* [*Seeing that he is not understood.*] Oh dear! Him, sir, him French *Mamamouchi,* and Madame French *Mamamouchie;* I can't say it more clearly. Good, here's the interpreter. Where are you going, anyway? We can't say a thing without you. Just tell him that the gentleman and the lady are persons of high rank, who have come to pay their respects to him, as my friends, and assure him of their services. [*To Dorante and Dorimène.*] You'll see how he'll answer.

Covielle *Alabala crociam acci boram alabamen.*

Cléonte *Catalequi tubal ourin soter amalouchan.*

Monsieur Jourdain You see?

Covielle He says: "May the rain of prosperities forever water the garden of your family!"

Monsieur Jourdain I told you, he speaks Turkish.

Dorante That's wonderful.

SCENE FIVE

Lucile, Monsieur Jourdain, Dorante, Dorimène, Cléonte, Covielle

Monsieur Jourdain Come here, daughter; closer. Come and give your hand to this gentleman, who is doing you the honor of asking to marry you.

Lucile What's this, father? What a get-up! Are you acting in a play?

Monsieur Jourdain No, no, it's no play, it's a very serious matter, and the most honorable for you that could be wished for. Here's the husband I am giving you.

Lucile Me, father?

Monsieur Jourdain Yes, you. Come on, give him your hand, and thank Heaven for your good fortune.

Lucile I don't want to get married.

Monsieur Jourdain I want you to, and I'm your father.

Lucile I'll do nothing of the kind.

Monsieur Jourdain Oh! What a lot of fuss! Come on, I tell you. Here, your hand.

Lucile No, father, I've told you, there is no power that can oblige me to take any other husband than Cléonte; and I'll go to any extremes rather than . . . [*Recognizing Cléonte.*] It is true that you are my father, I owe you entire obedience, and it is for you to dispose of me according to your will.

Monsieur Jourdain Ah! I'm delighted to see you return to your duty so promptly, and I'm really pleased to have an obedient daughter.

SCENE SIX

Madame Jourdain, Monsieur Jourdain, Lucile, Cléonte, Covielle, Dorante, Dorimène

Madame Jourdain How's this? What in the world is going on? They say you want to give your daughter in marriage to a Mardi Gras reveler.

Monsieur Jourdain Will you be quiet, you impertinent woman? You're always coming thrusting your silly notions into everything, and there's no way of teaching you to be reasonable.

Madame Jourdain You're the one there's no way of getting any sense into, and you go from folly to folly. What is your intention, and what do you mean to do with this motley crew?

Monsieur Jourdain I mean to marry our daughter to the son of the Grand Turk.

Madame Jourdain To the son of the Grand Turk!

Monsieur Jourdain Yes, have the interpreter here pay him your compliments.

Madame Jourdain I have no use for the interpreter, and I'll tell him perfectly well myself to his face that he shan't have my daughter.

Monsieur Jourdain Once more, will you be quiet?

Dorante What, Madame Jourdain, you oppose such good fortune as this? You refuse his Turkish Highness as a son-in-law?

Madame Jourdain Good Lord, sir, mind your own business.

Dorimène It's a great honor, which is not one to reject.

Madame Jourdain Madame, I beg you too not to bother yourself with what doesn't concern you.

Dorante It's our friendly feeling for you that makes us take an interest in whatever is to your advantage.

Madame Jourdain I'll get along fine without your friendly feeling.

Dorante Your daughter here consents to her father's will.

Madame Jourdain My daughter consents to marry a Turk!

Dorante Yes indeed.

Madame Jourdain She can forget Cléonte!

Dorante What won't a person do to be a great lady?

Madame Jourdain I'd strangle her with my own hands if she'd done a thing like that.

Monsieur Jourdain That's a lot of cackle. I tell you this marriage shall take place.

Madame Jourdain And *I* tell *you* that it shall not.

Monsieur Jourdain Oh, what a lot of fuss!

Lucile Mother.

Madame Jourdain Go on with you, you're a bad girl.

Monsieur Jourdain What? You're scolding her because she obeys me?

Madame Jourdain Yes: she belongs to me as well as to you.

Covielle [*to Madame Jourdain*] Madame.

Madame Jourdain You, what are you trying to tell me?

Covielle One word!

Madame Jourdain I don't want any part of your "word."

Covielle [*to Monsieur Jourdain*] Sir, if she will listen to a word in private, I promise you to get her to consent to what you want.

Madame Jourdain I won't consent to it one bit.

Covielle Just listen to me.

Madame Jourdain No.

Monsieur Jourdain Listen to him.

Madame Jourdain No, I won't listen.

Monsieur Jourdain He'll tell you . . .

Madame Jourdain I don't want him to tell me anything.

Monsieur Jourdain There's an obstinate woman for you! Will it hurt you to hear him?

Covielle Just listen to me; afterward you'll do as you please.

Madame Jourdain Well! What?

Covielle [*aside to Madame Jourdain*] Madame, we've been trying to make signs to you for an hour. Don't you see that all this is being done just to fall in with your husband's visions, that we're fooling him in this disguise, and that it's Cléonte himself who's the son of the Grand Turk?

Madame Jourdain [*aside to Covielle*] Aha!

Covielle [*aside to Madame Jourdain*] And I, Covielle, am the interpreter?

Madame Jourdain [*aside to Covielle*] Ah! In that case, I give in.

Covielle [*aside to Madame Jourdain*] Don't let on to a thing!

Madame Jourdain [*to Monsieur Jourdain*] Yes, that's settled, I consent to the marriage.

Monsieur Jourdain Ah! Now everybody's reasonable. You wouldn't listen to him. I knew perfectly well that he'd explain what it is to be the son of the Grand Turk.

Madame Jourdain He explained it to me very well, and I'm satisfied. Let's send for a notary.

Dorante That's very well said. And, Madame Jourdain, so that your mind may be completely at ease, and that you may lose today any jealousy you might have conceived about your honorable husband, let me say that this lady and I will use the same notary to be married.

Madame Jourdain I consent to that too.

Monsieur Jourdain [*aside to Dorante*] That's to pull the wool over her eyes.

Dorante [*aside to Monsieur Jourdain*] We simply have to delude her with this pretense.

Monsieur Jourdain [*aside*] Fine, fine. [*Aloud.*] Have the notary sent for, quick.

Dorante While he's coming and drawing up the contracts, let's see our ballet and offer it as an entertainment to his Turkish Highness.

Monsieur Jourdain That's a very good idea. Let's go take our seats.

Madame Jourdain What about Nicole?

Monsieur Jourdain I give her to the interpreter; and my wife to anyone that wants her.

Coviellе Sir, I thank you. [*Aside.*] If you can find anyone crazier, I'll go publish it in Rome.

The play concludes with the short Ballet of the Nations, which has nothing to do with the rest of the play and is omitted from this version.

The Imaginary Invalid

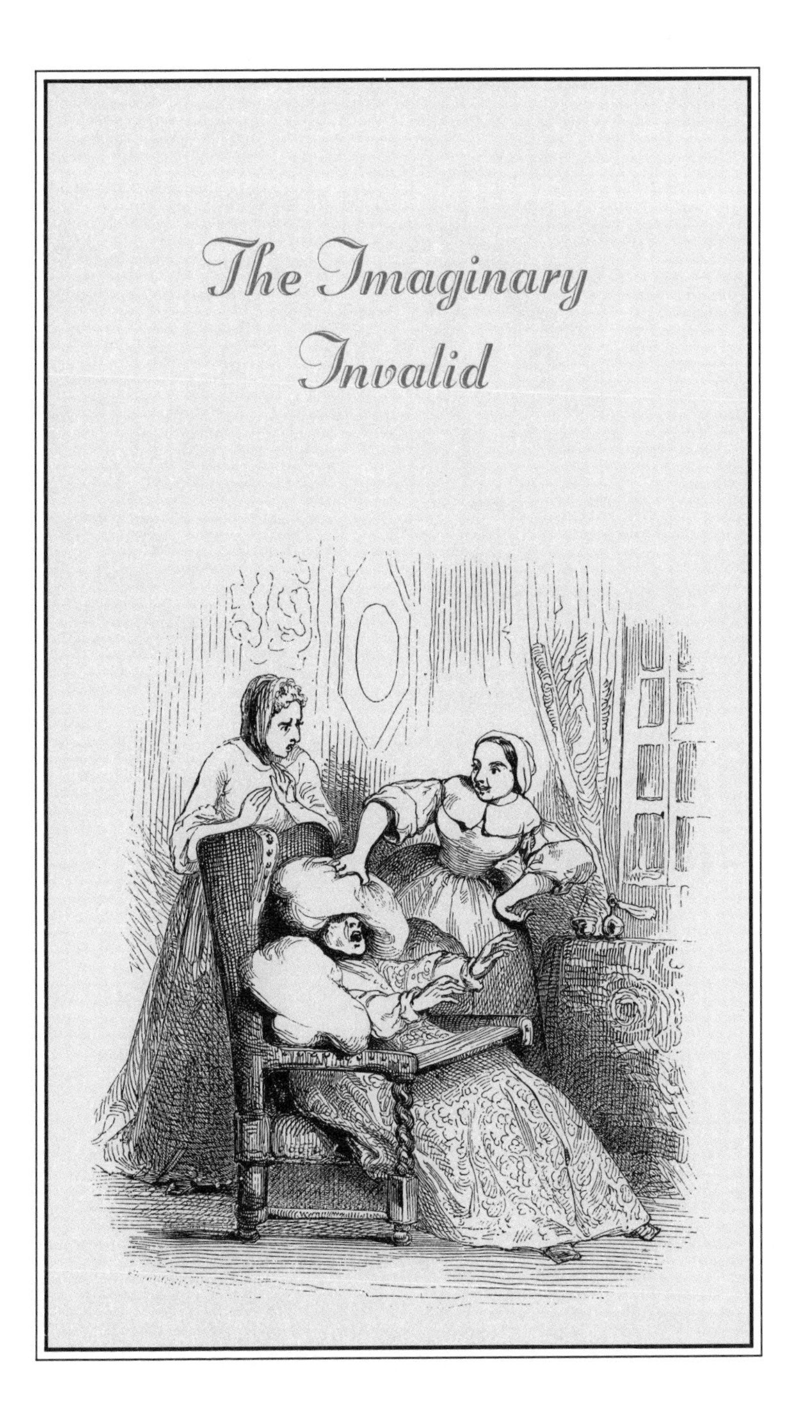

CHARACTERS

Argan, An imaginary invalid

Béline, Argan's second wife

Angélique, daughter of Argan by his first marriage, in love with Cléante

Louison, young daughter of Argan by his first marriage, sister of Angélique

Béralde, Argan's brother

Cléante, in love with Angélique

*Monsieur Diafoirus,** a doctor

Thomas Diafoirus, his son, suitor of Angélique

Monsieur Purgon, Argan's doctor

Monsieur Fleurant, an apothecary

Monsieur Bonnefoy, notary

Toinette, maidservant

The scene is Argan's bedroom in his house in Paris.

* Many of Molière's characters' names in this play are suggestive. Diafoirus would bc rather like Diarrheus or Diaturdus in English; Fleurant, like Sniffer or Smeller; Bonnefoy means Good Faith; Purgon speaks for itself.

PROLOGUE

At the first performance, on February 10, 1673, the play opened with a pastoral ballet honoring the recent military victories of Louis XIV in Holland. This was superseded in 1674 by a shorter one announcing the play but having no other relation to the action. Neither prologue is given here.

Act One

SCENE ONE
Argan

Argan [*sitting alone at a table in his bedroom, adding up his apothecary's bills with counters, and talking to himself as he does*] Three and two makes five, and five makes ten, and ten makes twenty. Three and two makes five. "Plus, on the twenty-fourth, a little enema, insinuative, preparatory, and emollient, to soften up, moisten, and refresh the gentleman's bowels." What I like about Monsieur Fleurant, my apothecary, is that his bills are always very civil: "the gentleman's bowels, thirty sous." Yes, but, Monsieur Fleurant, being civil isn't everything, you've got to be reasonable too, and not fleece your patients. Thirty sous for an enema! I'm your very humble servant, and I've told you so already. You put them down in my other bills at only twenty sous, and twenty sous in apothecary's language means ten sous. Here they are, ten sous [*dropping some counters into a slot*]. "Plus, on the said day, a good detergent enema composed of double catholicon, rhubarb, rose honey, etc., according to the prescription, to flush, clean, and scour the gentleman's lower intestine, thirty sous." With your permission, ten sous. "Plus, on the said day, in the evening, a hepatic, soporific, and somniferous julep compounded to put the gentleman to sleep, thirty-five sous." I've no complaint about that one, for it made me sleep well. Ten, fifteen, sixteen, and seventeen sous, six deniers.* "Plus, on the twenty-fifth, a good purgative and tonic concoction of fresh cassia with Levantine senna, etc., according to Monsieur Purgon's prescription, to expel and evacuate the gentleman's bile, four francs." Ah, Monsieur Fleurant, you're joking; you have to live with your patients. Monsieur Purgon didn't prescribe for you to put down four francs. Put down . . . put down three francs, if you please. Twenty . . . thirty sous. "Plus, on the said day, an anodyne and astringent potion, to make the gentleman rest, thirty sous." All right, ten . . . fifteen sous. "Plus, on the twenty-sixth, a carminative enema, to drive out the gentleman's wind, thirty sous." Ten sous, Monsieur Fleurant. "Plus, the gentleman's enema repeated in the evening, as above, thirty sous." Monsieur Fleurant, ten sous. "Plus, on the twenty-seventh, a good medicine compounded to speed along and drive out the gentleman's noxious humors, three francs." All right, twenty . . . thirty sous; I'm very glad you're being reasonable. "Plus, on the twenty-eighth, a dose of whey, clarified and edulcorated, to dulcify, lenify, temper, and refresh the gentleman's blood, twenty sous." All right, ten sous. "Plus a cordial and preservative potion, compounded with twelve grains of bezoar, lemon and pomegranate syrups, etc., according to the prescription, five francs." Ah! Monsieur Fleurant, gently, if you please; if you treat people like that, they won't want to be sick any more; content yourself with four francs. Twenty . . . and forty sous. Three and two makes five, and five makes ten, and ten makes twenty. Sixty-three francs four sous six deniers. So this month I've taken one, two, three, four, five, six, seven, eight doses of medicine and one, two, three, four, five, six, seven, eight, nine, ten, eleven, twelve enemas; and last month there were twelve doses of medicine and twenty enemas. I don't wonder that I'm not as well this month as last. I'll tell Monsieur Purgon this, so

* Twelve deniers make one sou, twenty sous make one franc. In all these calculations Argan plans—as was customary enough in his time—to pay exactly half of the apothecary's adjusted bill.

that he'll set this right. Come on, have all this taken away! . . . There's nobody here. No matter what I say, they always leave me alone; there's no way to keep them here. [*He rings a bell to summon his servants.*] They don't hear a thing, and my bell doesn't make enough noise. [*Ringing and calling out at the same time, more and more loudly and angrily.*] Ting-a-ling, ting-a-ling, ting-a-ling: nothing doing. Ting-a-ling a-ling a-ling: they're deaf. Toinette! Ting-a-ling a-ling a-ling: just as if I wasn't ringing. You slut, you hussy! Ting-a-ling a-ling a-ling: I'm getting mad. [*Throws away the bell and simply shouts.*] Ting-a-ling a-ling a-ling: you jade, go to the devil! Is it possible that they should leave a poor invalid all alone like this? Ting-a-ling a-ling a-ling: that's really pitiful! Ting-a-ling a-ling a-ling: oh, good Lord! They're going to leave me here to die. Ting-a-ling a-ling a-ling!

SCENE TWO

Toinette, Argan

Toinette [*coming into the room*] Here we are.

Argan Oh, you slut! Oh, you hussy . . . !

Toinette [*pretending to have bumped her head*] Confound your impatience! You hurry people so that I got a big bang on the head on the corner of the shutter.

Argan [*angrily*] Ah, you traitress . . . !

Toinette [*interrupting him and trying to keep him from shouting by always wailing*] Oh!

Argan It's been . . .

Toinette Oh!

Argan It's been an hour . . .

Toinette Oh!

Argan Since you left me . . .

Toinette Oh!

Argan Will you shut up, you hussy, and let me scold you?

Toinette Indeedy! My word! That's nice, after what I've done to myself.

Argan You made me shout myself hoarse, you slut.

Toinette And you, you made me bang my head; that's just as bad; we'll call it quits, if you like.

Argan What, you hussy . . . ?

Toinette If you scold me, I'll cry.

Argan You'd leave me, you traitress . . .

Toinette [*still interrupting him*] Oh!

Argan You wench, you want . . .

Toinette Oh!

Argan What! I won't even have the pleasure of scolding her?

Toinette Scold me, have your fill of it, I'm willing.

Argan You stop me, you wench, by interrupting me at every turn.

Toinette If you have the pleasure of scolding me, for my part, I must have the pleasure of crying. To each his own, that's only fair. Oh!

Argan All right, I've got to put up with it. Take this away, you hussy, take this away. [*Gets up from his chair.*] Did my enema today work well?

Toinette Your enema?

Argan Yes. Did I produce plenty of bile?

Toinette Faith! I don't get mixed up in those affairs. It's up to Monsieur Fleurant to poke his nose into it, since he makes his profit from it.

Argan See that they have some hot water ready, for the other that I'm to take in a while.

Toinette That Monsieur Fleurant and that Monsieur Purgon are having a gay old time over your body; they have a good milch cow in you; and I'd really like to ask them what ails you, for them to give you so many remedies.

Argan Be quiet, you ignoramus, it's not up to you to question the doctor's orders. Have my daughter Angélique sent in, I have something to say to her.

Toinette Here she comes of her own accord; she must have guessed what was on your mind.

SCENE THREE

Angélique, Toinette, Argan

Argan Come here, Angélique; you've come at a good time; I wanted to talk to you.

Angélique Here I am ready to hear you.

Argan [*running over to the basin*] Wait. Give me my stick. I'll be right back.

Toinette [*teasing him*] Go quick, sir, go. Monsieur Fleurant gives us plenty of business to do.

SCENE FOUR

Angélique, Toinette

Angélique [*confidentially, with a languishing look*] Toinette.

Toinette What?

Angélique Look at me a minute.

Toinette Well! I'm looking at you.

Angélique Toinette.

Toinette Well, what, "Toinette"?

Angélique Don't you guess what I want to talk about?

Toinette I have a pretty good suspicion: about our young suitor; for it's about him that all our conversations have been for six days; and you're not well if you're not talking about him every moment.

Angélique Since you know that, then why aren't you the first to talk to me about him, and why don't you spare me the pains of getting you started on the subject?

Toinette You don't give me time to, and you're so eager about it that it's hard to get ahead of you.

Angélique I confess to you that I couldn't possibly tire of talking about him, and that my heart warmly takes advantage of every chance to open itself to you. But tell me, Toinette, do you condemn the feelings I have for him?

Toinette I wouldn't dream of it.

Angélique Am I wrong to abandon myself to these sweet impressions?

Toinette I don't say that.

Angélique And would you have me be insensible to the tender protestations of the ardent passion he manifests for me?

Toinette God forbid!

Angélique Just tell me, don't you agree with me in seeing something providential, some act of destiny, in the unforeseen way we became acquainted?

Toinette Yes.

Angélique Don't you think that the act of coming to my defense without knowing me is the mark of a really gallant gentleman?

Toinette Yes.

Angélique That it's impossible to act more nobly?

Toinette Agreed.

Angélique And that he did all that with the best grace in the world?

Toinette Oh, yes!

Angélique Toinette, don't you think he's good looking?

Toinette Assuredly.

Angélique That he has the nicest manners in the world?

Toinette Beyond a doubt.

Angélique That there's something noble about his words as well as his actions?

Toinette That's sure.

Angélique That you could never hear anything more passionate than everything he says to me?

Toinette That's true.

Angélique And that there's nothing more irritating than the constraint I'm kept in, which blocks all communication of the sweet transports of that mutual ardor that Heaven inspires in us?

Toinette You're right.

Angélique But, my dear Toinette, do you think he loves me as much as he tells me he does?

Toinette Mm hmm! Those things are sometimes subject to caution. Love's grimaces are a lot like the real thing; and I've seen some great actors in that field.

Angélique Oh, Toinette! What are you saying? Alas! With the way he talks, would it really be possible that he wasn't telling me the truth?

Toinette In any case, you'll soon be enlightened about that; and his resolution, that he wrote you about yesterday, to ask for your hand in marriage, is a quick way to let you know whether he's telling you the truth or not. That will be the real proof of it.

Angélique Ah, Toinette! If that man deceives me, I'll never believe any man as long as I live.

Toinette Here's your father coming back.

SCENE FIVE

Argan, Angélique, Toinette

Argan [*sitting down in his chair*] Well now, daughter, I'm going to tell you a bit of news that you may not be expecting. Your hand is being requested in marriage. What's that?

You're laughing. That word *marriage* is amusing, yes; there's nothing more laughable for girls. Ah! Nature, nature! From what I can see, daughter, I have no need to ask you if you are willing to get married.

Angélique Father, I must do whatever you are pleased to order me to.

Argan I'm very glad to have such an obedient daughter. So the matter is settled, and I have promised your hand.

Angélique It is for me, father, to follow all your wishes blindly.

Argan My wife, your stepmother, wanted me to make you a nun, and your little sister Louison as well; she's been set on that all along.

Toinette [*aside*] That innocent creature has her reasons.

Argan She wouldn't consent to this marriage, but I won out, and my word is given.

Angélique Ah, father! How grateful I am to you for all your goodness!

Toinette In truth, I am grateful to you for that, and that's the most sensible thing you've done in your life.

Argan I haven't yet seen the person; but I've been told that I'd be pleased with him, and you too.

Angélique Certainly, father.

Argan What, have you seen him?

Angélique Since your consent authorizes me to be able to open my heart to you, I shall not hesitate to tell you that chance made us acquainted six days ago, and that the request made of you is an effect of the inclination that we formed for each other at first sight.

Argan They didn't tell me that; but I'm very glad of it, and so much the better that things are that way. They say he's a tall, nice looking young man.

Angélique Yes, father.

Argan Well built.

Angélique Undoubtedly.

Argan Personally attractive.

Angélique Yes indeed.

Argan Good looking.

Angélique Very good looking.

Argan Sensible, and well born.

Angélique Absolutely.

Argan A very fine chap.

Angélique As fine as can be.

Argan And speaking good Latin and Greek.

Angélique That I don't know.

Argan And he'll be accepted as a doctor in three days.

Angélique He, father?

Argan Yes. Didn't he tell you so?

Angélique No, really. Who told *you?*

Argan Monsieur Purgon.

Angélique Does Monsieur Purgon know him?

Argan A fine question! Indeed he must know him, since he's his nephew.

Angélique Cléante, Monsieur Purgon's nephew?

Argan What Cléante? We're talking about the man for whom your hand has been asked in marriage.

Angélique Indeed yes!

Argan Well, he's Monsieur Purgon's nephew, son of his brother-in-law the doctor, Monsieur Diafoirus; and this son's name is Thomas Diafoirus, not Cléante; and we arranged that marriage this morning, Monsieur Purgon, Monsieur Fleurant, and I; and tomorrow this prospective son-in-law is to be brought to see me by his father. What's the matter? You look all flabbergasted!

Angélique That, father, is because I now know that you were talking about one person, and I understood you to mean another.

Toinette What, sir? You could have made such a ludicrous plan? And with all the money you have you'd like to marry your daughter to a doctor?

Argan Yes. What business is it of yours, you impudent hussy?

Toinette Good Lord! Easy now. You start right in with invectives. Can't we reason together without getting into a temper? There now, let's talk calmly. What is your reason, if you please, for such a marriage?

Argan My reason is that, seeing myself sick and infirm as I am, I want to have doctors for a son-in-law and relatives, so as to assure myself of good assistance against my illness, to have in my family the sources of the remedies I need, and to be within reach of consultations and prescriptions.

Toinette Well, that's telling me a reason, and it's a pleasure to be answering one another gently. But, sir, put your hand on your conscience: are you sick?

Argan What, you wench, am I sick? Am I sick, you hussy?

Toinette Well then, yes, sir, you're sick, let's have no quarrel about that; yes, you're very sick, I grant you that, and sicker than you think: that's settled. But your daughter should marry a husband for herself; and since she's not sick, it's not necessary to give her a doctor.

Argan It's for me that I'm giving her this doctor; and a daughter with the right nature should be delighted to marry whatever is useful to her father's health.

Toinette Faith, sir! Do you want me to give you a piece of advice, as a friend?

Argan What is this advice?

Toinette Not to think of this marriage.

Argan And the reason?

Toinette The reason? That your daughter won't consent to it.

Argan She won't consent to it?

Toinette No.

Argan My daughter?

Toinette Your daughter. She'll tell you that she wants no part of Monsieur Diafoirus, nor of his son Thomas Diafoirus, nor of all the Diafoiruses in the world.

Argan Well, I want them. Besides, the match is more advantageous than you think. Monsieur Diafoirus has only that son for his sole heir, and what's more, Monsieur Purgon, who has neither wife nor children, will leave him his entire estate in view of this marriage; and Monsieur Purgon is a man who has a good eight thousand francs a year of income.

Toinette He must have killed a lot of people to get so rich.

Argan Eight thousand francs a year is something, without counting the father's money.

Toinette Sir, all that is very well and good; but I still come back to my point. I advise you, between ourselves, to choose her another husband, and she's not cut out to be Madame Diafoirus.

Argan And *I* want that to be.

Toinette Oh, fie! Don't say that.

Argan What do you mean, I shouldn't say that?

Toinette Why, no.

Argan And why shan't I say it?

Toinette People will say you don't know what you're saying.

Argan They'll say what they like; but I tell you, I want her to carry out the promise I've given.

Toinette No: I'm sure she won't do it.

Argan I'll darned well make her.

Toinette She won't do it, I tell you.

Argan She'll do it, or I'll put her in a convent.

Toinette You?

Argan I.

Toinette Fine.

Argan What do you mean, "fine"?

Toinette You won't put her in a convent.

Argan I won't put her in a convent?

Toinette No.

Argan No?

Toinette No.

Argan Well now! That's a good one! I won't put my daughter in a convent if I want to?

Toinette No, I tell you.

Argan Who'll stop me?

Toinette You yourself.

Argan I?

Toinette Yes, you won't have the heart to do it.

Argan I will.

Toinette You're joking.

Argan I'm not joking one bit.

Toinette Fatherly affection will get the better of you.

Argan It won't get the better of me.

Toinette A little tear or two, two arms around your neck, a tenderly uttered "my dear little papa," will be enough to touch you.

Argan All that won't do a thing.

Toinette Yes, yes.

Argan I tell you I won't back down.

Toinette Fiddlesticks.

Argan You mustn't say "fiddlesticks."

Toinette Good Lord! I know you; you're naturally good.

Argan [*angrily*] I am not good, I'm bad when I want to be.

Toinette Gently, sir; you're forgetting that you're sick.

Argan I absolutely command her to prepare to take the husband I say.

Toinette And *I* absolutely forbid her to do anything of the sort.

Argan What are we coming to? And what kind of effrontery is that, for a slut of a maidservant to talk that way in front of her master?

Toinette When a master doesn't think what he's doing, a sensible servant has the right to correct him.

Argan [*running after Toinette*] Oh! You insolent hussy, I'll brain you!

Toinette [*running away from him*] It's my duty to oppose anything that may dishonor you.

Argan [*in a fury, chasing her around his chair, stick in hand*] Come here, come here, I'll teach you how to talk.

Toinette [*running around the chair ahead of Argan*] I'm concerned, as I should be, with not letting you do anything foolish.

Argan Slut!

Toinette No, I'll never consent to this marriage.

Argan Gallows bait!

Toinette I don't want her to marry your Thomas Diafoirus.

Argan Jade!

Toinette And she'll obey me rather than you.

Argan Angélique, won't you stop this hussy?

Angélique Oh, father! Don't make yourself sick.

Argan If you don't stop her for me, I'll put my curse on you.

Toinette And *I'll* disinherit her if she obeys you.

Argan [*weary of running after her, throwing himself into his chair*] Oh! Oh! I'm done for. It's enough to kill me.

SCENE SIX

Béline, Angélique, Toinette, Argan

Argan Ah! My wife, come here.

Béline What's wrong, my poor husband?

Argan Come over here and help me.

Béline What in the world is it, my sweet boy?

Argan My darling!

Béline My dearest!

Argan They've just made me angry!

Béline Alas! Poor little hubby! How did it happen, my dear?

Argan That scoundrelly Toinette of yours got more insolent than ever.

Béline Then don't get excited.

Argan She put me in a rage, darling.

Béline Easy, sweet boy.

Argan For one whole hour she opposed the things I want to do.

Béline There, there, gently.

Argan And had the effrontery to tell me I'm not sick.

Béline She's an impertinent hussy.

Argan You know, sweetheart, how it really is.

Béline Yes, sweetheart, she's wrong.

Argan My love, that slut will be the death of me.

Béline There now, there now!

Argan She's the cause of all the bile I'm producing.

Béline Don't get so upset.

Argan And I've been telling you for I don't know how long to dismiss her.

Béline Good Lord, dear boy! There are no servants, men or women, who don't have their faults. Sometimes one is forced to put up with their bad qualities on account of the good ones. This one is adroit, careful, diligent, and above all faithful; and you know that nowadays you need great precautions about the people you take on. Here now! Toinette!

Toinette Madame?

Béline Why in the world do you make my husband angry?

Toinette [*sweetly*] I, Madame? Alas! I don't know what you mean, and all I think of is pleasing the master in all things.

Argan Oh, the traitress!

Toinette He told us he wanted to give his daughter in marriage to the son of Monsieur Diafoirus; I answered that I thought it was an advantageous match for her, but that I thought he'd do better to put her in a convent.

Béline There's no great harm in that, and I think she's right.

Argan Ah, my love! You believe her! She's a scoundrel: she said all kinds of insolent things to me.

Béline Well, I believe you, my dear. There, pull yourself together. Listen, Toinette, if you ever make my husband angry, I'll put you out. Here, give me his fur-lined cloak and some pillows, so I can get him comfortable in his chair. You're all every which way. Pull your night cap well down over your ears; there's nothing like getting air in your ears for catching cold.

Argan Oh, my darling! I'm so grateful to you for all the care you take of me!

Béline [*putting the pillows around Argan and arranging them*] Get up, let me put this under you. Let's put this one here for you to lean on, and that one on the other side. Let's put this one behind your back, and that other one there to prop up your head.

Toinette [*putting a pillow roughly over his head and running off*] And this one to protect you from the evening dew.

Argan [*getting up in anger and throwing all the pillows at Toinette*] Ah, you scoundrel, you're trying to smother me!

Béline There now, there now! Why, what's the matter?

Argan [*out of breath, throwing himself into his chair*] Oh, oh, oh! I'm all in!

Béline Why do you get so angry? She meant well.

Argan My love, you don't know the malice of that she-devil. Ah! She's got me beside myself; and I'll need more than eight doses of medicine and a dozen enemas to make up for all this.

Béline There, there, my little sweet, calm down a bit.

Argan Honey, you're my only consolation.

Béline Poor dear boy.

Argan To try to show my gratitude for the love you bear me, sweetheart, I want, as I told you, to make my will.

Béline Ah, my darling! Let's not talk about that, I beg you. I can't abide the thought of it, and the very word *will* makes me shudder with pain.

Argan I had told you to speak to your notary about that.

Béline There he is in there; I brought him with me.

Argan Then have him come in, my love.

Béline Alas, my dear! When someone really loves her husband, she's hardly in any condition to think about all that.

SCENE SEVEN

The Notary, Béline, Argan

Argan Come here, Monsieur de Bonnefoy, come here. Have a seat, please. My wife has told me, sir, that you're a very reliable man and quite a good friend of hers; and I've asked her to speak to you about a will I want to make.

Béline Alas! I just can't talk about those things.

Notary She explained your intentions to me, sir, and the plan you have for her; and on that score I have this to tell you, that you can't give anything to your wife by your will.

Argan But why not?

Notary Common law opposes it. If you were in a region of statute law, that could be done; but in Paris and the regions of common law, at least most of them, that can't be done, and that disposition would be null and void. The only provision that man and woman conjoined in marriage can make for each other is a mutual gift *inter vivos;* even then there must be no children, whether of the two conjoined, or of either one of them, at the time of the decease of the first to die.

Argan That's a mighty impertinent common law, that a man can't leave anything to a wife who loves him tenderly and takes such care of him. I'd like to consult my lawyer to see how I might do something.

Notary It's not lawyers you should go to, for ordinarily they're strict about those things and imagine it's a great crime to deal with the law by fraud. They're people who make difficulties and are ignorant of the detours of conscience. There are other people to consult who are much more accommodating, who have expedients for quietly getting around the law and making something just that isn't permitted; who know how to smooth out the difficulties of an affair and find ways to elude the common law by some indirect advantage. Without that, where would we be every day? There has to be some facility in things; otherwise we wouldn't get anything done, and I wouldn't give you a sou for our business.

Argan Indeed, my wife had told me that you were very able, and a very reliable man. How can I go about it, if you please, to give her my estate and keep it from my children?

Notary How can you go about it? You can quietly pick out some intimate friend of your wife, to whom in your will you'll give in due form all that you can; and then this friend will give everything back to her. Or again, you can contract a large number of obligations, all above board, toward various creditors, who will lend their names to your wife, and will put into her hands a declaration that what they've done was only to serve her. You can also, while you are alive, put ready cash in her hands, or notes that you may have, made payable to the bearer.

Béline Good Lord! You mustn't worry yourself about all that. If ever I don't have you, my sweet boy, I don't want to stay in this world.

Argan My darling!

Béline Yes, my darling, if I'm unhappy enough to lose you . . .

Argan My dear wife!

Béline Life won't mean a thing to me any more.

Argan My love!

Béline And I'll follow in your footsteps, to let you know the affection I have for you.

Argan My darling, you're breaking my heart. Console yourself, please.

Notary These tears are out of season, and things haven't come to that yet.

Béline Ah, sir! You don't know what it is to have a husband you love tenderly.

Argan The only regret I'll have if I die, my darling, is not to have a child by you. Monsieur Purgon told me he'd have me have one.

Notary That may still come.

Argan I'll have to make my will, my love, in the way the gentleman says; but as a precaution, I want to put into your hands twenty thousand francs in gold, which I have in the panel of my alcove, and two notes payable to the bearer that are due me, one from Monsieur Damon, and the other from Monsieur Gérante.

Béline No, no, I don't want any of that at all . . . Ah! How much did you say there was in your alcove?

Argan Twenty thousand francs, my love.

Béline Don't talk to me about money, I beg you . . . Ah! How much are the two notes?

Argan My darling, one is for four thousand francs, and the other for six.

Béline All the money in the world, my darling, is nothing to me compared with you.

Notary Shall we proceed to the will?

Argan Yes, sir; but we'll be better in my little study. [*Gets up, then remembers his illness.*] My love, take me in, please.

Béline Come on, my poor sweet little boy.

SCENE EIGHT

Angélique, Toinette

Toinette There they are with a notary, and I heard them talking about a will. Your stepmother isn't falling asleep, and no doubt it's some conspiracy against your interests that she's pushing your father into.

Angélique Let him dispose of his money as he likes, provided he doesn't dispose of my heart. You see, Toinette, the plans they're making to do violence to it. Don't abandon me, I beg you, in the extremity I'm in.

Toinette I, abandon you? I'd rather die. Your stepmother can make me her confidante and try to get me to work for her all she likes, but I've never been able to have any inclination for her, and I've always been on your side. Leave it to me: I'll do everything to serve you; but to serve you more effectively I want to change my line of attack, cover up the zeal I have for you, and pretend to fall in with the feelings of your father and your stepmother.

Angélique Try, I beseech you, to let Cléante know about the marriage they've arranged.

Toinette I have no one to use for that purpose but my sweetheart Punchinello, the old usurer, and it will cost me a few sweet nothings that I'm willing to spend for you. For today it's too late; but tomorrow bright and early I'll send for him, and he'll be delighted to . . .

Béline [*offstage*] Toinette!

Toinette They're calling me. Good night. Rely on me.

FIRST INTERLUDE

Punchinello, coming to serenade his mistress, is interrupted by the violinists, then by the watch, whom he has to pay off to avoid being beaten. Since this interlude has nothing to do with the rest of the play, it is omitted here.

Act Two

SCENE ONE
Toinette, Cléante (disguised)

Toinette [*not recognizing Cléante*] What do you want, sir?

Cléante What do I want?

Toinette [*recognizing him*] Aha! It's you? What a surprise! What have you come here for?

Cléante To learn my destiny, speak to the lovely Angélique, inquire about the feelings of her heart, and ask her what she has resolved about this fatal marriage I've been informed about.

Toinette Yes, but you don't talk point-blank like that to Angélique. There have to be mysteries, and you've been told of the tight guard she's kept under, how they don't let her go out, or talk to anyone, and that it was only the curiosity of an elderly aunt of hers that got us permission to go to that play that was the scene of the birth of your passion; and we have taken good care not to speak of that adventure.

Cléante So I'm not coming here as Cléante and in the role of her sweetheart, but as a friend of her music teacher, who has authorized me to say that he's sending me in his place.

Toinette Here's her father. Go out for a bit, and let me tell him that you're here.

SCENE TWO

Argan, Toinette, Cléante

Argan Monsieur Purgon told me to take a walk in my room in the morning, twelve times up and back; but I forgot to ask him whether he meant lengthwise or crosswise.

Toinette Sir, here is a . . .

Argan Speak softly, you slut; you're shaking up my whole brain, and you forget that you mustn't speak so loud to the sick.

Toinette I wanted to tell you, sir . . .

Argan Speak low, I tell you.

Toinette Sir . . . [*Pretending to speak.*]

Argan Eh?

Toinette I tell you that . . . [*Pretending to speak.*]

Argan What's that you say?

Toinette [*shouting*] I tell you that there's a man who wants to speak to you.

Argan Have him come in. [*Toinette beckons to Cléante to come forward.*]

Cléante Sir . . .

Toinette [*teasing*] Don't speak so loud, for fear of shaking up the master's brain.

Cléante Sir, I'm delighted to find you up and around and to see that you're better.

Toinette [*pretending to be angry*] What do you mean, he's better? That's not true. The master is always ill.

Cléante I heard that the gentleman was better, and I think he looks well.

Toinette What do you mean, he looks well? The master looks very badly, and the people who told you he was better don't know what they're talking about. He's never been so ill.

Argan She's right.

Toinette He walks, sleeps, eats, and drinks just like anyone else; but that doesn't keep him from being very sick.

Argan That's true.

Cléante Sir, I'm terribly sorry. I've come on behalf of your daughter's singing teacher. He had to go to the country for a few days; and he sends me, as his intimate friend, in his place, to continue her lessons for him, for fear that by interrupting them she might come to forget what she already knows.

Argan Very well. Call Angélique.

Toinette I think, sir, it will be better for me to take the gentleman to her room.

Argan No; have her come.

Toinette He won't be able to give her a lesson properly unless they are alone.

Argan Yes he will, yes he will.

Toinette Sir, it will only deafen you, and it doesn't take anything to upset you in the state you're in, and shake up your brain.

Argan Not at all, not at all; I like music, and I'll be very glad to. . . . Ah! Here she is! You, go see if my wife is dressed.

SCENE THREE

Argan, Angélique, Cléante

Argan Come here, daughter; your music teacher has gone to the country, and here's someone he's sending in his place to teach you.

Angélique [*recognizing Cléante as he turns to face her*] Ah, Heavens!

Argan What is it? Why this surprise?

Angélique It's . . .

Argan What? What moves you so?

Angélique Father, it's a surprising coincidence I find here.

Argan How's that?

Angélique I dreamed last night that I was in the worst predicament in the world, and that someone who looked just like this gentleman presented himself. I asked him for help, and he came and got me out of the trouble I was in; and my surprise was great to see unexpectedly, on arriving here, what I had in mind all night.

Cléante That's no unhappy lot, to occupy your mind whether you're asleep or awake, and my happiness would unquestionably be great if you were in some trouble that you thought me worthy to get you out of; and there's nothing I wouldn't do to . . .

SCENE FOUR

Toinette, Cléante, Angélique, Argan

Toinette [*in derision*] Faith, sir, I'm for you now, and I take back all I was saying yesterday. Here are Monsieur Diafoirus the father and Monsieur Diafoirus the son, come to pay you a visit. How well son-in-lawed you will be! You're going to see the handsomest young fellow in the world, and the wittiest. He said just two words, which delighted me, and your daughter's going to be charmed with him.

Argan [*to Cléante, who pretends he wants to go*] Don't go away, sir. You see, I'm marrying off my daughter; and now they're bringing her her prospective husband, whom she hasn't yet seen.

Cléante That's doing me a great honor, to want me to be witness to such a charming interview.

Argan He's the son of an able doctor, and the marriage will take place in four days.

Cléante Very good.

Argan Just tell her music teacher about it, so he'll be at the wedding.

Cléante I won't fail to.

Argan I'm inviting you too.

Cléante You do me much honor.

Toinette Come, make room, here they are.

SCENE FIVE

Monsieur Diafoirus, Thomas Diafoirus, Argan, Angélique, Cléante, Toinette

Argan [*putting his hand to his hat without taking it off*] Sir, Monsieur Purgon has forbidden me to uncover my head. You're in the business, you know the consequences.

Monsieur Diafoirus In all our visits we are there to bring help to the sick, and not to bring them any discomfort.

Argan Sir, I receive . . .

They both speak at the same time, interrupting each other.

Monsieur Diafoirus We come here, sir . . .

Argan With great joy . . .

Monsieur Diafoirus My son Thomas and I . . .

Argan The honor you do me . . .

Monsieur Diafoirus To let you know, sir . . .

Argan And I would have wished . . .

Monsieur Diafoirus The delight that is ours . . .

Argan To be able to go to your house . . .

Monsieur Diafoirus For the kindness you do us . . .

Argan To assure you . . .

Monsieur Diafoirus In being willing to receive us . . .

Argan But you know, sir . . .

Monsieur Diafoirus Into the honor, sir . . .

Argan What a poor invalid is . . .

Monsieur Diafoirus Of an alliance with you . . .

Argan Who can do nothing else . . .

Monsieur Diafoirus And to assure you . . .

Argan Than to tell you now . . .

Monsieur Diafoirus That in all matters that depend on my profession . . .

Argan That he will seek every occasion . . .

Monsieur Diafoirus As well as in all others . . .

Argan To let you know, sir . . .

Monsieur Diafoirus We shall always be ready, sir . . .

Argan That he is entirely at your service.

Monsieur Diafoirus To demonstrate our zeal to you. [*Turning back to his son.*] Come on, Thomas, step forward. Pay your compliments.

Thomas Diafoirus [*a great simpleton, recently issued from the schools, who does everything clumsily and at the wrong time*] Isn't it the father I'm supposed to begin with?

Monsieur Diafoirus Yes.

Thomas Diafoirus Sir, I come to salute, recognize, cherish, and revere in you a second father; but a second father to whom I take the liberty of saying that I am more indebted than to the first. The first engendered me, but you have chosen me. He received me through necessity, but you have accepted me through kindness. What I have from him is a work of his body; but what I have from you is a work of your will; and the more the spiritual faculties are above the corporeal, the more I owe you, and the more I hold precious this future filiation, for which I come today to pay in advance my most humble and most respectful homage.

Toinette Hurrah for the schools, which produce such able men!

Thomas Diafoirus Was that all right, father?

Monsieur Diafoirus *Optime.*

Argan [*to Angélique*] Come on, greet the gentleman. [*Angélique curtsies.*]

Thomas Diafoirus Do I kiss?

Monsieur Diafoirus Yes, yes.

Thomas Diafoirus [*to Angélique*] Madame, it is with justice that Heaven has granted you the fair name of mother-in-law, since we . . .

Argan It's not my wife, it's my daughter you're speaking to.

Thomas Diafoirus Then where is she?

Argan She's coming.

Thomas Diafoirus Do I wait, father, till she comes?

Monsieur Diafoirus Go ahead and pay your compliment to Mademoiselle.

Thomas Diafoirus Mademoiselle, no more nor less than the statue of Memnon gave forth a harmonious sound when it came to be lit by the sun's rays, even so I feel myself animated by a sweet transport at the apparition of the sun of your beauties. And as the naturalists note that the flower named heliotrope turns incessantly toward that day star, so my heart shall henceforth always turn toward the resplendent stars of your adorable eyes, as toward its only pole. So permit me, Mademoiselle, to append to the altar of your charms the offering of this heart, which breathes and aspires to no other glory than to be all its life, Mademoiselle, your most humble, most obedient, and most faithful servant and husband.

Toinette [*mocking him*] That's what it is to study, you learn to say beautiful things.

Argan [*to Cléante*] Well! What do you say to that?

Cléante That the gentleman does wonders, and that if he's as good a doctor as he is an orator, it will be a pleasure to be a patient of his.

Toinette Yes indeed. It will be something wonderful if he cures as well as he makes speeches.

Argan Come, quick, my chair, and seats for everybody. You sit there, daughter. You see, sir, that everyone admires your son, and I think you're very fortunate to have a boy like that.

Monsieur Diafoirus Sir, it's not because I'm his father, but I may say that I have reason to be pleased with him, and that everyone who sees him speaks of him as a boy who has no wickedness in him. He has never had a very lively imagination, nor that sparkling wit that you notice in some; but it's by this that I have always augured well of his judgment, a quality required for the exercise of our art. When he was small, he never was what you'd call mischievous or lively. He was always mild, peaceful, and taciturn, never saying a word, and never playing all those little games that we call childish. We had all the trouble in the world in teaching him to read, and he was nine years old before he ever knew his letters. "All right," I used to say to myself, "the late-growing trees are the ones that bear the best fruit; you have much more trouble engraving on marble than on sand; but things are preserved there much longer, and this slowness of understanding, this heaviness of imagination, is the sign of a good judgment to come." When I sent him to school, he had trouble; but he stood firm against the difficulties, and his teachers always praised him to me for his assiduity and his hard work. Finally, by keeping hard at it, he succeeded in earning his *licence* gloriously; and I may say without vanity that in the two years he's been on the benches there is no candidate that has made more noise than he in all the disputations in our school. He's made himself redoubtable at this, and no act is ever passed without his arguing to the last ditch for the opposite proposition. He is firm in dispute, strong as a Turk on his principles, he never gives up his opinion, and he follows a line of reasoning down to the last recesses of logic. But what I like about him above all else, and in which he follows my example, is that he attaches himself blindly to the opinions of our ancients, and he has never been willing to understand or listen to the reasons and experiments of the so-called discoveries of our century, about the circulation of the blood, and other opinions of the same ilk.

Thomas Diafoirus [*drawing a great rolled thesis from his pocket and presenting it to Angélique*] I have maintained a thesis against the circulators, which, with the gentleman's permission, I make bold to present to Mademoiselle, as a homage I owe her of the first fruits of my mind.

Angélique Sir, that's a useless article for me, and I'm no expert in those matters.

Toinette Give it here, give it here; it's always worth taking for the picture; it will serve to decorate our bedroom.

Thomas Diafoirus Also with the gentleman's permission, I invite you to come one of these days, for your entertainment, to see the dissection of a woman, on which I am to make a dissertation.

Toinette That will be a delightful entertainment. There are some who put on a play for their sweethearts; but to put on a dissection is a much more gallant thing.

Monsieur Diafoirus [*confidentially, to Argan*] For the rest, as regards the qualities requisite for marriage and propagation, I assure you that, according to the rules of our doctors, he is just as one could wish; he possesses the prolific virtue to a laudable degree, and he is of the proper temperament to engender and procreate well-conditioned children.

Argan Isn't it your intention, sir, to push him at court and get him a position as a doctor there?

Monsieur Diafoirus To be frank with you, our profession among the great has never seemed agreeable to me, and I have always found it better for us to stick to the general public. The public is easy to deal with. You don't have to answer to anyone for your actions; and provided you follow the current of the rules of our art, you don't have to worry about anything that can happen. But what is annoying with the great is that when they fall ill they absolutely insist that their doctors cure them.

Toinette That's a funny one, and they are mighty presumptuous to insist that you gentlemen cure them; you're not there for that; you're there only to receive your fees and prescribe remedies for them; it's up to them to be cured if they can.

Monsieur Diafoirus That's true. We're obliged only to treat people according to the proper forms.

Argan [*to Cléante*] Sir, have my daughter sing a bit for the company.

Cléante I was awaiting your orders, sir, and it occurred to me, to entertain the company, to sing with Mademoiselle a scene from a little opera that was composed recently. [*To Angélique.*] Here, this is your part. [*Gives her a piece of paper.*]

Angélique Me? [*Gets up and takes the paper.*]

Cléante [*to Angélique*] Don't refuse, please, and let me make you understand what the scene is that we are to sing. [*To all.*] I have no singing voice, but it's enough here for me to make myself heard, and you will be good enough to excuse me because of the necessity I'm in to have Mademoiselle sing.

Argan Are the verses nice?

Cléante This is really a little impromptu opera, and all you'll hear sung is rhythmic prose, or a kind of free verse, such as passion and necessity can inspire in two persons who say what they say by themselves, and speak extemporaneously.

Argan Very well. Let's listen.

Cléante Here is the subject of the scene. A shepherd was attentive to the beauties of a performance, which had just begun, when his attention was distracted by a noise he heard nearby. He turns around and sees a brutish fellow mistreating a shepherdess with insolent words. Immediately he espouses the interests of a sex to which all men owe homage; and after giving the brute the punishment due to his insolence, he comes to the shepherdess and sees a young person who, from the two most beautiful eyes he had ever seen, was shedding tears, which he thought the most beautiful in the world. "Alas!" he says to himself, "is it possible for anyone to outrage so lovely a person? And what inhuman barbarian would not be touched by such tears?" He takes pains to stop them, these tears that he finds so beautiful; and the lovely shepherdess takes pains at the same time to thank him for this slight service of his, but in a manner so charming, so tender, and so passionate, that the shepherd cannot resist it; and each word, each glance is a flaming dart which he feels penetrating his heart. "Is there anything," he says, "that can deserve the lovely expression of such thanks? And what would a man not do, what service and what danger would he not hasten in delight to undergo, to win a single moment of the touching tenderness of so grateful a soul?"

The whole performance takes place without his paying any attention to it; but he complains that it is too short, because the end separates him from his adorable shepherdess; and from that first sight, from that first moment, he takes home with him all the greatest violence of several years of love. Now immediately he feels all the pangs of absence, and he is tormented at seeing no more what he has seen so little. He does all he can to see once again this vision, of which he retains night and day so dear an image; but the great constraint in which his shepherdess is kept deprives him of any means of doing so. The violence of his passion makes him resolve to ask to marry the adorable beauty without whom he can no longer live, and he obtains her permission to do so by a note which adroitly he succeeds in putting into her hands. But at the same time he is informed that the father of this beauty has arranged her marriage to another, and that all is being prepared to celebrate the ceremony.

Think what a cruel blow this is to the heart of this sad shepherd. Behold him stricken with a mortal sorrow. He cannot bear the frightful idea of seeing the one he loves in another's arms; and his love, in despair, makes him find a way to enter the house of his shepherdess, to learn her feelings and find out from her the destiny he must accept. There he finds the preparations for all he fears; there he sees the unworthy rival come whom a father's caprice opposes to the tenderness of his love. He sees this ridiculous rival, triumphant, with the lovely shepherdess, as with a conquest of which he is assured; and this sight fills him with an anger which he finds hard to master. He casts pained glances at the one he adores; and his respect, and the presence of her father, keep him from saying anything except with his eyes.

But finally he overcomes all constraint, and the transport of his love obliges him to speak to her thus:
[*Sings.*]

Fair Phyllis, too much pain have I;
Break this harsh silence, tell me how you feel.
My destiny you must reveal:
Am I to live or shall I die?

Angélique [*singing in response*]

You see me, Tircis, sad and melancholy,
Confronted by this marriage that you dread;
I raise my eyes to Heaven, I look at you, I sigh,
And that is enough said.

Argan Well, well! I didn't think my daughter was good enough to sing at sight like that without hesitation.

Cléante

Alas! O lovely Phyllis,
Can it be true that ever-loving Tircis
Has such rapture for his part
As to hold some small place within your heart?

Angélique

I've no defense in my extreme distress:
Tircis, I love you, yes.

Cléante

O words full of delight!
Alas! Can I have heard aright?
Say them again, Phyllis, and put my doubts to flight.

Angélique

Yes, Tircis, I love you.

Cléante

Pray, Phyllis, one more time.

Angélique

I love you.

Cléante

Begin again a hundred times, and never tire.

Angélique

I love you, I love you,
Yes, Tircis, I love you.

Cléante

O Gods, O kings, who see the world beneath your feet,
Can you compare your happiness with mine?
But, Phyllis, there's one thought
That comes to mar my bliss:
A rival, a rival . . .

Angélique

Ah! I hate him more than death.
And his presence is to me,
A torment, as it is to you.

Cléante

But your father's will can set your hopes awry.

Angélique

I'd rather, rather die
Than ever to comply,
Rather, rather die, rather die.

Argan And what does the father say to all that?

Cléante [*back to earth, after a pause*] He doesn't say a thing.

Argan That's a stupid father, that father, to put up with all that nonsense without saying a thing.

Cléante [*sings*]

Ah! My love . . .

Argan No, no, that's enough of that. That play sets a very bad example. The shepherd Tircis is an impertinent fellow, and the shepherdess Phyllis an impudent girl, to talk that way in front of her father. Show me that paper. [*Angélique hands it over reluctantly.*] Aha! Why, where are the words you spoke? There's nothing written here but music.

Cléante Don't you know, sir, that they've recently invented a way to write the words with the notes themselves?

Argan Very well. I'm your servant, sir; good-by. We could have gotten along very nicely without your silly opera.

Cléante I thought it would entertain you.

Argan Stupid things aren't entertaining. Ah! Here's my wife.

SCENE SIX

Béline, Argan, Toinette, Angélique, Monsieur Diafoirus, Thomas Diafoirus

Argan My love, here is the son of Monsieur Diafoirus.

Thomas Diafoirus [*beginning a memorized compliment, but unable to continue when his memory fails him*] Madame, it is with justice that Heaven has granted you the fair name of mother-in-law, since we see on your face . . .

Béline Sir, I am delighted to have come here at the right time to have the honor of seeing you.

Thomas Diafoirus Since we see on your face . . . since we see on your face . . . Madame, you interrupted me in the middle of my sentence, and that has troubled my memory.

Monsieur Diafoirus Thomas, save that for another time.

Argan Honey, I wish you'd been here just now.

Toinette Ah, Madame! You missed a lot by not being here for the second father, the statue of Memnon, and the flower called heliotrope.

Argan Come, daughter, take the gentleman's hand, and plight him your troth as your husband.

Angélique Father.

Argan Well then! "Father?" What does that mean?

Angélique I beseech you, don't hurry things. At least give us the time to come to know each other, and to see within us the birth of that inclination for one another that is so necessary to make up a perfect union.

Thomas Diafoirus As for me, Mademoiselle, it is already full born in me, and I have no need to wait any longer.

Angélique If you are so prompt, sir, it is not the same with me, and I admit to you that your merit has not yet made enough impression on my soul.

Argan Oh, well, well! There'll be plenty of time for that to develop when you're married to each other.

Angélique Ah, father! Give me time, I beg you. Marriage is a bond that should never be imposed on a heart by force; and if the gentleman is an honorable man, he must not want to accept a person who would belong to him by constraint.

Thomas Diafoirus *Nego consequentiam,*★ Mademoiselle, and I can be an honorable man and still be willing to accept you from the hands of your father.

Angélique That's a bad way to make someone love you, to do her violence.

Thomas Diafoirus We read of the ancients, Mademoiselle, that it was their custom to carry off by force from the fathers' house the daughters they were taking to marry, so that it should not seem that it was by their own consent that they flew off in a man's arms.

Angélique The ancients, sir, are the ancients, and we are the people of today. Pretences are not necessary in our time; and when we are pleased with a marriage, we are perfectly capable of going to it without being dragged. Have patience: if you love me, sir, you should want everything I want.

Thomas Diafoirus Yes, Mademoiselle, up to but not including the interests of my love.

Angélique But the great mark of love is to submit to the will of the one you love.

Thomas Diafoirus *Distinguo,* Mademoiselle. In what does not concern the possession of her, *concedo;* but in what concerns it, *nego.*†

Toinette [*to Angélique*] There's no use your arguing. The gentleman is fresh out of school, and he'll always have the upper hand. Why do you resist so, and refuse the glory of being attached to the staff of the Faculty?

Béline Perhaps she has some other inclination in her head.

Angélique If I had, Madame, it would be such a one as reason and decency would permit.

Argan Well! I'm playing a funny part here.

★ "I deny the consequence," a phrase used in scholastic debate.

† *Distinguo,* "I make a distinction." *Concedo,* "I concede the point." *Nego,* "I deny it."

Béline If I were you, dear boy, I wouldn't force her to get married, and I know very well what I'd do.

Angélique I know what you mean, Madame, and the kindness you have for me; but perhaps your advice won't have the good fortune to be carried out.

Béline That's because decent well-behaved daughters like you laugh at being obedient and submissive to their fathers' will. It was better in the old days.

Angélique A daughter's duty has limits, Madame, and reason and the laws do not extend it to every kind of matter.

Béline That is to say that your thoughts are all for marriage, but you want to choose a husband to suit your fancy.

Angélique If my father won't give me a husband I like, I shall at least conjure him not to force me to marry one I cannot love.

Argan Gentlemen, I beg your pardon for all this.

Angélique Everyone has his own aim in getting married. As for me, since I want a husband only to love him truly, and since I mean to attach myself entirely to him for life, I admit I want some precautions. There are some women who take a husband only to extricate themselves from the constraint of their parents and get in a position to do whatever they want. There are others, Madame, who make of marriage a matter of pure self-interest, who marry only to get inheritances, only to get rich by the death of the men they marry, and run without scruple from husband to husband to appropriate their spoils. Those persons, in truth, are not so particular, and care little who the person may be.

Béline You're quite a reasoner today, and I'd very much like to know what you mean by that.

Angélique I, Madame? What should I mean except what I say?

Béline You're so stupid, my dear, you're really unbearable.

Angélique Madame, you'd like to provoke me into some impertinent reply; but I warn you that you shall not have that advantage.

Béline I've never seen the like of your insolence.

Angélique No, Madame, it's no use your talking.

Béline And you have a ridiculous pride, an impertinent presumption, that makes people shrug their shoulders.

Angélique All that, Madame, will be no use. I'll be well-behaved in spite of you; and to deprive you of any hope of being able to succeed in what you want, I'm going to remove myself from your sight.

Argan Listen, there's no middle ground in this. Make up your mind to marry, within four days, either this gentleman, or a convent. *Exit Angélique.*

Don't worry. I'll bring her around.

Béline I'm sorry to leave you, sweet boy, but I have business in town that I must attend to. I'll be back soon.

Argan Go ahead, my love, and stop at your notary's, so that he'll expedite you know what.

Béline Good-by, my little darling.

Argan Good-by, my dear. *Exit Béline.*

There's a woman who loves me so. . . . It's incredible.

Monsieur Diafoirus Sir, we're going to take leave of you.

Argan I beg you, sir, just to tell me how I am.

Monsieur Diafoirus [*taking his pulse*] Come on, Thomas, take the gentleman's other arm, to see if you can make a good judgment about his pulse. *Quid dicis?*

Thomas Diafoirus *Dico* that the gentleman's pulse is the pulse of a man who is not well.

Monsieur Diafoirus Good.

Thomas Diafoirus That it is a wee bit hardish, not to say hard.

Monsieur Diafoirus Very good.

Thomas Diafoirus Beating strongly.

Monsieur Diafoirus *Bene.*

Thomas Diafoirus And even a little capricious.

Monsieur Diafoirus *Optime.*

Thomas Diafoirus Which indicates an intemperance in the splenic parenchyma, that is to say the spleen.

Monsieur Diafoirus Very good.

Argan No. Monsieur Purgon says it's my liver that's sick.

Monsieur Diafoirus Oh, yes! If anyone says *parenchyma,* he says both, because of the close sympathy they have with each other, by means of the *vas breve* of the *pylorus,* and often of the *choledochal meatuses.* No doubt he orders you to eat a lot of roast meat?

Argan No, nothing but boiled.

Monsieur Diafoirus Oh, yes! Roast, boiled, all the same thing. He prescribes for you very prudently, and you couldn't be in better hands.

Argan Sir, how many grains of salt should one put on an egg?

Monsieur Diafoirus Six, eight, or ten, in even numbers; just as with medicines, in odd numbers.

Argan Good-by, sir.

SCENE SEVEN

Béline, Argan

Béline Before I go out, dear boy, I've come to inform you about something you must watch out for. As I passed in front of Angélique's room, I saw a young man with her, who ran away as soon as he saw me.

Argan A young man with my daughter?

Béline Yes. Your little daughter Louison was with them, and can tell you some things about it.

Argan Send her here, my love, send her here. Ah, the brazen girl! No wonder she resisted so.

SCENE EIGHT

Louison, Argan

Louison What do you want, papa? My stepmother said you're asking for me.

Argan Yes, come here. Come nearer. There. Turn around, raise your eyes, look at me. Well?

Louison What, papa?

Argan Here now.

Louison What?

Argan Haven't you anything to tell me?

Louison If you want, I'll tell you, to divert you, the story of the Ass's Skin or the fable of the Fox and the Crow, which was taught me recently.

Argan That's not what I'm asking.

Louison What, then?

Argan Ah, you sly girl! You know very well what I mean.

Louison I beg your pardon, papa.

Argan Is this how you obey me?

Louison What?

Argan Didn't I ask you to come and tell me right away anything you see?

Louison Yes, papa.

Argan Have you done that?

Louison Yes, papa. I came and told you everything I've seen.

Argan And haven't you seen anything today?

Louison No, papa.

Argan No?

Louison No, papa.

Argan Are you sure?

Louison I'm sure.

Argan Oh, now really! *I'm* going to make you see something. [*He goes and picks up a switch.*]

Louison Oh, papa!

Argan Aha! You little minx, you didn't tell me that you saw a man in your sister's room.

Louison Papa!

Argan Here's something that'll teach you to lie.

Louison [*falling on her knees*] Oh, papa, I ask your pardon. You see, sister had told me not to tell you; but I'm going to tell you everything.

Argan First you've got to have a whipping for lying. Then afterward we'll see about the rest.

Louison Forgive me, papa!

Argan No, no.

Louison Dear papa, don't give me a whipping!

Argan You shall have it.

Louison In Heaven's name, papa, don't whip me!

Argan [*taking hold of her to whip her*] Come on, come on.

Louison Oh, papa, you've hurt me! Stop, I'm dead. [*She plays dead.*]

Argan Hey! What's this? Louison! Louison! Oh, good Lord! Louison! Oh, my daughter! Oh, unhappy me, my poor daughter is dead! What have I done, wretch that I am? Oh, blast this switch! Plague take all switches! Oh, my poor daughter, my poor little Louison!

Louison There, there, papa, don't cry so hard, I'm not dead—quite.

Argan Will you look at that little trickster? Oh, all right! I forgive you this time, provided you really tell me everything.

Louison Oh, yes, papa!

Argan Anyway, be good and sure you do, for here's my little finger that knows everything and will tell me if you lie.

Louison But, papa, don't tell my sister I told you.

Argan No, no.

Louison The fact is, papa, a man did come into sister's room while I was there.

Argan Well?

Louison I asked him what he wanted, and he told me he was her singing teacher.

Argan Oho! So that's the game. Well?

Louison Then sister came.

Argan Well?

Louison She said to him: "Go, go, go! Good Lord, go! You're driving me to despair."

Argan Well?

Louison Well, *he* didn't want to go.

Argan What did he say to her?

Louison He said I don't know how many things.

Argan And then what?

Louison He told her all this and all that, that he loved her dearly, and that she was the most beautiful girl in the world.

Argan And after that?

Louison And after that, he got on his knees before her.

Argan And after that?

Louison And after that, he kissed her hands.

Argan And after that?

Louison And after that, my stepmama came to the door, and he ran away.

Argan There's nothing else?

Louison No, papa.

Argan But here's my little finger mumbling something. [*Put-*

ting his finger to his ear.] Wait! Eh? Aha! Yes? Oho! Here's my little finger telling me there's something you saw and that you haven't told me.

Louison Oh, papa! Your little finger's a liar.

Argan Take care!

Louison No, papa, don't believe it, it's lying, I assure you.

Argan Oh, all right, all right! We'll see about that. Run along, and keep an eye out for everything. Go on.

Exit Louison.

Ah! There are no children any more. Oh! What a lot of troubles! I don't even have time to think about my illness. Really, I'm done for. [*Sits down in his chair again.*]

SCENE NINE

Béralde, Argan

Béralde Well, brother, what's up? How are you?

Argan Ah, brother! Very bad.

Béralde How do you mean, very bad?

Argan Yes, I'm so weak you wouldn't believe it.

Béralde That's too bad.

Argan I haven't even the strength to be able to speak.

Béralde I've come here, brother, to propose to you a match for my niece Angélique.

Argan [*speaking furiously, and rising from his chair*] Brother, don't talk to me about that wicked girl! She's an impertinent, brazen hussy, and I'll put her into a convent before two days are up.

Béralde Oh! That's fine. I'm very glad that your strength is coming back a bit, and that my visit is doing you good. Oh, well, we'll talk about business later. I'm bringing you an entertainment I came across that will banish your melancholy and make your soul better disposed for the things we have to talk about. They are Gypsies dressed as Moors, who put on dances mingled with songs. I'm sure you'll enjoy them, and they'll do you as much good as one of Monsieur Purgon's prescriptions. Come on.

SECOND INTERLUDE

A troop of Gypsies dance and sing songs in praise of love, and their pet monkeys join in one of the dances. Since the songs have nothing to do with the rest of the play, they are omitted here.

Act Three

SCENE ONE

Béralde, Argan, Toinette

Béralde Well, brother, what do you say to that? Isn't that as good as a dose of senna?

Toinette Hm! Good senna is good.

Béralde Well, now! Would you like to have a little talk together?

Argan Be patient a bit, brother, I'll be back.

Toinette Wait, sir, you're forgetting that you can't walk without a stick.

Argan You're right.

SCENE TWO

Béralde, Toinette

Toinette Please don't abandon your niece's interests.

Béralde I'll do everything I can to get her what she wants.

Toinette It's absolutely necessary to prevent this crazy marriage that he's taken into his head, and I had thought to myself that it would have been a good idea to be able to bring in here a doctor of our own choosing, to give him a distaste for his Monsieur Purgon and disparage his methods. But since we have no one in hand for that, I've resolved to play a trick out of my head.

Béralde How's that?

Toinette It's a wild idea. Maybe it will be more lucky than it is sensible. Leave it to me; for your part, do what you can. Here's our man.

SCENE THREE

Argan, Béralde

Béralde Allow me, brother, to ask you above all not to get excited during our conversation.

Argan That's settled.

Béralde To answer any things I may say to you without bitterness.

Argan Yes.

Béralde And to reason together on the things we have to talk about with a mind detached from any passion.

Argan Good Lord, yes! That's a lot of preamble.

Béralde How does it happen, brother, that with the money you have, and no children but one daughter, for I'm not counting the little one, how does it happen, I say, that you're talking about putting her into a convent?

Argan How does it happen, brother, that I am master in my family to do what seems good to me?

Béralde Your wife doesn't fail to advise you to get rid of both your daughters thus, and I have no doubt that, out of a spirit of charity, she would be delighted to see both of them be good nuns.

Argan Aha! Here we go. You've got my poor wife into it right away: she's the one who does all the harm, and everyone has it in for her.

Béralde No, brother; let's let her be; she's a woman who has the best intentions in the world for your family, free of any sort of self-interest, who has a marvelous tenderness for you, and displays for your children an affection and a kindness which are inconceivable; that's certain. Let's not talk about her, and let's come back to your daughter. What's your idea, brother, in wanting to give her in marriage to a doctor's son?

Argan My idea, brother, is to give myself the kind of son-in-law I need.

Béralde That, brother, isn't the thing for your daughter, and there's a match available that's more suitable for her.

Argan Yes, brother, but this one is more suitable for me.

Béralde But, brother, should the husband she is to take be for her or for you?

Argan He should be, brother, both for her and for me, and I want to bring into my family the people I need.

Béralde On that reasoning, if your little one was grown up, you'd give her in marriage to an apothecary?

Argan Why not?

Béralde Is it possible that you will always be infatuated with your apothecaries and your doctors, and that you intend to be sick in spite of everyone and of nature herself?

Argan How do you mean that, brother?

Béralde I mean, brother, that I don't see one single man who is less sick than you, and that I wouldn't ask for a better constitution than yours. One great sign that you are healthy and that you have a perfectly well set up body is that with all the cares you have taken you haven't yet succeeded in ruining the soundness of your system, and that you haven't burst with all the medicines they've had you take.

Argan But do you realize, brother, that that's what's keeping me alive, and that Monsieur Purgon says I would succumb if he went even three days without taking care of me?

Béralde If you're not careful, he'll take such care of you that he'll send you into the other world.

Argan But let's discuss this a little, brother. So you don't believe in medicine?

Béralde No, brother, and I don't believe it's necessary, for our salvation, to believe in it.

Argan What? You don't believe in the truth of a thing established by everyone, and which every age has revered?

Béralde Very far from believing in its truth, I consider it, between us, one of the greatest follies there is among men; and looking at things as a philosopher, I can see no more comical piece of mummery, I can see nothing more ridiculous, than one man wanting to undertake to cure another.

Argan Brother, why won't you allow that one man can cure another?

Béralde For this reason, brother: that the functioning of our machine is a mystery in which up to now men can't see a thing, and nature has put before our eyes veils too thick to allow us to know anything about it.

Argan So the doctors don't know anything, by your account?

Béralde Oh yes, they do, brother. Most of them know a lot in the humanities, know how to talk in fine Latin, know how to name all the diseases in Greek, define them, and classify them; but as for curing them, that's what they don't know how to do at all.

Argan But still you must agree that on this matter the doctors know more than others.

Béralde Brother, they know what I've told you, which doesn't cure anyone of very much; and the whole excellence of their art consists of a pompous mumbo-jumbo, a specious chatter, which gives you words for reasons, and promises for results.

Argan But after all, brother, there are people as wise and as clever as you; and we see that in time of sickness, everyone has recourse to the doctors.

Béralde That's a sign of human weakness, and not of the truth of their art.

Argan But the doctors must certainly believe their art is true, since they use it for themselves.

Béralde That's because there are some among them who themselves share the popular delusion, by which they profit, and others who profit by it without sharing it. Your Monsieur Purgon, for example, doesn't try to fool anybody: he's a man who's all doctor, from head to foot, a man who believes in his rules more than in all the demonstrations of mathematics, and who would think it a crime to want to examine them; who sees in medicine nothing obscure, nothing doubtful, nothing difficult, and who, with impetuous prejudice, rigid self-confidence, brutish common sense and reason, gives purgations and bleedings right and left and never ponders a thing. You mustn't bear him ill will for anything he may do to you; it's in the best faith in the world that he'll expedite you; and in killing you he will do only what he's done to his wife and children, and what, if the need arose, he would do to himself.

Argan The fact is, brother, you've always had it in for him. But anyway, let's come to the point. Then what should you do when you're sick?

Béralde Nothing, brother.

Argan Nothing?

Béralde Nothing. All you have to do is rest. Nature, by herself, when we let her be, gently makes her way out of the disorder into which she has fallen. It's our anxiety, our impatience that spoils everything, and almost all men die of their remedies, and not of their diseases.

Argan But you must agree, brother, that we can assist nature in certain ways.

Béralde Good Lord, brother, those are pure notions that we like to feed on; and in every age there have been pretty fancies that have insinuated themselves among men, which we come to believe because they flatter us and because it would be most desirable that they should be true. When a doctor talks to you about aiding, helping, relieving nature, taking away from it what harms it and giving it what it lacks, setting it right again and restoring it to a full state of ease in its functions; when he talks to you about rectifying the blood, tempering the bowels and the brain, deflating the spleen, redressing the lungs, repairing the liver, fortifying the heart, re-establishing and conserving the natural heat, and having secrets to extend your life for many long years, he is telling you precisely the fairy tale of medicine. But when you come down to truth and experience, you find nothing of all that, and it's like those beautiful dreams that leave you, when you wake, nothing but chagrin at having believed them.

Argan That is to say that all the knowledge in the world is enclosed in your head, and you claim to know more about it than all the great doctors of our time.

Béralde Your great doctors are two different kinds of people in words and in deeds. Hear them talk: the ablest men in the world. See them at work: the most ignorant of all men.

Argan Well! You're a great doctor, I can see that; and I wish there was one of those gentlemen here to refute your arguments and humble your chatter.

Béralde Brother, I don't take it upon myself to combat medicine; and everyone, at his own risk and peril, may believe all he likes. What I'm saying about it is just between us, and I would have liked to be able to bring you a little way out of the error you're in, and, to amuse you, take you to see one of Molière's comedies on the subject.

Argan He's a really impertinent fellow, your Molière, with his comedies, and it's very amusing of him to go and make fun of worthy men like the doctors.

Béralde It's not the doctors he makes fun of, but the absurdities of medicine.

Argan I suppose it's his business to undertake to criticize medicine. He's a fine kind of impertinent fool to ridicule consultations and prescriptions, to attack the medical profession, and to put on his stage venerable people like those gentlemen!

Béralde What would you have him put on his stage but the

various professions of men? Every day they put on princes and kings, who are of just as good birth as the doctors.

Argan By all that's holy—or unholy! If I were a doctor, I'd take revenge on his impertinence; and when he's sick, I'd let him die without any help. He could say or do what he likes, I wouldn't prescribe the slightest little bleeding, the least little enema; and I'd say to him: "Croak! Croak! That'll teach you another time to make fun of the Faculty of Medicine!"

Béralde You really are angry at him!

Argan Yes, he's a stupid joker, and if the doctors are smart they'll do what I'm saying.

Béralde He'll be even smarter than your doctors, for he won't ask them for any help.

Argan So much the worse for him, if he doesn't have recourse to any remedies.

Béralde He has his reasons for not wanting any, and he maintains that they are permissible only for vigorous, robust people who have strength to spare to bear the remedies as well as the disease; but that for his part he has only just strength enough to bear his illness.

Argan What stupid arguments those are! Look, brother, let's not talk about that man any more, for it rouses my bile, and it would bring on my illness.

Béralde I'm perfectly willing, brother; and to change the subject, I will tell you that just because your daughter shows some slight opposition, you shouldn't make the violent resolve to put her into a convent; that in choosing a son-in-law, you shouldn't blindly follow the passion that carries you away; and that in this matter one should make some accommodation to a daughter's inclinations, since it's for her whole life, and since on that depends the whole happiness of a marriage.

SCENE FOUR

Monsieur Fleurant (syringe in hand), Argan, Béralde

Argan Ah, brother, with your permission . . .

Béralde How's that? What do you want to do?

Argan Take this little enema; I'll be done soon.

Béralde You must be joking. Can't you go one moment without an enema or a dose of medicine? Put it off for another time, and take a little rest.

Argan Monsieur Fleurant, I'll see you this evening, or tomorrow morning.

Monsieur Fleurant [*to Béralde*] What business is it of yours to oppose the prescriptions of medicine, and to keep the gentleman from taking my enema? Your audacity is mighty comical!

Béralde Come, sir, it's easy to see that you're not accustomed to talking to people's faces.

Monsieur Fleurant A person has no business making fun of remedies and making me waste my time. I came here only on a proper prescription, and I'm going to tell Monsieur Purgon how I've been kept from executing his orders and performing my function. You'll see, you'll see . . .

Exit.

Argan Brother, you're going to be the cause of some misfortune here.

Béralde A great misfortune, not to take an enema that Monsieur Purgon prescribed! Once again, brother, is it possible that there's no way to cure you of the malady of doctors, and that you want to be buried in their remedies all your life?

Argan Good Lord, brother! You're talking about this as a well man; but if you were in my place, you'd really change your tune. It's easy to talk against medicine when you're in perfect health.

Béralde But what illness *do* you have?

Argan You're enough to drive me crazy. I wish *you* had my illness, to see if you'd prattle so much. Oh! Here's Monsieur Purgon.

SCENE FIVE

Monsieur Purgon, Argan, Béralde, Toinette

Monsieur Purgon I've just learned, here at the door, a pretty piece of news: that people have made light of my prescriptions, and have refused to take the remedy I had prescribed.

Argan Sir, it wasn't . . .

Monsieur Purgon That's a great piece of audacity, an extraordinary rebellion by a patient against his doctor!

Toinette That is frightful.

Monsieur Purgon An enema that I had taken pleasure in concocting myself!

Argan It wasn't I . . .

Monsieur Purgon Invented and fashioned according to all the rules of the art!

Toinette He was wrong.

Monsieur Purgon And that was destined to have a marvelous effect on the bowels.

Argan Brother?

Monsieur Purgon To send it away with disdain!

Argan He's the one . . .

Monsieur Purgon It's an unconscionable act.

Toinette That's true.

Monsieur Purgon A shocking attack on medicine.

Argan He's the cause . . .

Monsieur Purgon A crime of *lèse-faculté,* which cannot be punished severely enough.

Toinette You're right.

Monsieur Purgon I declare to you that I am breaking off relations with you.

Argan It was my brother . . .

Monsieur Purgon That I want no more family alliance with you.

Toinette You'll be doing the right thing.

Monsieur Purgon And that to end all dealings with you, here is the donation I was making to my nephew in favor of the marriage. [*Tears it up.*]

Argan It was my brother that did all the harm.

Monsieur Purgon To disdain my enema!

Argan Bring it here, I'll take it right away.

Monsieur Purgon I would have got you out of this in next to no time.

Toinette He doesn't deserve it.

Monsieur Purgon I was going to clean out your body and completely evacuate the evil humors.

Argan Ah, brother!

Monsieur Purgon And all I wanted was another dozen doses of medicine to empty the bottom of the sack.

Toinette He is unworthy of your care.

Monsieur Purgon But since you wouldn't be cured at my hands . . .

Argan It wasn't my fault.

Monsieur Purgon Since you absconded from the obedience that a man owes to his doctor . . .

Toinette That cries for vengeance.

Monsieur Purgon Since you have declared yourself a rebel against the remedies I was prescribing for you . . .

Argan Oh! Not at all!

Monsieur Purgon I have this to tell you: that I abandon you to your bad constitution, to the intemperance of your bowels, to the corruption of your blood, to the bitterness of your bile, and to the turbidity of your humors.

Toinette Well done!

Argan Good Lord!

Monsieur Purgon And I will that before four days are up you get into an incurable state.

Argan Ah! Mercy!

Monsieur Purgon That you fall into bradypepsia . . .*

Argan Monsieur Purgon!

Monsieur Purgon From bradypepsia into dyspepsia . . .

Argan Monsieur Purgon!

Monsieur Purgon From dyspepsia into apepsia . . .

Argan Monsieur Purgon!

Monsieur Purgon From apepsia into lientery . . .

Argan Monsieur Purgon!

Monsieur Purgon From lientery into dysentery . . .

Argan Monsieur Purgon!

Monsieur Purgon From dysentery into dropsy . . .

Argan Monsieur Purgon!

Monsieur Purgon And from dropsy into loss of life, to which your folly will have led you.

SCENE SIX

Argan, Béralde

Argan Oh, good Lord! I'm a dead man. Brother, you've ruined me.

Béralde What? What's the matter?

Argan I'm done for. Already I feel medicine taking its revenge.

* Bradypepsia: slow digestion. Dyspepsia: bad digestion. Apepsia: lack of digestion. Lientery: a form of diarrhea.

Béralde Faith, brother! You're crazy, and I wouldn't for anything want to have you be seen doing what you're doing. Examine yourself a bit, please, come back to yourself, and don't give so much play to your imagination.

Argan Brother, you heard the awful diseases he threatened me with.

Béralde What a simpleton you are!

Argan He says I'll become incurable in less than four days.

Béralde And what he says, what has that to do with the case? Was it an oracle that spoke? It seems, to hear you, that Monsieur Purgon holds the thread of your days in his hands, and that by supreme authority he lengthens it and shortens it for you as he pleases. Remember that the principles of your life are in yourself, and that the wrath of Monsieur Purgon is as little capable of making you die as are his remedies of making you live. Here is an adventure, if you will, to rid you of doctors; or, if you are born to be unable to do without them, it is easy to get another, with whom, brother, you might run a little less risk.

Argan Ah, brother! He knows my whole constitution and the way I have to be treated.

Béralde I must confess to you that you're a man of great obstinacy, and that you see things through a strange pair of eyes.

SCENE SEVEN

Toinette, Argan, Béralde

Toinette Sir, there's a doctor here asking to see you.

Argan And what doctor?

Toinette A doctor of doctoring.

Argan I ask you who he is?

Toinette I don't know him, but he and I look as much alike as two peas in a pod; and if I wasn't sure that my mother was an honest woman, I'd say that he's probably some little brother she'd given me since my father's death.

Argan Show him in. *Exit Toinette.*

Béralde You're served to your heart's content: one doctor leaves you, another presents himself.

Argan I'm very much afraid that you'll be the cause of some misfortune.

Béralde Again? You're still coming back to that?

Argan You see, I have all these illnesses I don't know anything about on my mind, these . . .

SCENE EIGHT

Toinette (disguised as a doctor), Argan, Béralde

Toinette Sir, allow me to come and pay you a visit and offer you my modest services for any bleedings and purges you may need.

Argan Sir, I am much obliged to you. [*To Béralde.*] My word, he looks just like Toinette herself!

Toinette Sir, I beg you to excuse me; I forgot to give an order to my valet; I'll be right back.

Argan Eh! Wouldn't you say it really is Toinette?

Béralde It's true that the resemblance is extremely great. But this is not the first time that this sort of thing has been observed, and the histories are only too full of these freaks of nature.

Argan For my part, I'm surprised, and . . .

SCENE NINE

Toinette, Argan, Béralde

Toinette [*having shed her doctor's gown so fast that it's hard to believe that it was she who appeared as a doctor*] What do you want, sir?

Argan What?

Toinette Didn't you call me?

Argan I? No.

Toinette My ears must have been burning.

Argan Stay here a bit to see how much this doctor looks like you.

Toinette Yes indeed! I've plenty to do downstairs, and I've seen him enough. *Exit.*

Argan If I didn't see them both, I'd think there was only one of them.

Béralde I've read some surprising things about this kind of resemblance, and we've seen some in our time that fooled everybody.

Argan As for me, I would have been fooled by this one, and I would have sworn it was the same person.

SCENE TEN

Toinette (as a doctor), Argan, Béralde

Toinette Sir, with all my heart I ask your pardon.

Argan That's amazing!

Toinette If you please, you won't take amiss the curiosity I've had to see an illustrious invalid like yourself; and your reputation, which has spread everywhere, may excuse the liberty I have taken.

Argan Sir, I am your servant.

Toinette I see, sir, that you're looking at me fixedly. How old do you really think I am?

Argan I think you may be twenty-six or twenty-seven at the very most.

Toinette Ha, ha, ha, ha, ha! I'm ninety.

Argan Ninety?

Toinette Yes. You see one effect of the secrets of my art, to keep myself fresh and vigorous in this way.

Argan Faith! Here's a handsome young old man for ninety!

Toinette I'm a traveling doctor, who goes from town to town, from province to province, from kingdom to kingdom, seeking illustrious subjects for my capacity, trying to find patients worthy of my attention, capable of exercising the fine great secrets I have discovered in medicine. I disdain to waste my time on that petty jumble of ordinary illnesses, on those trifles rheumatism and catarrhs, on those pathetic little fevers, those vapors, and those migraines. I want important illnesses: good continuous fevers with spells of delirium, good scarlet fevers, good plagues, good well-formed dropsies, good pleurisies with inflammation of the lungs: that's what I enjoy, that's where I triumph. And I wish, sir, that you had all the illnesses I've just mentioned, that you were abandoned by all the doctors, desperate, in agony, to show you the excellence of my remedies and my keen desire to do you service.

Argan I am obliged to you, sir, for all your kindness to me.

Toinette Give me your pulse. Come on now, beat properly. Aha! I'll make you work as you should all right. Hey, this pulse is trying to be impertinent: I see very well that you don't know me yet. Who is your doctor?

Argan Monsieur Purgon.

Toinette That man is not inscribed on my list among the great doctors. What does he say you're sick with?

Argan He says it's the liver, and others say it's the spleen.

Toinette They're all ignoramuses: it's in the lungs that you're sick.

Argan The lungs?

Toinette Yes. What do you feel?

Argan From time to time I have headaches.

Toinette Precisely, the lungs.

Argan It seems to me sometimes that I have a veil before my eyes.

Toinette The lungs.

Argan I sometimes have pains in my heart.

Toinette The lungs.

Argan Now and then I feel a weariness in every limb.

Toinette The lungs.

Argan And sometimes I have pains in my stomach, as if it were colic.

Toinette The lungs. You have an appetite for what you eat?

Argan Yes, sir.

Toinette The lungs. You like to drink a little wine?

Argan Yes, sir.

Toinette The lungs. You get a little sleepy after a meal, and feel glad of a nap?

Argan Yes, sir.

Toinette The lungs, the lungs, I tell you. What does your doctor prescribe for your diet?

Argan He prescribes soup.

Toinette Ignoramus.

Argan Poultry.

Toinette Ignoramus.

Argan Veal.

Toinette Ignoramus.

Argan Broths.

Toinette Ignoramus.

Argan Fresh eggs.

Toinette Ignoramus.

Argan And some little prunes in the evening as a laxative.

Toinette Ignoramus.

Argan And above all to drink my wine mixed with a lot of water.

Toinette *Ignorantus, ignoranta, ignorantum.* You must drink your wine straight; and to thicken your blood, which is too thin, you must eat good fat beef, good fat pork, good Holland cheese, gruel and rice, and chestnuts and wafers, to bind and conglutinate. Your doctor is an ass. I mean to send you one of my own choosing, and I'll come and see you from time to time while I'm in town.

Argan I'm much obliged to you.

Toinette What the devil do you do with that arm?

Argan How's that?

Toinette That's an arm I'd have cut off right away, if I were you.

Argan And why?

Toinette Don't you see that it's drawing all the nourishment to itself, and keeping that whole side from profiting?

Argan Yes, but I need my arm.

Toinette You also have a right eye there that I'd have put out, if I were in your place.

Argan Put out an eye?

Toinette Don't you see that it's disadvantaging the other one and stealing its nourishment? Believe me, have it put out as soon as possible, you'll see better out of the left eye.

Argan There's no hurry.

Toinette Good-by. I'm sorry to leave you so soon, but I've got to be at a big consultation to be held for a man who died yesterday.

Argan For a man who died yesterday?

Toinette Yes, to deliberate and see what should have been done to cure him. Good-by.

Argan You know that patients don't show you out.

Exit Toinette.

Béralde There's a doctor who really seems very able.

Argan Yes, but he goes about things pretty fast.

Béralde All great doctors are like that.

Argan Cut off one of my arms, and put out one of my eyes, so that the other one will be healthier? I'd much rather it wasn't so healthy. A fine operation, to make me one-eyed and one-armed!

SCENE ELEVEN

Toinette, Argan, Béralde

Toinette [*calling offstage*] Come, come, I'm your servant, I'm not in the mood for fun.

Argan What is it?

Toinette Faith, your doctor! He wanted to feel my pulse.

Argan What do you know! At ninety!

Béralde Now then, brother, since your Monsieur Purgon is on bad terms with you, won't you let me talk to you about the suitor who's seeking my niece's hand?

Argan No, brother; I want to put her in a convent, since she has opposed my wishes. I see very well that there's some little love affair at the bottom of this, and I've found out about a certain secret interview that they don't know I've found out about.

Béralde Well, brother, even if there were some slight inclination, would that be so criminal, and can anything offend you when it all leads only to honorable things like marriage?

Argan Be that as it may, brother, she shall be a nun; that's settled.

Béralde You're trying to please someone.

Argan I understand you: you always come back to that, and you have my wife on the brain.

Béralde Well, yes, brother, since I must speak open-heartedly, it is your wife that I mean; and no more than your infatuation with medicine can I bear the infatuation you have for her, or see you fall head down into all the traps she lays for you.

Toinette Ah, sir, don't speak of Madame! She's a woman against whom there's nothing to be said, a woman without artifice, and who loves Monsieur, who loves him . . . you can't put it into words.

Argan [*to Béralde*] Just ask *her* how she caresses me.

Toinette That's true.

Argan How worried she is about my illness.

Toinette Unquestionably.

Argan And the care and trouble she takes for me.

Toinette That's certain. [*To Béralde.*] Do you want me to convince you, and show you right now how Madame loves Monsieur? [*To Argan.*] Sir, allow me to show him how childish he is, and undeceive him.

Argan How?

Toinette Madame is just coming back. Stretch out full length in this chair and pretend to be dead. You'll see what her grief is like when I tell her the news.

Argan I'm willing.

Toinette Yes, but don't leave her long in despair, for she might well die of it.

Argan Leave it to me.

Toinette [*to Béralde*] You, hide yourself in that corner.

Argan Isn't there some danger in pretending to be dead?

Toinette No, no. What danger could there be? Just stretch out there. [*Whispering, to Argan.*] It'll be a pleasure to confound your brother. Here's Madame. Keep good and still.

SCENE TWELVE

Béline, Toinette, Argan, Béralde

Toinette [*wailing loudly*] Oh, good Lord! Oh, what a shame! What a terrible accident!

Béline What is it, Toinette?

Toinette Oh, Madame!

Béline What's the matter?

Toinette Your husband is dead.

Béline My husband is dead?

Toinette Alas! Yes. The poor deceased has passed on.

Béline Are you quite sure?

Toinette Quite sure. No one knows it's happened yet, and I was here all alone. He's just passed away in my arms. Look, there he is stretched out full length in this chair.

Béline Heaven be praised! I'm delivered from a heavy burden. How stupid you are, Toinette, to take on over his death.

Toinette Madame, I thought I ought to cry.

Béline Come, come, it's not worth it. What are we losing in him? And what good on earth was he? A man who was a nuisance to everyone, dirty, disgusting, always with an enema or a dose of medicine in his stomach; always blowing his nose, coughing, and spitting; devoid of wit, boring, bad-humored, constantly wearying people, and scolding all the servants day and night.

Toinette That's a nice funeral oration.

Béline Toinette, you must help me carry out my plan, and believe me, in serving me your reward is sure. Since by a stroke of good fortune no one is yet informed of the matter, let's carry him to his bed and keep this death quiet until I've done some business of mine. There are some papers, there's some money I want to get hold of, and it isn't fair that I should have spent the best years of my life with him without some reward. Come on, Toinette, first let's take all his keys.

Argan [*rising suddenly*] Gently.

Béline [*surprised and terrified*] Oh!

Argan Yes, my lady and wife, so that's how you love me?

Toinette Ha, ha! The deceased isn't dead.

Argan [*to Béline*] I'm very glad to see how you love me and to have heard the fine panegyric you gave about me.

Exit Béline.

There's a warning to the reader that will make me wiser in the future and keep me from doing a lot of things.

Béralde [*coming out of his hiding-place*] Well, brother, you see the way it is.

Toinette Upon my word, I never would have believed it. But I hear your daughter; get back the way you were, and let's see how she receives your death. That's a thing that it's not bad to test out; and while you're at it, that way you'll learn the feelings your whole family has for you.

SCENE THIRTEEN

Angélique, Argan, Toinette, Béralde

Toinette [*wailing*] O Heavens! Ah, what a sad thing! Unhappy day!

Angélique What's the matter, Toinette, and what are you crying about?

Toinette Alas! I have sad news to give you.

Angélique Why, what?

Toinette Your father is dead.

Angélique My father is dead, Toinette?

Toinette Yes. There you see him. He's just died, just now, of a spell of weakness that seized him.

Angélique O Heaven! What a misfortune! What a cruel blow! Alas! Must I lose my father, the only thing left to me in the world? And moreover, to add to my despair, lose him at a time when he was irritated with me? What is to become of me, wretched girl that I am, and what consolation can I find after so great a loss?

SCENE FOURTEEN

Cléante, Angélique, Argan, Toinette, Béralde

Cléante Why, what's wrong, lovely Angélique? And what misfortune is making you weep?

Angélique Alas! I'm weeping for the dearest and most precious thing I could lose in life: I'm weeping for the death of my father.

Cléante O Heavens! What a calamity! What an unexpected blow! Alas! After I'd implored your uncle to ask your hand of him on my behalf, I was coming to present myself to him and try, by my respects and my prayers, to make his heart disposed to grant you to my wishes.

Angélique Ah, Cléante, let's not talk any more about any of that. Let's leave behind all thoughts of marriage. After the loss of my father, I want no part of the world any more, and I give it up forever. Yes, father, if I resisted your wishes just now, I want to follow at least one of your intentions, and thereby make amends for the unhappiness I blame myself for having given you. Allow me, father, to give you my word for this here and now, and to kiss you to testify my feeling to you.

Argan [*rising*] Ah, my daughter!

Angélique [*frightened*] Oh!

Argan Come. Don't be afraid, I'm not dead. Come, come, you are my own flesh and blood, my true daughter; and I'm delighted to have seen how good your nature really is.

Angélique Oh, what a delightful surprise, father! Since, by extreme good fortune, Heaven restores you to my love, allow me here and now to throw myself at your feet to beseech you for one thing. If you are not favorable to the inclination of my heart, if you refuse me Cléante for a husband, I conjure you at least not to force me to marry another. That's all the boon I ask of you.

Cléante [*throwing himself on his knees*] Ah, sir, let yourself be touched by her prayers and mine, and don't take a stand against the mutual ardor of such a fair inclination.

Béralde Brother, can you hold out against that?

Toinette Sir, will you be insensible to so much love?

Argan Let him become a doctor, and I'll consent to the marriage. Yes, become a doctor, and I'll give you my daughter.

Cléante Very gladly, sir; if that's all that's needed to be your son-in-law, I'll become a doctor, even an apothecary, if you want. That's no great matter, and I'd do far more than that to win the lovely Angélique.

Béralde But, brother, a thought occurs to me: become a doctor yourself. The convenience would be even greater, to have everything you need in yourself.

Toinette That's true. That's the real way to get well soon; and there is no illness so daring as to trifle with the person of a doctor.

Argan Brother, I think you're making fun of me. Am I of an age to be a student?

Béralde Be a student? That's a good one! You're learned enough; and there are many of them who are no smarter than you.

Argan But you have to know how to speak Latin well, and know the illnesses and the remedies you need to use for them.

Béralde As you receive the doctor's cap and gown you'll learn all that, and afterward you'll be even smarter than you want.

Argan What? A man knows how to discourse upon illnesses when he has that costume?

Béralde Yes. One has only to talk with a cap and gown on. Any gibberish becomes learned, and any nonsense becomes reason.

Toinette Look here, sir, if all you had was your beard, that's already a lot, and a beard makes more than half a doctor.

Cléante In any case, I'm ready for anything.

Béralde Do you want to have the thing done right away?

Argan What do you mean, right away?

Béralde Yes, and in your own house.

Argan In my own house?

Béralde Yes. I have friends on the Faculty who will come right away and perform the ceremony here in your room. It won't cost you a thing.

Argan But for my part, what am I to say, what am I to answer?

Béralde They'll give you instructions in a few words, and give you in writing what you have to say. Go along and put on proper clothes; I'm going to send for them.

Argan All right, let's see about it. *Exit.*

Cléante What do you mean, and what do you have in mind with these friends on the Faculty . . . ?

Toinette What's your plan, anyway?

Béralde To have a little fun this evening. I have some actors who have composed a little act about accepting a man as a doctor, with music and dances. I want us to enjoy the entertainment together, and I want my brother to play the leading part.

Angélique But, uncle, it seems to me that you're making a bit too much fun of my father.

Béralde But, niece, it's not so much making fun of him as accommodating ourselves to his fancies. All this is just between us. We can also each of us take a part, and thus put on a comedy for one another. Carnival time authorizes that. Let's go quickly and get everything prepared.

Cléante [*to Angélique*] Do you consent?

Angélique Yes, since my uncle is leading the way.

FINALE

A burlesque, with recitative, song, and dance, of the conferral of the degree of Doctor of Medicine on a candidate (a Bachelor) by the Faculty. It is in macaronic Latin—sprinkled with French and a little Italian in Molière's text, with English here—easily intelligible to Molière's audience.

Several attendants, to music, prepare the room and set out the benches. Then enter the whole assembly—eight syringe-bearers, six apothecaries, twenty-two doctors, the candidate (Bachelierus, in this case Argan), eight surgeons dancing and two singing. All take their places according to their ranks. The Presiding Officer (Praeses) takes his place in a pulpit.

Praeses

Learnedissimi doctores,
Medicinae professores,
Qui hic assemblati estis,
Et vos, altri Messiores,
Sententiarum facultatis
Fideles executores,
Surgeoni, apothecari,
Atque tota company,
Salus, honor, et argentum,
Atque bonum appetitum.

Non possum, docti Confreri,
In me satis admirari
Qualis bona inventio
Est medici professio,
How fine a thinga est, et well trovata,
Medicina illa benedicta,
Quae suo nomine solo,
Surprisingi miraculo,
For such a longo tempore
Has made à gogo vivere
So many omni genere.

Per totam terram videmus
Grandam vogam ubi sumus,
Et quod omnes, great and small,
Sunt infatuated with us all.
Totus mundus, currens ad nostros remedios,
Nos regardat sicut Deos;
Et nostris ordonnanciis
Principes et reges submissive videtis.

Therefore 'tis nostrae sapientiae,
Boni sensus atque prudentiae,
Sturdily to laborare
A nos bene conservare
In tali credito, voga, et honore,
And take good care to non receivere
In nostro docto corpore
Quam personas capabiles,
Et totas dignas to fillire
Has plaças honorabiles.

This is why nunc convocati estis:
Et credo quod findabitis
Dignam materiam medici
In learned man whom here you see,
Whom, in thingsis omnibus,
Dono ad interrogandum,
Et in depth examinandum
Vostris capacitatibus.

Primus Doctor

Si mihi licentiam dat Dominus Praeses,
Et tanti docti Doctores,
Et assistantes illustres:
Very learned Bacheliero,
Quem estimo et honoro,
Demandabo causam et rationem quare
Opium facit dormire.

Bachelierus [*Argan*]

Mihi by docto Doctore
Demandatur causam et rationem quare
Opium facit dormire:
To which respondeo
Quia est in eo
Virtus dormitiva,
Cuius est natura
Sensus stupefire.

Chorus

Bene, bene, bene, bene respondere:

Dignus, dignus est entrare
In nostro docto corpore.

Secundus Doctor

Cum permissione Domini Praesidis,
Doctissimae Facultatis,
Et totius his nostris actis
Companiae assistantis,
Demandabo tibi, docte Bacheliere,
Quae sunt remedia
Quae in maladia
Known as hydropisia
Convenit facere.

Bachelierus [*Argan*]

Enema donare,
Postea bleedare,
After that purgare.

Chorus

Bene, bene, bene, bene respondere:
Dignus, dignus est entrare
In nostro docto corpore.

Tertius Doctor

Si bonum seems Domini Praesidi,
Doctissimae Facultati,
Et companiae praesenti,
Demandabo tibi, docte Bacheliere,
Quae remedia eticis,
Pulmonicis, atque asmaticis,
You think it right to facere.

Bachelierus [*Argan*]

Enema donare,
Postea bleedare,
After that purgare.

Chorus

Bene, bene, bene, bene respondere:
Dignus, dignus est entrare
In nostro docto corpore.

Quartus Doctor

Super illas maladias
Doctus Bachelierus dixit marvelias,
But si non annoyo Dominum Praesidem,
Doctissimam Facultatem,
Et totam honorabilem
Companiam listenantem,
Faciam illi unam quaestionem.
Yesterday maladus unus
Fellavit into meas manus;
Habet grandam feveram cum redoublamentis,
Grandam dolorem capitis,
Et grandum malum in the side,
Cum granda difficultate
Et paina to respirare:
Be so kind as to tell mihi,
Docte Bacheliere,
Quid illi facere?

Bachelierus [*Argan*]

Enema donare,
Postea bleedare,
After that purgare.

Quintus Doctor

But if maladia,
With obstinacia,
Non vult se curire,
Quid illi facere?

Bachelierus [*Argan*]

Enema donare,
Postea bleedare,
After that purgare.

Chorus

Bene, bene, bene, bene respondere:
Dignus, dignus est entrare
In nostro docto corpore.

Praeses

Juras keepare statuta

Per Facultatem praescripta
Cum sensu et judgeamento?

Bachelierus [*Argan*]

Juro.*

Praeses

Essere in omnibus
Consultationibus
True to opinion oldo,
Aut bono,
Aut baddo?

Bachelierus [*Argan*]

Juro.

Praeses

Never to usire
Any remediis
But only those of doctae Facultatis,
Though maladus croakare,
Et mori de suo malo?

Bachelierus [*Argan*]

Juro.

Praeses

Ego, cum isto boneto
Venerabili et docto,
Dono tibi et concedo
Virtutem et poweriam
Medicandi,
Purgandi,
Bleedandi,
Pierceandi,
Carvandi,
Cutandi,
Et killendi
Impune per totam terram.

* It was here or hereabouts that at the fourth performance of the play (February 17, 1673) Molière suffered an attack of his lung trouble that made him cough up blood. He finished the performance but died that evening.

All the surgeons and apothecaries come and do reverence to Argan, to music.

Bachelierus [*Argan*]

Grandes doctores doctrinae
Of rhubarb and of senna,
'Twould be no doubt the action of a foola,
Inepta et ridicula,
If I went and m'engageare
Praises unto you donare,
And undertook to add-on-are
Any lightas to the sunno,
And any staras to the skyo,
Waveas to the oceano,
And rosas to the springo.
Pray allow that with one wordo,
As grateful as you ever heardo,
I give thanks to corpori tam docto.
Vobis, vobis debeo
Much more than to naturae and to patri meo:
Natura et pater meus
Hominem me habent factum;
But vos me—a great big plus—
Havetis factum medicum,
Honor, favor, et gratia
Qui, in hoc corde you have here,
Imprimant ressentimenta
Which will endure in saecula.

Chorus

Vivat, vivat, vivat, vivat, a hundred times vivat
Novus Doctor, qui tam bene speakat!
Mille, mille annis et eatet et drinkat
Et bleedet et killat!

All the surgeons and apothecaries dance to the sound of instruments and voices, hand-clapping, and apothecaries' mortars.

Chirurgus

May he see doctas
Suas ordonnancias
Omnium chirurgorum

Et apothecarum
Fill up the shoppas!

Chorus

Vivat, vivat, vivat, vivat, a hundred times vivat
Novus Doctor, qui tam bene speakat!
Mille, mille annis et eatet et drinkat,
Et bleedet et killat!

Chirurgus

May all his anni
Be to him boni
And favorable,
And always be full
Of pestas, poxas,
Feveras, pleurisias,
Of bloody fluxions and dysenterias!

Chorus

Vivat, vivat, vivat, vivat, a hundred times vivat
Novus Doctor, qui tam bene speakat!
Mille, mille annis et eatet et drinkat
Et bleedet et killat!

This Franklin Library edition of

MOLIÈRE COMEDIES

is set in Bembo, a classic typeface

developed in the fifteenth century.

The wood engravings that illustrate the text were created

by the celebrated nineteenth-century painter and etcher, Tony Johannot.

The acid-free paper is

60-pound Franklin Library Olde Style Cream,

made to archival standards by

the S. D. Warren Paper Company

of Cumberland Mills, Maine, for The Franklin Library.

The book was printed by R. R. Donnelley & Sons Co.,

Chicago, Illinois.